INSTITUTE OF ADVANCED LEGAL STUDIES

Union Catalogue No.1 (4th ed.)

UNION LIST
OF LEGAL PERIODICALS

A Location Guide to Holdings of Legal Periodicals in Libraries in the United Kingdom

FOURTH EDITION

UNIVERSITY OF LONDON
INSTITUTE OF ADVANCED LEGAL STUDIES

17, Russell Square,
London WC1B 5DR

1978

ISBN 0 901190 20 9

Printed in England by
The Chameleon Press Limited
5-25 Burr Road, London, SW18 4SG

PUBLICATIONS IN THIS SERIES

No.1 Union List of Legal Periodicals: A Location Guide to Holdings of Legal Periodicals in Libraries in the United Kingdom, 4th edition, 1978.

No.2 Union List of Commonwealth and South African Law, 1963 edition. A Location Guide to Commonwealth and South African Legislation, Law Reports and Digests held by Libraries in the United Kingdom at May 1963.

No.3 Union List of United States Law Literature in Libraries in Oxford, Cambridge and London, 2nd edition, 1967.

No.4 Union List of Air and Space Law Literature in the Libraries of Oxford, Cambridge and London, 2nd edition, 1975.

No.5 Union List of West European Legal Literature: Publications held by Libraries in Oxford, Cambridge and London, 1966.

PREFACE

In 1934 the Legal Education Committee which had been set up by the Lord Chancellor under the chairmanship of Lord Atkin envisaged that one of the tasks of an institute of advanced legal studies, the establishment of which was recommended in its report (Cmd. 4663), would be that of making known the contents of other law libraries. In trying to perform this task, this Institute publishes five "union lists" (listed on p.ii), which give the location in the United Kingdom of a wide variety of legal materials. These have simplified the task of librarians and readers in finding, without waste of time, volumes which might not otherwise have been readily available, and have also provided a basis for rationalisation of holdings.

The need for such union lists is continually growing, since the increase in the number of titles, the lack of funds and shortage of accommodation make it impossible for any one library to acquire everything its readers need.

The present Union List is the 4th edition of a publication first brought out in 1949 under the title "A survey of legal periodicals: union catalogue of holdings in British libraries", but it is a completely new compilation. Like its predecessors, it covers only law reviews; legislation, law reports, and collections of treaties are excluded. Libraries with significant legal holdings (those of institutions of higher education which teach law, those of the legal profession and of certain government departments, some public libraries and a number of specialist libraries) were asked to insert details of their holdings on prepared lists and to make a return of their holdings of periodicals not contained in the lists. The co-operation which the Institute received from those libraries is most gratifying and shows their appreciation of the need to have available an up-to-date statement of all such holdings in the United Kingdom. The closing dates for entries vary from library to library and range from January to December 1977.

The first edition (1949) recorded 464 titles in 34 libraries, the 2nd edition (1957) 1026 titles in 76 libraries, and the 3rd edition (1968) 1831 titles in 87 libraries. This 4th edition lists nearly 3000 titles in 114 libraries. Holdings of 23 libraries outside London were included in 1949, of 35 in 1957, and of 49 in 1968. This edition includes the holdings of 69 libraries outside London.

The attention of readers is drawn to the Introduction which will facilitate the use of this Union List.

The Institute would like to thank the contributing libraries for making the publication of this Union List possible and to record its appreciation of the work done by the members of the Institute's staff in the Readers' Services Department, who are responsible for the preparation of the bibliographical publications of the Institute.

March 1978

AUBREY L. DIAMOND
DIRECTOR

TABLE OF CONTENTS

INTRODUCTION

The information for the 4th edition of the Union List has been obtained from checklists marked up and returned by libraries over a period of 11 months. Although some libraries supplied supplementary information on alterations to their stock after sending in their main return, it must be appreciated that the Union List cannot be considered completely current at the time of publication. The compilers could only use the information as supplied, and therefore cannot accept responsibility for any errors which have occurred, although naturally it is hoped that these are minimal.

All bibliographical details have been checked and verified as far as possible and librarians have helped us by confirming details from their own copies of journals on many occasions.

In the following notes we have tried to be brief, hoping that the simple alphabetical arrangement of the List will make it easy to use and understand. There are certain points, however, which we felt justified a special note, and these are set out below.

We hope that this publication will benefit all our colleagues, for whose help in its compilation we express our thanks.

1. Titles selected for inclusion

The basic requirement for selection was that a periodical should contain articles or doctrinal writings and its subject should be law. Some fringe periodicals have been included because of their legal interest, and a few foreign law reports because they have sections devoted to articles or doctrinal writings.

The following types of publication have normally been excluded: ephemeral series, such as newsletters etc.; non-legal periodicals; law reports; legislative series; annual administrative reports; reports of conferences; monographic series, including studies/studia/studi where they are monographic in nature.

2. Filing order of entries

The alphabetical order is word by word, not letter by letter, e.g. "Law weekly review" precedes "Lawasia"; "d'" precedes "de"; "Bulletin - University..." precedes, and may be widely separated from, "Bulletin of the University...".

Case and gender endings as well as articles (other than initial articles) are taken into account, and therefore affect the alphabetical order. Periodicals with the same title are arranged alphabetically by place of publication, and then, if from the same town, chronologically. Titles starting with abbreviations or acronyms occur at the beginning of each alphabetical section.

3. Form of entry

This is based on: ISBD(S) International Standard Bibliographic Description for Serials published by the International Federation of Library Associations' Committee on Cataloguing, 1974.

Main entry: entry is under latest known title.

Foreign language titles which are not in roman script appear in a transliterated form. Because of varying library practice, consistency in transliteration has not always been possible, and the form given may be that of the holding library.

All conference proceedings, reports, studies, yearbooks, journals, bulletins etc., are entered directly under the title as published on the volume itself. Where there is no grammatical connection, such generic terms are followed by a statement of authorship, which is preceded by a dash (-) e.g. Bulletin - Copyright Society of the U.S.A.

Parallel titles in other languages on the title page are preceded by an equals sign (=).

"Unofficial" translations of titles are sometimes included in brackets after the distinctive title.

Where it is considered helpful, a statement of authorship follows a distinctive title, and this is preceded by an oblique stroke (/).

Publication dates have been used rather than coverage dates, which are added in brackets if different. Volume numbers have occasionally been given for clarity.

Annotations to main entry: the history of any change of title is given after the main entry. The usual format used is: "Continues:" followed by the previous title, dates, volume numbers (if included) and the ISSN for the previous title in brackets. If more than one change is given, titles are listed in chronological order. Library holdings are all listed under the latest title, with references from other earlier titles to the main entry.

Mergers: journals which have merged are treated as separate titles, with their own list of holdings until the date of merger.

4. Interpretation of holdings

For library symbols and any relevant notes, see next section.

Holdings are complete where the library symbol stands alone.

Details of incomplete holdings are stated after the library symbol, and are given in years rather than volume numbers, but volume numbers are added in brackets where known.

Note that although holdings are shown under the latest title, they apply to the journal throughout its history.

Please refer to the examples following.

Abbreviations and notes used in holdings

imp. = imperfect	Shows that the holdings for either the whole run of the title or the period of coverage stated are imperfect, and that the gaps are too numerous to list or are not known.
w. = wanting	Shows that the holdings as stated are complete except that they lack the years or volumes as stated in brackets after the "w".
A full stop	Has been used after a year to emphasise that no further holdings are held beyond that single year. It shows that the continuation sign was not omitted in error.
No holdings notified	It was considered helpful to include bibliographical information where this was known to be correct, although there are no known locations.
Not on checklist circulated so other/ some holdings possible	Some titles have come to our notice since our original checklists were circulated. In these cases we feel that users should know that other/some locations are possible.

Examples of holdings for some imaginary titles commencing in 1920 (not taken from actual entries)

1. LO/U24	holdings complete from beginning of title, 1920-
2. LO/U24 imp.	holdings run from 1920-, but with some gaps throughout
3. LO/U24 (1930-35 imp.)	holdings run from 1920-, with imperfect holdings for the years specified in brackets (cf. no.8 below)
4. LO/U24 (w.1940;1943-45) or (w.v. 21; 24-26)	holdings run from 1920-, but the library lacks the years or volumes specified in brackets
5. LO/U24 1926-	holdings complete from 1926-
6. LO/U24 1950-56	holdings complete from 1950 to 1956 inclusive

7.	LO/U24 1922- imp.	holdings run from 1922-, but with some gaps throughout
8.	LO/U24 1945-55 imp.	holdings run from 1945 to 1955 inclusive, with some gaps throughout (cf. no. 3 above)
9.	LO/U24 1930- (1957-60 imp). or 1930-56;1957-60 imp.,1961-	either version used, meaning that holdings run from 1930-, but that holdings for 1957 to 1960 inclusive have some gaps
10.	LO/U24 1950- (w.1960-62) or 1950-59;1963-	either version used, meaning that holdings run from 1950-, but the library lacks the volumes for 1960 to 1962 inclusive

Other minor variations may occur, usually for reasons of space, or because the holding library gave the information in a different form.

5. Library symbols

The symbols used in this 4th edition of the Union List of Legal Periodicals are based on those devised by the National Central Library which now appear in the *Directory of Library Codes* issued by the British Library Lending Division. There are, however, points of difference which should be noted.

In cases where no such code has been traced, the compilers have assigned codes distinguished by a hyphen instead of an oblique stroke, e.g. LO-MT.

In the case of law or social science libraries which are part of a larger system, the address and telephone number of the law library has been preferred to those of the main library appearing in the British Library Directory, e.g. LO/C15, LO/N17, QS/Q13, QS/Q29.

Some British Library symbols do not appear in its Directory of October 1977, but have been retained in the Union List.

An alphabetical list of all symbols used follows these notes.

Notes on library facilities

No attempt has been made to indicate the accessibility of materials held by libraries which have contributed to the Union List. For libraries listed in the Directory of Library Codes mentioned above, that publication may be useful as a guide. In other cases, information as to opening hours, restrictions on admission, etc., may be obtained either direct from the contributing library, or from guides such as: Mangles, B. *Directory of Law Libraries in the British Isles* (1976) or the International Association of Law Libraries' *European Law Libraries Guide* (1971).

Alphabetical list of symbols

		Telex	Telephone
AB/N-1	National Library of Wales, Aberystwyth, Dyfed. SY23 3BU	35165	0970-3816
AB/U-1	University Library, University College of Wales, Hugh Owen Building, Penglais, Aberystwyth, Dyfed. SY23 3DZ	35181	0970-3111
AD-A	The Library, Society of Advocates in Aberdeen, Advocates' Hall, Concert Court, Aberdeen, AB1 1AR	-	0224-20079
AD/U-6	Aberdeen University Library, Law Library, Taylor Building, Aberdeen, AB9 2UB	73458	0224-40241
BC-UC	The Library, University College at Buckingham, Buckingham, MK18 1EG	-	02802-4161
BH-LS	Birmingham Law Library, Birmingham Law Society, 8, Temple Street, Birmingham, B2 5BT	-	021-643 9116
BH/P-1	Birmingham Public Libraries, Central Libraries, Paradise, Birmingham, West Midlands, B3 3HQ	33455	021-235 4543
BH/U-1	Main Library, Birmingham University, P.O. Box 363, Edgbaston, Birmingham, West Midlands, B15 2TT	338160	021-472 1301
BL-LS	The Library, Incorporated Law Society of Northern Ireland, Royal Courts of Justice, Belfast, BT1 3JX	-	0232-31614
BL/U-1	University Library, Queens University, Belfast, BT7 1LS	74487	0232-45133
BR/U-1	University of Bristol Library, Tyndall Avenue, Bristol, Avon, BS8 1TJ	449174	0272-24161
BT/U-1	University of Sussex Library, Brighton, East Sussex, BN1 9QL	87394	0273-66755
CA/U-1	University of Cambridge Library, West Road, Cambridge, CB3 9DR	81395	0223-61441
CA/U13	Squire Law Library, Old Schools, Cambridge, CB2 1TN	-	0223-58933
CA/U37	Radzinowicz Library, University of Cambridge Institute of Criminology, 7 West Road, Cambridge, CB3 9DT	-	0223-68511

CB/U-1	University Library, University of Kent, Canterbury, Kent, CT2 7NU	965449	0227-66822
CC/U-1	University Library, University of Essex, P.O. Box 24, Colchester, Essex, CO4 3VA	98440	0206-44144
CH-CI	The Library, Chelmer Institute of Higher Education, Victoria Road South, Chelmsford, Essex, CM1 1LL	-	0245-54491
CR/U-1	Arts and Social Studies Library, University College, P.O. Box 98, Cardiff, South Glamorgan, CF1 1XQ	49635	0222-44211
CV/C-1	The Library, Lanchester Polytechnic, Priory Street, Coventry, CV1 5FB	-	0203-24166
CV/U-1	The Librarian, University of Warwick Library, Gibbet Hill Road, Coventry, West Midlands, CV4 7AL	31406	0203-24011
DG-LS	The Library, Isle of Man Law Society, 20 Athol Street, Douglas, Isle of Man	-	0624-3391
DN/U-1	University Library, University of Dundee, Perth Road, Dundee, DD1 4HN	76293	0382-23181
DR/U-1	University Library, University of Durham, Palace Green, Durham, DH1 3RN	537351	0385-61262
DR/U-4	Durham University Library, Oriental Library, Elvet Hill, Durham, DH1 3TH	-	0385-64371
ED/N-1	National Library of Scotland, George IV Bridge, Edinburgh, EH1 1EW	72638	031-226 4531
ED/S10	Signet Library, Parliament Square, Edinburgh, EH1 1RF	-	031-225 6138
ED/S11	Advocates' Library, Parliament House, Edinburgh, EH1 1RF	-	031-225 5002
ED-SLC	The Library, Scottish Law Commission, 140, Causewayside, Edinburgh, EH9 1PR	-	031-668 2131
ED/U-1	University Library, University of Edinburgh, George Square, Edinburgh, EH8 9LJ	-	031-667 1011
EX/U-1	University Library, University of Exeter, Prince of Wales Road, Exeter, EX4 4PT	42894	0392-77911

GL/U-1	University Library, University of Glasgow, Hillhead Street, Glasgow, G12 8QE	778421	041-334 2122
GL/U-2	University of Strathclyde, Andersonian Library, Richmond Street, Glasgow, G1 1QX	77472	041-552 4156
HL/U-1	Brynmor Jones Library, University of Hull, Hull, North Humberside, HU6 7RX	52530	0482-46311
JE-LS	The Library, Jersey Law Society, 2, Hill Street, St. Helier, Jersey, C.I.	-	0534 25332
KL/U-1	University Library, University of Keele, Keele, Staffs, ST5 5BG	36113	0782-621111
LA/U-1	University Library, University of Lancaster, Bailrigg, Lancaster, LA1 4YH	65111	0524-65201
LC/C-1	Library, Leicester Polytechnic, P.O. Box 143, Leicester, LE1 9BH	34429	0533-50181
LC/U-1	University Library, University of Leicester, University Road, Leicester, LE1 7RH	341198	0533-50000
LD/C-1	Library, Leeds Polytechnic, Calverley Street, Leeds, LS1 3HE	-	0532-41101
LD/P-1	Leeds Central Library, Municipal Buildings, Leeds, LS1 3AB	556237	0532-31301
LD/U-1	Brotherton Library, University of Leeds, Leeds, LS2 9JT	-	0532-31751
LO/C-3	The Library, Polytechnic of the South Bank, Borough Road, London, SE1 OAA	-	01-928 8989
LO/C-5	The Library, Ealing College of Higher Education, St. Mary's Road, London, W5 5RF	-	01-579 4111
LO/C10	Reference Library, Kingston Polytechnic, Penrhyn Road, Kingston-upon-Thames, Surrey, KT1 2EE	928530	01-549 1366
LO/C14	Polytechnic of North London Library Service, Holloway Road, London, N7 8DB	25228	01-607 2789
LO/C15	The Law Library, Polytechnic of Central London, 235 High Holborn, London, WC1V 7DN	-	01-405 3144

LO/C18	The Library, Thames Polytechnic, Wellington Street, London, SE18 6PF	-	01-854 2030
LO/C25	The Library, North East London Polytechnic, Barking Precinct, Longbridge Road, Dagenham, Essex, RM8 2AS	897099	01-597 2417
LO/C27	The Librarian, Middlesex Polytechnic, The Burroughs, Hendon, London, NW4 4BT	-	01-202 6545
LO/C47	City of London Polytechnic, Calcutta House Library, Calcutta House, Old Castle Street, London, E1 7NT	8812073	01-283 1030
LO-CBL	City of London Libraries, City Business Library, Gillett House, London, EC2V 5BX	887955	01-638 8215/6
	N.B. Titles marked with an asterisk (LO-CBL*) are transferred to the Guildhall Library (see LO/P-6) after 5 years.		
LO/M32	The Nuffield Library, British Medical Association, Tavistock Square, London, WC1H 9JP	-	01-387 4499
LO-MT	Middle Temple Library, Middle Temple Lane, London, EC4Y 9BT	-	01-353 4303
LO/N-1	Department of Printed Books, British Library Reference Division, Great Russell Street, London, WC1B 3DG	21462	01-636 1544
LO/N-5	Department of Industry Solicitors' Library, Kingsgate House, 66-74 Victoria Street, London, SW1E 6SQ	-	01-215 3901
LO/N14	Science Reference Library, British Library Reference Division, 25 Southampton Buildings, Chancery Lane, London, WC2A 1AW	266959	01-405 8721
LO/N17	Foreign and Commonwealth Office Library, Room E213, Downing Street, London, SW1A 2AL	-	01-233 3166
LO/N26	House of Commons Library, Westminster, London, SW1A 0AA	-	01-219 3666
LO/N27	Home Office Library, Legal and Political Library, 50 Queen Annes Gate, London, SW1H 9AT	24986	01-213 4227/3646

LO/N46	House of Lords Library, Westminster, London, SW1A OPW	-	01-219 5242
LO/P-6	City of London Libraries, Guildhall Library, Aldermanbury, London, EC2P 2EJ	-	01-606 3030
LO-PC	The Library, Privy Council Office, (Judicial Dept.), Whitehall, London, SW1A 2AT	-	01-233 4896
LO/R74	Law Commission Library, Conquest House, 37-38 John Street, Theobalds Road, London, WC1N 2BQ	-	01-242 0861
LO/S14	The Library, Royal Institute of International Affairs, Chatham House, 10 St. James's Square, London, SW1Y 4LE	-	01-930 2233
LO/S28	The Library, Institute of Bankers, 10 Lombard Street, London, EC3V 9AS	-	01-623 3531
LO/S55	India House Library, High Commission for India, India House, Aldwych, London, WC2B 4NA	-	01-836 8484
LO/S65	The Library, Royal Commonwealth Society, 18 Northumberland Avenue, London, WC2N 5BJ	-	01-930 6733
LO-SC	Supreme Court Library, Royal Courts of Justice, Strand, London, WC2A 2LL	-	01-405 7641
LO-TS	The Library, Treasury Solicitor's Dept., 3 Central Buildings, Matthew Parker Street, London, SW1H 9NN	-	01-930 7363/1124
LO/U-1	University of London Library, Senate House, Malet Street, London, WC1E 7HU	269400	01-636 4514
LO/U-2	The Library, University College London, Gower Street, London, WC1E 6BT	-	01-387 7050
LO/U-3	British Library of Political and Economic Science, London School of Economics, Houghton Street, Aldwych, London, WC2A 2AE	-	01-405 7686
LO/U11	The Library, King's College London, Strand, London, WC2R 2LS	-	01-836 5454

LO/U12	The Library, Queen Mary College, Mile End Road, London, E1 3NS	-	01-980 4811
LO/U14	The Library, School of Oriental and African Studies, Malet Street, London, WC1E 7HP	-	01-637 2388
LO/U19	The Library, Institute of Historical Research, Senate House, Malet Street, London, WC1E 7HU	-	01-636 0272
LO/U24	The Library, Institute of Advanced Legal Studies, 17 Russell Square, London, WC1B 5DR	-	01-637 1731
LO/U28	The Library, Brunel University, Kingston Lane, Uxbridge, Middx. UB8 3PH	261173	0895 37188
LV-LP	The Library, Liverpool Polytechnic, 1 Rumford Place, Liverpool, L3 9RH		051-227 5581
LV/P-1	Bib. Services Division, Liverpool City Libraries, Brown Picton and Hornby Libraries, William Brown Street, Liverpool, L3 8EW	62500	051-207 2147
LV/U-1	University Library, University of Liverpool, P.O. Box 123, Liverpool, L69 3DA	627095	051-709 6022
MA/P-1	Manchester Central Library, St. Peter's Square, Manchester, M2 5PD	669475	061-236 9422
MA/U-1	John Rylands University Library of Manchester, Oxford Road, Manchester, M13 9PL	668932	061-273 3333
NO/U-1	University Library, University of Nottingham, Nottingham, NG7 2RD	37346	0602 56101
NW/U-1	University Library, University of Newcastle upon Tyne, Queen Victoria Road, Newcastle upon Tyne, NE1 7RU	53654	0632 28511
OX/U-1	Bodleian Library, University of Oxford, Broad Street, Oxford, OX1 3BG	83656	0865 44675
OX/U-9	Rhodes House Library, University of Oxford, South Parks Road, Oxford, OX1 3RG	-	0865 55762
OX/U13	Indian Institute, University of Oxford, Broad Street, Oxford OX1 3BE	-	0865 44675

OX/U15	University of Oxford Law Library, St. Cross Building, Manor Road, Oxford, OX1 3UR	83656	0865 49631
OX/U25	Codrington Library, All Souls College, High Street, Oxford, OX1 4AL	-	0865 22251
QE/C76	The Library, Trent Polytechnic, Burton Street, Nottingham, NG1 4BU	-	0602 48248
QG/C25	The Library, Polytechnic of Wales, Llantwit Road, Treforest, Pontypridd, Mid-Glamorgan, CF37 1DL	-	0443 405133
QL/D15	Manchester Polytechnic, Inter-Library Loans Unit, Central Library, All Saints Building, Grosvenor Square, Manchester, M15 6BH	667915	061-228 6171
QM/C48	The Library, Birmingham Polytechnic, Perry Barr, Birmingham B42 2SU	-	021-356 6911
QM/C68	The Librarian, North Staffordshire Polytechnic, College Road, Stoke-on-Trent, ST4 2DE	-	0782 45531
QN/C70	The Library, Newcastle upon Tyne Polytechnic, Ellison Building, Ellison Place, Newcastle upon Tyne, NE1 8ST	-	0632 26002
QS/Q12	Interlending Department, London Borough of Hammersmith Public Library, Shepherds Bush Road, Hammersmith, London, W6 7AT	-	01-748 6032
QS/Q13	Camden Public Library, Holborn Reference Library, 32-38 Theobalds Road, London, WC1X 8PA	-	01-405 2705
QS/Q29	City of Westminster Public Library, Central Reference Library, St. Martin's Street, London, WC2H 7HP	-	01-930 3274
QS/S-4	The Library, Gray's Inn, 5 South Square, Gray's Inn, London, WC1R 5EU	-	01-242 8592
QS/S-5	The Library, Institute of Classical Studies, 31 Gordon Square, London, WC1H OPY	-	01-387 7697
QS/S-6	Inner Temple Library, Temple, London, EC4Y 7DA	-	01-353 2959
QS/S-7	Lincoln's Inn Library, London, WC2A 3TN	-	01-242 4371

QS/S-8	Law Society Library, Law Society's Hall, 113 Chancery Lane, London, WC2A 1PL	261203	01-242 1222
QW/C73	Police College Library, Bramshill House, Hartley Wintney, Hants, RG27 OJW	-	025-126 2931
QW/D12	Bolland Library, Bristol Polytechnic, Coldharbour Lane, Bristol, BS16 1QY	-	0272 656261
RE/U-1	University Library, University of Reading, Whiteknights, Reading, Berks, RG6 2AE	847813	0734 84331
SH/U-1	University Library, University of Sheffield, Western Bank, Sheffield, S10 2TN	54348	0742 78555
SO/U-1	University Library, University of Southampton, University Road, Highfield, Southampton, SO9 5NH	47661	0703 559122
SW/U-1	University Library, University College of Swansea, Singleton Park, Swansea, West Glamorgan, SA2 8PP	48358	0792 25678
XM/C10	The Library, Wolverhampton Polytechnic, St. Peters Square, Wolverhampton, WV1 1RL	336301	0902 27371
XY/N-1	British Library Lending Division, Boston Spa, Wetherby, West Yorkshire, LS23 7BQ	557381	0937 843434
YK/U-1	University of York Library, Heslington, York YO1 5DD	57933	0904 59861

ALI-ABA-CLE review/ American Bar Association Committee on Continuing Professional Education. -- Philadelphia, 1966-
Co-sponsor: American Law Institute
ISSN 0044-7560

No holdings notified

APLA bulletin/ American Patent Law Association. -- Washington D.C., 1952-

XY/N-1 1963-

APLA quarterly journal/ American Patent Law Association. -- Arlington, Va., 1972-
ISSN 0091-0538

No holdings notified

ARSP: Archiv für Rechts- und Sozialphilosophie. -- Munich, etc., 1934 (vol.27)-
Continues: Archiv für Rechts- und Wirtschaftsphilosophie, 1907-1933 (vol.26 no.3) and: Archiv für Rechtsphilosophie, 1933 (vol.26 no.4)
ISSN 0001-2343

AD/U-6 1952-
CA/U-1 imp.
CR/U-1 1972-
DN/U-1 1966-
ED/U-1
GL/U-1 1967-
LO/U-2 1971-
LO/U-3
LO/U24 1936-1938 imp., 1960-
MA/U-1 1966-
OX/U15 (1939/40 imp)
XY/N-1 1964 (v.50)-

ASDA bulletin/ Association Suisse de Droit Aérien et Spatiale = SVLR bulletin/ Schweizerische Vereinigung für Luft- und Raumrecht. -- Zurich, 1952-
ISSN 0487-8213

LO/U24
XY/N-1 1969-74 imp.

Abogada internacional/ Federacion Internacional de Abogadas. -- Detroit, 1953?-
ISSN 0567-5111

XY/N-1 1965(13)-

Abstracts on criminology and penology. -- Deventer, 1969 (vol.9)-
Continues: Excerpta criminologica, 1961-1968 (vol.8)
ISSN 0001-3684

AD/U-6
BL/U-1
BR/U-1 1976 (v.16)-
BT/U-1 1974 (v.14)-
CA/U37
CB/U-1
CR/U-1 1969-
CV/U-1 1968-
DR/U-1 1965-68
ED/U-1
EX/U-1
GL/U-1
HL/U-1
KL/U-1 1969-
LC/U-1
LD/U-1
LO/C-3 1970 (v.10)-
LO/C14 1974 (v.14)-
LO/C15 1972 (v.12)-
LO/N-1 1969 (v.9)-
LO/N27
LO/U-2 1967-
LO/U-3 1962-
LO/U24 1965-68;1969-72 imp., 1973-
LO/U28 1970 (v.10)-
NW/U-1 1968-
OX/U15
QE/C76 1961-
QW/C73 1962-
RE/U-1 1966-
SH/U-1
SO/U-1
SW/U-1 1967 (v.7)-
XY/N-1

Acta Academiae Universalis Jurisprudentiae Comparativae = Mémoires de l'Académie Internationale de Droit Comparé. -- Paris, 1928-1957 (vol.3 no.6)

LO/U-2 1953-57   LO/U24 (w.v.2,pt.1)   OX/U15

Acta criminologiae et medicinae legalis japonica see Nippon hoigaku zasshi

Acta criminologica see Criminologie

Acta Facultatis Politico-iuridicae Universitatis Scientarium Budapestinensis. -- Budapest, 1939-

CA/U13 1966-68; 1970-

Acta juridica/ Faculty of Law, University of Capetown. -- Capetown, 1958-
Continues: Butterworths' South African law review, 1954-1957
ISSN 0065-1346

AB/U-1 1969-	ED/U-1	NO/U-1 1958-
AD/U-6	EX/U-1	OX/U15
BH/U-1	LC/U-1 1958-	OX/U25
BL/U-1 1958-	LD/U-1 1954-57	QS/S-4
CA/U13	LO/U-1 1958-74	SH/U-1 1958-
CA/U37 1959-75 (v.17)	LO/U-2	SO/U-1 1958-60; 1967.
CR/U-1 1970-	LO/U11 1958-	XY/N-1 1964-
DN/U-1 1958-	LO/U14 1967-	
ED/S11	LO/U24	
	MA/U-1 1956-	

Acta juridica Academiae Scientiarum Hungaricae. -- Budapest, 1959-
ISSN 0001-592X

BL/U-1 1967-	LO/U-3	XY/N-1 1960 (v.2); 1966 (v.8)-
CA/U13 1966-	LO/U24 1966 (v.8)-	
LO/N-1	OX/U15	

Acta juridica et politica. -- Szeged, 1955-

CA/U13 1960- imp.   OX/U-1   XY/N-1

Acta juris Hungarici: revue trimestrielle de droit hongrois. -- Budapest, 1932.

LO/N-1

Acta medicinae legalis et socialis. -- Brussels, 1948-
ISSN 0065-1397

DN/U-1 1950-75   XY/N-1 1965-67 (v.18-20)

Acta salmanticensia. Derecho. -- Salamanca, 1946-

AD/U-6 1966 (v.18); 1968 (v.22).	GL/U-1 1946-68	OX/U15
CA/U-1 1946.	LO/N-1	XY/N-1 1946-71 (v.31)

Acta Universitatis Carolinae <u>see</u> next entry

Acta Universitatis Carolinae. Iuridica. -- Prague, 1958-
Continues in part: Acta Universitatis Carolinae, 1954-1957, (ISSN 0515-3174)
ISSN 0515-3212

CA/U-1 1954- LO/U24 1960- OX/U15
GL/U-1 1954-

Actes de la Société Suisse des Juristes <u>see</u> Verhandlungen des Schweizerisches Juristenvereins

Actualité juridique: droit administratif. -- Paris, 1945-
ISSN 0001-7728

BH/U-1 1960-
CV/U-1 1972 (v.28 no.3)-
DN/U-1 1958-68 imp., 1969-
ED/U-1 1962-
HL/U-1 1966-
LD/U-1 1964.
LO/U24 1960 (v.16)-
OX/U15 1960-
SH/U-1 1960 (v.16)-
XY/N-1 1963 (v.19)-

Adelaide law review. -- Adelaide, 1960-
ISSN 0065-1915

AB/U-1 1972 (v.4)-
CA/U13
LD/U-1
LO/U12 June 1963-
LO/U24
NO/U-1
NW/U-1 1960 (v.1 no.3)-
OX/U15
SH/U-1
XY/N-1 1969 (v.3, no.3)-

Administration publique: revue du droit public et des sciences administratives. -- Brussels, 1976-
Continues: Recueil de jurisprudence du droit administratif, 1946-1975 (vol.30)

OX/U15 1964 (v.19)-

Administrative law bulletin <u>see</u> next entry

Administrative law review/ American Bar Association Section of Administrative Law. -- Chicago, 1960 (vol.13)-
Continues: Administrative law bulletin, 1949-1960 (vol.12)
ISSN 0001-8368

LC/U-1
LO-MT 1970 (v.23)-
LO/U24
QN/C70 1970-
XY/N-1 1967 (v.19 no.2)-

Advertising law anthology. -- Arlington, Va., 1973-
ISSN 0093-1985

No holdings notified

Advocate. -- Ife, 1968-

OX/U15 1968 (v.1 no.1).

Advocate. -- London, 1875.

LO/N-1

Advocate/ Vancouver Bar Association. -- Vancouver, 1943-

LO/U24 OX/U15 1946-

Advocates chronicle. -- Madras, 1932.

LO/N-1

Advokatbladet/ Danske Advokatsamfund. -- Copenhagen, 1921-

No holdings notified

African Law Association in America newsletter/ Columbia University School of Law. -- New York, 1965 (no.1) - 1967 (no.5)
ISSN 0568-1375

LO/U24

African law digest. -- Addis Ababa, 1966-
ISSN 0002-0052

No holdings notified

African law studies. -- New York, 1969-
ISSN 0002-0060

LO/U14	OX/U15	XY/N-1 1975 (12)-
LO/U24		

Agrarrecht: Zeitschrift für das gesamte Recht der Landwirtschaft, der Agrarmärkte und des ländlichen Raumes. -- Hiltrup/Westf., 1971-

XY/N-1 1975 (Bd.5)-

Air Force law review. -- Maxwell AFB, Ala., 1974 (vol.16)-
Continues: JAG bulletin, 1959-1964, and: United States Air Force JAG law review, 1965-1973 (vol.15), (ISSN 0021-3527)
ISSN 0094-8381

LO/N-1 1974 (v.16)-	LO/U24 1971 (v.13)-	XY/N-1 1974 (v.16)-
LO/U11 1967-73 imp., 1974-		

Air law. -- Deventer, 1975-

AD/U-6	LO/N-5	LO/U24
BH/U-1	LO/U-2	XY/N-1

Air law review. -- New York, 1930-1941 (vol.12)

AD/U-6	LO/U-3 (w.v.1 nos. 2-4)	LO/U24
CA/U13		OX/U15

Akron law review. -- Akron, Ohio, 1967-
ISSN 0002-371X

LO/U24 XY/N-1 1972 (v.5)-

Alabama Bar bulletin <u>see</u> Alabama lawyer

Alabama law journal. -- Birmingham, Ala., 1925-1930 (vol.5)

OX/U15

Alabama law review. -- University, 1948-
ISSN 0002-4279

BH/U-1 1967 (v.20)-
BR/U-1 1967 (v.20)-
DN/U-1 1967-
ED/U-1 1967-74 (v.20 -26) imp.
EX/U-1 1967 (v.20)-
LO/U24
OX/U15
XY/N-1 1969 (v.22)-

Alabama lawyer. -- Montgomery, 1940 (vol.1)-
Continues: Alabama Bar bulletin, 1939 (vol.1)
ISSN 0002-4287

LO/U24
OX/U15 1960 (v.21)-
XY/N-1 1968 (v.29)-

Alabama State Foundation bulletin. -- Montgomery,

OX/U15 1966 (v.4)-

Alaska Bar brief. -- Anchorage, 1972-
Continues in part: Alaska law journal, 1963-1971 (ISSN 0002-452X)
ISSN 0093-1039

No holdings notified

Alaska law journal. -- Juneau, 1963-1971 (vol.9 no.5)
Continued by: Alaska Bar brief, q.v., and: UCLA-Alaska law review, q.v.
ISSN 0002-452X

No holdings notified

Albany law journal. -- Albany, N.Y., 1870-1908 (no.70)

ED/S10 1876-87
ED/S11 1880-1908
LO-MT 1878-80; 1882-1904
LO/N-1
OX/U15

Albany law review. -- Albany, N.Y., 1948 (vol.12)-
Continues: Albany law review of recent decisions, 1931-1942 (vol.11)
ISSN 0002-4678

CA/U13 1967 (v.32)-
LO/U24
OX/U15
XY/N-1 1969 (v.34)-

Albany law review of recent decisions <u>see</u> previous entry

Alberta law quarterly. -- Edmonton, 1934-1945

LO/U24
OX/U15

Alberta law review. -- Edmonton, 1955-
ISSN 0002-4821

BL/U-1 1963-
LO/U24
MA/U-1 1970 (v.8)-
OX/U15
SH/U-1 1974 (v.12)-
SO/U-1 1974-
XY/N-1

Alert: women's legislative review. -- Middletown, Conn., 1972-

No holdings notified

Aligarh law journal. -- Aligarh Muslim University, 1964-
ISSN 0568-9996

LO/U14 1964.	OX/U15 1964-65 (nos.1-2); 1969 (no.4).

All India reporter: Journal section. -- Nagpur, 1914-
ISSN 0002-5593

BL/U-1 1950-	LO/N17 1963-74	OX/U15
CA/U13	LO/U14 1920-21; 1923-	QS/S-6
LO-MT 1921-		

Allahabad law journal. -- Allahabad, 1904-

CA/U13 1952-62	LO/U14	OX/U15
LO/N-1 1907-43; 1957-71		

Allahabad law review. -- Allahabad, 1969-

LO/U14

Allahabad law times. -- Lahore, 1923-

LO/N-1 1933-41	LO/U14 1923-63; 1966-

Állam-és jogtudomány. -- Budapest, 1957-
1957-1961 entitled: Állam-és jogtudomány intézet értesítoje
ISSN 0002-564X

LO/N-1 1961 (v.4)-	LO/U-3 1965-77	XY/N-1 1964 (v.7)-

Állam-és jogtudomány intézet értesítoje <u>see</u> previous entry

Allgemeine deutsche Strafrechtszeitung. -- Leipzig, 1861-1873 (vol.13)

LO/N-1

Allgemeine Telegraph für die deutsche Gesetzkunde. -- Stuttgart, etc., 1840 (n.s.v.1).
Continues: Archiv für die neueste Gesetzgebung aller deutschen Staaten, 1832-1839 (vol.9)

LO/N-1

American Association for Labor Legislation legislative review <u>see</u> American labor legislation review

American bankruptcy law journal. -- Bangor, Me., 1971 (vol.45)-
Continues: Journal of the National Association of Referees in Bankruptcy, 1926-1965 (vol.39), and: Journal of the National Conference of Referees in Bankruptcy, 1966-1970 (vol.44)
ISSN 0027-9048

LO/U24 1971 (v.45)-

American Bar Association
Periodicals with distinctive titles issued by the ABA and its sections are entered under title

American Bar Association journal. -- Chicago, 1915-
ISSN 0002-7596

BH/U-1 1968-	LA/U-1 1969-	NO/U-1 1973 (v.59)- imp.
BL/U-1 1954-	LC/C-1 1974-	OX/U15
CA/U13 1926-	LO-MT	QS/S-4 1958-
CR/U-1 1971-	LO/U11 1959-	QS/S-7 1947-71
ED/S11 1931-	LO/U24	XY/N-1 1940 (v.26)-
HL/U-1 1975 (v.61)-		

American Bar Foundation research journal. -- Chicago, 1976-

LO-MT	XY/N-1

American Bar news. -- Chicago, 1956-1976 (vol.21)
ISSN 0002-760X

HL/U-1 1975 (v.20).	LO/U24 1967-76 (v.12-21)

American business law journal. -- Bloomington, Ind., 1963-
Continues: Bulletin - American Business Law Association, 1956-1962 (vol.6 no.1) (ISSN 0517-0338)
ISSN 0002-7766

CH-CI 1973 (v.11)-	CV/U-1 1968 (v.6)-	QW/D12 1975 (v.13)-
CV/C-1 1969-72 (v.7-10)	LO/U24 1976 (v.14)-	XY/N-1 1967 (v.7)-

American criminal law quarterly <u>see</u> next entry

American criminal law review/ A.B.A. Section of Criminal Law. -- Chicago, 1971 (vol.10)-
Continues: Criminal law quarterly, 1962-1963 (vol.1 no.2) and: American criminal law quarterly, 1963 (vol.1 no.3)- 1970 (vol.9) (ISSN 0002-8118)

CA/U37	LO/U28 1970 (v.8)-	QN/C70 1969 (v.8)-
LO/U11 1976 (v.14)-	OX/U15	XY/N-1 1965 (v.5)-
LO/U24		

American Foreign Law Association newsletter. -- New York, 1969-

No holdings notified

American Indian law review. -- Norman, Okla., 1973-
ISSN 0094-002X

No holdings notified

American journal of comparative law. -- Ann Arbor, Mich., 1952-
ISSN 0002-919X

AB/U-1	BR/U-1	CV/U-1
AD/U-6	CA/U13	DN/U-1
BH/U-1	CB/U-1	DR/U-1
BL/U-1	CR/U-1 1954-	ED/S11 (cont'd)

American journal of comparative law (cont'd).

ED-SLC 1966-
ED/U-1
EX/U-1
GL/U-1
HL/U-1 1965-
LA/U-1 1952-76
LC/U-1
LD/U-1
LO/C10 1973-
LO/C15 1972-
LO/C25 1975-
LO/C27 1973-
LO/C47 1954-
LO/N-1
LO/N-5
LO/R74 1965-
LO/U-2
LO/U-3
LO/U11
LO/U12
LO/U14 1973-
LO/U24
LO/U28
LV/U-1
MA/U-1
NO/U-1
OX/U15
QE/C76 1960-
QW/D12
SH/U-1
SO/U-1
XM/C10
XY/N-1

American journal of criminal law. -- Austin, Tex., 1972-
ISSN 0092-2315

CR/U-1
LO-MT
LO/U24
XY/N-1

American journal of international law. -- Washington, D.C., 1907-
ISSN 0002-9300

AB/N-1 1960- imp.
AB/U-1 1920-
AD/U-6
BC-UC 1961-74 imp.
BH/U-1 1933-
BL/U-1 1920-
BR/U-1
BT/U-1 1940-
CA/U-1
CA/U13
CB/U-1 1966 (v.60)-
CH-CI 1971 (v.65)-
CR/U-1 1938-52
CV/U-1
DN/U-1 1907-26; 1948-
DR/U-1 (w.1927-30)
ED/S11
ED/U-1 (v.22 imp.)
EX/U-1 1964-
GL/U-1
GL/U-2 1972-
HL/U-1
KL/U-1
LA/U-1 1959-75
LC/U-1
LD/C-1 1971 (v.65)-
LD/U-1
LO/C-3 1970-
LO/C-5 1935; 1970 (v.64)-
LO/C10 1971-
LO/C14 1970 (v.64)-
LO/C15 1950-
LO/C25 1971-75
LO/C47 1974-
LO-MT
LO/N-1
LO/N17
LO/S14 1945-
LO/U-1 1956-
LO/U-2
LO/U-3
LO/U11 1938-
LO/U12 (w.1927-38)
LO/U24
LO/U28
LV-LP 1973-
LV/P-1 1913-42; 1960-
LV/U-1
MA/P-1 1907-40 (w.1913; 1918)
MA/U-1
NO/U-1
NW/U-1 1923-39 imp., 1949-
OX/U15
OX/U25
QE/C76 1972-
QM/C68 1975 (v.69)-
QS/Q12 1940-47 imp., 1948-
QS/S-4 1970-
QS/S-6 1912-imp.
QS/S-7
QW/D12
RE/U-1
SH/U-1 1934-37 imp., 1938-
SO/U-1
XY/N-1 1929-34 imp., 1935 (v.29)-

American journal of jurisprudence. -- Notre Dame, Ind., 1969 (vol.14)-
Continues: Natural law forum, 1956-1968 (vol.13)
ISSN 0065-8995

AB/U-1
AD/U-6 1957-
BH/U-1
BL/U-1
BR/U-1
BT/U-1
CA/U13 1959-
CV/C-1 1957 (v.2)- (w.1968 v.13)
DN/U-1 1963-68 imp., 1969-
DR/U-1
ED/U-1 1961; 1963-65; 1969-
HL/U-1 1971 (v.16)-
LC/U-1
LD/U-1 1956-68
LO/C10 1972 (v.17)-
LO/C15 1972 (v.17)-
LO-MT 1957 (v.2)-
LO/N-1 1969 (v.14)-
LO/U-2 1957-59 imp., 1960-
LO/U24
LV-LP 1973-
LV/U-1
NO/U-1 1959-68 (cont'd)

American journal of jurisprudence (cont'd).

OX/U15
RE/U-1
SH/U-1 1963-68 imp., 1973-
SO/U-1 1961.
SW/U-1
XY/N-1 1968 (v.13)-

American journal of law and medicine. -- Boston, 1975-

XY/N-1 1977 (v.3)-

American journal of legal history. -- Philadelphia, 1957-
ISSN 0002-9319

AB/U-1
BH/U-1
BL/U-1
BR/U-1
CA/U13
CR/U-1
ED/U-1 1966-
EX/U-1
HL/U-1 1964-
LD/C-1 1973 (v.17)-
LD/U-1 1966-
LO/N-1 1957-74
LO/U-2 1975-
LO/U-3
LO/U11 1963-
LO/U19
LO/U24
LV/U-1 1961-
MA/U-1 1963-
NO/U-1 1970 (v.14)-
OX/U15
QN/C70 1971-
SH/U-1
SW/U-1
XY/N-1
YK/U-1 1963-76

American journal of police science. -- Chicago, 1930-1932 (vol.3 no.2)
Absorbed by: Journal of criminal law and criminology, q.v.

No holdings notified

American jurist and law magazine <u>see</u> American law magazine

American labor legislation review. -- New York, 1911-1942 (vol.32 no.4)
Continues: American Association for Labor Legislation legislative review, 1909-1910

BL/U-1 1915 imp.
LO/U-3 1909-10 imp., 1911-42

American Law Institute-ABA-CLE review <u>see</u> ALI-ABA-CLE review

American law journal. -- Philadelphia, 1848-1852 (vol.11)
Continues: Pennsylvania law journal, 1842-1848 (vol.7)

LO/N-1 1847-52

American law journal/ Ed. John E. Hall. -- Philadelphia, 1808-1817 (vol.6)
1808-1813(vol.4)as American law journal and miscellaneous repertory.
Continued by: Journal of jurisprudence, q.v.

ED/S11
LO-MT
LO/N-1

American law journal and miscellaneous repertory <u>see</u> previous entry

American law magazine. -- Philadelphia, 1843-1846 (vol.6)
Continues: American jurist and law magazine, 1829-1843 (vol.28)

ED/S11 LO/N-1 LO/U24 1842 (v.27).
LO-MT 1829-43 (w.1833)

American law register see University of Pennsylvania law review

American law review see United States law review

American law school review see Journal of legal education

American law times. -- New York, 1905-1906 (vol.1 no.5)

LO/N-1

American lawyer see Lawyer (Brooklyn)

American legislator/ Council of State Governments. -- Lexington, Ky., 1971-
ISSN 0002-9750

LO/N-1

American Patent Law Association bulletin see APLA bulletin

American Patent Law Association quarterly journal see APLA quarterly journal

American University. Washington College of Law intramural law review see next entry

American University law review. -- Washington D.C., 1957 (vol.6)-
Continues: American University. Washington College of Law intramural law review, 1952-1956 (vol.5)
ISSN 0003-1453

LO/U24 XY/N-1 1971 (v.21)-

Amtliche Nachrichten des Reichsversicherungsamts. -- Berlin, 1884-1919

LO/N-1 1884-87; 1916-19

Analecta juris pontifici. -- Rome; Paris, 1855-1891 (vol.29)

LO/N-1 OX/U-1 1855-89

Analele Facultăţii de drept de Cluj. -- Cluj, 1939-

OX/U15 1939.

Analele Universitaţii Bucureşti. Seria ştiinţe filozofie, istorie, drept. -- Bucharest, 1974-
Continues: Analele... Seria ştiinţe sociale, 1954-1963 (anul 12) (ISSN 0524-8248), and: Analele... Seria ştiinţe juridice, 1964 (anul 13)-1973 (ISSN 0068-3310)

CA/U-1 1971-
OX/U-1 1974-
OX/U15 1959/60-73
XY/N-1 1961 (anul 10)- imp.

Analele Universitaţii Bucureşti. Seria ştiinţe juridice see previous entry

Analele Universitaţii Bucureşti. Seria ştiinţe sociale see Analele... Seria ştiinţe filozofie, istorie, drept

Anales de la Academia Nacional de Derecho y Ciencias Sociales. -- Buenos Aires, 1950?-

No holdings notified

Anales de la Catedra Francisco Suárez. -- Granada, 1960?-

OX/U15 1965 (no.5)-

Anales de la Facultad de Ciencias Jurídicas Politicas y Sociales/ Universidad Católica. -- Santiago de Chile, 1945?-

No holdings notified

Anales de la Facultad de Ciencias Juridicas y Sociales/ Universidad de Chile. -- Santiago, 1935-

CA/U-1 1935-36
GL/U-1 1935-36
LO/U-1 1935-36
LO/U24 1952-57 (3 epoca, v.4)
OX/U-1 1935-51 (v.1-14) imp.

Anales de la Facultad de Ciencias Juridicas y Sociales/ Universidad Nacional de La Plata. -- La Plata, 1926-

CA/U-1 1942-48 (v.13,14,16)
LO/U-3 1926-48 (t.16 no.1)
LV/U-1 1941 no.1; 1942-43
OX/U15 1926-27

Anales de la Facultad de Derecho y Ciencias Sociales/ Universidad de Buenos Aires. -- Buenos Aires, 1902-1919 (no.20)

LO/U24 1918 (v.18-19)
OX/U15 1915.

Anali Pravnog Fakulteta u Beogradu. -- Belgrade, 1953-
ISSN 0003-2565

GL/U-1 (Soviet Studies Branch Library) 1964-
LO/N-1 1958-
LO/U-3 1953-77
LO/U11 1956

Angelicum/ Pontificium Athenaeum Angelicum. -- Rome, 1924-
ISSN 0003-3081

CA/U-1 1973-
XY/N-1 1959 (v.36 no.2)-

Anglo-American law review. -- Chichester, 1972-

AB/N-1 1975-
AB/U-1
BH/U-1
BL/U-1
BR/U-1 1974 (v.3)-
CA/U-1
CA/U13
CB/U-1 1974 (v.3)-
CH-CI
CR/U-1
ED/S11
ED-SLC
ED/U-1
EX/U-1 1974-
HL/U-1
LC/C-1
LD/C-1
LO/C-5
LO/C14
LO/C15
LO/C25 1975-
LO/C27 1974-
LO/C47
LO/N-1
LO/N-5
LO/N26
LO/R74
LO/U-2
LO/U11 1972-75
LO/U12
LO/U24
LO/U28
LV/U-1
MA/U-1
NO/U-1 1973 (v.2)-
OX/U15
QE/C76
QM/C48
QM/C68
QN/C70
QS/S-4
QS/S-6
QW/C73
QW/D12
SH/U-1
SO/U-1
XY/N-1

Annalen der deutschen und ausländischen Criminalrechtspflege. -- Berlin, etc., 1828-1837 (vol.17); 1837-1855 (N.S. vol.73)

LO/N-1

Annalen der grossherzoglich-badischen Gerichte see Badische Rechtspraxis

Annalen der Justiz und Verwaltung im Bezirke des K. Appellationsgerichts und der K. Regierung zu Cassel. -- Cassel, 1853-1885 (vol.28)
Vols 1-14 entitled: Annalen der Justizpflege und Verwaltung in Kurhessen

LO/N-1

Annalen der Justizpflege und Verwaltung in Kurhessen see previous entry

Annalen der preussischen innern Staatsverwaltung. -- Berlin, 1817-1839

LO/N-1
LO/U-3 (1831; 1834 imp.)

Annalen des Deutschen Reichs für Gesetzgebung, Verwaltung und Volkswirtschaft. -- Berlin; Munich, 1868-1931 (vol.64 no.2)
1868-1869 entitled: Staatshandbuch für Gesetzgebung... des Norddeutschen Bundes...

LO/N-1
LO/U-3 1870-1931 (w.1926)

Annales africaines. -- Paris, 1954-
ISSN 0066-202X

BT/U-1 1961-
ED/U-1 1962-
LD/U-1 1965-
LO/N-1 (w.1955;1957)
LO/U14
LO/U24
OX/U15
XY/N-1 1967-

Annales criminelles. -- Dresden, 1868.

LO/N-1

Annales d'études internationales = Annals of international studies/ Association des Anciens Etudiants de l'Institut Universitaire de Hautes Etudes Internationales (Genève). -- Brussels, 1970-
ISSN 0066-2135

LO/N-1
LO/S14
LO/U-3
OX/U-1
SH/U-1 1973 (v.4)-

Annales d'hygiène publique et de médecine légale *see* next entry

Annales d'hygiène publique, industrielle et sociale. -- Paris, 1923 (5e série t.1)-1950 (5e série t.28)
Continues: Annales d'hygiène publique et de médecine légale, 1829-1922 (in 188 vols.)

No holdings notified

Annales de droit: revue trimestrielle de droit belge. -- Louvain, 1965 (vol.25)-
Continues: Annales de l'Association des Anciens Etudiants de la Faculté de Droit de l'Université de Louvain, 1930-1938, and: Annales de droit et de sciences politiques, 1939-1964 (vol.24)

BL/U-1 1965-
ED/U-1 1965-
LO/U-3 1957-
LO/U24 1958 (v.18) imp., 1961 (v.21)-
XY/N-1 1953 (v.13 no.51)-

Annales de droit commercial et industriel français, étranger et international. -- Paris, 1886-1914; 1920-1939
1886-1895(vol.10)as Annales de droit commercial français, étranger et international

CA/U13 1921-30; 1932-38
LO/N-1 1886-1939

Annales de droit commercial français, étranger et international *see* previous entry

Annales de droit et de sciences politiques *see* Annales de droit: revue trimestrielle de droit belge

Annales de droit international médical. -- Monaco, 1957-
ISSN 0517-8517

LO/M32
XY/N-1 1968; 1970 (v.20)-

Annales de l'Association des Anciens Etudiants de la Faculté de Droit de l'Université de Louvain *see* Annales de droit: revue trimestrielle de droit belge

Annales de l'Enseignement Supérieur de Grenoble *see* Annales de l'Université de Grenoble. Section lettres-droit

Annales de l'Institut de Droit Comparé/ Université de Paris. -- Paris, 1934-1938

CA/U13
OX/U15

Annales de l'Université de Grenoble <u>see</u> next entry

Annales de l'Université de Grenoble. Section lettres-droit. -- Grenoble, 1924 (n.s. vol.1)- 1947 (n.s. vol.22)
Continues in part: Annales de l'Enseignement Supérieur de Grenoble, 1889-1894 (vol.6) and: Annales de l'Université de Grenoble, 1895 (vol.7)- 1923 (vol.34)

CA/U-1 1889-1946 LO/U-1 1924-47 OX/U-1 1924-47
ED/U-1 1912-47

Annales de l'Université de Lyon. Nouvelle série 3: Droit. -- Lyon, 1936-
Continues in part: its Annales, 1891-1898 and: Nouvelle série 2: Droit, lettres, 1899-1934 (no.48)

LO/N-1 1952- LV/U-1 1899-1925

Annales de l'Université de Madagascar <u>see</u> Annales malgaches: droit

Annales de la Faculté de Droit, d'Economie et de Sciences Sociales de Liège. -- Liège, 1976 (vol.21 no.4)-
Continues: Annales de la Faculté de Droit de Liège,1956-1976 (vol. 21 no.3), (ISSN 0457-8023)

BL/U-1 1966- LO/U24 1959 (v.4)- OX/U15
CA/U13 1961-

Annales de la Faculté de Droit d'Istanbul. -- Istanbul, 1951-
ISSN 0578-9745

CA/U13 1951-64 LD/U-1 1953- OX/U15 1951-57; 1959 (v.9 no.12); 1967-
DR/U-4 1963 (v.19). LO/N-1 1951- XY/N-1 1966 (v.16)-
GL/U-1 1955-59 imp., 1970- LO/U14 imp.
LO/U24

Annales de la Faculté de Droit de Liège see Annales de la Faculté de Droit, d'Economie et de Sciences Sociales de Liège

Annales de la Faculté de Droit et des Sciences Economiques/ Université de Clermont-Ferrand. -- Clermont-Ferrand, 1964-
ISSN 0578-4999

LO/N-1 XY/N-1 1971 (v.8)-

Annales de la Faculté de Droit et des Sciences Economiques/ Université Saint Joseph de Beyrouth. -- Beirut, 1945-
Has sub-series, entitled: Proche-Orient, études juridiques q.v.

LO/N-1 1956-73 LO/U-3 imp. LO/U14 imp.

Annales de la Faculté de Droit et des Sciences Economiques d'Aix en Provence. -- Aix en Provence, 1907-1913; n.s. 1918-
Continues: Annales des Facultés de Droit et de Lettres, 1905-1906 (vol.2)

AD/U-6 1905-13; 1918-63 CA/U-1 1907-14; 1918-26; 1937-39 LO/N-1 1945-72
LO/U-1 1940-65

(cont'd)

Annales de la Faculté de Droit et des Sciences Economiques d'Aix en Provence (cont'd).

LO/U-3 1907-13 (June); 1918- imp.	LO/U24 1960/61 (n.s.no.52)-	OX/U15 1906- XY/N-1 1971 (no.57)-

Annales de la Faculté de Droit et des Sciences Economiques de Toulouse. -- Toulouse, 1953-
ISSN 0563-9727

LO/N-1 1960-   LO/U-2 1973-   XY/N-1 1968-

Annales de la Faculté de Droit, Université de Bordeaux see Revue juridique et économique du Sud-Ouest...

Annales de la législation et de la jurisprudence françaises. -- Paris, 1834-1838

LO/N-1

Annales de la propriété industrielle, artistique et littéraire. -- Paris, 1855-

LO-MT 1958 (t.92)-   LO/U24 1959 (t.93)-   XY/N-1 1969 (t.103)-

Annales de législation et de jurisprudence. -- Geneva, 1820-1822 (vol.3)

LO/N-1 1820-21

Annales de médecine légale, de criminologie et de police scientifique see Médecine légale et dommage corporel

Annales des Facultés de Droit et de Lettres see Annales de la Faculté de Droit et de Sciences Economiques d'Aix en Provence

Annales des justices de paix see next entry

Annales des tribunaux. -- Paris, 1959-1969
Continues: Annales et journal spécial des justices de paix, 1784-1862, and: Annales des justices de paix, 1863-Oct. 1959

LO/N-1 1850 (yr.57)-1969

Annales du notariat et de l'enregistrement. -- Brussels, 1896-1970
Merged with: Revue pratique du notariat belge
to form: Revue du notariat belge, q.v.

No holdings notified

Annales et journal spécial des justices de paix see Annales des tribunaux

Annales internationales de criminologie. -- Paris, 1962-
ISSN 0003-4452

AB/U-1	ED/U-1	OX/U15
BH/U-1	LO/U-3 1968 (v.7)-	RE/U-1 1965-
CA/U37	LO/U28 1970 (v.9)-	XY/N-1 1966 (v.5 no.2)-

Annales juridiques, politiques, économiques et sociales. -- Algiers, 1955-1957 (vol.3 no.2)
ISSN 0517-8584

AD/U-6 (w.v.1, nos. 1-2)	CA/U13	LO/U14 (v.3 imp)
	ED/N-1 1956-57	OX/U15 imp.
BL/U-1 imp.	LO/U-3	

Annales malgaches: droit/ Université de Madagascar. Faculté de Droit et des Sciences Economiques. -- Paris, 1963-
ISSN 0570-1724

LO/N-1	LO/U24 1963-71 (v.8)	XY/N-1
LO/U14		

Annales Universitatis Mariae Curie-Sklodowska. Sectio G: Ius. -- Lublin, 1954-
ISSN 0458-4317

GL/U-1	LO/U-3 1954-75 (v.22)	XY/N-1

Annales Universitatis Saraviensis. Serie Rechts- und Wirtschaftswissenschaften <u>see</u> next entry

Annales Universitatis Saraviensis. Serie Rechts- und Wirtschaftswissenschaftliche Abteilung. Schriftenreihe. -- Saarbrücken, 1963 (no.1)-
Continues: its Serie Rechts- und Wirtschaftswissenschaften, 1952-1961 (vol.9), (ISSN 0558-0706)
ISSN 0563-1475

CA/U-1 1963-	LO/N-1	OX/U-1
DR/U-1 1952.	LO/U-1 imp.	OX/U15
GL/U-1	LO/U-3 1952-61	XY/N-1 1966 (no.23); 1969 (no.39)-
LD/U-1 1952-61	LV/U-1	

Annales Universitatis Scientiarum Budapestinensis de Rolando Eötvös nominatae. Sectio juridica. -- Budapest, 1959-
ISSN 0524-899X

CA/U-1	LO/N-1	OX/U15
CA/U13 1966-	LO/U24 1962 (v.3)- (w.1967;1969-70 (v.8; 10-12))	XY/N-1 1964 (v.5)-
CC/U-1 1967-73		
GL/U-1		

Annali del Seminario Giuridico/ Università di Catania. -- Naples, 1946 (n.s. vol.1)-1953 (n.s. vol.7)

GL/U-1 1917-	LO/U24	OX/U15
LO/U-2		

Annali del Seminario Giuridico della [Regia] Università di Palermo. -- Palermo, 1912 (vol.2)- (Vol.1 published in 1916)

AD/U-6 1917; 1921 (v.9); 1949 (v.20)-	ED/U-1	LO/U24 1912-30 (v.14)
	LO/U-2	OX/U15
	LO/U-3	QS/S-5 1936-44
CA/U13 1912-30;1949-		

Annali dell'Istituto di Diritto Aeronautico. -- Milan, 1969-

No holdings notified

Annali della Facoltà di Giurisprudenza/ Università degli Studi di Genova. -- Genova, 1962-

LO/U-2 1967-

Annali della Facoltà di Giurisprudenza/ Università di Bari. -- Bari, 1927-

OX/U15 1938-61 (v.16,n.s.)(w.1948/49)

Annali di diritto e procedura penale. -- Turin, 1932-

RE/U-1 1934-42

Annali di diritto internazionale see Diritto internazionale

Annali di diritto teorico pratico. -- Naples, 1856-1859 (tom.5)

CA/U-1 LO/N-1

Annali di storia del diritto. -- Milan, 1957-
ISSN 0570-1767

LO/N-1 OX/U15 XY/N-1
LO/U24 1957-73 (v.17)

Annals of international law and international relations. -- Lwów, 1938-

OX/U15 1938.

Annals of international studies see Annales d'études internationales

Annals of the Chinese Society of International Law. -- Taipei, 1964-

CA/U13 LO/U14 OX/U15 1964-66 (no.3)
LO/U-2 1970-72

Année canonique. -- Paris, 1952-
ISSN 0570-1953

CA/U-1 1953-62; 1968- (v.2-8,12-) XY/N-1 1973 (no.17)-

Année juridique: sélection et commentaire pratique des lois et décisions de jurisprudence de l'année. -- Paris, 1947-

No holdings notified

Annuaire - Association Internationale pour la Protection de la Propriété Industrielle. -- Paris, 1897-
1939-45; 1948-49 not published

LO/U-3 (w.1903) XY/N-1 1967-

Annuaire - Institut de Droit International. -- Basel, etc., 1875-1937; 1947-
ISSN 0073-8182

AD/U-6 1875-1913*
CA/U13
ED/S11 1875-1904 imp.
ED/U-1 1875;1957-73
GL/U-1 1913-75
LO-MT 1877-1928 (w.1926); 1947-73
LO/N-1 1875-1923 imp., 1950; 1952-
LO/U-2 1875-1937 imp., 1947-73
LO/U-3 1887-
LO/U11 1875-1913; 1947-
LO/U24 1892-96*; 1922-25; 1929-
OX/U15 1947-
OX/U25 1875-1971
QS/S-6 1875-1913*
QS/S-7 1877-1922
XY/N-1 1967 (v.52)-

* Libraries holding Abridged edition 1875-1913 in 6 vols. with 1 vol. of tables

Annuaire canadien de droit international see Canadian yearbook of international law

Annuaire de droit aérien et spatial see Yearbook of air and space law

Annuaire de droit maritime et aérien. -- Nantes, 1974-

LO/U24

Annuaire de l'A.A.A./ Association des Auditeurs et Anciens Auditeurs de l'Académie de Droit International de la Haye = Yearbook of the A.A.A./ Association of Attenders and Alumni of the Hague Academy of International Law. -- The Hague, 1951 (vol.21)-
Continues its Bulletin, 1925-1950 (vol.20) English title varies: 1951-1954 as Annuary, 1955-1959 as Annual
ISSN 0066-8923

CA/U13 1957-59;1961-
LO/U24 1955 (no.25)-
OX/U15 1964 (no.34)-
SH/U-1 1964-
XY/N-1 1966 (no.36)-

Annuaire de l'Association des Auditeurs et Anciens Auditeurs... see previous entry

Annuaire de l'Association Yougoslave de Droit International. -- Belgrade, 1931-1937

CA/U-1 1934-37
CA/U13
LO/U-3
LO/U11 1934-37
OX/U15

Annuaire de l'Ecole des Législations Religieuses. -- Paris, 1950-
ISSN 0475-7645

CA/U-1 1950-52/53

Annuaire de l'Institut International de Droit Public. -- Paris, 1929-1938

CA/U-1
HL/U-1
LO/U-2 1932-33
LO/U-3 1931-38 imp.
LO/U24 1930-37 (w.1935)
OX/U15

Annuaire de l'Institut International de Philosophie du Droit et de Sociologie Juridique. -- Paris, 1935 (vol.1, 1934/35)-1938 (vol.3, 1937/38)

LO/U24 1935 (v.1). OX/U15

Annuaire de l'Université de Sofia. Faculté de Droit = Godishnik na Sofiiskija Universitet. Juridicheski Fakultet. -- Sofia, 1908 (vol.5)-
Continues: Godishnik na Sofiiskija Universitet, 1904-1908 (vol.3/4)

AD/U-6 1967 (v.58)-	LO/N-1 1908 (v.5)-	LO/U24 1968 (v.59)-
CA/U-1 1950 (v.44)- imp.	LO/U11 1955-	

Annuaire de la Faculté de Droit de Sarajevo see Godishnjak Pravnog Fakulteta u Sarajevu

Annuaire de la législation du travail. -- Brussels, 1897-1923 (vol.23, 1919)

OX/U15 1898-1901

Annuaire de la marine marchande. -- Paris, 1968 (no.19)-
Continues: Marine marchande, 1948-1967
Annual review published by Journal de la marine marchande

XY/N-1 1967 (no.18)-

Annuaire de législation étrangère see Annuaire de législation française et étrangère

Annuaire de législation française/ Société de Législation Comparée. -- Paris, 1881-1933 (vol.53)
Absorbed by: Annuaire de législation française et étrangère (see next entry)

BH/U-1 1928-32	LO/U-1 1922-33	LV/U-1
ED/S11 1886-1917	LO/U-3	QS/S-6
LO-MT	LO/U24 1904-33 (v.23-53) (w.v.31-33,36-37,39,43)	QS/S-7
LO/N-1		
LO/N17 1882-85		

Annuaire de législation française et étrangère. -- Paris, 1956 (n.s.,tom.5)-
Continues: Annuaire de législation étrangère, 1872-1938; 1954 (n.s.,tom.1, 1938-1949)-1955 (n.s.,tom.4)
Absorbed: Annuaire de législation française, q.v.

BH/U-1 1938-	LO/N17 1872-1936	LV/U-1 1872-1971
CA/U13 1938-	LO/U-1 1919-37	OX/U15 1938-
CV/U-1 1950 (t.2)-	LO/U-3 1872-1931; 1958-	QS/S-6 1872-1936; 1938-49
HL/U-1 1964-	LO/U11 1964-	QS/S-7 1872-1936
LO-MT 1872-1936; 1938-55	LO/U24 1904 (t.3)- (w.t.14,16)	XY/N-1 1961 (t.10)-
LO/N-1		

Annuaire du tiers monde: droit et politique. -- Paris, 1976-

LO/N-1

Annuaire européen = European yearbook. -- The Hague, 1955-
ISSN 0071-3139

AB/N-1	LA/U-1	LV/P-1
AB/U-1 1956-	LC/U-1 1955-67	LV/U-1 1962-73
BH/P-1	LD/U-1	MA/P-1 1955-63
BR/U-1 1962-	LO-CBL*	NO/U-1 1956 (v.2)-
BT/U-1 1956-	LO/N-1	OX/U-1
CA/U13	LO/N17	OX/U15 1956 (v.2)-
CB/U-1 1956-	LO/P-6	QS/Q29
DN/U-1	LO/R74 1964-67	RE/U-1
DR/U-1 1956-	LO/S14	SH/U-1
ED/N-1 1955-56	LO/U-1	SO/U-1 1956-
ED/U-1	LO/U-2 1955-74	XM/C10 1970.
EX/U-1	LO/U-3	XY/N-1 1960;1964-
GL/U-1 1958-	LO/U11	
HL/U-1 1956 (v.2)-	LO/U24	

Annuaire français de droit international. -- Paris, 1955-
ISSN 0066-3085

AD/U-6 1968 (v.14)-	LO/N-1	LV/U-1 1955-74
BL/U-1	LO/N17 1969 (v.15)-	MA/U-1
CA/U13	LO/S14	NO/U-1
DR/U-1 1970-	LO/U-2	OX/U15
ED/U-1	LO/U-3	OX/U25
KL/U-1	LO/U11	XY/N-1 1962;1965-
LD/U-1	LO/U24	

Annuaire français des droits de l'homme. -- Paris, 1974-

LO/U24

Annuaire suisse de droit international <u>see</u> Schweizerisches Jahrbuch für internationales Recht

Annual conference of the Nigerian Society of International Law <u>see</u> Papers of the ... annual conference ...

Annual Institute on Estate Planning/ University of Miami. -- Indianapolis, 1967-

LO/U24 1971 (5th)-

Annual law review <u>see</u> University of Western Australia law review

Annual legal bibliography/ Harvard Law School Library. -- Cambridge, Mass., 1961-
Monthly supplement entitled: Current legal bibliography
ISSN 0073-0793

AB/U-1	LD/U-1	NO/U-1
BH/U-1	LO/N-5 1963-	OX/U15
BL/U-1 1971-74	LO/N17	QL/D15 1964 (v.4)-
CA/U13	LO/R74	QS/S-6
ED/U-1	LO/U-2	XM/C10
GL/U-1	LO/U24	XY/N-1 1969 (v.9)-
HL/U-1	LO/U28 1972 (v.12)-	
LC/U-1 1964-72 (v.4-12)	LV/U-1 1961-76	

Annual of industrial property law. -- London, 1975-

CA/U-1	LO/N-5	QN/C70
CA/U13	LO/N14 1975.	QS/S-6
LO-CBL	OX/U15	QW/D12
LO/N-1	QE/C76	XY/N-1

Annual report - Association of the Bar of the City of New York
see Yearbook - Association of the Bar ...

Annual review of the Law School of New York University see New York University law review

Annual survey of African law. -- London, 1970 (1967)-
ISSN 0066-4405

AB/N-1	CB/U-1	LO/U14
BH/U-1	CR/U-1	LO/U24
BL/U-1	EX/U-1 1967.	OX/U15
BT/U-1 1967-69 (v.1-3)	HL/U-1 1970 (v.4).	QS/S-6
	LC/U-1	SO/U-1
CA/U-1	LO/N-1	XY/N-1
CA/U13	LO/N17	

Annual survey of American law. -- New York, 1942-
ISSN 0066-4413

AB/U-1 (w.1946-60)	LA/U-1	LV/U-1 (w.1945;1951; 1971-72)
AD/U-6 1960-	LC/U-1	
BH/U-1	LD/U-1	MA/U-1
BL/U-1	LO-MT	NO/U-1
BR/U-1 1942- imp.	LO/R74	OX/U15
CA/U13	LO/U-1 1942-55,1958-60,1963.	OX/U25
CB/U-1 1942-54 imp., 1955-		QN/C70 1970-
	LO/U-2 1954;1956-	QS/Q12 1950-
CR/U-1 1970-	LO/U-3 1942-53	QS/S-4 1942-49
DN/U-1 1969-74	LO/U11 1960-74	RE/U-1
DR/U-1 (w.1951)	LO/U12	SH/U-1
ED/U-1 (w.1945)	LO/U24	SO/U-1
EX/U-1 1942-47;1961-	LO/U28	XY/N-1 1953;1966-
GL/U-1 1947-		

Annual survey of California law see Survey of California law

Annual survey of Commonwealth law. -- London, 1965-
ISSN 0570-2658

AB/N-1	CV/C-1	LO/C10 1965-73
AB/U-1	DN/U-1	LO/C15 1971-
AD/U-6	DR/U-1	LO/C25 1968;1973.
BH/U-1	ED/S11	LO/C47
BL/U-1	ED/U-1	LO-MT
BR/U-1	EX/U-1	LO/N-1
BT/U-1 1967-75	GL/U-1	LO/N17
CA/U-1 1970-	GL/U-2	LO/N46
CA/U13	HL/U-1	LO/R74
CB/U-1	LA/U-1 1965-74	LO-SC
CH-CI 1970-	LC/U-1	LO/U-2
CR/U-1	LD/U-1	LO/U-3 (cont'd)

Annual survey of Commonwealth law (cont'd).

LO/U11	NO/U-1	QS/S-6
LO/U12	OX/U15	QS/S-7
LO/U14	OX/U25	QW/D12
LO/U24	QE/C76	RE/U-1
LO/U28	QM/C68 1972-	SH/U-1
LV-LP 1967-	QN/C70 1971-	SO/U-1
LV/U-1	QS/Q12	XM/C10
MA/U-1	QS/S-4 1965-73	XY/N-1 1968-

Annual survey of English law. -- London, 1928-1940; 1945.
N.B. Holdings shown as complete may not have the 1945 volume

AB/N-1 1929-40	HL/U-1	MA/P-1 1932-40
AB/U-1 1932-40	LC/U-1 1928-40	NO/U-1 1928-40
BH-LS	(w.1930)	NW/U-1
BH/P-1 1928-40	LD/U-1	OX/U15
BH/U-1	LO/C10 1931-40	OX/U25
BL/U-1 (w.1930,	LO-MT	QS/Q12 1928;1934;
1945)	LO/N-1	1937-40
BR/U-1 1933-40	LO/N46 1937-40	QS/S-4 1940.
CA/U-1	LO/U-1 1928-40	QS/S-6 1928-29;
CA/U13	LO/U-2 1928-40	1931-40
CR/U-1 1929-40	LO/U-3	SH/U-1 1928-40
DR/U-1	LO/U11 1932-33;	SO/U-1 1930;1932;
ED/S11	1940.	1934-40
EX/U-1	LO/U24	SW/U-1 1929-40
GL/U-1 1932-40	LV/U-1	XM/C10 1936-39

Annual survey of Indian law. -- New Delhi, 1965-
ISSN 0570-2666

BL/U-1 1972-	LO/U14	XY/N-1 1973 (v.9).
CA/U13	OX/U15 1965-73 (v.9)	

Annual survey of Massachusetts law. -- Boston, 1954-
ISSN 0570-2674

LO/N-1 1969-

Annual survey of South African law. -- Cape Town, etc., 1947-

AD/U-6	EX/U-1 1953.	LO/U24
BH/U-1 1952-	GL/U-1 1952-	MA/U-1 1952-
BL/U-1 1949-	LC/U-1 1950-(w.1951,	NO/U-1
CA/U-1 1952.	1952,1958)	OX/U15
CA/U13 (w.1948,1951)	LD/U-1 1952	QS/S-4 1948-52
CB/U-1 1972-	LO-MT	QS/S-6 1953;1963.
DN/U-1 1947-59 imp.,	LO/N17 1949-59 imp.	QS/S-7 1952-53
1961-73	LO/U-2 1950;1953-74	SO/U-1 1960-
ED/S11 1952-	LO/U11 1952-53	XY/N-1 1970
ED/U-1 1950;1953-	LO/U14 1968-	

Annuario di diritto comparato e di studi legislativi. -- Rome, 1927-
ISSN 0003-5149

CA/U-1 1933-34	LO/U-3 1927-34	OX/U25 1927-37
CA/U13	LO/U24	XY/N-1 1969 (v.43);
LO/N-1 (v.1-24)	OX/U15	1972 (v.45)-

Annuario di diritto internazionale. -- Naples, 1965-
ISSN 0570-2747

LO/U24 1965. XY/N-1 1966.

Annuario di dottrina di legislazione e di giurisprudenza. -- Milan, 1889-1891 (no.3)

LO/N-1

Ansul/ Dalhousie Law School. -- Halifax, N.S., 1968-
ISSN 0587-3266

No holdings notified

Antitrust bulletin. -- New York, 1955-
ISSN 0003-603X

BH/U-1 1965-
BL/U-1 1967-76
CB/U-1 1961- (1964 imp.)
CV/U-1 1971 (v.16)-
DR/U-1 1975-
LO/C-3 1965-
LO/C-5 1975-
LO/C47 1972-
LO/N-5 1966-
LO/U24
OX/U15 1964 (v.9)-
QL/D15 1972 (v.17)-
XY/N-1 1963 (v.8)-

Antitrust law and economics review. -- McLean, Va., 1967-
ISSN 0003-6048

LO/N-5 1968- LO/U24 XY/N-1 (w.v.1, no.1)

Antitrust law journal/ American Bar Association Section of Antitrust Law. -- Chicago, 1966 (vol.32)-
Continues: Proceedings - A.B.A. Section of Antitrust Law, 1952-Apr. 1966 (vol.31)
ISSN 0003-6056

LO/U24 XY/N-1 1970 (v.39, no.3)-

Antitrust law symposium/ New York State Bar Association Section of Antitrust Law. -- Chicago, 1949-
ISSN 0066-4901

LO/U24 1959 (11th)-

Anuario - Instituto de Ciencias Penales/ Universidad Central de Venezuela. -- Caracas, 1967-

OX/U15

Anuario de derecho/ Universidad de Panamá. -- Panama, 1955-1972 (año 10)
Ceased publication

CA/U13 1955-62 (año 5); 1970-72 (año 9-10)
LO/U24
OX/U15 w.1972 (año 10)
XY/N-1 1969-71 (año 8-9)

Anuario de derecho aragonés. -- Zaragoza, 1944-

LO/N-1

Anuario de derecho civil. -- Madrid, 1948-

LD/U-1 1950-51 imp. LO/U24 (w.1953 (v.6)) XY/N-1 1966;1976 (v.29)-
LO-MT 1948-50 imp.

Anuario de derecho internacional/ Universidad de Navarra. Facultad de Derecho. -- Pamplona, 1975-

LO/N-1

Anuario de derecho penal y ciencias penales. -- Madrid, 1948-

CA/U37 XY/N-1 1974 (v.27 no.3)-

Anuario de filosofía del derecho. -- Madrid, 1953-

LO/N-1 LO/U-3 OX/U15

Anuario de historia del derecho español. -- Madrid, 1924-

CA/U-1 v.16-25;29-
LO/N-1
LO/U-1 1925-
LO/U24 1946 (v.17); 1970-71 (v.40-41)
LV/U-1 1936-44
OX/U15
RE/U-1 1964-65 (v.34-35)
XY/N-1 1974 (v.44)-

Anuario de la Sociedad Panameña de Derecho Internacional. -- Panama, [1931?]-

CA/U-1 1938-41;1944-46

Anuario ecuatoriano de derecho internacional. -- [Quito], 1965 (vol.1, 1964/65)-
ISSN 0570-4251

LO/U24

Anuario Hispano-luso-americano de derecho internacional. -- Madrid 1959-
ISSN 0570-4316

OX/U15

Anuario historico juridico ecuatoriano. -- Guayaquil, 1970-

OX/U-1

Anuario interamericano de derechos humanos = Inter-American yearbook on human rights. -- Washington D.C., 1968 (1960-1967)-

LO/S14 Session 1-32

Anuario jurídico interamericano = Inter-American juridical yearbook. -- Washington D.C., 1948-1955/57

CA/U13 (w.1948) LO/U-3 1948;1949. OX/U15
LO/S14 LO/U24 1950/51.

Anuario uruguayo de derecho internacional. -- Montevideo, 1962-
ISSN 0570-443X

LO/U24 1966 (v.4). OX/U15 1962-1965/66 (v.4)

Apollinaris: commentarius juris canonici. -- Rome, 1928-

CA/U-1 1935-44;1946- LO/N-1 1953- XY/N-1 1972 (v.45)-

Approved schools gazette <u>see</u> Community home schools gazette

Arbeit und Arbeitsrecht: Zeitschrift für sozialistische Arbeit und Arbeitsrecht. -- Berlin, D.D.R., 1947-

LO/U-3 1947 (Jg.2)- XY/N-1 1968-

Arbeit und Recht: Zeitschrift für Arbeitsrechtspraxis. -- Cologne, 1953-
ISSN 0003-7648

OX/U15 XY/N-1 1969 (Bd.17)-

Arbeits- und Sozialrecht. -- Stuttgart, 1946-
ISSN 0003-7664

LO/U-3 1946-61 imp. XY/N-1 1972 (Bd.21)-

Arbeitsrecht <u>see</u> Deutsches Arbeitsrecht

Arbeitsrecht der Gegenwart: Jahrbuch für das gesamte Arbeitsrecht und die Arbeitsgerichtsbarkeit. -- Berlin, 1964-
ISSN 0066-586X

LO/N-1 1963- OX/U15 XY/N-1

Arbeitsrecht und Arbeitslosenversicherung = Droit du travail et assurance chômage. -- Zurich, 1953-
ISSN 0003-777X

No holdings notified

Arbitration. -- London, 1954 (n.s. vol.20 no.3)-
Continues: Journal of the Institute of Arbitrators, 1915-1954 (n.s. vol.20 no.2). (Oct. 1927-Dec. 1928 entitled: Arbitrator; Jun. 1953-Jun. 1954 entitled: Arbitration journal)
ISSN 0003-7877

AB/N-1 1927-51
BL/U-1 1966-72 imp.
CA/U-1
ED/S11 1927-
LO-CBL last 4 years
LO-MT 1945-55
LO/N-1
LO/N26 last 2 years
LO/U24 1948-55 imp., 1956 (v.22)-
LV/P-1 1956-72 (v.39)
MA/P-1 Apr. 1959-
OX/U15
QW/D12 1973- imp.
RE/U-1 1968 (n.s.v.34)-imp.
XY/N-1 1961 (v.27)-

Arbitration journal (London) <u>see</u> previous entry

Arbitration journal. -- New York, 1937-1942; 1945-
1945 entitled International arbitration journal.
Absorbed: Arbitration magazine, 1943-1945
ISSN 0003-7893

BH/P-1 1937-42
CA/U13 1937-42 imp., 1949-66 imp., 1968-
CV/U-1 1937-42 imp.
HL/U-1 1937-42; 1946-52
LO/C47 1954-70
LO/U-3 (w.v.21,no.1)
LO/U24 1971 (v.26)-
XY/N-1 1965 (v.20)-

Arbitration magazine. -- New York, 1943-Oct. 1945 (vol.3)
Absorbed by: Arbitration journal, q.v.

LO/U-3

Arbitrator see Arbitration

Archeion buzantinou dikaiou. -- Athens, 1930-1933

AD/U-6 LO/N-1 1930-31 OX/U-1

Archeion ekklesiastikou kai kanonikou dikaiou. -- Athens, 1946-

LO/N-1 OX/U-1

Archeion idiotikou dikaiou = Archives de droit privé. -- Athens, 1934-

CA/U13 1934- imp. LO/N-1 1934-

Archiv der Forst- und Jagdgesetzgebung der deutschen Bundesstaaten. -- Freiburg, etc., 1834-1847

LO/N-1

Archiv der Kirchenrechtswissenschaft. -- Frankfurt, 1830-1835

QS/S-7 1830-33

Archiv des Criminalrechts. -- Halle; Brunswick, 1798-1857
1816-1834 entitled: Neues Archiv des Criminalrechts

LO/N-1

Archiv des öffentlichen Rechts. -- Freiburg; Tübingen, 1885-1944; 1948-
Vols 1-26 entitled: Archiv für öffentliches Recht
ISSN 0003-8911

CA/U-1
CV/U-1 1966 (Bd.91)-
ED/U-1 1968-
GL/U-1 1968-
LO-MT 1958 (Bd.83)-
LO/N-1
LO/U24 1948 (Bd.74)-
OX/U15 1886-1917 imp., 1918-
OX/U25 1886-1901
XY/N-1 1966 (Bd.91)-

Archiv des preussischen Rechts see Neues Archiv der preussischen Gesetzgebung und Rechtsgelehrsamkeit

Archiv des Völkerrechts. -- Tübingen, 1948-
ISSN 0003-892X

BH/U-1 1974-
CA/U13
ED/U-1
LO/S14 1948-64
LO/U-2 1951/52-
LO/U24
OX/U15
XY/N-1 1966 (Bd.13)-

Archiv for danske og norske Criminalhistorier. -- Copenhagen, 1834.

LO/N-1

Archiv for Lov og Ret i Danmark. -- Copenhagen, 1824-1834

LO/N-1

Archiv for Retsvidenskaben og dens Anvendelse. -- Copenhagen, 1824-1831

LO/N-1

Archiv für bürgerliches Recht. -- Berlin, 1888-1919 (Bd.43)
Continues: Archiv für Theorie und Praxis des allgemeinen deutschen Handels- und Wechselrechts, 1862-1888 (Bd.48).
Absorbed by: Archiv für die civilistische Praxis, q.v.

LO/N-1 OX/U15 1907-10 OX/U25 1889.

Archiv für das Civil- und Criminalrecht der königlichen preussischen Rhein-Provinzen see Rheinisches Archiv für das Civil- und Criminalrecht...

Archiv für das Handelsrecht. -- Hamburg, 1818-1821

LO/N-1

Archiv für das öffentliche Recht des deutschen Bundes. -- Giessen, 1850-1863

LO/N-1

Archiv für das Strafrecht und das öffentliche Gerichtsverfahren in dem Grossherzogthum Hessen... Mainz, 1850-1852

LO/N-1

Archiv für deutsches Wechselrecht (und Handelsrecht) see Dr. Siebenhaar's Archiv für deutsches Wechselrecht und Handelsrecht

Archiv für die civilistische Praxis. -- Tübingen, 1818-1944; 1948-
1919 absorbed: Archiv für bürgerliches Recht, q.v.
ISSN 0003-8997

AD/U-6 1952-
CA/U13 1820-1941; 1948-
DN/U-1 1949-
ED/U-1 1959-
EX/U-1 1948-
GL/U-1 1973-
LO/C47 1962 only
LO-MT 1958/59 (Bd.157)-
LO/N-1
LO/U24 1841-42;1883-1916;1917-39 imp.,1941 (Bd.146)-
OX/U15 1818-1914;1948-
XY/N-1 1970?-

Archiv für die Gesetzgebung und Reform des juristischen Studiums. -- Landshut, 1808-1814

LO/N-1

Archiv für die neueste Gesetzgebung aller deutschen Staaten see Allgemeine Telegraph für die deutsche Gesetzkunde

Archiv für die neueste Gesetzgebung in den deutschen Bundes-Staaten. -- Erlangen, 1848-1850

LO/N-1

Archiv für die Rechtspflege und Gesetzgebung im Grossherzogthum Baden. -- Freiburg, 1830-1839

LO/N-1

Archiv für Funkrecht. -- Berlin, 1928-1937

LO/U24 1928-33;1934-35 imp., 1936; 1937 imp. XY/N-1 1937.

Archiv für gemeines deutsches und für preussisches Strafrecht see Goltdammer's Archiv für Strafrecht

Archiv für gerichtliche Medizin und Kriminologie see Nippon hoigaku zasshi

Archiv für Gesetzgebung, Rechtsprechung und Verwaltung im Deutschen Reiche und in Preussen. -- Berlin, 1884.

LO/N-1

Archiv für katholisches Kirchenrecht. -- Innsbruck; Mainz, 1857-
ISSN 0003-9160

CA/U-1 1942- imp. OX/U-1 1857-1922 imp. XY/N-1 1971 (Bd.140)-
LO/N-1 1929-

Archiv für Kriminalanthropologie und Kriminalistik see next entry

Archiv für Kriminologie. -- Leipzig; Lübeck, 1898-1944; 1955-
1898-19? (Bd.65) entitled: Archiv für Kriminalanthropologie und Kriminalistik

CA/U37 OX/U15 1955 (Bd.115)- XY/N-1 1960 (Bd.125)-

Archiv für Luftrecht. -- Berlin, 1931-1943

CA/U13 1931-38 OX/U15 1931-39

Archiv für öffentliches Recht see Archiv des öffentlichen Rechts

Archiv für preussisches Strafrecht see Goltdammer's Archiv für Strafrecht

Archiv für Rechts- und Sozialphilosophie see ARSP: Archiv für Rechts- und Sozialphilosophie

Archiv für Rechts- und Wirtschaftsphilosophie see ARSP: Archiv für Rechts- und Sozialphilosophie

Archiv für Rechtsfälle. -- Berlin, 1851-1880

LO/N-1

Archiv für Rechtspflege in Sachsen, Thüringen und Anhalt. -- Leipzig, 1924-1940 (Bd.17)
Continues: Sächsisches Archiv für bürgerliches Recht und Prozess, 1891-1905 (Bd.15) and: Sächsisches Archiv für Rechtspflege, 1906-1923

LO/N-1 1891-1939

Archiv für Rechtsphilosophie see ARSP: Archiv für Rechts- und Sozialphilosophie

Archiv für rechtswissenschaftliche Abhandlungen. -- Berlin, 1861-1862

LO/N-1

Archiv für soziale Gesetzgebung und Statistik see next entry

Archiv für Sozialwissenschaft und Sozialpolitik. -- Tübingen, etc., 1904 (Bd.19)-1933 (Bd.69)
Continues: Archiv für soziale Gesetzgebung und Statistik, 1888-1903 (Bd.18)

LO/N-1

Archiv für Strafrecht see Goltdammer's Archiv für Strafrecht

Archiv für Strafrecht und Strafprozess see Goltdammer's Archiv für Strafrecht

Archiv für Theorie und Praxis des allgemeinen deutschen Handels- und Wechselrechts see Archiv für bürgerliches Recht

Archiv für Urheber- Film- Funk- und Theaterrecht. -- Berlin, etc., 1928-1944; 1954-
1928-1944 (Bd.17) entitled: Archiv für Urheber- Film- und Theaterrecht
ISSN 0003-9454

LO/N14 1954-	LO/U24 1939-44;1962 (Bd.36)-	OX/U15
LO/U-3 1959-73		XY/N-1 1969 (Bd.52)-

Archiv für Urheber- Film- und Theaterrecht see previous entry

Archives d'histoire du droit oriental. -- Brussels, 1937-1953
Merged with (1952) and continued by (1954): Revue internationale des droits de l'antiquité, q.v.

CA/U-1 1937-38	LO/U-2	OX/U15
LO/N-1	LO/U14	

Archives de droit et de législation. -- Brussels, 1837-1841 (vol.5)

LO/N-1

Archives de droit international et de législation comparée. -- Ghent, 1874.

CA/U-1	LO/N-1	QS/S-7

Archives de droit privé see Archeion idiotikou dikaiou

Archives de philosophie du droit. -- Paris, 1931-1940; 1952-
1931-1940 entitled: Archives de philosophie du droit et de sociologie juridique
ISSN 0066-6564

AD/U-6 1959-64 (v.4-9); 1968 (v.13)-	ED/U-1 1952-	LO/U24 (w.1933 (v.3); v.4 imp.)
BL/U-1 1970-	GL/U-1 1952-	LV/U-1 1932.
CA/U-1	LO/U-2 1952-65;1968-	MA/U-1 1952-
CB/U-1 1967 (v.12)-	LO/U-3 1931-40; 1952- imp.	OX/U15
		OX/U25

Archives de philosophie du droit et de sociologie juridique see previous entry

Archives of criminal psychodynamics. -- Washington D.C., 1955-1962 (vol.5)
ISSN 0570-698X

LO/M32 1955-57; 1959-62

Archivio di diritto pubblico. -- Palermo, 1891-1896 (vol.6)

LO/N-1 1891 (v.1) imp.

Archivio giuridico "Filippo Serafini". -- Bologna, etc., 1868-

LO/U24 1961 (v.160)-	OX/U-1	XY/N-1 1969 (v.176)-

Archivio penale. -- Rome, 1945-
ISSN 0004-0304

XY/N-1 1967 (March)-

Archivo de derecho público. -- Granada, 1948-1959

GL/U-1 1953-55	LO/U-3	LO/U24 1948-56 (v.9); 1959 (v.12).

Archivo de derecho publico y ciencias de la administracion. -- Caracas, 1968-

XY/N-1 1968/69-1970/71 (v.2)

Archivo de medicina legal. -- Lisbon, 1922-

BL/U-1 1930-42	LO/N-1	LV/U-1 1935-
ED/U-1 1930-35		

Archivum iuridicum cracoviense. -- Wroclaw, 1968-
ISSN 0066-6882

LO/N-1	XY/N-1 1969 (v.2)-

Archiwum komisji prawniczej/ Polska Akademia Umiejetności. -- Cracow, 1895-1936 (t.10)
Ceased publication?

CA/U-1 1897.

Argentine law bulletin. -- Buenos Aires, 1962-

LO/U-2 1962.

Arhiv za pravna i društvene nauke. -- Belgrade, 1945-
ISSN 0004-1270

LO/N-1 LO/U11 1956- XY/N-1 1966.

Arhiva contabilă: revistă de teorie, tehnică si jurisprudenţă contabilă. -- Bucharest, Jan.-Dec. 1936.

LO/N-1

Arizona Bar journal. -- Phoenix, Ariz., 1965-
ISSN 0004-1424

No holdings notified

Arizona law review. -- Tucson, 1959-
ISSN 0004-153X

LO/U24 1971 (v.13)- OX/U15 XY/N-1 1969 (v.11)-

Arizona State law journal. -- Tempe, 1974-
Continues: Law and the social order, 1969-1973

CR/U-1 1969-73 OX/U15 SO/U-1
LO/U24

Arkansas law review. -- Fayetteville, 1946-
ISSN 0004-1831

BL/U-1 1964- OX/U15 XY/N-1 1967 (v.21)-
LO/U24

Arkiv for luftrett. -- Oslo, 1958-
ISSN 0004-2072

LO/U24 XY/N-1

Arkiv for sjørett. -- Oslo, 1951-
ISSN 0004-2102

LO/N-5 1957 (v.4)-1966 (v.8); 1972 (v.12)- LO/U24 1956 (v.3)- (w.v.3 nos. 2-7; v.7 no.4) SO/U-1 XY/N-1 1965 (v.8)-

Army lawyer/ Judge Advocate General's School. -- Charlottesville, Va., 1971-

LO/N-1 1972- LO/U24 1976- XY/N-1 1974 (March)-

Ars aequi: juridisch studentenblad. -- Zwolle, 1951-
ISSN 0004-2870

LO/U24

Articled clerk. -- London, 1867-1868 (no.13)

ED/S11 LO/N-1 1-13 pt.1 Conveyancing OX/U15

Articled clerk and debater. -- London, 1866.

LO/N-1 nos. 3-4 OX/U-1 nos.1,3,4

Articled clerks' annual. -- Halifax, 1912-1949

OX/U15 1912-14; 1926-29; 1932-38

Articled clerks' journal and examiner. -- London, 1879-1881

ED/S11 LO/N-1 OX/U15 (w.1880 (Jan.-Aug.))

Asian comparative law review <u>see</u> Revue asienne de droit comparé

Assize: the journal of Queen Mary College Law Society. -- London, 1967-1973

LO/N-1 LO/U12 OX/U15 1967 (v.1).

Association Nationale des Docteurs en Droit. Cahiers <u>see</u> Droit et économie

Association of Trial Lawyers of America law journal <u>see</u> Journal of the American Trial Lawyers' Association

Association Suisse de Droit Aérien et Spatiale bulletin <u>see</u> ASDA bulletin

Ateneo law journal. -- Manila, Philippines, 1951-
ISSN 0519-2676

LO/U24 1959 (v.9)-

Atomic energy law journal. -- Boston, 1959-
ISSN 0004-7104

OX/U15 XY/N-1

Atti della Società Svizzera dei Giuristi <u>see</u> Verhandlungen des Schweizerischen Juristenvereins

Auckland University law review. -- Auckland, 1968-
ISSN 0067-0510

AB/U-1 1970- OX/U15 SO/U-1 1972-
LO/U24

Ausländisches Strafrecht der Gegenwart. -- Berlin, 1955-

OX/U15 1976 (63)-

Auslandsrecht: Blätter für Industrie und Handel see Rabels Zeitschrift ...

Aussenwirtschaftsdienst des Betriebs-Beraters: Recht der internationalen Wirtschaft see Recht der internationalen Wirtschaft: Aussenwirtschaftsdienst des Betriebs-Beraters

Australian and New Zealand journal of criminology. -- Melbourne, 1968-
ISSN 0004-8658

CA/U37	LO/U11 1976 (v.9)-	OX/U15
LO/U-3 1968-77 (v.10)	LO/U24	XY/N-1 1969 (v.2)-

Australian Bar gazette. -- Sydney, 1963-1970
Continues: Bar gazette/ New South Wales Bar Association, 1961-1963 (no.6)

OX/U15

Australian business law review. -- Sydney, 1973-
ISSN 0310-1053

LO/N-1	OX/U15	XY/N-1
LO/U24	SO/U-1	

Australian conveyancer and solicitors' journal see Australian lawyer

Australian current law review. -- Sydney, 1969-1971 (vol.2 no.6)
ISSN 0045-0413

LO/U24	OX/U15	QS/Q12

Australian industrial law review. -- Artarmon, N.S.W., 1959-
ISSN 0084-7445

No holdings notified

Australian journal of forensic sciences. -- Chatswood, N.S.W., 1968-
ISSN 0045-0618

CA/U37	DN/U-1	XY/N-1

Australian journal of public administration. -- Sydney, 1976 (vol.35)-
Continues: Public administration, 1937-1975 (vol.34) (ISSN 0033-328X)
ISSN 0313-6647

BT/U-1 1949- imp.	LO/N-1 1963-	QE/C76 1975-
DR/U-1 1970-	LO/N17 1951- imp.	QN/C70 1970 (v.30)- imp.
ED/U-1 1964-	LO/U24 1947-70 imp.	
LD/U-1 1964-	LV/U-1 1965-75	XY/N-1 1937-48 imp., 1966 (v.25)-

Australian law journal. -- Sydney, 1927-
ISSN 0004-9611

AB/U-1	KL/U-1	LO/U24
AD/U-6 1952-	LC/U-1	LO/U28
BH/U-1 1956-	LD/C-1 1967/68 (v.41)-	LV/U-1
BL/U-1	LD/U-1	MA/U-1
BR/U-1	LO/C-3	NO/U-1
CA/U13	LO/C15 1971-	OX/U15
CB/U-1	LO-MT 1948-56 imp., 1963-64; 1968 (v.42)-	QE/C76 1975-
CV/C-1 1974 (v.48)-	LO/N-1	QN/C70
CV/U-1 1967 (v.41)-	LO/R74 1965-	QS/S-4
DR/U-1 (w.1947, 1964-66)	LO/S65 1927-76	QS/S-7 1967-
ED/U-1	LO/U-2	RE/U-1 1970 (v.44)-
EX/U-1	LO/U-3	SH/U-1 1967 (v.41)-
GL/U-1	LO/U12	SO/U-1 1951-
GL/U-2 1972 (v.46)-		XM/C10 1972-
HL/U-1 1970 (v.44)-		XY/N-1 1950 (v.24)-

Australian law news. -- Melbourne, 1977 (vol.12 no.2)-
Continues: Law Council newsletter, 1964-1977 (vol.12 no.1), (ISSN 0047-4177)

LO/U24	OX/U15

Australian law times. -- Melbourne, 1879-1884 (vol.5)
Vols.6-49, 1884-1928 contain only reports of cases; holdings not recorded

LO-SC	LO/U24	OX/U15

Australian lawyer. -- Sydney, 1960 (vol.1)-1968 (vol.7)
Continues: Australian conveyancer and solicitors' journal, 1948-1959 (vol.12). Vols 1 and 2 also numbered vols 13 and 14 of that journal

LO/N-1 1963-68	LO/U24	OX/U15 1960/68

Australian tax review. -- Sydney, 1971-

LO/U24	XY/N-1

Australian yearbook of international law. -- Sydney, 1965-
ISSN 0084-7658

AD/U-6 1967-	ED/U-1	LO/U24
BH/U-1 1970/73-	LC/U-1 1965-66	MA/U-1
BL/U-1 1970/73.	LD/U-1	NO/U-1
CA/U13 (w.1966)	LO/C15 1967-	OX/U15
CB/U-1	LO/N17	XY/N-1

Badische Rechtspraxis. -- Karlsruhe, 1900-1901
Continues: Annalen der grossherzoglich-badischen Gerichte, 1833-1899

LO/N-1

Baltisches Recht; das Recht Estlands, Lettlands und Litauens in Vergangenheit und Gegenwart. -- Munich, 1962-
ISSN 0067-3102

ED/N-1 Sonderheft 1968; 1969-70 (Hft.9-11)

Banaras law journal. -- Benares, 1965-
ISSN 0522-0815

LO/U14 imp.   OX/U15

Banca, borsa e titoli di credito: revista di dottrina e giurisprudenza. -- Milan, 1934-43;1948-

No holdings notified

Banca ve ticaret hukuku dergisi. -- Ankara, 1962-

LO/U14

Bank of England quarterly bulletin. -- London, 1960-
ISSN 0005-5166

AD/U-6	LO/C-5	MA/P-1 March 1961-
BL/U-1	LO/C25 1969- imp.	QM/C68 1968 (v.8 no.3)-
BR/U-1	LO/N-1	QN/C70
BT/U-1	LO/N-5	QW/C73
CA/U-1	LO/S14 1965 (v.5)-	QW/D12
DR/U-1	LO-TS	XM/C10
HL/U-1	LO/U-1	XY/N-1
LC/C-1 1968-	LO/U-2 1960-	
LC/U-1	LV-LP (w.1962, v.2, no.4)	
LO/C-3 1968-		

Bankers magazine <u>see</u> next entry

Banking law journal. -- Boston, Mass., 1889-
1932 absorbed: Business law journal
1943 absorbed: Bankers magazine
ISSN 0005-5506

LO/N-1	LO/U-3 1943-68	OX/U15 1960 (v.77)-
LO/S28 1910-	LO/U24 1972 (v.89)-	XY/N-1 1969 (v.86)-

Bar/ West Virginia Bar Association <u>see</u> West Virginia law review

Bar and legal world. -- London, Nov. 1903.
Nos 1 and 2 only published

LO/N-1   OX/U15

Bar briefs <u>see</u> North Dakota law review

Bar bulletin/ New York County Lawyers Association. -- New York, 1943-

LO/U24

Bar examination annual. -- London, 1893-1894
Continues: Bar examination journal, 1871-1892

CA/U-1 LO/N-1 OX/U15 1877-94

Bar examination guide. -- London, 1895-1899

CA/U-1 LO/N-1 OX/U15 1896-99

Bar examination journal see Bar examination annual

Bar examiner. -- Denver etc., 1931-
ISSN 0005-5824

No holdings notified

Bar gazette/ New South Wales Bar Association see Australian Bar gazette

Barrister. -- Toronto, 1894-1897

OX/U15

Barrister/ American Bar Association Young Lawyers' Section. -- Chicago, 1974-
ISSN 0094-5277

HL/U-1 1975 (v.2)- LO/U24

Bayerische Verwaltungsblätter see Deutsche Verwaltungsblätter

Baylor law review. -- Waco, Texas, 1948-
ISSN 0005-7274

LO/U24 OX/U15 XY/N-1 1966 (v.18)-

Beiträge zur Erläuterung des deutschen Rechts. -- Berlin, 1857-1933
Continues: Beiträge zur Erläuterung des preussischen Rechts und Praxis, 1857-1871 and: Beiträge zur Erläuterung des deutschen Rechts, in besonderer Beziehung auf das preussische Recht mit Einschluss des Handels- und Wechselrechts, 1872-1896

LO/N-1 OX/U25 1887-89,1893.

Beiträge zur Erläuterung des preussischen Rechts see Beiträge zur Erläuterung des deutschen Rechts

Beiträge zur Revision der preussischen Gesetzgebung. -- Berlin, 1830-1832

LO/N-1

Belang en Recht. -- Amsterdam, 1896-1918

LO/N-1

Belgian review of international law see Revue belge de droit international

Belgique judiciaire. -- Brussels, Dec. 1842-1940

KL/U-1 1871-97   LO/N-1

Belgisch tijdschrift voor internationaal recht see Revue belge de droit international

Bell yard. -- London, 1927-1939

AB/N-1 1931-39	LC/U-1	LV/U-1
BH/U-1	LD/U-1	NO/U-1
BR/U-1	LO-MT	NW/U-1
CA/U-1 1935-39	LO/N-1 1928-39 imp.	OX/U15
CA/U13	LO/U-2 1927-34; 1936-39	QS/S-8
ED/S11 1935-39		SH/U-1
ED/U-1	LO/U-3	
GL/U-1	LO/U24	

Bench and Bar review see Forum (Baltimore)

Bengal and Assam journal of lawyers. -- Calcutta, 1936-

No holdings notified

The Bergin Hall review. -- Santa Clara, 1951.
ISSN 0405-4512

No holdings notified

Berichte der Deutschen Gesellschaft für Völkerrecht. -- Karlsruhe, 1957 (1955)-

OX/U15

Bestuurswetenschappen. -- The Hague, 1946-1977

LO/U-3 1946-47; 1954-77

Der Betrieb : Wochenzeitschrift für Betriebswirtschaft, Steurrecht, Wirtschaftsrecht, Arbeitsrecht. -- Düsseldorf, 1948-
ISSN 0005-9935

ED/U-1 1963-   XY/N-1 1972 (v.25)-

Der Betriebs-Berater. -- Heidelberg, 1946-
Title varies

CA/U13 1964-75	GL/U-1 1973-	OX/U15 1950-
ED/U-1 1968-	LO/U-3	XY/N-1 1966 (v.21)-

Bibliotheca visseriana dissertationum jus internationale illustrantium; cura Facultatis iuridicae Lugduno-Batavae edita. -- Lugduni Batavorum [i.e. Leiden], 1923-

BL/U-1 1940 (v.15); 1951 (v.17).
CA/U13 1923-63
LD/U-1
LO-MT 1923-63
LO/N-1
LO/U-2
LO/U-3
LO/U24
LV/U-1 1923-26 (v.1-4;6)
OX/U15
QS/S-7 1924.

Biennial survey of Israel law. -- Jerusalem, 1958/59-
ISSN 0067-852X

CA/U13 1963/64.
LO/U14 1960/61-
OX/U15 1960/61, 1962/63.

Bill of rights journal/ National Emergency Civil Liberties Committee. -- New York, 1968-
ISSN 0006-2499

No holdings notified

Birmingham Law Society bulletin. -- Birmingham, 1941.

BH/P-1 1941 (nos.1-2).

Biuletyn - Naczelna Rada Adwokacka <u>see</u> Palestra

Black law journal. -- Sausalito, Cal., 1971-
ISSN 0045-2181

XY/N-1 1972 (v.2 no.1).

Blatt für Patent- Muster- und Zeichenwesen. -- Berlin, etc., 1894/95-1944; 1948-
ISSN 0006-4602

LO/N-1 1962-
OX/U15
XY/N-1 1894/95-1940 (Jg.46)

Blätter für administrative Praxis <u>see</u> Deutsche Verwaltungsblätter

Blätter für gerichtliche Anthropologie <u>see</u> Friedreichs Blätter für gerichtliche Medicin und Sanitäts-polizei

Blätter für internationales Privatrecht. -- Munich,etc., 1926-1931
Supplement to: Leipziger Zeitschrift für deutsches Recht, q.v.

LO/U-3 1927; 1930-31
LO/U24

Boletim - Sociedade Brasileira de Direito Internacional. -- Rio de Janeiro, 1945-
Revives the Boletim begun and ended in 1915

CA/U13 1945-50
LO/U-3 1945-54 (w.1952)

Boletim da Faculdade de Direito. -- Coimbra, 1914-

LO/N-1 1953-   LO/U24 1925-26 1940-46 imp., 1949 (v.25)-   XY/N-1 1970-

Boletim do Ministério da Justiça. -- Lisbon, 1940-

LO/U24 1947-57 imp., 1958 (no.72)-

Boletín - Colegio de Abogados de Guatemala. -- Guatemala City, 1952-
ISSN 0588-0289

LO/U24 1960-   XY/N-1 1960 (v.8)-

Boletín - Colegio de Abogados de Lima. -- Lima, 1970-

LO/U24

Boletín - Facultad de Derecho y Ciencias Sociales. -- Cordoba, 1921-

LO/U24 1956-68 imp., 1969-   XY/N-1 1970 (año 34)-

Boletín - Instituto Centroamericano de Derecho Comparado. -- Tegucigalpa, Honduras, 1962/3-
ISSN 0494-9722

LO/U24

Boletín - Instituto de Derecho Civil, Universidad Nacional de Córdoba <u>see</u> Cuadernos de los Institutos/ Instituto de Derecho Civil, Universidad Nacional de Córdoba

Boletín - Instituto de Derecho Comparado. -- Quito, 1951-
Early volumes entitled: Boletín de la Sección de Investigaciones de Derecho Comparado (Sidec)
ISSN 0480-8118

LO/U24 1951-63 imp., 1964-   OX/U15 1951-52

Boletín - Instituto de Derecho Comparado de Mexico <u>see</u> Boletín Mexicano de derecho comparado

Boletín - Instituto de Derecho Comparado del Peru. -- Lima, 1964-
ISSN 0459-4215

LO/U24 1964-65 imp.

Boletín - Instituto de Derecho Privado. -- Caracas, 1966-
ISSN 0020-3823

BL/U-1 1966-71 (v.10)   LO/U24   OX/U15

Boletín - Instituto de Ensenanza Practica. -- Santa Fé, 1942-

OX/U15 1942 (no.2).

Boletín de derecho de autor see Copyright bulletin : quarterly review

Boletín de jurisprudencia. -- Santiago, 1972-

LO/N-1 XY/N-1

Boletín de la Revista de los tribunales. -- Madrid, 1878-

LO/U24 1878-82 (v.5)

Boletín de la Revista general de legislación y jurisprudencia. Periódico oficial del ilustre Colegio de Abogados de Madrid. -- Madrid, 1854 - Sept./Oct. 1937. 1854-56 as Boletín semenal de...

No holdings notified

Boletín de la Sección de Investigaciones de Derecho Comparado see Boletín - Instituto de Derecho Comparado (Quito)

Boletín de legislación extranjera. -- Madrid, 1943 (Epoca 4, año 1)-
Earlier series entitled: Boletín de legislación y documentos parlamentarios extranjeros. Holdings not recorded

LO/N-1 1946 (v.8 no.40)- LO/U24 1968 (v.35)-

Boletín informativo del Seminario de Derecho Político. -- Salamanca, 1955-

OX/U15

Boletín juridico y legislativo. -- Guatemala City, 1956-
ISSN 0473-2952

No holdings notified

Boletín mensual del Seminario de Ciencias Juridicas y Sociales see Revista jurídica de Buenos Aires

Boletín Mexicano de derecho comparado. -- Mexico, 1968-
Continues: Boletín - Instituto de Derecho Comparado de Mexico, 1948-1967 (vol.20)
ISSN 0041-8633

CA/U-1 1950-65 imp.
CA/U13 1948- (1966 imp.)
LO/N-1 1968-
LO/U-3 1953-67
LO/U24 1948-51 imp., 1952-
OX/U15

Boletín penitenciario. -- Bogotá, 1935-

No holdings notified

Boletín semenal de la Revista general de legislación y jurisprudencia see Boletín de la Revista general de legislatión...

Bollettino dell'aviazione civile e del traffico aereo. -- Rome, 1926-

XY/N-1 1932-35 (v.11-14)

Bollettino dell'Ufficio della Proprietà Letteraria e Scientifica. -- Rome, 1945 -

LO/N-1 1963-

Bollettino di informazioni/ Associatione Italiana di Diritto Marittimo. -- Rome, 1954-1964

LO/U24

Bollettino di informazioni costituzionali e parlamentari/ Camera dei Deputati. -- Rome,

LO/N-1 1948-   XY/N-1 1973 (anno 24)-

Bollettino di legislazione comparata. -- Rome, 1966-
ISSN 0523-9362

LO/N-1

Bollettino informativo dell'Istituto Giuridico Spagnolo in Roma. -- Rome, 1953-

LO/U24 1955-

Bombay law journal. -- 1923-1946

LO/N-1 1936-46   LO/U14 1930-46 (v.7-24) imp.

Bombay law reporter. -- 1899-

LO/N-1 1944 (v.46)-   OX/U15 (w.1905 (v.7))   QS/S-6 1929-59 (v.31-61)
LO/U14 1904 (v.6)-

Boston College industrial and commercial law review. -- Brighton, Mass., 1959-
ISSN 0006-7954

LO/U24 1971/72 (v.13)-   OX/U15   XY/N-1 1963 (v.5)-

Boston University law review. -- Boston, 1921-
ISSN 0006-8047

BL/U-1 1964-   LO/U24   XY/N-1 1970 (v.50)-
CA/U13 1949-   OX/U15

Bouwrecht. -- Deventer, 1975-

No holdings notified

Bracton law journal/ University of Exeter law students. -- Exeter, 1965-

EX/U-1   OX/U15 1969-   QG/C25 1976-

Brief. -- Lancaster, Pa., 1887-
Publication suspended June 1888-December 1899

LO/U24 1900-08 imp., 1936-56 imp.   OX/U15 1949-

Brief case <u>see</u> NLADA briefcase

Brigham Young University law review. -- Provo, Utah, 1975-
ISSN 0360-151X

No holdings notified

British Columbia law notes. -- Victoria, B.C., 1894 (vol.1 nos.1-2).

LO/U24
OX/U15

British Insurance Law Association bulletin. -- London, 1964-

LO/N-1

British journal of administrative law. -- London, 1954-1957/58 (vol.3)
In 1958 merged with Public law q.v.
ISSN 0524-6334

AB/N-1
AD/U-6
BH/U-1
BL/U-1
BR/U-1
CA/U-1
CA/U13
CR/U-1
DR/U-1
ED/S11
ED/U-1
EX/U-1
GL/U-1
HL/U-1
KL/U-1
LD/U-1
LO/C15 1954-1956/57
LO-MT
LO/N-1
LO/N-5
LO/N26
LO-TS 1954-56
LO/U-2 1954-56/57
LO/U-3
LO/U11 1954-56/57
LO/U24
LV/P-1 1956/57.
LV/U-1 1956/57.
NO/U-1
OX/U15
QS/S-4
QS/S-6
QS/S-8
RE/U-1
SH/U-1
SO/U-1

British journal of criminology, delinquency and deviant social behaviour. -- London, 1960-
Continues: British journal of delinquency, 1950-1960
ISSN 0007-0955

AB/N-1
AB/U-1 1960-
AD/U-6 1958-60; 1967 (v.7)-
BH/P-1
BH/U-1
BL/U-1 1951-
BR/U-1
BT/U-1
CA/U-1
CA/U37
CB/U-1
CC/U-1
CH-CI
CR/U-1
CV/U-1 1960-
DN/U-1 1953-
DR/U-1 (w.1961)
ED/N-1
ED-SLC 1961-
ED/U-1
EX/U-1 1952- imp.
GL/U-1 1950-51 imp., 1952-
GL/U-2 1960-
HL/U-1
KL/U-1
LA/U-1
LC/U-1
LD/C-1 1971 (v.11)-
LD/P-1 1960-
LD/U-1
LO/C-3 1960-
LO/C-5 1973-
LO/C10
LO/C14 1960-
LO/C15 1968-
LO/C25 1950-70;1972-
LO/C27 1973-
LO/M32 1960-75
LO-MT 1960-
LO/N-1
LO/N26 1957-
LO/N27
LO/N46 1977-
LO/R74 1967-
LO-SC 1951-
LO/U-1
LO/U-2
LO/U-3
LO/U11
LO/U12 1960-
LO/U24
LO/U28 1960-63;1965-
LV-LP 1970 (v.10)- (v.13-14 imp.)
LV/P-1
LV/U-1
MA/P-1
MA/U-1 imp.
NW/U-1
OX/U15
OX/U25
QE/C76 1960-
QG/C25 1974-
QL/D15 1960- (cont'd)

British journal of criminology, delinquency and deviant social behaviour (cont'd).

QM/C48 1976-
QM/C68 1968-73
QN/C70 1960-
QS/S-6
QW/C73
QW/D12 1960-
RE/U-1 1951 (v.2 no.2); 1952 (v.3)-
SH/U-1
SO/U-1
SW/U-1 (w.1952)
XM/C10 1975-
XY/N-1
YK/U-1 1950-60;1963-

British journal of delinquency <u>see</u> previous entry

British journal of industrial relations. -- London, 1963-
ISSN 0007-1080

AB/U-1 1964-
AD/U-6
BH/P-1
BH/U-1
BL/U-1
BR/U-1
BT/U-1
CA/U-1
CA/U13
CB/U-1
CC/U-1
CR/U-1
DN/U-1
ED/N-1
ED/U-1
EX/U-1
GL/U-1
GL/U-2
HL/U-1
KL/U-1
LA/U-1
LC/C-1
LC/U-1
LD/C-1
LD/U-1
LO/C-3 1967 (v.5, no.3)-
LO/C-5 1974 (v.12)-
LO/C14 1972 (v.10)-
LO/C15
LO/C25 1967;1969-
LO/C27
LO/C47
LO-CBL last 5 years
LO/N-1
LO/N26
LO/U-1
LO/U-2
LO/U-3
LO/U11 1976-
LO/U12
LO/U24
LO/U28
LV-LP 1965 (v.3)- imp.
LV/P-1
LV/U-1
MA/P-1
NW/U-1
OX/U-1
OX/U15
QE/C76 1972-
QG/C25 1965-
QM/C68
QN/C70
QS/Q12
QS/Q29
QW/D12
SH/U-1
SO/U-1
SW/U-1
XM/C10
XY/N-1
YK/U-1

British journal of law and society. -- London, 1974-

AB/N-1
AB/U-1
AD/U-6
BH/U-1
BL/U-1
BR/U-1
CA/U-1
CA/U13 imp.
CB/U-1
CH-CI
CR/U-1
CV/U-1
DR/U-1
ED/S11
ED/U-1
EX/U-1
GL/U-1 (Social Sciences Faculty Library)
GL/U-2
HL/U-1
LA/U-1
LC/C-1
LC/U-1
LD/U-1
LO/C-3
LO/C-5
LO/C10
LO/C14
LO/C15
LO/C25
LO/C47 1975-
LO-MT
LO/N-1
LO/N27
LO/R74
LO/U-2
LO/U11 1976 (v.3)-
LO/U12
LO/U24
LO/U28
LV-LP
LV/U-1
MA/U-1
NO/U-1
OX/U15
QE/C76
QG/C25
QL/D15
QM/C48 (w.v.1,no.1)
QM/C68
QN/C70
QW/C73 1976 (v.3)-
QW/D12
SH/U-1
SO/U-1
XY/N-1
YK/U-1

British tax review. -- London, 1956-
ISSN 0007-1870

AB/N-1
AB/U-1
AD-A
AD/U-6 1963-
BC-UC 1975-
BH/P-1 1959-
BH/U-1
BL-LS
BL/U-1
BR/U-1
BT/U-1 1961-67 imp., 1976-
CA/U-1
CA/U13
CB/U-1 1957-
CH-CI 1957-
CR/U-1
DN/U-1
DR/U-1
ED/S10
ED/S11
ED-SLC 1963-
ED/U-1
EX/U-1
GL/U-1 1957-
GL/U-2 1958- imp.
HL/U-1
KL/U-1 1957
LA/U-1 1969-
LC/U-1
LD/C-1 1966-
LD/U-1
LO/C-3 1969-
LO/C15
LO/C18 1964-
LO/C25 1963-
LO/C47
LO-CBL 1959-
LO-MT
LO/N-1
LO/N-5
LO/N26
LO/P-6 1959-
LO/R74
LO/S28 1956-
LO-SC
LO-TS
LO/U-2
LO/U-3
LO/U11 1956-
LO/U12
LO/U24
LO/U28
LV-LP 1957-
LV/P-1 1957-
LV/U-1
MA/P-1
MA/U-1
NO/U-1
NW/U-1
OX/U15
QE/C76 1968-
QG/C25 1976-
QL/D15 1957;1961;1965-
QM/C48 1972-
QM/C68 1965-
QN/C70
QS/S-4
QS/S-6
QS/S-7
QS/S-8
QW/D12
RE/U-1
SH/U-1
SO/U-1
SW/U-1 1964-
XY/N-1 (w.1st issue, June 1956)
YK/U-1 1962-

British yearbook of international law. -- London, 1920-
ISSN 0068-2691

AB/N-1
AB/U-1
AD/U-6
BC-UC imp.
BH/P-1
BH/U-1
BL/U-1
BR/U-1
BT/U-1 1921-
CA/U-1
CA/U13
CB/U-1 (w.1958,1959)
CC/U-1 1961-72/73
CH-CI
CR/U-1 1920-29;1932; 1944-
CV/U-1 1921 (v.2)-
DN/U-1
DR/U-1
ED/S11
ED/U-1
EX/U-1 1920/21-
GL/U-1
GL/U-2 1969 (v.43)-
HL/U-1
KL/U-1
LC/U-1 (w.1959,1965)
LD/P-1 1929-
LD/U-1
LO/C10 1950 (v.27)-
LO/C15
LO/C47 1946- imp.
LO/N-1
LO/N-5
LO/N17
LO/N26 1921/22-
LO/N46
LO/R74 1963-
LO/S14
LO-SC 1920-50;1957-67;1970-
LO-TS
LO/U-1
LO/U-2
LO/U-3
LO/U11
LO/U12 (w.1946-47; 1950;1957-59;1962)
LO/U14 1971-72/73
LO/U24
LO/U28 1921/22-30; 1963-67;1970-
LV-LP 1920-57;1963-67; 1970-
LV/P-1 1920-44 imp., 1946-
LV/U-1 (w.1947)
MA/P-1 1920-53 imp., 1954-
MA/U-1
NO/U-1
NW/U-1
OX/U15
OX/U25
QG/C25 1972/73-
QM/C68 1955/56-64 imp. 1970-
QN/C70
QS/Q12 1921-29;1931-35;1944;1947-
QS/Q29 1924-64 imp., 1965/66-
QS/S-4
QS/S-6

(cont'd)

British yearbook of international law (cont'd).

QS/S-7 | RE/U-1 1920-45;1948- | XY/N-1 1923/24-26;
QS/S-8 1921- | SH/U-1 | 1944-53 imp.,
QW/D12 | SO/U-1 (w.1947) | 1965-

Brooklyn barrister. -- Brooklyn, N.Y., 1950-
ISSN 0007-232X

No holdings notified

Brooklyn journal of international law. -- Brooklyn, N.Y., 1975-

XY/N-1

Brooklyn law review. -- Brooklyn, N.Y., 1932-
Publication suspended July 1943 - February 1947
ISSN 0007-2362

BL/U-1 1961-63 imp., 1963 (v.30)- | CA/U13 1966- | OX/U15
LO/U24 | XY/N-1 1969 (v.36)-

Buffalo law review. -- Buffalo, N.Y., 1951-
ISSN 0023-9356

CA/U13 1958- | OX/U15 | XY/N-1 1969 (v.19)-
LO/U24

Bulletin - American Academy of Psychiatry and the Law. --
Pittsburgh, Pa., 1972-
ISSN 0091-634X

No holdings notified

Bulletin - American Bar Association. Section of International and Comparative Law <u>see</u> International lawyer/ American Bar Association. Section of International Law

Bulletin - American Bar Association. Section of Taxation <u>see</u> Tax lawyer

Bulletin - American Business Law Association <u>see</u> American business law journal

Bulletin - American Foreign Law Association. -- New York,1950-1951
Absorbed by: American journal of comparative law, q.v.
ISSN 0401-815X

LO/U24

Bulletin - Association Canadienne des Bibliothèques de Droit <u>see</u> Newsletter - Canadian Association of Law Libraries

Bulletin - Association des Auditeurs et Anciens Auditeurs ... <u>see</u> Annuaire de l'A.A.A.

Bulletin - Association des Ingénieurs-Conseils en matière de Propriété Industrielle <u>see</u> Bulletin - Syndicat des Ingénieurs-Conseils en matière de Propriété Industrielle

Bulletin - Association Suisse de Droit Aérien et Spatiale <u>see</u> ASDA bulletin

Bulletin - Bureau International de l'Edition Mécanique <u>see</u> next entry

Bulletin - Bureau International des Sociétés gérant les Droits d'Enregistrement et de Réproduction Mécanique. -- Paris, 1963-
Continues: Bulletin - Bureau International de l'Edition Mécanique, 1959-1962 (ISSN 0407-9361)
ISSN 0572-7529

LO/N14

Bulletin - Columbia Society of International Law <u>see</u> Columbia journal of transnational law

Bulletin - Commercial Law League of America <u>see</u> Commercial law journal

Bulletin - Copyright Society of the U.S.A. -- New York, 1953-
ISSN 0010-8642

CB/U-1 1973 (v.20)-	LO/U-3 1953-58	OX/U15
LO/N14	LO/U24	XY/N-1 1969 (v.16 no.3)-

Bulletin - Far Eastern American Bar Association. -- Shanghai, 1916-1923 (no.8)

LO/U14 1916-20

Bulletin - Fédération Internationale des Conseils en Propriété Industrielle. -- Paris, 1970 (vol.18)-
Continues: Bulletin - Fédération Internationale des Ingénieurs-Conseils en Propriété Industrielle, 1947-1969 (vol.17)

LO/N14

Bulletin - Fédération Internationale des Ingénieurs-Conseils en Propriété Industrielle <u>see</u> previous entry

Bulletin - Industrial Law Society <u>see</u> Industrial law journal

Bulletin - Institute of Medieval Canon Law <u>see</u> Bulletin of medieval canon law

Bulletin - International Association of Law Libraries <u>see</u> International journal of law libraries

Bulletin - International Bar Association. -- New York, 1947-

No holdings notified

Bulletin - International Society for Labor Law and Legislation <u>see</u> Comparative labor law

Bulletin - New York State Bar Association <u>see</u> New York State Bar journal

Bulletin - Patent and Trademark Institute of Canada. -- Ottawa, 1926?-

LO/N14 1962-

Bulletin - Schweizerische Vereinigung für Luft- und Raumrecht <u>see</u> ASDA bulletin

Bulletin - Syndicat des Ingénieurs-Conseils en matière de Propriété Industrielle. -- Paris, 1884-1923
1906-1911 as Bulletin - Association des Ingénieurs-Conseils...

LO/N14 (w.v.7 nos.1-3)

Bulletin administratif et judiciaire des Annales forestières. -- Paris, 1844-1866

LO/N-1

Bulletin argentin de droit international privé. -- Buenos Aires, 1903-1910

LO/U24 imp.

Bulletin d'information du Comité International de Droit Comparé de l'Association Internationale des Sciences Juridiques. -- Barcelona, 1956-1966 (no.11)
ISSN 0443-8167

LO/U24 OX/U15

Bulletin de droit des gens. -- Brussels, 1952-1958
ISSN 0405-3052

GL/U-1 LO/U-2

Bulletin de droit nucléaire/ Agence pour l'Energie Nucléaire. -- Paris, 1968-
1968-1972 Organisation entitled Agence Européenne pour l'Energie Nucléaire. For English edition <u>see</u> Nuclear law bulletin

No holdings notified

Bulletin de droit tchécoslovaque. -- Prague, 1925-1938; 1947-
For English edition <u>see</u> Bulletin of Czechoslovak law

LO-MT 1925-38	LO/U-3 1925-59	OX/U15 1925-38 imp., 1948-59
LO/N-1 1948-67	LO/U24 1951-59 (v.9-17)	QS/S-7 1925-38
LO/S14 1948-59		

Bulletin de jurisprudence des tribunaux indigènes du Ruanda-Urundi. -- Usumbura, 1946-1955

LO/U14

Bulletin de l'Académie de Droit International, Centre d'Etudes <u>see</u> Annuaire de l'A.A.A...

Bulletin de l'Académie de Législation see Recueil de l'Académie de Législation de Toulouse

Bulletin de l'Association Française pour la Protection de la Propriété Industrielle. -- Paris, 1899/1900-

LO/N14 1899/1900-1935/36

Bulletin de l'Institut de Droit Comparé de Lyon. -- Lyon, 1938-1940

LO/U-3 1938-39 imp. LO/U24 imp.

Bulletin de l'Institut Intermédiaire International see next entry

Bulletin de l'Institut Juridique International. -- The Hague, 1919-1940
1919-1933 entitled: Bulletin de l'Institut Intermédiaire International

CA/U-1
CA/U13
LO-MT 1919-36
LO/N-1
LO/N17
LO/U-3 imp.
LO/U24 (w.v.37; v.36 imp.)

Bulletin de l'Organisation Internationale de Métrologie Légale. -- Paris, 1960-
ISSN 0473-2812

AB/N-1 OX/U15 XY/N-1

Bulletin de l'Union Internationale de Droit Pénal see Mitteilungen der Internationalen kriminalistischen Vereinigung

Bulletin de la Société d'Etudes Législatives. -- Paris, 1901-1928?

LO/N-1 1902-28

Bulletin de la Société de Législation Comparée see Revue internationale de droit comparé

Bulletin de la Société Générale des Prisons see Revue pénitentiaire et de droit pénal et études criminologiques

Bulletin de législation comparée. -- Paris, 1941-1948
Continues: Bulletin de statistique et de législation comparée. -- Paris, 1877-1940

CA/U-1 LO/U-3 1896-97;1903,1906,1912 imp., 1913-48

Bulletin de législation libanaise. -- Beirut, 1954?-
Title varies
ISSN 0570-8915

LO/U14 1959- imp.

Bulletin de médecine légale et de toxicologie médicale see next entry

Bulletin de médecine légale, urgence médicale, Centre anti-poisons/ Association Lyonnaise de Médecine Légale. -- Lyon, 1976 (vol.19)-
Continues: Bulletin de médecine légale et de toxicologie médicale, 1957-1975 (ISSN 0007-4365)

CA/U37 1962-72 LO/M32 1965-72 (v.18-25) NW/U-1 1968-72
DN/U-1 1969- XY/N-1 1960 (v.13)-

Bulletin de statistique et de législation comparée see Bulletin de législation comparée

Bulletin des juridictions indigènes et du droit coutumier congolais see Bulletin des tribunaux coutumiers

Bulletin des tribunaux: moniteur de la Cour de Cassation et du Conseil d'Etat: journal judiciaire. -- Paris, 1863-1865

LO/N-1

Bulletin des tribunaux coutumiers. -- Elisabethville, 1933-1963
1933-1960 entitled: Bulletin des juridictions indigènes et du droit coutumier congolais
1964 absorbed by: Revue juridique du Congo, afterwards Revue juridique du Zaïre, q.v.

LO/U14 1951-63 imp. NW/U-1 1955-63 (v.23-31)(v.28 imp.) XY/N-1 1941-58 (9e-26e année) imp.

Bulletin du droit d'auteur see Copyright bulletin: quarterly review

Bulletin économique et juridique. -- Algiers, 1936-

ED/N-1 1949-63 LO/U14 1951-63 imp. OX/U-1 1949-63
LO/U-3 1949-63 imp.

Bulletin for international fiscal documentation. -- Amsterdam, 1946-
ISSN 0007-4624

CA/U13 1964- LO/U-3 (w.v.19 no.9) OX/U15 1964-
EX/U-1 1969- LO/U24 XY/N-1 1966 (v.20)-
LO/N-1 MA/P-1 1964-

Bulletin international de recherches sur le droit en Europe de l'est see International bulletin for research on law in eastern Europe

Bulletin judiciaire de l'Algérie see Revue algérienne des sciences juridiques...

Bulletin juridique/ Fédération Nationale des Organismes de Sécurité Sociale. -- Paris,

LO/N-1 1959-

Bulletin of Canadian welfare law. -- Ottawa, 1972-

CA/U13	LO/U-3 1976 (v.4)-	OX/U15

Bulletin of comparative labour relations. -- Deventer, 1970-

BH/U-1	HL/U-1	QN/C70 1976 (no.72)-
BL/U-1 1975-		

Bulletin of current research in Soviet and East European law.
-- Bethlehem, Pa., 1971-

No holdings notified

Bulletin of Czechoslovak law. -- Prague, 1960-
For French ed., <u>see</u>: Bulletin de droit tchécoslovaque
ISSN 0521-7245

AB/U-1 1962-	HL/U-1 1967 (v.8)-	NO/U-1
AD/U-6	LC/U-1	OX/U15
BL/U-1	LO/N-1 imp.	RE/U-1
CA/U13 1974-	LO/S14 1960-68	SO/U-1
CR/U-1	LO/U-2 1960-68;1971-	XY/N-1 1962 (v.3 no.3/4)-
EX/U-1 1974-	LO/U-3	
GL/U-1 Soviet Studies Branch Lib. 1972-	LO/U24	

Bulletin of legal developments/ British Institute of International and Comparative Law -- London, 1966-
ISSN 0007-4969

AB/N-1	EX/U-1 1973-	LO/U11 1968-
AB/U-1 1968-	GL/U-2 1974-	LO/U12
AD/U-6	HL/U-1 1966-75	LO/U24 imp.
BH/U-1	LC/U-1 1969-	LV/U-1
BL/U-1	LO/C-3 1974-	MA/U-1
CA/U-1 1966-	LO/C15	NO/U-1 1968-
CA/U13	LO/C47	OX/U15
CH-CI 1973-	LO-MT 1973-	QE/C76 1972-
CR/U-1 1971-	LO/N-1	QG/C25 1976-
DN/U-1	LO/N-5	QS/Q12
ED/S11	LO/N17	QW/D12 1972-
ED-SLC 1966-	LO/R74	RE/U-1 1974-
ED/U-1	LO/U-2 1966-76	SH/U-1 1966-74

Bulletin of medieval canon law/ University of California Institute of Medieval Canon Law. -- Berkeley, Cal., (n.s.) 1971-
Continues: Bulletin - Institute of Medieval Canon Law 1955-1970.Issued with Traditio, vol.11-26, 1955-1970

AB/N-1 1971-	HL/U-1 1971-	OX/U25 1971-
CA/U-1 1971-	LO/N-1	XY/N-1 1974 (v.4).
DN/U-1 1971-	MA/U-1 1971-	

Bulletin of the Anglo-Soviet Law Association. -- London, 1947?-1953

LO/N-1 imp.

Bulletin of the Harvard International Law Club see Harvard international law journal

Bulletin of the International Commission of Jurists. -- Geneva, 1954-1968 (no.36)
Merged with: Journal of the International Commission of Jurists, q.v., to become: Review - International Commission of Jurists,q.v.
Editions also in French and German
ISSN 0534-8242

AB/U-1
AD/U-6 1955-67
BL/U-1
BR/U-1 1955-68
CA/U13 1960-68
CB/U-1 1968 (nos.34-36).
DR/U-1 1963-68 imp.
ED/S10 1955-68
ED/S11
ED/U-1 1955-68
EX/U-1 1967/68.
GL/U-1 1955-68
HL/U-1
LD/U-1
LO-MT 1955-68
LO/N17
LO/S14 1955-68
LO/U-2 1955-68
LO/U11 1957-68 imp.
LO/U12 1960-68
LO/U24
LV/U-1 1965-68
NO/U-1 1956-68 (w.v.30)
OX/U15
QS/Q12 1958-68
QS/Q29 1956-68
QS/S-6
QS/S-7 1955-68
RE/U-1 1957-58 (nos.7-8);1960-68 (nos.10-36)
SH/U-1 1958-68 (nos. 5-36)
SO/U-1 1955-68 imp.
SW/U-1 1963-68
XY/N-1 1956-68 (nos. 5-36)

Bulletin of the State Bar Association of Wisconsin see Wisconsin Bar bulletin

Bulletin of the United States Trade-Mark Association. -- New York, 1877-1940
Absorbed by: Trade mark reporter, q.v.

LO/N14 1906-40

Bulletin officiel de la propriété industrielle. -- Paris, 1884-
Published in 5 parts
ISSN 0007-5183

XY/N-1 1937 (54e année)-

Bulletin spécial des commissaires de police. -- Paris, 1858-1859

LO/N-1

Bulletin spécial des décisions des juges de paix et des tribunaux de simple police, recueil mensuel... -- Paris, 1859-1943

LO/N-1 1859-1943 (v.1-70;83-85)

Bulletin trimestriel - Institut Belge de Droit Comparé see Revue de droit international et de droit comparé

Bulletin trimestriel de la Société de Législation Comparée see Revue internationale de droit comparé

Bulletin zur Ostrechtsforschung in den Ländern des Europarates see International bulletin for research on law in eastern Europe

Bullettino dell'Istituto di Diritto Romano "Vittorio Scialoja". -- Rome, 1888-

AD/U-6	GL/U-1 1934-	OX/U15
CA/U13	LO/U-2 (w.v.23)	QS/S-5
ED/U-1	LO/U24 1921 (v.31)-	XY/N-1 1969 (v.72=ser. 3 v.11)-

Burma Law Institute journal. -- Rangoon, 1958-1960
Publication suspended 1960
ISSN 0525-2415

CA/U13	LO/U24	OX/U13
LO/U14		

Business and law. -- Wellington, N.Z., 1966 (vol.1 nos 1-2).
ISSN 0525-2644

LO/U24

Business law journal. -- New York, 1923-1932 (vol.19)
Absorbed by: Banking law journal, q.v.

No holdings notified

The Business law review; a journal of commercial law and practice. -- Ipswich, 1954-1958 (vol.5)
ISSN 0408-0181

BH/U-1	LO/C47 1954-56	LV/P-1 1954-56 (v.3)
CA/U13 1955-58	LO-MT 1954-57 (v.4)	OX/U15 1955-58
DR/U-1 imp.	LO/N-1	QW/D12
ED/S11	LO/U-3	XY/N-1 1956-57 (v.3-4)
EX/U-1 1955-58	LO/U24	

Business lawyer. -- Chicago, July 1946-
ISSN 0007-6899

CA/U13 1958- imp.	EX/U-1 1974-	LO/U24
CV/C-1 1968-73 (v.24-28)	LO/C10 1972-	OX/U15
CV/U-1	LO-MT	XY/N-1 1966 (v.21 no.4)-
	LO/U12	

Businessman's law/ Ed. by A.S. Silke and Ellison Kahn. -- Capetown, 1971-
ISSN 0045-3668

LO/U24

Butterworths' fortnightly notes <u>see</u> New Zealand law journal

Butterworths' South African law review <u>see</u> Acta juridica (Capetown)

Byulleten verkhovnogo suda R.S.F.S.R. -- Moscow,

GL/U-1 Soviet Studies Branch Library 1964-	LO/U-2 1961-69	OX/U15 1964-

Byulleten verkhovnogo suda SSSR. -- Moscow,

GL/U-1 Soviet Studies Branch Library 1957-	LO/U-2 1957-70	OX/U15 1957-

CLU journal/ American Society of Chartered Life Underwriters. -- Bryn Mawr, Pa., 1946-
ISSN 0007-8573

No holdings notified

Cahiers - Association Nationale des Docteurs en Droit see Droit et économie

Cahiers de bibliographie juridique. -- Barcelona, 1962-1964
ISSN 0068-5003

CA/U13	LO/U-3	OX/U15

Cahiers de droit/ Université Laval. -- Quebec, 1954-
ISSN 0007-974X

BL/U-1 1966-	LO/U24	OX/U15 1966-
DN/U-1		

Cahiers de droit: édition du centenaire/ Université Laval see University of British Columbia law review: centennial edition

Cahiers de droit comparé. -- Brussels, 1964-
ISSN 0575-0601

LO/U24	LV/U-1 1964-71	XY/N-1 1971 (no.2/3)-

Cahiers de droit européen. -- Louvain, 1965-
ISSN 0007-9758

AB/U-1	EX/U-1 1976-	LO/U24
BH/U-1	GL/U-1	NO/U-1
BR/U-1 1973 (v.9)-	LC/U-1 1966 (v.2)-	OX/U15
BT/U-1	LD/U-1	QN/C70 1972 (v.8)-
CA/U13	LO-MT	QS/S-6
CB/U-1	LO/N-5 1966-	QW/D12 1973 (v.9)-
CR/U-1 1976-	LO/N17 1967-	SH/U-1
DN/U-1 1972-	LO/S14	SO/U-1 1966,1968-
ED-SLC 1965-	LO/U-2 imp.	XY/N-1 1968 (v.4)-
ED/U-1	LO/U11 1976-	

Cahiers de droit familial. -- Brussels, 1973-

HL/U-1 1973 (no.1-3).		OX/U15

Cahiers de droit fiscal international = Studies on international fiscal law = Schriften zum internationalen Steuerrecht/ International Fiscal Association. -- Rotterdam, 1939-

LO/N-1 1939-62	LO/U24	XY/N-1 1967 (v.52)-
LO/U-3 1939;1947- imp.		

Cahiers de législation et de bibliographie juridique de l'Amérique latine. -- Paris [ca 1947]-1956 (vol.28)

LO/N-1 1955/56.	LO/U24	OX/U15
LO/U-3		

Cahiers du Centre d'Etude des Coutumes/ Faculté de Droit et des Sciences Economiques, Université de Madagascar. -- Tananarive, 1966-

LO/U14

Cahiers du droit de l'énergie atomique. -- Paris, 1968-

No holdings notified

Cahiers suisse de la sécurité du travail. -- Lucerne, 1956-

LO/N14	XY/N-1 1977 (no.125)-

Cahiers trimestriels: la paix mondiale par le droit. -- Geneva, 1968-

LO/U24

Cal law, trends and developments <u>see</u> Golden Gate University law review

Calcutta law journal. -- Calcutta, 1905-

LO-MT 1905-09;1912-39;1940-42 imp., 1943-48	LO/N-1 1907-31	LO/U14 1905-09
	LO-PC 1905-43	

California law review. -- Berkeley, 1912-
ISSN 0008-1221

AD/U-6	ED/U-1	MA/U-1 imp.
BL/U-1 1964-	KL/U-1	NO/U-1 1961 (v.49)-
CA/U13 1948-	LC/U-1 1945 (v.33)-	OX/U15
CB/U-1	LO/C15 1972-	SH/U-1 1960 (v.48)-
CR/U-1	LO/U-2	SO/U-1 1973-
CV/U-1 1967 (v.55)-	LO/U12 1950-	XY/N-1 1967 (v.55 no.2)-
DR/U-1 1950-	LO/U24	

California State Bar journal. -- Los Angeles, Calif., 1972 (vol.47)-
Continues: State Bar journal of the State Bar of California, 1926-1942 (vol.17), and: Journal of the State Bar of California, 1943-1971 (vol.46)
ISSN 0039-002X

LO-MT 1972 (v.47)-	LO/U24 1972 (v.47)-	XY/N-1 1973 (v.48)-

California Western international law journal. -- San Diego, 1970-

AD/U-6
BL/U-1 1972-76
LO/N-1
LO/U24
NO/U-1 1973 (v.4)-
XY/N-1 1973 (v.4)-

California Western law review. -- San Diego, 1965-
ISSN 0008-1639

BL/U-1
CA/U13
LO/U24
XY/N-1

Cambrian law review. -- Aberystwyth, 1970-
ISSN 0084-8328

AB/U-1
BH/U-1
BL/U-1
BR/U-1 1975-
CA/U-1
CA/U13
CB/U-1 1973 (v.4)-
CR/U-1
ED/S11
ED/U-1
EX/U-1
HL/U-1
LA/U-1 1970-75
LO/C47 1975.
LO/N-1 1975-
LO/U12
LO/U24
LV-LP 1971-
LV/U-1
NO/U-1 1971 (v.2)-
OX/U15
QG/C25 1976-
QM/C48 1971-
QS/S-4
SO/U-1
XY/N-1

Cambridge law journal. -- London, 1921-
ISSN 0008-1973

AB/N-1
AB/U-1
AD/U-6
BC-UC 1957-
BH/U-1
BL/U-1
BR/U-1
BT/U-1
CA/U-1
CA/U13
CA/U37 1959-74
CB/U-1
CC/U-1 1967-
CH-CI
CR/U-1
CV/C-1 1939 (v.7)-
CV/U-1
DN/U-1 1951-
DR/U-1
ED/S10 1942-58
ED/S11
ED-SLC
ED/U-1
EX/U-1
GL/U-1 1923-
GL/U-2
HL/U-1 1922-
KL/U-1
LA/U-1 1921-74
LC/C-1 1924-
LD/C-1 1924-
LD/P-1 1954-69
LD/U-1
LO/C-3 1924-
LO/C-5 1960-
LO/C10
LO/C14 1924-
LO/C15
LO/C18 1967 (v.25)-
LO/C25 1951-
LO/C27
LO/C47
LO-MT
LO/N-1
LO/N-5 1967-
LO/N17 1948-
LO/N46
LO/R74
LO-SC 1939-66;1972-
LO-TS 1954-
LO/U-1
LO/U-2
LO/U-3
LO/U11
LO/U12
LO/U24
LO/U28
LV-LP 1924- (v.30; 32 imp.)
LV/P-1 1956-
LV/U-1
MA/U-1
NO/U-1
NW/U-1
OX/U15
OX/U25
QE/C76
QG/C25 1976-
QL/D15 1924-50;1951 (v.11) imp., 1954-
QM/C48 1924 (v.2)-
QM/C68
QN/C70
QS/Q12 1939-53 imp., 1957-
QS/Q13 1971-72;1974-
QS/Q29 1962-66;1969-
QS/S-4
QS/S-6
QS/S-7
QS/S-8
QW/D12
RE/U-1
SH/U-1
SO/U-1
SW/U-1 1933-
XM/C10 1924-
XY/N-1 1967 (v.25)-

Canada law journal. -- Montreal, 1867 (vol.3)-1868 (vol.4)
Continues: Lower Canada law journal, 1866-1867

LO/U24
OX/U15

Canada law journal. -- Toronto, 1868-1922 (vol.58, n.s.)
Continues: Upper Canada law journal and local courts' gazette, 1855-1864 (vol.10) and: Upper Canada law journal, 1865-1867
Merged with: Canadian law times q.v., to become Canadian Bar review q.v.

ED/S11 1858-1922	LO/N-1 1865-1922	OX/U15
LO-MT 1865-73	LO/U24 1881-1922 (v.17-58) (w.v.57)	QS/S-6 1855-75

Canadian Bar journal <u>see</u> National/ Canadian Bar Association

Canadian Bar review. -- Toronto, 1923-
Merger of: Canada law journal, q.v., and: Canadian law times, q.v.
ISSN 0008-3003

AB/U-1 1923- imp.	KL/U-1 1973 (v.51)-	LO/U12 1945-
AD/U-6 1952.	LC/U-1 1923- (w.1934-44, 1950,1960)	LO/U24
BH/U-1	LD/U-1	LO/U28
BL/U-1 1944-	LO/C-3	LV/U-1 (w.1950)
CA/U13	LO/C10 1950-	MA/U-1
CB/U-1 (w.1936,1960)	LO/C14 1960-73 (v.51)	NO/U-1
CH-CI	LO/C15 1973-	NW/U-1 1963-72 (v.41-50)
CR/U-1	LO/C27 1974-	OX/U15
CV/C-1 1974 (v.52).	LO/C47 1972-	OX/U25 1934-
CV/U-1 1967 (v.45)-	LO-MT	QM/C48 1976 (v.54)-
DR/U-1 (w.v.8,12-18,20-22)	LO/N-1 1970-	QN/C70 1970 (v.48)-
ED/S11	LO/R74 1965-	QS/S-4
ED-SLC 1974-	LO/S65 1923-73 imp.	QS/S-6 1946-
ED/U-1	LO/U-2	QS/S-7 1953-
EX/U-1 1948-	LO/U-3 1923- (1923 imp.)	RE/U-1 1974 (v.52)-
GL/U-1 1945-	LO/U11 1955-	SH/U-1
GL/U-2 1966-		SO/U-1
HL/U-1 1947-		XM/C10 1972-
		XY/N-1 1950 (v.28)-

Canadian business law journal = Revue canadienne du droit de commerce. -- Agincourt, 1975-
ISSN 0319-3322

LO/U24

Canadian environmental law news. -- Toronto, 1972-
ISSN 0317-6517

LO/U24

Canadian journal of corrections <u>see</u> next entry

Canadian journal of criminology and corrections = Revue canadienne de criminologie. -- Ottawa, 1971 (vol.13)-
Continues: Canadian journal of corrections = Revue canadienne de criminologie, 1958-1970 (ISSN 0008-4069)
ISSN 0315-5390

CA/U37	KL/U-1	LO/U24
CB/U-1 1970 (v.12)-	LO/N-1 1971-	OX/U15
ED/U-1 1968 (v.10)-	LO/U-3	XY/N-1 1963 (v.5)-

Canadian law review. -- Toronto, 1901-1907 (vol.6)
Absorbed by: Canadian law times, q.v.

OX/U15

Canadian law times. -- Toronto, 1881-1922 (vol.42)
Absorbed: Canadian law review, q.v.
Merged with: Canada law journal, q.v., to become: Canadian Bar review, q.v.

LO/N-1 1893-1917　　LO/U24 1881-1919; 1920-22 imp.　　OX/U15

Canadian legal studies: journal of the Association of Canadian Law Teachers. -- Toronto, 1964-
ISSN 0576-5625

LO/U24　　OX/U15 1964-68 (v.5)　　XY/N-1

Canadian municipal journal. -- Toronto, 1891-1892

OX/U15

Canadian Society of Forensic Science journal. -- Ottawa, 1968-
ISSN 0008-5030

GL/U-2　　LO/U24

Canadian Tax Foundation conference see Report of proceedings of the annual Tax Conference...

Canadian tax journal. -- Toronto, 1953-
ISSN 0008-5111

GL/U-1 1959-　　LO/U24 1964 (v.12)-　　XY/N-1 1963 (v.11)-
LO/U-3

Canadian yearbook of international law = Annuaire canadien de droit international. -- Vancouver, 1963-
ISSN 0069-0058

AB/U-1	HL/U-1	LO/U24
AD/U-6	LD/U-1	MA/U-1
BH/U-1	LO/C15 1970-	NO/U-1
BL/U-1 1963-64	LO/N-1	OX/U15
CA/U13	LO/N17	SH/U-1
DR/U-1	LO/U-2	SO/U-1
ED/U-1	LO/U-3	XY/N-1

Cape law journal see South African law journal

Capital University law review. -- Columbus, Ohio, 1972-

XY/N-1

Caribbean law journal. -- Kingston, Jamaica, 1952-1953
ISSN 0528-130X

LO/U24

Carl Heymann's kritisches Literaturblatt für Rechts- und Staatswissenschaft. -- Berlin, 1879.
Continues: Carl Heymann's Literaturblatt für Rechts- und Staatswissenschaft, 1874-1878

LO/N-1

Carl Heymann's Literaturblatt für Rechts- und Staatswissenschaft
see previous entry

Cartel: quarterly review of monopoly developments and consumer protection. -- London, 1950-1964 (vol.14)
ISSN 0576-8349

BL/U-1 1960-64	LO/N-1	LV/U-1 1955 (v.5 no.3)-1964
ED/N-1	LO/U-3	OX/U-1
KL/U-1	LO/U24	XY/N-1 1963-64 (v.13-14)

Case and comment. -- Rochester, N.Y., 1894-
ISSN 0008-7238

LO/N-1 1901-07 imp.	LO/U24 1906-44 imp., 1946-	OX/U15 1961-
LO/U-2 1965-		

Case Western Reserve journal of international law. -- Cleveland, Ohio, 1968-
ISSN 0008-7254

LO/U24	XY/N-1 1972 (v.5)-

Case Western Reserve law review. -- Cleveland, Ohio, 1967 (vol.19)-
Continues: Western Reserve law review, 1949-1967
ISSN 0008-7262

LO/U24 1971 (v.23)-	OX/U15	XY/N-1 1970 (v.22)-

Casopis pro mezinárodní právo = Czechoslovak journal of international law. -- Prague, 1957-
ISSN 0008-736X

LO/U24 1963-71 (v.7-15)	OX/U15	XY/N-1 1967-71 (v.11-15)

Catholic lawyer. -- Brooklyn, N.Y., 1955-
ISSN 0008-8137

CA/U13 1971 imp.	OX/U15	XY/N-1 1971 (v.17)-
LO/U24	QS/S-7	

Catholic University law review. -- Washington D.C., 1950-
1950-1975 (vol.24) entitled: Catholic University of America law review
ISSN 0008-8390

CA/U13 1969-	OX/U15	XY/N-1 1973 (v.23)-
LO/U24		

Catholic University of America law review <u>see</u> previous entry

Cauris. -- Strasbourg, 1972-

LO/U14 1973 (v.4)-

Central law journal. -- St. Louis, Mo., 1874-1927

LO/N-1

Central law monthly <u>see</u> Chicago law journal

Central-organ für das deutsche Handels- und Wechselrecht. -- Cologne, 1865-1873
Continues: Central-organ für den deutschen Handelsstand 1862-1864

LO/N-1

Central-organ für den deutschen Handelsstand <u>see</u> previous entry

Centralblatt für Rechtswissenschaft <u>see</u> Zentralblatt der Rechtswissenschaft

Ceylon labour law journal. -- Colombo, 1962-

No holdings notified

Ceylon law college review. -- Colombo, 1955-1962

LO/N-1

Ceylon law journal. -- Colombo, 1892.

LO/N-1

Ceylon law journal. -- Colombo, 1936-

No holdings notified

Ceylon law review. -- Colombo, 1899-1912 (vol.7)

LO/U24 1903 (v.3).

Ceylon Law Society journal. -- Colombo, 1954-1971?
ISSN 0528-7626

LO/N-1 1956-68 LO/U24 (v.1 & 3 imp.)

Ceylon law students magazine. -- Colombo, 1910-

No holdings notified

Ceylon law weekly. -- Colombo, 1931-

LO/N-1 1931-73 LO/U14 1937- (w.v.28) OX/U15 1936 (v.6)-

Chancery miscellanies. -- London, 1850-1851

ED/S11 LO/N-1 OX/U15

Chartered Life Underwriters journal <u>see</u> CLU journal

Chartered secretary <u>see</u> Professional administration

Cheng fa yen chiu: zheng-fa yanjiu (fa lu ch'u pan she). -- Peking, 1954-
ISSN 0577-6430

LO/N-1 1958-64 LO/U14 1954-64 imp.

Cheng-ta fa-hsüeh p'ing-lun (Chengchi law review)/ Department of Law, National Chengchi University. -- Taipei, 1969-

LO/U14

Chicago Bar Association record <u>see</u> next entry

Chicago Bar record. -- Chicago, 1934 (vol.16)-
Continues: Chicago Bar Association record, 1910-1932
Not published, Apr. 1932-Oct. 1934

LO/U24 OX/U15 1949 (v.31)- XY/N-1 1970 (v.51 no.4)-

Chicago-Kent law review. -- Chicago, 1938 (vol.17)-
Continues: Chicago-Kent review, 1923-1938

BL/U-1 1969- LO/U24 XY/N-1 1969 (v.46)-
CA/U13 1966-

Chicago-Kent review <u>see</u> previous entry

Chicago law journal. -- Chicago, [1883]-1907 (vol.24, 3rd series)
Continues: Central law monthly, 1880- Jan., 1883

No holdings notified

China law review = Fa-hsüeh tsa-chih/ Law Department, Soochow University. -- Shanghai, 1922-June 1937; 1940-

LO/U14 1922-26 imp.

Chinese law and government: a journal of translations. -- White Plains, N.Y., 1968-
ISSN 0009-4609

CA/U-1 LO/U14 XY/N-1 1973 (v.6 no.4)-
LD/U-1

Chitty's law journal. -- Toronto, 1950-
ISSN 0009-4889

AB/U-1 1976- OX/U15 XY/N-1 1976 (v.24 no.6)-
LO/U24

Chŏsut'isŭ = The Justice. -- Seoul, 1957-[1964?]

LO/N-1 1958 (v.2)-

Chronique européenne du droit des affaires see Droit et C.E.E. affaires international

Chün-fa chuan-k'an = The Military law journal. -- T'ai Pei, 1952-
ISSN 0529-5483

LO/N-1 Aug.1956-Dec.1957 (v.5 no.8)

Chuo law review see Hōgaku shimpō

Ciencia penal. -- Sao Paulo, 1973-

No holdings notified

City of London law review: journal of the Mansfield Law Club, City of London Polytechnic. -- London, 1974-

AB/N-1
AB/U-1
CA/U-1
CA/U13 Lent,1975.
CB/U-1 1975-
LO/C15
LO/C27 1975-
LO/C47
LO-MT
LO/N-1
LO/S28
LO/U24
LV-LP
OX/U15
QE/C76
QL/D15
QM/C68 Michaelmas,1974-
QN/C70
QW/D12 1975-
XM/C10 1975-76
XY/N-1

Civil and military law journal. -- New Delhi, 1965-
ISSN 0045-7043

No holdings notified

Civil liberties docket/ National Lawyers' Guild. -- Berkeley, Calif., 1955-1969 (no.14)
ISSN 0578-378X

LO/U24 1957-68 imp. OX/U15 1967-69 (nos.13-14)

Civil liberties review. -- New York, 1973-
ISSN 0093-6383

GL/U-1 Social Sciences Faculty Library
XY/N-1

Clearinghouse review/ National Clearinghouse for Legal Services. -- Chicago, 1967-
ISSN 0009-868X

CA/U13 1969 (v.3) imp., 1970 (v.4)-
CB/U-1 1973 (v.7)-
XY/N-1 1975 (v.8)-

Cleveland-Marshall law review see next entry

Cleveland state law review. -- Cleveland, 1969 (vol.18, no.3)-
Continues: Cleveland-Marshall law review, 1951-1969
ISSN 0009-8876

CA/U13 1967- OX/U15 XY/N-1 1970 (v.19, no.2)-
LO/U24

Code reporter: a monthly law journal. -- New York, 1848-1853 (vol.3)

LO/N-1

Codicillus/ Faculty of Law, University of South Africa. -- Pretoria, 1960-
ISSN 0010-020X

LO/U14 1969- LO/U24 OX/U15

Collected studies in criminological research: reports presented to the Conference of Directors of Criminological Research Institutes. -- Strasbourg, 1967 (1963/65)-

AD/U-6 LA/U-1 1969 (v.4). MA/P-1 1963/65 (v.1); 1967 (v.3)-
CA/U37 LC/U-1
DR/U-1 LO/U-1 OX/U15
GL/U-1 LO/U-2 (w.v.2) RE/U-1
HL/U-1 (w.v.9) LO/U24 SH/U-1

Colombo law review. -- Colombo, Sri Lanka, 1969-
ISSN 0069-5939

BL/U-1 1971- LO/N17 1969-72 (v.1-3) LO/U24 1969-72 (v.3)
LO/N-1 OX/U15 1969-72 (v.3)

Columbia human rights law review. -- New York, 1971 (vol.4)-
Continues: Columbia survey of human rights law, 1967-1971 (ISSN 0010-2008)
ISSN 0090-7944

BL/U-1 1973- SO/U-1 1973 (v.5)- XY/N-1 1970 (v.3)-
OX/U15

Columbia journal of environmental law. -- New York, 1974-

OX/U15 XY/N-1

Columbia journal of law and social problems. -- New York, 1965-
ISSN 0010-1923

BL/U-1 LO/U24 SH/U-1
CA/U13 1967- OX/U15 1966 (v.2)- XY/N-1 1967 (v.3)-
CR/U-1

Columbia journal of transnational law. -- New York, 1964 (vol.3)-
Continues: Bulletin - Columbia Society of International Law, 1961-1963 (vol.2 no.1), and: International law bulletin, 1963 (vol.2 no.2)
ISSN 0010-1931

BH/U-1 CB/U-1 LO/S14 1971 (v.10)-
BL/U-1 DR/U-1 LO/U-2
CA/U13 1962- imp. HL/U-1 1963- LO/U24 (cont'd)

Columbia journal of transnational law (cont'd).

MA/U-1 1968-	OX/U15	XY/N-1 1965 (v.4)-
NO/U-1	SO/U-1	

Columbia law review. -- New York, 1901-
ISSN 0010-1958

AB/U-1	GL/U-1	LO/U12 1920-
AD/U-6	HL/U-1	LO/U24
BH/U-1	KL/U-1	LO/U28
BL/U-1	LC/U-1	LV/U-1
BR/U-1	LD/C-1 1974 (v.74)-	MA/U-1
BT/U-1 1975-	LD/U-1 1928-	NO/U-1
CA/U13	LO/C-3 1953-	OX/U15
CB/U-1	LO/C10 1950 (v.50)-	OX/U25 1909-
CH-CI	LO/C15 1945-	QM/C68 1950-
CR/U-1	LO/C25 1960-	QN/C70
CV/C-1 1960 (v.60)-	LO/C27 1973-	QS/S-7
CV/U-1 imp.	LO/C47 1971-	QW/D12
DN/U-1 1940-	LO-MT	RE/U-1
DR/U-1 1945-	LO/N-1	SH/U-1
ED/S11 1944-	LO/R74 1968 (v.68)-	SO/U-1
ED/U-1	LO/U-2	XY/N-1 1930 (v.30)-
EX/U-1	LO/U-3	

Columbia survey of human rights law <u>see</u> Columbia human rights law review

Commercial and municipal law reporter. -- Port Elizabeth, 1959-
Continues: Commercial law reporter, 1948-1958

LO/U24 1949-51	OX/U15 1959-	XY/N-1 1969 (Sep.-Dec.).

Commercial law annual. -- London, 1871-1874

CA/U-1 1874.	LO/N-1	OX/U15 (w.1872)

Commercial law journal. -- Chicago, 1930 (vol.35 no.8)-
Continues: Bulletin - Commercial Law League of America, 1888-1923 (vol.28 no.8), and: Commercial Law League journal, 1923 (vol.28 no.9)-1930 (vol.35 no.7)
ISSN 0010-3055

LO/U24 1972 (v.77)-	XY/N-1 1967 (v.72)-

Commercial Law League journal <u>see</u> previous entry

Commercial law reporter <u>see</u> Commercial and municipal law reporter

Common Market law review. -- Leyden, 1963-
ISSN 0010-3292

AB/N-1 imp.	BT/U-1	DR/U-1
AB/U-1	CA/U-1	ED/S11
AD/U-6	CA/U13	ED-SLC 1962-
BC-UC 1976-	CB/U-1	ED/U-1
BH/U-1	CR/U-1	EX/U-1
BL/U-1	CV/U-1 (w.v.2)	GL/U-1
BR/U-1	DN/U-1	GL/U-2 (cont'd)

Common Market law review (cont'd).

HL/U-1
KL/U-1
LA/U-1 1969-
LC/C-1 1973-
LC/U-1
LD/C-1
LD/U-1
LO/C-3
LO/C-5 1972 (v.9 no.3)-
LO/C10 1973-
LO/C14 1970 (v.7)-
LO/C15
LO/C25
LO/C47
LO-CBL 1969-*
LO-MT
LO/N-1
LO/N-5
LO/N17
LO/N26
LO/N46
LO/R74
LO/S14
LO-SC (w.v.3-4; 7;9)
LO-TS
LO/U-1 1973-
LO/U-2 imp.
LO/U-3
LO/U11
LO/U12 (w.1965-66; 1967-69)
LO/U24
LO/U28 1972 (v.9)-
LV-LP
LV/U-1
MA/P-1
MA/U-1
NO/U-1
OX/U15
OX/U25
QE/C76
QG/C25 1973-
QL/D15 1963-65; 1966/67;1970-
QM/C48 1963/64-66/67; 1972-
QM/C68
QN/C70
QS/Q13 1966-72
QS/S-4
QS/S-6
QS/S-7 1966-
QS/S-8
RE/U-1
SH/U-1
SO/U-1
XY/N-1

Commonwealth judicial journal/ Commonwealth Magistrates' Association. -- London, 1973-

LO/N17
LO/U14

Commonwealth law bulletin/ Commonwealth Secretariat. -- London, 1974-

AB/N-1
BL/U-1
CA/U-1
CA/U13
LO/C47
LO-MT
LO/N-1
LO/N17
LO/R74
LO-SC
LO/U-3 1972 (no.2)-
LO/U24
OX/U15
QM/C68
QN/C70 1975 (no.2)-
QS/S-4 1976-
QS/S-6
QS/S-7
RE/U-1
XY/N-1 1975 (no.2)-

Commonwealth law review. -- Melbourne, 1903-1909 (vol.6)

LO/N-1 imp.
LO/U24
OX/U15

Community home schools gazette. -- Baschurch, etc? 1975 (vol.69)-
Continues: Approved schools gazette, 1918-1970 (vol.63), and: Community schools gazette, 1970 (vol.64)-1975 (vol.68)

CA/U-1 1959-
ED/U-1 1968 (v.62)-
HL/U-1 1949 (v.42)-
LO/C-3 1968-Mar.1970
LO/N-1
OX/U15 1967-
XY/N-1 1950 (v.44)-

Community schools gazette see previous entry

Comparative and international law journal of southern Africa = Tydskrif vir regsvergelyking en internasionale reg van suidelike Afrika = Jornal de direito comparativo e internacional para os países do sul da Africa = Journal de droit comparé et international des pays de l'Afrique australe = Zeitschrift für Rechtsvergleichung und internationales Recht des südlichen Afrika. -- Pretoria, S.A., 1968-
ISSN 0010-4051

AD/U-6	ED/U-1	LO/U14
BH/U-1	EX/U-1 1973-	LO/U24
BL/U-1	LC/U-1 1973 (v.6)-	OX/U15
CA/U13	LO/C47 1974-	SH/U-1
CR/U-1 1972-	LO/U-3	XY/N-1

Comparative juridical review. -- Coral Gables, Fla., 1964-
ISSN 0069-7893

AD/U-6 1969 (v.6)-	LC/U-1	LV/U-1 1965-
BR/U-1 1967-	LD/U-1	OX/U15
EX/U-1 1975-	LO/U-2 1967-	SH/U-1 1973 (v.10)-
GL/U-1 1965-	LO/U24	XY/N-1 1973 (v.10)-

Comparative labor law. -- Los Angeles, 1976-
Continues: Newsletter/ Bulletin - International Society for Labor Law and Legislation, 1967-1975

OX/U15

Competition and trade regulation <u>see</u> Wirtschaft und Wettbewerb

Computers and law: the newsletter of the Society for Computers and Law Ltd. -- London, 1975 (no.3)-
Continues: Newsletter - Society for Computers and Law Ltd., 1974 (nos.1-2)

LO/U24	OX/U15

Comunicazione e studi/ Istituto di Diritto Internazionale e Straniero della Università di Milano. -- Milan, 1942-

CA/U13 1942-69	LO/U24	XY/N-1 1966-69 (v.12-13)
LO/U-2	OX/U15	

Comunitá internazionale. -- Rome, 1946-
ISSN 0010-5066

LO/U24 1952 (v.7 no.2)-	XY/N-1 1949 (v.4)-

Concord: Journal of the International Arbitration and Peace Association. -- London, 1887 (vol.3)-1917 (vol.30)
Continues: International Arbitration and Peace Association monthly journal, 1885-1887

LO/N-1

Concurrence et marché <u>see</u> Wirtschaft und Wettbewerb

Conference on charitable foundations, New York University <u>see</u> Proceedings of the... biennial conference...

Conference on labor, New York University see Proceedings - Conference...

Conference series - Law School, University of Chicago. -- Chicago, Ill., [ca 1939]-
ISSN 0412-0310

No holdings notified

Congrès international - Société Internationale de Droit Pénal Militaire et de Droit de la Guerre see Société Internationale de Droit Pénal Militaire et de Droit de la Guerre

Connecticut Bar journal. -- Hartford, Conn., 1927-
Contains: Law review/ University of Connecticut School of Law, in vol.31-42, 1957-1968, afterwards: Connecticut law review, q.v.,
ISSN 0010-6070

LO/U24 OX/U15 1946 (v.20)- XY/N-1 1970 (v.44)-

Connecticut law review. -- W. Hartford, Conn., 1968-
Continues: Law review/ University of Connecticut School of Law, in: Connecticut Bar journal, q.v.
ISSN 0010-6151

LO/U24 OX/U15 XY/N-1

Conservateur: revue de droit international. -- Utrecht, 1867-1870 (vol.2)

LO/U24

Constitutional and parliamentary information/ Association of Secretaries-General of Parliaments. -- Geneva, 3rd series 1948-
Continues: Informations constitutionelles et parlementaires, 1st series 1936-1938 and: Constitutional and parliamentary information, new series 1939/47 - 1947/48 (vol.2)
ISSN 0010-6623

BH/P-1 1967 (3rd series no.69)-
ED/U-1 1958 (3rd series no.33)-
HL/U-1 1957-76 (3rd series nos.29-108)
LO/N-1 1936-39;1948-
LO/S14
LO/U-2 1950 (no.3)- (w.nos. 20,37)
LO/U24 1960 (3rd series no.44)-
XY/N-1 1967 (3rd series no.69)-

Constitutional and parliamentary information, new series see previous entry

Contemporary drug problems. -- New York, 1971-
ISSN 0091-4509

XY/N-1

Contents of current legal periodicals. -- Wilmington, Del., 1972-
ISSN 0300-7391

CA/U13 1976 (v.5 no.9)- OX/U15 XY/N-1 1975(?)-

Conveyancer <u>see</u> next entry

Conveyancer and property lawyer. -- London, 1936 (vol.1)-
Continues: Conveyancer, 1915-1936 (vol.21) and index vol. (vol.22), 1939
ISSN 0010-8200

AB/N-1 Je 1916-
AB/U-1
AD/U-6 1972 (v.36)-
BH-LS
BH/U-1
BL-LS
BL/U-1 1936-
BR/U-1
BT/U-1 1975-
CA/U-1 1971-
CA/U13
CB/U-1
CH-CI
CR/U-1
CV/U-1 (w.v.10-11)
DN/U-1 1956-
DR/U-1
ED/S11
ED-SLC 1936-
ED/U-1 1972 (v.36)-
EX/U-1
GL/U-1 1960 (v.24 no.6)-
GL/U-2 1976 (v.40)-
HL/U-1 1936-
KL/U-1 1915-62 (v.26)
LA/U-1 1958-61
LC/C-1 1936-
LC/U-1
LD/C-1 1936-
LD/P-1 1936-
LD/U-1
LO/C-3 1936-
LO/C-5 1960 (v.24)-
LO/C14 1965 (v.29)-
LO/C15
LO/C25 1960-
LO/C27 1936-
LO/C47 1972-
LO-MT (w.1936,(v.21))
LO/N-1
LO/N-5 1956-
LO/R74 1956;1958-
LO-SC 1915-36;1950-53;1958;1960-
LO-TS 1948 (v.12)-
LO/U-1 1936-
LO/U-2
LO/U-3 1936-
LO/U11 1936-
LO/U12 1915-40;1946-
LO/U24
LO/U28 1937-38;1940-
LV-LP 1961;1970 (v.34)-
LV/P-1 1960 (v.24)-
LV/U-1
MA/U-1 1970-
NO/U-1 1936-
NW/U-1
OX/U15
OX/U25 1952-
QE/C76 1936- (w.1937-39;1946-47)
QG/C25 1975-
QL/D15 1915-36;1956;1958;1960-69;1971-
QM/C48 1950-53;1958;1960-
QM/C68 1963-
QN/C70 1936-
QS/Q12 1953-
QS/S-4 (w.1944 (v.8); 1946 (v.10))
QS/S-6
QS/S-7
QS/S-8
QW/D12
RE/U-1
SH/U-1
SO/U-1
XM/C10
XY/N-1 1918-35;1950-59;1960 (v.24)-

Conveyancers' year book. -- London, 1940-1951 (vol.12)

AB/N-1
AB/U-1
BH/U-1 1940.
CA/U13
ED/S11
EX/U-1
HL/U-1 1946-51
LC/U-1
LD/P-1
LO-MT 1940,1944,1946.
LO/N-1
LO/U24
LV/U-1
NO/U-1 1941-42, 1947-51
OX/U15
OX/U25
QS/Q12 1946.
QS/S-7
QS/S-8
RE/U-1

Conveyancing review. -- Glasgow, 1957-1963 (vol.3)
Absorbed by: Journal of the Law Society of Scotland, q.v.

AB/N-1
AD/U-6
CA/U13
ED/S10
ED/S11
ED/U-1
GL/U-1
GL/U-2
LO/U24
OX/U15

Copyright: geistiges Eigentum. -- Zurich, Leiden, 1938 (vol.4 no.2)-1940 (vol.5 no.4)
Continues: Geistiges Eigentum, 1935-1938 (vol.4 no.1)

LO/N14

Copyright: monthly review of the United International Bureaux for the Protection of Intellectual Property. -- Geneva, 1965-
English edition of: Droit d'auteur, 1888- (ISSN 0012-6365)
ISSN 0010-8626

LO/N14
LO/U24
SO/U-1
XY/N-1 1969 (v.5)-

Copyright bulletin see next entry

Copyright bulletin: quarterly review. -- Paris, 1967 (vol.1)-
Editions also in French and Spanish.
Continues: Copyright bulletin = Bulletin du droit d'auteur = Boletin de derecho de autor, 1948-1967 (vol.19)
ISSN 0010-8634

AB/N-1 imp.
BH/P-1
BT/U-1 1948-66 imp. 1967-
CA/U-1
CR/U-1 1954- imp.
ED/N-1
GL/U-1 1948-63 imp. 1969-
LC/U-1 1968 (v.2)-
LD/U-1
LO/C47 1972-
LO/N-1
LO/N-5 1967-
LO/N14
LO/N17 1969-
LO/U-1
LO/U-3
LO/U24
MA/P-1 (1968 imp.)
OX/U-1
QS/Q12 1956-
QS/Q29
XY/N-1 1952 (v.5); 1967 (v.1)-

Copyright law symposium/ American Society of Composers, Authors and Publishers. -- New York, 1938-1940; 1952 (no.4)-

AD/U-6 1956-
CA/U13 1967-71 (nos.15-19)
ED/S11 1954-
LO/U-2 1952 (no.4)-
LO/U24 1952 (no.4) -1968 (no.16); 1971 (no.19).
LV/P-1 1957-58;1963; 1966;1968.
OX/U15 1952-69 (no.17)
XY/N-1 1958 (no.9)- imp.

Copyright Society of the United States. Bulletin see Bulletin - Copyright Society of the U.S.A.

Cornell international law journal. -- Ithaca, N.Y., 1968-
ISSN 0010-8812

CA/U-1
CA/U13
LO/U24
NO/U-1 1970 (v.3)-
OX/U15
XY/N-1

Cornell law quarterly see next entry

Cornell law review. -- Ithaca, N.Y., 1967 (vol.53)-
Continues: Cornell law quarterly, 1915-1967
ISSN 0010-8847

BL/U-1 1964-
CA/U13
CR/U-1
CV/U-1 1970 (v.56)-
ED/U-1
LO/C27 1973-
LO/C47 1953-
LO/N-1 1961-
LO/U-3
LO/U24
NO/U-1 1960-72
OX/U15
QN/C70 1970 (v.56)-
XY/N-1 1950 (v.36)-

Corporate practice commentator. -- Chicago, Ill., 1959-
ISSN 0010-8995

LO/U24 1965 (v.7)-

Correo judicial. -- Buenos Aires, 1834.

LO/N-1

County courts chronicle and gazette of bankruptcy. -- London, 1847-1920 (vol.47)

AB/N-1 1883-88 imp. 1912-20	ED/S11 1847-62	OX/U15
CA/U-1 1847-1919 (w.1857)	LO/N-1	

Court: the journal of legal practice in Magistrates' Courts. -- St. Albans, 1976-
ISSN 0308-3764

AB/N-1	OX/U15	QS/S-8
LO-SC	QN/C70	QW/D12
NO/U-1		

Creighton law review. -- Omaha, Neb., 1968-
ISSN 0011-1155

XY/N-1

Crime and delinquency. -- New York, 1961 (vol.7)-
Continues: NPPA journal, 1955-1960 (vol.6)
ISSN 0011-1287

AD/U-6 1973-	KL/U-1 1972 (v.18)-	LO/U28 1971 (v.17)-
BH/U-1	LA/U-1 1974-	OX/U15 1965-
CA/U37	LO/N-1 1971-	QL/D15 1976-
CB/U-1	LO/N27 1964-	QN/C70 1972 (v.18)-
DR/U-1 1968-	LO/U-3 (w.1966 no.1)	QW/C73 1973-
ED/U-1 1968 (v.14)-	LO/U11 1976-	RE/U-1 1969 (v.15)-
EX/U-1 1966-	LO/U24 1955-68 (v.14); 1969- imp.	SW/U-1 1969-
GL/U-1 1970.		XY/N-1 1960 (v.6, no.3)-
HL/U-1		

Crime and delinquency abstracts/ National Clearinghouse for Mental Health Information. -- Bethesda, Md., 1966-1972
Continues: International bibliography on crime and delinquency, 1963-1966
ISSN 0590-0824

BL/U-1 1966-69 imp.	LC/U-1 1967-72 (v.5-8)	QW/C73
BT/U-1 1966-67		RE/U-1 1965-72 (v.8)
CA/U37	LO/U24 (w.v.5)	XY/N-1 1966-72 (v.4-8) imp.
HL/U-1 1965/66-69	OX/U15 1965 (v.3, no.3)-1972	

Crime and detection <u>see</u> Criminologist

Crime and social justice/ University of California School of Criminology. -- Berkeley, Cal., 1974-
1975 absorbed: Issues in criminology, q.v.
ISSN 0094-7571

CA/U37	LO/U-2	QL/D15
LO/C27 1976 (no.5)-	LO/U24	

Crime, punishment and correction see South African journal of criminal law and criminology

Criminal justice/ American Bar Association. Section of Criminal Law. -- Chicago, 1973-
ISSN 0092-2498

LO/U24	XY/N-1 1974 (v.2)-

Criminal justice periodical index. -- High Wycombe, 1960-

CA/U37 1975-

Criminal law bulletin. -- New York, 1965-
ISSN 0011-1317

CA/U13	OX/U15 1971 (v.7)-	XY/N-1 1968 (v.4)-
LO/U24	SH/U-1 1973-74 (v.9-10)	

Criminal law journal. -- Sydney, etc., 1977-

LO/U24	OX/U15

Criminal law magazine and reporter. -- Jersey City, N.J., 1880-1896 (vol.18)

LO/U24 1880-88 (v.10); 1893 (v.15).	OX/U15

Criminal law quarterly (Chicago) see American criminal law review

Criminal law quarterly. -- Toronto, 1958-
ISSN 0011-1333

BL/U-1 1969-	LO/U24	QN/C70 1970 (v.13)-
CA/U13	NO/U-1 1962 (v.5)-	SH/U-1
ED/U-1 1969 (v.12)-	OX/U15	XY/N-1 1962 (v.5)-

Criminal law review. -- London, 1954-
ISSN 0011-135X

AB/N-1	CV/C-1 1966-	LD/P-1
AB/U-1	CV/U-1	LD/U-1
AD/U-6	DN/U-1	LO/C-3
BC-UC 1957-	DR/U-1	LO/C-5 imp.
BH-LS	ED/S11	LO/C10
BH/U-1	ED-SLC	LO/C14
BL-LS	ED/U-1	LO/C15
BL/U-1	EX/U-1	LO/C18 1960-
BR/U-1	GL/U-1 Law Faculty Library	LO/C25
BT/U-1		LO/C27
CA/U-1	GL/U-2	LO/C47 1969-
CA/U13	HL/U-1	LO-MT
CA/U37	JE-LS	LO/N-1
CB/U-1	KL/U-1	LO/N-5
CC/U-1 1967-	LC/C-1	LO/N17
CH-CI	LC/U-1	LO/N26
CR/U-1	LD/C-1	LO/N27 1964-

(cont'd)

Criminal law review (cont'd).

LO/N46
LO/R74
LO-SC
LO-TS 1956-
LO/U-1
LO/U-2
LO/U-3
LO/U11
LO/U12
LO/U24
LO/U28
LV-LP (w.May 1971; Jan 1972)
LV/U-1
MA/U-1
NO/U-1
NW/U-1
OX/U15
OX/U25
QE/C76
QG/C25 1971-
QL/D15
QM/C48
QM/C68
QN/C70
QS/Q12 1958-
QS/Q13 1965-
QS/Q29 1955-58;1962-
QS/S-4
QS/S-6
QS/S-7
QS/S-8
QW/C73
QW/D12
RE/U-1
SH/U-1
SO/U-1
XM/C10 1962;1964-67; 1969-
XY/N-1 1954-57 imp., 1959-

Criminal law review/ Association of Lawyers of the Criminal Courts of Manhattan. -- New York, 1954-
ISSN 0590-0905

CA/U13 1958-61

Criminalhistorier, aeldre og nyere. -- Copenhagen, 1866-1867 (vol.2)

LO/N-1

Criminalistische Zeitschrift für die preussischen Staaten. -- Berlin, 1841-1842 (vol.2)

LO/N-1

Criminologica <u>see</u> Criminology

Criminologie. -- Montreal, 1975 (vol.8)-
Continues: Acta criminologica, 1968-1974 (vol.7), (ISSN 0065-1168)
ISSN 0316-0041

AD/U-6 1968-74 (v.6)
CA/U37
ED/U-1
KL/U-1 1974 (v.7)-
LO/C-3 1970-
LO/N-1
OX/U15
XY/N-1

Criminologist. -- London, 1967 (no.5, August)-
Continues: Crime and detection, 1966-1967 (nos.1-4)
ISSN 0011-1376

AD/U-6 1966-67 (nos.1-4)
BT/U-1
CA/U-1
CA/U37
CB/U-1 1971 (v.6)-
ED/U-1 1971 (v.6 no.19)-
LO/C15 1973 (v.8 no.27)-
LO/N-1
OX/U15 1966-74 (no.34)
QL/D15 1966 (no.2)-
QW/C73

Criminology. -- Beverly Hills, Cal., 1971 (vol.8)-
Continues: Criminologica, 1963-1970
ISSN 0011-1384

AD/U-6 1972/73 (v.10)-
BH/U-1
BL/U-1 1975-
CA/U37
CB/U-1
DR/U-1 1972 (v.9)-
GL/U-2 1971/72 (v.9)-
KL/U-1 1974 (v.12)-
LA/U-1 1975-
LO/C10 1974-
LO/N27 1973-

(cont'd)

Criminology (cont'd)

LO/U28 1972 (v.9)-   QW/C73   XY/N-1 1967 (v.5)-
LV-LP 1973 (v.11)-   SH/U-1

Criminology. -- Longfield, 1963-1964
ISSN 0590-093X

AB/N-1   OX/U15   XY/N-1 1963 (v.1 no.1).
ED/S11

Critisches Archiv der neuesten juridischen Litteratur und Rechtspflege in Teutschland [sic]. --Tübingen, 1801-1807 (vol.6)

LO/N-1

Cuaderno de la Facultad de Derecho y Ciencias Políticas/ Universidad de Panamá. -- Panama, [ca 1960]-

LO/N-1   LO/U24 1966-68 (nos.4-5)   MA/U-1

Cuadernos de derecho angloamericano. -- Barcelona, 1953-1961 (no.17)
ISSN 0590-1790

LA/U-1 1953-60   LO/U24   OX/U15
LO/U-3

Cuadernos de derecho francés. -- Barcelona, 1953-1961 (no.17)
ISSN 0590-1804

LO/U24   OX/U15 1953-60   XY/N-1 1960 (nos.14-15).

Cuadernos de los institutos/ Instituto de Derecho Civil, Universidad Nacional de Córdoba. -- Córdoba, 1957-
Continues: Boletín - Instituto de Derecho Civil, Universidad Nacional de Córdoba, 1934-[1949]

OX/U15 1938-40 (año 4-5 no.1);
1949 (año 14 no.3/4);
1957- imp.

Cuadernos del Instituto Juridico Español. -- Rome, 1952-
ISSN 0538-1320

LO/N-1   XY/N-1 1956 (nos.5-6).

Cultura jurídica. -- Caracas, 1941-

No holdings notified

Cumberland law review. -- Birmingham, Ala., 1975 (vol.6)-
Continues: Cumberland-Samford law review, 1970-1974 (ISSN 0045-9275)

No holdings notified

Cumberland-Samford law review <u>see</u> previous entry

Current Australian and New Zealand legal literature index. -- Sydney, 1973-

LO/U24 OX/U15 RE/U-1

Current bibliography of Hebrew law and allied subjects <u>see</u> Dine Israel: an annual of Jewish law and Israeli family law

Current law and social problems. -- Toronto, 1960-1963 (vol.3)
ISSN 0590-3971

BH/U-1
BL/U-1 1963.
LO/U24
LV/P-1
LV/U-1 1960.
OX/U15

Current legal bibliography <u>see</u> Annual legal bibliography/ Harvard Law School Library

Current legal problems. -- London, 1948-

AB/N-1
AB/U-1
AD/U-6
BC-UC 1948;1965; 1970-75
BH-LS 1952-63
BH/P-1 1961- (w.1964, 1966)
BH/U-1
BL/U-1
BR/U-1
BT/U-1 1955;1957; 1960;1963-
CA/U-1
CA/U13
CB/U-1 1949 (v.2)-
CC/U-1 1948-59
CH-CI 1951-
CR/U-1
CV/C-1 1961 (v.14)-
CV/U-1 imp.
DN/U-1
DR/U-1
ED/S11
ED-SLC 1951-
ED/U-1
EX/U-1
GL/U-1
GL/U-2
HL/U-1
KL/U-1
LC/C-1 1966-
LC/U-1
LD/P-1 1962;1964; 1966;1971.
LD/U-1
LO/C10 1948;1951 (v.4)-
LO/C15 1951-
LO/C25 1962-74 imp.
LO/C47 1951-62 imp., 1965-
LO-MT
LO/N-1
LO/N-5 1969-
LO/N17
LO/N26 1951-
LO/N27 1968-
LO/N46
LO/R74
LO-SC 1975-
LO-TS
LO/U-1
LO/U-2
LO/U-3
LO/U11
LO/U12 1951-
LO/U14 1948.
LO/U24
LO/U28 imp.
LV-LP 1958 (v.11)- (w. 1964 (v.17))
LV/P-1 1951-74
LV/U-1
MA/P-1
MA/U-1
NO/U-1
NW/U-1
OX/U15
OX/U25
QE/C76
QG/C25
QM/C68 1970-
QN/C70 imp.
QS/Q12
QS/S-4
QS/S-6
QS/S-7 1953;1955;1963-
QS/S-8 1963-
QW/D12 1957 (v.10)-
RE/U-1
SH/U-1
SO/U-1
SW/U-1 1961; 1966-68
XM/C10
XY/N-1 1967 (v.20)-

Current legal thought. -- New York, 1935-1948 (vol.14)

LO/U24

Current property law. -- London, 1952-1953
Absorbed by: Journal of planning and property law, afterwards: Journal of planning and environment law, q.v.
ISSN 0526-4529

AB/N-1	LO-MT	QS/Q12
BL/U-1	LO/N-1	QS/S-4
CA/U13	LO/U24	QS/S-6
ED/S11	OX/U15	RE/U-1
EX/U-1		

Current publications in legal and related fields. -- Chicago, 1953-

OX/U15 1965-

Current research in law. -- Baltimore, 1929-1930

CA/U-1

Cuttack law times. -- Cuttack, 1935-

LO/N-1	LO/U14 (w.1952-54,1961-62)

Czasopismo prawno-historyczne. -- Warsaw, 1948-

CA/U-1	LO/U-1 1948-55;1964.	XY/N-1 1955;1959;1965; 1969 (t.21)-
CA/U13	LO/U24	
LO/N-1	OX/U15	

Czechoslovak journal of international law see Casopis pro mezinárodní právo

Czechoslovak yearbook of international law: hlídka mezinárodního práva. -- London, 1942.

CA/U-1	LO/U-2	NW/U-1
CA/U13	LO/U-3	OX/U15
LO/N-1	LO/U24	QS/S-7
LO/S14	LV/U-1	

D.C. Bar journal see Journal - Bar Association of the District of Columbia

Dakota law review. -- Grand Forks, N.D., 1927-1932

OX/U15

Dalhousie law journal. -- Halifax, Nova Scotia, 1973-

BL/U-1 1975 (v.2)-	LO/U-2	OX/U15
BR/U-1 1976 (v.3)-	LO/U24	XY/N-1

Dar es Salaam law journal see next entry

Dar es Salaam University law journal. -- Dar es Salaam, 1971 (vol.3)-
Continues: Dar es Salaam law journal, 1963 (vol.1 no.1) (ISSN 0418-3770) and: Journal of the Denning Law Society, 1963/66-1969
Vol.4 (1972) not published

LO/N17 1963/66-71; 1973 (v.5).
LO/U14 1963-69;1973-
LO/U24 1963/66-1969; 1973 (v.5)- (v.2 imp.)
OX/U15 imp.

Datenverarbeitung im Recht. -- Berlin; New York, 1972-
ISSN 0301-2980

LO/U24

De jure/ Fakulteit regsgeleerdheid, Universiteit van Pretoria. -- Pretoria, S.A., 1966-

LO/U24 1975 (Jg.8)-

De jure/ University of Cape Town publication, Law Faculty Society. -- Cape Town, 1960-1963
ISSN 0416-8135

LO/U24
OX/U15

De Paul law review. -- Chicago, 1951-
ISSN 0011-7188

BL/U-1 1963-
LO/U24
OX/U15
XY/N-1 1971 (v.21)-

Defense law journal. -- Indianapolis, 1957-
ISSN 0011-7587

XY/N-1 1967 (v.16)-

Defensor legis. -- Helsinki, 1920-

LO/U24 1960 (v.41)-
QS/S-6 1967-
XY/N-1 1966 (v.47)-

Delhi law review. -- Delhi, 1972-

No holdings notified

Delikt en delinkwent. -- Leyden, 1970/71-
Continues: Tijdschrift voor strafrecht, 1886/87-1943; 1946-1970 (vol.79)
ISSN 0045-9879

CA/U37 1960-
LO/N-1 1970/71-
LO/U-3 1886-1929 (w.1923,1925)
LO/U24 1960 (v.69)-
OX/U15
XY/N-1 1968-

Demokratie und Recht. -- Cologne, 1973-

No holdings notified

Demokratyczny przegląd prawniczy <u>see</u> Nowe pravo

Den'gi i kredit. -- Moscow, 1938-1952; 1954-
Continues: Kredit i khozraschet. Suspended July 1941-Dec.1945. Merged with Sovetskie finansy July 1952-June 1954 to form Finansy i kredit SSSR. Continued as Den'gi i kredit July 1954
ISSN 0011-8362

LO/N-1 1954- XY/N-1 1951-54 imp.,1955-

Denver Bar Association record see Denver law journal

Denver journal of international law and policy. -- Denver, Col., 1971-

LO/S14 OX/U15 XY/N-1 1975 (v.5)-
LO/U24

Denver Law Center journal incorporating Dicta see next entry

Denver law journal. -- Denver, Col., 1966 (vol.43)-
Continues: Denver Bar Association record, 1923-1928 (vol.5); Dicta/Denver Bar Association... 1928 (vol.6)-1962 (vol.39); and: Denver Law Center journal incorporating Dicta, 1963 (vol.40)-1965 (vol.42)
ISSN 0011-8834

LO/U24 OX/U15 XY/N-1 1969 (v.46)-

Derecho/Pontificia Universidad Catolica del Peru. -- Lima, 1944-

LO/N-1 1944-64 LO/U24 1971-73 (nos.29-31)

Derecho: revista del Colegio de Abogados. -- Medellín, Colombia, 1927-1956?
ISSN 0301-9063

No holdings notified

Derecho de la integración. -- Buenos Aires, 1967-
ISSN 0420-0039

LO/S14 LO/U24 XY/N-1 1971 (no.8)-
LO/U-3

Derecho y reforma agraria/ Universidad de los Andes. -- Merida, Venezuela, 1969?-

LO/U24 1971 (no.3)- XY/N-1 1971 (no.3)-

Detroit Bar journal see Detroit lawyer

Detroit College of Law review. -- Detroit, Mich., 1975-
Continues: Detroit law review, 1931-1948 (vol.9)
Publication suspended June 1938-Dec. 1947

AB/U-1 1975- LO/U24 1931-48 (w.v.4,6; v.5 imp.) OX/U15 1931-48

Detroit law journal. -- Detroit, 1898-1917

No holdings notified

Detroit law review <u>see</u> Detroit College of Law review

Detroit lawyer. -- Detroit, 1931-
Continues: Detroit Bar journal
ISSN 0011-9652

No holdings notified

Deutsche Aussenwirtschafts-Rundschau. -- Munich; Bonn, 1959-1969 (vol.19)
Ceased publication?
Continues: Deutsche Devisen-Rundschau, 1951-1959
ISSN 0415-5483

OX/U15

Deutsche Devisen-Rundschau <u>see</u> previous entry

Deutsche Erfinder-Post: internationales Fachblatt für Erfindungen, Fortschritte und Neuerungen. -- Berlin, 1950-1963

LO/N14 XY/N-1 1961-63 imp.

Deutsche Gerichts-Zeitung. -- Berlin, 1861 (vol.3 no.44)- 1867
Continues: Preussische Gerichts-Zeitung, 1859-1861 (vol.3 no.43)

LO/N-1 1859-66

Deutsche Juristen-Zeitung. -- Berlin, 1896-1936 (Bd.41)
Absorbed by: Zeitschrift der Akademie für Deutsches Recht, q.v.

CA/U13 1907-13; 1930-36 LO/N-1 1917-21 imp. LO/U24

Deutsche Justiz: Rechtspflege und Rechtspolitik. -- Berlin, 1933 (vol.95 no.47)-1945?
Continues: Justizministerial-Blatt für die preussische Gesetzgebung und Rechtspolitik, 1839-1933 (vol.95 no.39) and: Preussische Justiz; Rechtspflege und Rechtspolitik, 1933 (vol.95 no.40-46)

LO/U24 1934;1936-45 imp. RE/U-1 1934-41 (v.96-103) imp.

Deutsche Notariats-Zeitung. -- Nördlingen; Munich, 1872-1899

LO/N-1

Deutsche Rechtspflege <u>see</u> Deutsche Richterzeitung

Der Deutsche Rechtspfleger. -- Bielefeld, 1893?-

XY/N-1 1972 (Bd.80 Hft.5)-

Deutsche Rechtswissenschaft. -- Hamburg, 1936-1943?

OX/U15 1936-43

Deutsche Rechtszeitschrift. -- Tübingen, 1946-1950 (vol.5)
Merged with: Süddeutsche Juristenzeitung, q.v., to become: Juristenzeitung, q.v.

CA/U13 1949-50 LO/U12 1950. LO/U24
ED/U-1

Deutsche Richterzeitung. -- Berlin, 1909-1935; 1950-
1936-1939 as Deutsche Rechtspflege which was absorbed by Deutsches Recht, Ausgabe B, q.v., 1939-1945

No holdings notified

Deutsche Steuer-Zeitung. -- Berlin, 1912-1945; 1947-
ISSN 0012-0774 (Ausgabe A)
0012-0782 (Ausgabe B)

LO/U-3 1919/20-45 LO/U24 1920-26 (Bd.9-15) OX/U15 Ausg.A, 1950 (Bd.38)-

Deutsche Verkehrssteuer-Rundschau. -- Konstanz; Bonn,

OX/U15 1958 (v.44)-

Deutsche Versicherungszeitschrift für Sozialversicherung und Privatversicherung. -- Munich; Berlin, 1951 (vol.6)-1971 (vol.25)
Ceased publication?
Continues: Versicherungswissenschaft, Versicherungspraxis, Versicherungs-Medizin, 1947-1951 (vol.5)

OX/U15 1947-71 (v.25) XY/N-1 1967 (June.)-1971 (Dec.)

Deutsche Verwaltung. -- Berlin, 1924-1945 (vol.22 no.2)
Merger of: Reich und Länder and: Deutsche Verwaltungsblätter, q.v., in 1938

No holdings notified

Deutsche Verwaltung. -- Hamburg, 1948-1950
Absorbed by: Deutsches Verwaltungsblatt q.v.

ED/U-1 LO/U-3 OX/U15

Deutsche Verwaltungsblätter. -- Munich; Nördlingen, 1923-1937
Continues: Blätter für administrative Praxis, 1851-1922 and: Bayerische Verwaltungsblätter, 1925-1933
United with: Reich und Länder to form: Deutsche Verwaltung, q.v., in 1938

LO/N-1 1851-1922

Deutsche Zeitschrift für die gesamte gerichtliche Medizin <u>see</u> Zeitschrift für Rechtsmedizin

Deutsche Zeitschrift für Kirchenrecht. -- Berlin, 1891-1917
Continues: Zeitschrift für Kirchenrecht, 1861-1889

CA/U-1 1861-76 LO/N-1 OX/U-1

Deutsches Arbeitsrecht. -- Berlin, Aug.1933-Apr.1944?
Continues: Arbeitsrecht, 1914-1933

No holdings notified

Deutsches Recht, Ausgabe A. -- Berlin, 1939 (Jg.9)-1945 (Jg.15 Hft.13)
Continues: Deutsches Recht, 1931-1939 (Jg.9), which absorbed Juristische Wochenschrift, q.v. to form Ausgabe A (weekly)

LO/U24 1934-45 (Jg.4-15 Hft.4)
OX/U15 1934-42 (Jg.4-12)
RE/U-1 1934-42 imp.

Deutsches Recht, Ausgabe B. -- Berlin, 1939 (Jg.9)-1945 (Jg.15)
Continues: Deutsches Recht, 1931-1939 (Jg.9), which absorbed Deutsche Rechtspflege, q.v., to form Ausgabe B (monthly)

LO/U24 1940 (Jg.10 Hft.17-24).
OX/U15 1939-42

Deutsches Recht, Ausgabe B (Wiener Ausgabe). -- Vienna, 1938-1945 (Jg.8 Hft.2)
First issue entitled: Deutsches Recht in Österreich

LO/U24 1938-39 (Jg.2)

Deutsches Recht in Österreich <u>see</u> previous entry

Deutsches Steuerrecht. -- Munich, Oct. 1962-
ISSN 0012-1347

OX/U15
XY/N-1

Deutsches Strafrecht; Strafrecht, Strafrechtspolitik, Strafprozess... <u>see</u> Goltdammer's Archiv für Strafrecht

Deutsches Verwaltungsblatt. -- Cologne, 1950-
Continues: Preussisches Verwaltungsblatt, 1880-1929 (vol.49 no.14); Reichsverwaltungsblatt und preussisches Verwaltungsblatt, 1929-1934 (vol.55 no.39); and: Reichsverwaltungsblatt, 1934-1941 (vol.62)
Publication suspended 1944-1950
Absorbed: Deutsche Verwaltung, q.v., in Apr. 1950.
Has Verwaltungsarchiv appended as a quarterly supplement, 1957-1964
ISSN 0012-1363

ED/U-1 1950-
LO/U-3 1950-
LO/U24 1960 (Bd.75)-
OX/U15 1950-
XY/N-1 1969 (Bd.84)-

Devisenarchiv. -- Berlin, 1936-1945

LO/U-3 1936; 1939-43 (Oct.)

Dickinson law review. -- Carlisle, Pa., 1908 (vol.13)-
Continues: Forum of the Dickinson School of Law, 1897-1908 (vol.12)
ISSN 0012-2459

CA/U13 1967-71 (v.72-75);1972 (v.77)-
LO-MT 1966-
LO/U24
OX/U15
XY/N-1 1969 (v.74)-

Dicta/Denver Bar Association see Denver law journal

Dine Israel: an annual of Jewish law and Israeli family law. -- Tel Aviv, 1969-
Continues: Current bibliography of Hebrew law and allied subjects, 1966-1969
ISSN 0070-4903

LO/U14

O Direito. -- Lisbon, 1868-

LO/U24 1961 (año 93)- XY/N-1 1971 (año 103, Julho)-

Diritto aereo. -- Rome, 1962-
ISSN 0012-3390

CA/U13 OX/U15 XY/N-1 1963 (v.2)-
LO/U24

Diritto comunitario e degli scambi internazionali. -- Milan, 1975 (vol.14)-
Continues: Diritto negli scambi internazionali, 1962-1974 (vol.13) (ISSN 0419-3938)

GL/U-1 1973- LO-MT 1968-74 (v.7-13) LO/U24
LO/C47 1963-70 XY/N-1 1970 (v.9)-

Diritto del lavoro. -- Rome, 1927-
ISSN 0012-3404

LO/U-2 1927-28 imp. LO/U-3 XY/N-1 1974 (v.48)-

Diritto dell'economia. -- Milan; Turin, 1955-
ISSN 0417-6758

LO/N-1 1967 (v.13)- 1971 XY/N-1 1966 (v.12)-

Diritto delle radiodiffusioni e delle telecomunicazioni. -- Rome, 1969-
ISSN 0012-3412

No holdings notified

Il Diritto di autore. -- Rome, 1930-
ISSN 0012-3420

LO/N-1 1930-43,1962- LO/U-3 1930-38 RE/U-1 1930-42
LO/N14 1953- LO/U24 1959 (v.30)-

Diritto di famiglia e delle persone. -- Milan, 1972-

OX/U15

Diritto e giurisprudenza: rassegna di dottrina e di giurisprudenza civile della Corte di Napoli e delle Corti meridionali. -- Naples, 1886-
Sub-title varies
ISSN 0012-3439

LO/U24 1960 (v.75=ser.III v.16)- XY/N-1 1969 (v.84=ser.III v.25)-

Diritto e società. -- Florence, 1973-

OX/U15 XY/N-1 1975-

Diritto ecclesiastico (e rassegna di diritto matrimoniale). -- Milan, 1926 (vol.37)-
Continues: Rivista di diritto ecclesiastico, 1890-1907 (vol.17) and 1922-1926 (vol.36); and: Diritto ecclesiastico italiano, 1908-1921 (vol.31)
ISSN 0012-3455

LO/N-1 1955- XY/N-1 1972-

Diritto ecclesiastico italiano see previous entry

Diritto europeo dei trasporti see European transport law

Diritto internazionale: rivista trimestrale di dottrina e documentazione. -- Milan, 1959 (vol.13)-1971 (vol.25)
Continues: Diritto internazionale, 1937-1941; and: Annali di diritto internazionale, 1949-1953 (vol.11)
Not published 1942-1948, 1954-1958
ISSN 0012-3471

CA/U13 1959-71
LO/N-1 1959-71
LO/U24 1937-41;1950-71 (v.8-25) (w.v.12)
OX/U15
XY/N-1 1966-71 (v.20-25)

Diritto marittimo. -- Genoa, 1899-
ISSN 0012-348X

LO/N-1 1959- LO/U24 1959 (v.61)- XY/N-1 1969 (v.71)-

Diritto negli scambi internazionali see Diritto comunitario e degli scambi internazionali

Il Diritto tributario del Mercato Comune see Intertax: European tax review

The Docket. -- St. Paul, Minn., 1942/44 (vol.6).
Continues: West Publishing Co.'s Docket, 1909-1941 (vol.5)

LO/N-1 1919-44 LO/U24 1913-44 imp.

Docket (and the barrister). -- Toronto, 1889-1898?

LO/N-1 Dec.1895 (7(i)).

Documentación jurídica. -- Madrid, 1974-
Continues: Información jurídica, 1941-1973 (no.319)

LO/N-1 1951-73
LO/U-3 1953-73 (no.316)
LO/U24 1948-54 imp., 1956-
XY/N-1 1968-

Documents and decisions - European Commission of Human Rights see Yearbook of the European Convention on Human Rights

Dr. Siebenhaar's Archiv für deutsches Wechselrecht und Handelsrech
-- Leipzig, 1870-1874
Continues: Archiv für deutsches Wechselrecht, 1850-1854 and: Archi
für deutsches Wechselrecht und Handelsrecht, 1855-1869

LO/N-1

Doshisha hogaku. -- Kyoto,
In Japanese

BL/U-1 1970 (no.117)- LO/U14 1969 (no.114)- XY/N-1 1966 (no.96)- imp.

Doshisha law review, international edition. -- Kyoto, 1956-
ISSN 0418-0046

BH/U-1 | CR/U-1 1971- | LO/U24 1958-69 (nos.3-6)

Drake law review. -- Des Moines, Iowa, 1951-
ISSN 0012-5938

BL/U-1 1963- | LO/U24 | XY/N-1 1967 (v.17)-

Droit aérien <u>see</u> Revue générale de l'air et de l'espace

Droit bulgare: doctrine, jurisprudence, legislation. -- Sofia, 1968-
ISSN 0085-0098

LO/N-1 | OX/U15 | XY/N-1
LO/U24

Droit d'auteur. -- Berne, 1888-
For ed. in English, 1965-, <u>see</u> Copyright: monthly review of the United International Bureaux for the Protection of Intellectual Property
ISSN 0012-6365

LO/N14 1901-64 | LO/U-3 1955-77 | OX/U15
LO/N17 1888-1953 | LO/U24 1960-64 (v.73-77)

Droit de l'espace. -- Paris, 1967-
ISSN 0419-747X

CA/U13 | LO/U24 1968-71 imp. | XY/N-1 nos. 3 and 4 (n.d.)
LO/S14 1971-72/73 | OX/U15

Droit du travail: revue mensuelle. -- Paris, 1950-
ISSN 0416-3575

OX/U15 1966 (v.17)-

Droit du travail et assurance chômage <u>see</u> Arbeitsrecht und Arbeitslosenversicherung

Droit du travail et sécurité sociale. -- Paris, 1954-
Title varies: Revue de droit industriel et de sécurité sociale
ISSN 0416-3583

No holdings notified

Droit et C.E.E. affaires see next entry

Droit et C.E.E. affaires international. -- Paris, 1975 (no.300)-
Continues: Chronique européenne du droit des affaires: Le droit et les affaires, bi-mensuel du Marché Commun, 1962-1969 and: Droit et C.E.E. affaires, 1970 (no.167)-1975 (no.299)

XY/N-1 1968-

Droit et économie. -- Paris, 1969-
Continues: Cahiers - Association Nationale des Docteurs en Droit, 1958-1968
ISSN 0012-639X

XY/N-1 1966 (v.8)-

Droit et économie politique see Revue "al qanoun wal iqtised"

Le Droit et les affaires: le bi-mensuel du Marché Commun see Droit et C.E.E. affaires international

Droit et pratique du commerce international = International trade law and practice. -- Paris, 1975-
English or French with summaries in the other language

BH/U-1	LO/U24	XY/N-1
LO/N26 last 5 years		

Droit européen. -- Paris, 1958-1963 (vol.6)
ISSN 0418-078X

LO/U24

Droit européen des transports see European transport law

Droit maritime. -- Brussels, 1910-1918

LO/N-1

Droit maritime français. -- Paris, 1923-1939; 1949-
1923-1939 issued as supplement to: Revue de droit maritime comparé, q.v. and: Journal de la Marine Marchand
ISSN 0012-642X

CA/U13	LO/N-1	OX/U15 1923-39;1953-
ED/U-1 1928-33 imp.	LO/U-3 imp.	XY/N-1 1968 (v.20)-
HL/U-1 1923-35 imp.	LO/U24 1927-32 (v.11 no.1);1961 (v.13)-	

Droit polonais contemporain. -- Warsaw, 1963-
ISSN 0070-7325

CA/U-1	LO/U-2	OX/U15
LD/U-1 1966-	LO/U-3	XY/N-1 1968 (no.9)-
LO/N-1	LO/U24	

Droit social. -- Paris, 1938-
ISSN 0012-6438

CA/U13 1977-	LO/U-3	OX/U15 (1938,1940 imp.)
ED/U-1 1966- (1967 imp.)	LO/U24 1938; 1960 (v.23)-	XY/N-1 1966-
LO-MT 1968-		

Droits de l'homme <u>see</u> Revue des droits de l'homme

Drug abuse law review. -- Buffalo, New York, 1971-
ISSN 0070-7341

XY/N-1 1973 (v.2)-

Dublin University law journal. -- Dublin, 1976-
Continues: Dublin University law review, 1969-1970, (ISSN 0012-6896)

AB/N-1 1969.	LO/N-1 1969-70	LV/U-1 1969-70
BL/U-1 1969-70 imp.	LO/U-3	OX/U15 1969-70
CA/U-1 1969-70	LO/U24 1969-70	SH/U-1 1969.

Dublin University law review <u>see</u> previous entry

Duke Bar Association journal. -- Durham, N.C., Mar. 1933-1941/42 (vol.10)

No holdings notified

Duke Bar journal <u>see</u> next entry

Duke law journal/ Duke University. -- Durham, N.C., 1959-
Continues: Duke Bar journal, 1951-1958 (vol.7)
ISSN 0012-7086

CA/U13 1964-	NO/U-1 1961-72	XY/N-1 1968-
LO/U24	OX/U15	

Duquesne law review. -- Pittsburgh, Pa., 1968/69 (vol.7)-
Continues: Duquesne University law review, 1963/64-1967/68 (vol.6) (ISSN 0012-7213)

BL/U-1 1965-	OX/U15	XY/N-1 1969 (v.8)-
LO/U24		

Duquesne University law review <u>see</u> previous entry

Earth law journal. -- Leiden, 1975-

EX/U-1	QE/C76	SO/U-1
LO/U24	QW/D12	XY/N-1 1976 (v.2)-

East African journal of criminology. -- Nairobi, 1977-

CA/U37

East African law journal.-- Nairobi, 1965-
ISSN 0070-797X

BH/U-1	LO/N-1	LO/U24
BL/U-1 1965.	LO/N17 1965-68	OX/U15
CA/U13 imp.	LO/U-3	XY/N-1
CR/U-1	LO/U14	

East Anglian law clerks' and students' journal. -- Ipswich, 1909.

LO/N-1	OX/U15 1909 (June).

Eastern Africa law review. -- Dar es Salaam, 1968-
ISSN 0012-8678

BL/U-1 1970-	LO/N17 1968-74 (v.7)	OX/U15
CA/U13 imp.	LO/U14	XY/N-1
CR/U-1	LO/U24	

Eastern journal of international law. -- Madras, 1969-
ISSN 0012-8821

XY/N-1

Ecology law quarterly. -- Berkeley, Cal., 1971-
ISSN 0046-1121

CA/U13	LO/U24	XY/N-1 1972 (v.2)-

Economic legislation review <u>see</u> Przegląd ustawodawstwa gospodarczego

Ediin zasag, erkhiin asuudal (Questions of economics and public law). -- Ulan-Bator, 1965?-
In Mongolian; Russian title: Ekonomika i pravo
ISSN 0422-5600

LO/N-1 1961 (11)-

Edinburgh law journal. -- Edinburgh, 1831-1837

ED/S10	ED/U-1 1831-32	LO/N-1 1831 (1-4)
ED/S11		

Ehe und Familie im privaten und öffentlichen Recht <u>see</u> Zeitschrift für das gesamte Familienrecht

Ekonomika i pravo <u>see</u> Ediin zasag, erkhiin asuudal

Emory law journal. -- Atlanta, Ga., 1974 (vol.23)-
Continues: Journal of public law, 1952-1973
ISSN 0094-4076

BL/U-1 1954-	CR/U-1	OX/U15
BT/U-1 1975-76	LO/C15 1972-	QN/C70 1972 (v.21)-
CA/U13	LO/U24	XY/N-1 1963 (v.12)-

Employee relations law journal. -- New York, 1975-
ISSN 0098-8898

No holdings notified

Environment law review. -- Albany, 1970-
ISSN 0071-0830

CV/U-1	XY/N-1 1971 (v.2)-

Environmental affairs. -- Boston, 1971-
ISSN 0046-2225

XY/N-1 1972 (v.2)-

Environmental law. -- Portland, Ore., 1970-
ISSN 0046-2276

LO/C10 1970-73	XY/N-1 1971 (v.1 no.2)-

Environmental policy and law/ International Council of Environmental Law. -- Lausanne, 1975-

BH/U-1	LO/N26	SO/U-1
HL/U-1	QE/C76 1976 (v.2)-	XY/N-1

Epeteris tou archeiou tes historias tou dikaiou <u>see</u> next entry

Epeteris tou kentrou ereunes tes historias tou dikaiou. -- Athens, 1963?-
Continues: Epeteris tou archeiou tes historias tou dikaiou, 1948-1962, of which title varies

OX/U15 1948-1969 (v.13 1966)

Ephemerides juris canonici. -- Rome, 1945-
ISSN 0013-9491

CA/U-1	OX/U-1	XY/N-1 1972 (v.28)-

Ephemeris hellenikes kai allodapes nomologias = Journal de jurisprudence hellénique et étrangère. -- Athens, 1942-1960
Continues: Ephemeris hellenikes kai gallikes nomologias, 1881-1941

LO/U24 1942-43; 1944-45 imp., 1953-60	OX/U15 1953-60	OX/U25 1953-58

Ephemeris hellenikes kai gallikes nomologias <u>see</u> previous entry

Ephemeris ton hellenon nomikon. -- Athens, 1934-

LO/N-1

Epitheoresis demosiou dikaiou kai dioiketikou dikaiou = Revue du droit public et de la science administrative. -- Athens, 1957-
Summary in French
ISSN 0423-281X

LO/N-1

Epitheoresis nautiliakou dikaiou. -- Athens, 1973-

No holdings notified

Epitheoresis tou emporikou dikaiou. -- Athens, 1950-
ISSN 0425-1563

LO/U24 1960 (v.11)-
XY/N-1 1971 (v.22)-

Esprit international = The international mind. -- Paris, 1927-1940

AB/U-1 1927-39
BH/U-1
BL/U-1 (w.1939(v.13), 1940 (v.15))
CA/U-1
CA/U13 1927-39
ED/N-1 1928-40
GL/U-1 1927-39
HL/U-1 1934-40
LO-MT
LO/N-1
LO/U-1
LO/U-3
LV/U-1
NW/U-1 1927-39
OX/U-1
OX/U25
SW/U-1 1930 (July)-1940
XY/N-1 1927 imp., 1928-40

Estates gazette. -- London, 1858-
ISSN 0014-1240

AB/N-1 1912-
AB/U-1 1967-
AD/U-6 1971 (v.217)-
BH-LS 1943-
BH/P-1 current year only
BH/U-1 1965-
BL/U-1 1970-
BR/U-1 1966-
CA/U-1 1971-
CA/U13 1949-
CB/U-1 1970 (v.214)-
CH-CI 1972 (v.222)-
CR/U-1 1973-
CV/U-1 1972 (Sep.)-
DR/U-3 1968-73
ED/S11 1948-
ED/U-1 1966-
GL/U-1 1964-
LC/C-1 1962-
LC/U-1 1957- imp.
LD/P-1 1959-63 imp., 1964-
LD/U-1 1952-69 imp., 1974-
LO/C47 current year
LO-CBL 1957-*
LO-MT 1948-
LO/N-1
LO/N26 last 2 years
LO/P-6 1957 (July)-
LO/R74 1967 (May)-
LO-SC 1969-71;1974-
LO-TS 1957-
LO/U-2 1963;1969- imp.
LO/U12 July 1973-
LO/U24 1952 (v.159)-
LO/U28 1975-
LV/P-1 1900-June 1903;1904-
LV/U-1 1965-
MA/P-1 Oct. 1960-
MA/U-1 1966 (v.197)-
NO/U-1 1959-64, imp., 1966-
NW/U-1 1971-75
OX/U-1 1949-
OX/U15 1964-
QE/C76 last 5 years
QG/C25 1968-
QL/D15 1973- (v.227 imp.)
QM/C68 1976-
QN/C70 1968-
QS/Q12 1952-
QS/Q29 1930-48 imp., 1949-72;1973 imp., 1974-
QS/S-4 1969-
QS/S-6 1943 (March)-
QS/S-7 1940-
QS/S-8 1943-
QW/D12 1972.
RE/U-1 1950-
SH/U-1 1957-
SO/U-1 1967-
XM/C10 1975-
XY/N-1 1965 (v.195)-

Estudios de derecho/ Universidad de Antioquia. -- Medellín, Colombia, 1939-
ISSN 0014-1461

LO/U24 1953-55 imp., 1957 (v.17)-
XY/N-1 1969 (v.28)-

Estudios de derecho penal y criminología/ Universidad de Buenos Aires. -- Buenos Aires, 1961-
ISSN 0425-3523

OX/U15

Estudios de Deusto. -- Bilbao, 1953-
ISSN 0423-4847

LO/U-3

Estudios visigóticos. -- Rome, 1956-
(Cuadernos del Instituto Juridico Español)
ISSN 0425-3868

LO/N-1
OX/U15 1956-62 (v.3)

Etudes et documents - Conseil d'Etat. -- Paris, 1947-

AD/U-6
BH/U-1
CA/U13
CV/U-1 1956-
DR/U-1 1948.
ED/U-1 1950;1955-
GL/U-1 (w.1965-70)
LC/U-1 1957 (v.11)-
LO/N-1
LO/U-3 (w.fasc.19)
LO/U24
LV/U-1 1960-61;1964-69;1971.
NO/U-1 1960 (v.14)-
OX/U15
QS/S-6
XY/N-1 1971-

Europäische Steuer-Zeitung <u>see</u> Intertax: European tax review

Europäisches Transportrecht <u>see</u> European transport law

Europarecht. -- Munich, 1966-
ISSN 0531-2485

BH/U-1
BT/U-1 1975-
CA/U13
CB/U-1 1970-
CR/U-1 1966-
ED-SLC
ED/U-1
EX/U-1
GL/U-1
LC/U-1
LD/U-1
LO-MT
LO/N-1
LO/N-5
LO/U-2
LO/U-11 1976-
LO/U12
LO/U24
OX/U15
QW/D12 1973-76
SH/U-1 1966-74 (v.9)
SO/U-1
XY/N-1

European industrial relations review. -- London, 1974-

OX/U15

European law review. -- London, 1975/76-

AB/N-1
AB/U-1
AD/U-6
BC-UC
BH/U-1
BR/U-1
BT/U-1
CA/U-1
CA/U13
CR/U-1
DR/U-1
ED/U-1 (cont'd)

European law review (cont'd).

GL/U-1	LO/N17	QM/C48
GL/U-2	LO/N26	QM/C68
HL/U-1	LO-SC	QN/C70
LD/C-1	LO-TS	QS/S-8
LO/C-3	LO/U-3	QW/C73
LO/C15	LO/U11	QW/D12
LO/C25	LO/U24	RE/U-1
LO/C27	LV/U-1	SH/U-1
LO/C47	NO/U-1	SO/U-1
LO-MT	OX/U15	XM/C10
LO/N-1	QE/C76	XY/N-1
LO/N-5	QG/C25	

European taxation. -- Amsterdam, 1961-
ISSN 0014-3138

CA/U13	LO-CBL last 5 years	QL/D15 1973 imp., 1974-
CB/U-1 1972 (v.12)-	LO/C25 1968-	
DN/U-1 1971-	LO-MT	QM/C68 1973 (v.13)-
ED/U-1	LO/N26 1965-	QS/S-6
EX/U-1 1969-	LO/U-2 1974-76	SO/U-1
GL/U-1 1963-	LO/U24	XM/C10 1971-
HL/U-1 1973 (v.13)-	LV/P-1 1961-75	XY/N-1
LD/U-1 1973-74	OX/U15	YK/U-1

European transport law = Droit européen des transports = Europäisches Transportrecht = Diritto europeo dei trasporti = Europees vervoerrecht. -- [Louvain], 1966-
ISSN 0014-3154

BH/U-1 1970-	LC/U-1	LO/U24
CA/U13	LO-MT	OX/U15
CB/U-1 1970 (v.5)-	LO/N-5 1976-	QN/C70
ED/U-1	LO/N26 last 5 years	SO/U-1 1970-
GL/U-1	LO/U-2	XY/N-1

European yearbook <u>see</u> Annuaire européen

Europees vervoerrecht <u>see</u> European transport law

Everybody's law magazine. -- New York, Jan.-June 1928.

LO/N-1

Examination of articled clerks <u>see</u> Leguleian, (1856-1865)

The Examiner = L'Observateur. -- Quebec, Jan.-Mar. 1861.

CA/U13	OX/U15

Excerpta criminologica <u>see</u> Abstracts on criminology and penology

Exchange of information between the member states on their legislative activity and regulations/ Council of Europe, Directorate of Legal Affairs. -- Strasbourg, 1964-1966, n.s. 1967-
1966- contains section on criminal law, previously issued separately as: International exchange of information on bills and draft regulations on penal matters, q.v.

LO/U24
Not on checklist circulated, so other holdings possible

Ezhedel'nik sovetskoi iustitsii <u>see</u> Sovetskaía iustitsiía

Fa lü p'ing-lun = Law weekly review. -- Peking, 1923-

No holdings notified

Fa-hsüeh tsa-chih/ Law Department, Soochow University <u>see</u> China law review

Faculty of Law review/ University of Toronto <u>see</u> University of Toronto Faculty of Law review

Family law. -- Chichester, 1971-
ISSN 0014-7281

AB/N-1
AB/U-1
BH/U-1
BR/U-1
BT/U-1 1975-
CA/U-1
CA/U13
CB/U-1
CH-CI
CR/U-1 1973-
CV/U-1
DN/U-1
DR/U-1 1973-
ED/S11
ED/U-1
EX/U-1
GL/U-2
LC/C-1
LC/U-1
LD/C-1
LD/P-1
LD/U-1
LO/C-3
LO/C-5 1973-
LO/C10
LO/C14
LO/C15
LO/C25
LO/C27
LO-MT
LO/N-1
LO/N27
LO/R74
LO-SC
LO/U-2 1973 (v.3)-
LO/U-3
LO/U11
LO/U12
LO/U24
LO/U28 1973 (v.3)-
LV-LP
LV/U-1
MA/P-1
MA/U-1
NO/U-1
NW/U-1 1972 (v.2)-
OX/U15
QE/C76
QG/C25 1976-
QL/D15 1972-
QM/C48 only 10 years to be kept
QM/C68
QN/C70
QS/Q13
QS/S-4
QS/S-6
QS/S-7
QS/S-8
QW/D12
RE/U-1
SH/U-1
SO/U-1
XM/C10 1975-
XY/N-1

Family law quarterly/ American Bar Association, Section of Family Law. -- Chicago, 1967-
ISSN 0014-729X

BH/U-1	LO/C10	LO/U24
CA/U13	LO/C14	OX/U15
CR/U-1	LO/C15 1972-	SH/U-1
CV/U-1 1972 (v.6)-	LO/R74	XY/N-1 1969 (v.3).
HL/U-1 1975 (v.9)-	LO/U-2 1974-	

Far Eastern law review/ Far Eastern University. -- Manila, 1953-
ISSN 0046-3272

LO/U24 1960 (v.7 no.4)- XY/N-1 1969 (v.16 no.4)-

Federal Bar Association journal <u>see</u> next entry

Federal Bar journal. -- Washington, 1944/45 (vol.6)-
Continues: Federal Bar Association journal, Sept. 1931-1943/44 (vol.5)
ISSN 0014-9039

LO/U24	OX/U15	XY/N-1 1969 (v.29)-

Federal Bar news. -- Washington D.C., 1952-
ISSN 0014-9047

No holdings notified

Federal Communications Bar journal. -- Washington D.C., 1937-

LO/U24 1972 (v.25)-

Federal law journal <u>see</u> Supreme Court journal

Federal law journal of India <u>see</u> Supreme Court journal

Federal law review. -- Canberra, 1964-
ISSN 0067-205X

AB/U-1 1970-	LO/N-1 1968-	NO/U-1 (w.v.1 no.1)
BL/U-1	LO/U12	OX/U15
CA/U13	LO/U24	XY/N-1
LC/U-1 1966 (v.2)-		

Federal probation. -- Washington D.C., 1938-
Continues: Federal probation newsletter, 1937.
ISSN 0014-9128

BT/U-1 1965 no.3-	ED/N-1 1949-	LO/U-3 1943- imp.
CA/U37	ED/U-1 1967 (v.31 no.4)-	LO/U24
CB/U-1 1975 (v.39)-		OX/U15
CR/U-1 1971-	HL/U-1 1973 (v.37)-	XY/N-1 1967 (v.31)-
DR/U-1 1955-62 imp., 1964-	KL/U-1 1970 (v.34)-	
	LO/N-1 June 1948-	

Federal probation newsletter <u>see</u> previous entry

Federal rules decisions. -- St. Paul, Minn., 1941-

CA/U13
CR/U-1 1941-72
LO-MT
LO/24
OX/U15
QS/S-4
QS/S-6

Federation of Insurance Counsel quarterly. -- Champaign, Ill., 1950-
ISSN 0430-2583

LO/U24 1971 (v.22)-

Fiat justitia/ Malaysian and Singapore Students' Law Society, U.K. -- London, 1966 (vol.1 no.1).

BL/U-1
LO-MT
LO/U24
OX/U15
QS/S-6

Fides: monthly law journal/ Seoul National University College of Law, 1954?-
ISSN 0428-3007

LO/N-1 1965 (12)-

Il Filangieri: rivista giuridica, dottrinale e pratica. -- Naples, 1876-1919
Sub-title varies

LO/N-1

Film und Recht. -- Munich, 1957-
ISSN 0015-1440

No holdings notified

The Final. -- London, 1869-1886

LO/N-1 1869-79
OX/U15 1869-79;1886 (no.1).

Finansy i kredit SSSR see Den'gi i kredit

Finsk tidskrift för vitterhet, vetenskap, konst och politik. -- Helsinki, 1876-
ISSN 0015-248X

No holdings notified

Fiscaal tijdschrift voor de Euromarkt see Intertax: European tax review

La Fiscalité du Marché Commun see Intertax: European tax review

Fischers Zeitschrift für Praxis und Gesetzgebung der Verwaltung see next entry

Fischers Zeitschrift für Verwaltungsrecht. -- Leipzig, 1924 (vol.56)-1941 (vol.79)
Continues: Zeitschrift für Rechtspflege und Verwaltung, 1838-1879; Zeitschrift für Praxis und Gesetzgebung der Verwaltung, 1880 (vol.1)-1899 (vol.20); and: Fischers Zeitschrift für Praxis und Gesetzgebung der Verwaltung, 1900-1923 (vol.55)

ED/U-1 1838-63 LO/N-1 1838-1939

Florida Bar journal. -- Tallahassee, Fla., 1953 (vol.27 no.7)-
Continues: Florida State Bar Association law journal, Aug.1927-May 1934 (vol.8 no.1) and: Florida law journal, June 1934-June 1953 (vol.27 no.6)
ISSN 0015-3915

LO/U24 1972 (v.46)-

Florida law journal see previous entry

Florida State Bar Association law journal see Florida Bar journal

Florida State University law review. -- Tallahassee, 1973-
ISSN 0096-3070

LO/U24

Focus see NCCD news

Food and agriculture: international law journal see International journal of law and legislation relating to food and agriculture

Food, drug, cosmetic law journal/ Commerce Clearing House. -- Chicago, 1950 (vol.5)-
Continues: Food, drug, cosmetic law quarterly, 1946-1949 (vol.4)
ISSN 0015-6361

LO/U24 SO/U-1 1974- XY/N-1 1956 (v.11)-

Food, drug, cosmetic law quarterly see previous entry

Fordham law review. -- New York, 1914-
Publication suspended 1918-1934
ISSN 0015-704X

BL/U-1 1963- LO/U24 XY/N-1 1971 (v.40)-
CA/U13 1958- OX/U15

Fordham urban law journal. -- New York, 1972-

XY/N-1 1975 (v.4)-

Foreign exchange bulletin see International legal education newsletter

Forensic science. -- Lausanne, 1972 (vol.1)-
Continues: Journal of forensic medicine (Johannesburg), 1953-1971 (vol.18) (ISSN 0022-1171)
ISSN 0300-9432

AD/U-6
BL/U-1
DN/U-1 1953-71 imp., 1972-
ED/U-1
LD/U-1
LO/M32
LO/U24 1971 (v.18)-
NW/U-1 1961
OX/U15 1953-75 (v.6 n.s.)
XY/N-1 1962 (v.9 no.3)-

El Foro: organo de la Barra Mexicana, Colegio de Abogados, 1918-

LO/U24 1953-58 imp., 1959 (no.26)- 1969 (no.16)

El Foro: periódico de jurisprudencia y administración. -- Barcelona, 1861-1862

LO/N-1

El Foro: revista mensual de derecho legislación y jurisprudencia, ciencias sociales y politicas. -- San José, Costa Rica, 1905/06-1921?

LO/U24 1914-18 (v.10-14) imp.

Foro internacional. -- Mexico City, 1960-
ISSN 0015-7821

LO/N-1
LO/S14
LO/U-1 1960-61 (v.1)
HL/U-1 1960-75/76 (v.16)
XY/N-1 1965 (v.6)-

Foro italiano. -- Rome, 1876-
ISSN 0015-783X

CA/U13 1931-
LO-MT 1958-
LO/U24 1932-33;1951-53 imp., 1955 (v.78)-
OX/U15
RE/U-1 1915-37 (v.40-62)
XY/N-1 1967 (v.92 no.5)-

Foro Napoletano: rivista di dottrina e di giurisprudenza. -- Rome, 1951-
ISSN 0015-7848

Not on checklist circulated, so some holdings possible

Il Foro Padano: rivista mensile di giurisprudenza Italiana e di dottrina. -- Milan, 1946-
Sub-title varies
ISSN 0015-7856

Not on checklist circulated, so some holdings possible

Foro penale: rivista critica di diritto e giurisprudenza penale. -- Rome, 1891-1901

LO/N-1 1895 imp.

Foro penale: rivista trimestrale di dottrina, giurisprudenza e legislazione. -- Naples, 1946-
ISSN 0015-7864

XY/N-1 1968-70 (v.23-25)

Forschungsstelle für Völkerrecht und ausländisches öffentliches Recht. Mitteilungen. -- Hamburg, 1959.

OX/U15 1959 (nos.1-2)

Forsete, et Tidsskrivt for Udvalg af Høiesterets-Sager og for andre retsvidenskabelige Gjenstande. -- Copenhagen, 1823-1824

LO/N-1

Fortnightly law journal. -- Toronto, June 1931-March 1948 (vol.17)

LO/N-1 | LO/U24 1931;1936-39 (v.6-8) imp., 1939-48 (v.9-17) | OX/U15

Forum. -- Baltimore; New York, 1874-Oct. 1875
Continues: Bench and Bar review; Forum review, 1874 (vol.1 no.1) and: Forum law review, 1874 (vol.1 no.2)

ED/S11 1874.

Forum/ American Bar Association, Section of Insurance, Negligence and Compensation Law. -- Chicago, 1965-
ISSN 0015-8356

HL/U-1 | LO/U24 | XY/N-1 1970 (v.5 no.2)-

Forum/ Federal Bar Association. -- Washington D.C., 1963-
ISSN 0015-8305

No holdings notified

Forum law review see Forum (Baltimore)

Forum of the Dickinson School of Law see Dickinson law review

Forum review see Forum (Baltimore)

Förvaltningsrättslig tidskrift. -- Stockholm, 1938-

LO/U24 (w.1953 v.16 no.2) | XY/N-1 1969 (v.32)-

France judiciaire. -- Paris, 1876-1910

LO/N-1

Friedensrecht. -- Vienna, June 1921-December 1930

LO/U24 1923/24 (Bd.3).

Friedensvertrag: Zeitschrift für Rechts- und Wirtschaftsfragen. -- Berlin, 1921-1923
Sub-title varies
Absorbed by: Juristische Wochenschrift, Apr. 1923, q.v.

LO/U24 1921-22 (Bd.2)

Friedenswarte. -- Berlin, 1899-1966, 1974-

CA/U-1 1908-	LO/N-1	OX/U15 1944-66,1974-
CA/U13 1926-41	LO/U-3 1899-1908; 1912-66 imp.	XY/N-1 1950-59 (Bd. 50-55)

Friedreichs Blätter für gerichtliche Medicin <u>see</u> next entry

Friedreichs Blätter für gerichtliche Medicin und Sanitätspolizei. -- Nuremberg, 1873 (vol.24)-1914
Continues: Blätter für gerichtliche Anthropologie, 1850-1862 (vol.13) and: Friedreichs Blätter für gerichtliche Medicin, 1863-1872 (vol.23)

LO/N-1

Fukuoka daigaku hōgaku ronsō = Fukuoka University review of law. -- Fukuoka, Japan, 1956-
ISSN 0429-8411

LO/N-1 1960 (v.5)-

Fukuoka University review of law <u>see</u> previous entry

GRC revue trimestrielle <u>see</u> R.C.M.P. quarterly

Gazette du Palais. -- Paris, 1881-
Sub-title varies

AD/U-6 current & pre-current years only	CA/U13 1913-	LO/U24
	GL/U-1 1925-	OX/U15 1897-
	LO/U12 1950-	

Gazette fiscale, commerciale et industrielle. -- Alexandria, 1948-

No holdings notified

Gazette of the Incorporated Law Society of Ireland. -- Dublin, 1907-

BL/U-1 1969-	LO/N-1	OX/U15 1972-
CA/U13 1971 (v.65)-	LO/U24 1967-68 imp., 1969 (v.63)-	QS/S-8 1964-
CR/U-1 1976-		

Gazette of the Incorporated Law Society of Northern Ireland. -- Belfast, 1964-
ISSN 0019-3526

BL-LS	LO/N-1	QS/S-8
BL/U-1 imp.	LO/U24	

Geistiges Eigentum <u>see</u> Copyright: geistiges Eigentum

Gema-Nachrichten. -- Berlin, 1948-
For English edition <u>see</u> next entry

LO/N14 1948-64

Gema news/ Gesellschaft für musikalische Aufführungs- und mechanische Vervielfältigungsrechte = Gema nouvelles = Gema novedades. -- Berlin, 1964-
ISSN 0433-2865

LO/N14

Gema nouvelles <u>see</u> previous entry

Gema novedades <u>see</u> Gema news

Der Gemeindetag. -- Stuttgart, 1948?-

OX/U15 1958 (Jg.11)- XY/N-1 1974 (Jg.27 Hft.6)-

George Washington law review. -- Washington D.C., Nov. 1932-
ISSN 0016-8076

CA/U13	OX/U15	XY/N-1
LO/U24		

Georgetown law journal. -- Washington D.C., Nov. 1912-1917/18; 1919/20-
Vol.7 not published
ISSN 0016-8092

CA/U13 1955-	OX/U15 1957 (v.46)-	XY/N-1 1971 (v.60)-
LO/U24		

Georgia Bar journal <u>see</u> Georgia State Bar journal

Georgia journal of international and comparative law. -- Athens, Ga., 1970-
ISSN 0046-578X

CA/U13	LO/N-1	LO/U24
CB/U-1	LO/U-2 1972 (v.2 suppl.2).	XY/N-1
CH-CI 1975-		

Georgia law review. -- Athens, Ga., 1966-
ISSN 0016-8300

LO/U24	XY/N-1 1970 (v.5)-

Georgia State Bar journal. -- Macon, Ga., Aug. 1964-
Continues: Georgia Bar journal, Apr. 1938-May 1964
ISSN 0016-8416

LO/U24 1971 (v.8)-
(1973/74 v.10 imp.)

Der Gerichtssaal. -- Erlangen; Stuttgart, 1849-1942

LO/N-1 1849-1940

German journal of air and space law see Zeitschrift für Luft- und Weltraumrecht

German yearbook of international law: Jahrbuch für internationales Recht. -- Berlin, 1976 (Bd.19)-
Continues: Jahrbuch für internationales und ausländisches öffentliches Recht, 1948-1949; and: Jahrbuch für internationales Recht, 1950 (Bd.3)-1975 (Bd.18) (ISSN 0021-3993)

CA/U13	LO/U-3 1948-71	OX/U15
LO/S14	LO/U24 1948-54;1960-	XY/N-1 1967 (Bd.13)-

Germanien, eine Zeitschrift für Staats-Recht, Politik und Statistik von Deutschland. -- Giessen, 1808-1811

LO/N-1

Geschiedenis der Nederlandsche rechtswetenschap. -- Amsterdam, 1937-

CA/U13 1937-62

Gesetzgebung und Rechtspraxis des Auslandes. -- Berlin, 1925-1930

LO/U-3 imp.

Gewerblicher Rechtsschutz und Urheberrecht. -- Weinheim, 1896-1944; 1948-
1936 (vol.41)-1951 (vol.53) issued in two sections: Deutscher Teil and Auslands- und internationaler Teil (irregular). 1952 (vol.54)- issued separately
ISSN 0016-9420

ED/U-1 1968-76	LO/N14	OX/U15 1930-44 (Kurzausgabe); 1948-
LO-MT 1961-	LO/U24 1933-34; 1969 (Bd.71)-	

Gewerblicher Rechtsschutz und Urheberrecht. Auslands- und internationaler Teil see Gewerblicher Rechtsschutz und Urheberrecht. Internationaler Teil

Gewerblicher Rechtsschutz und Urheberrecht. Deutscher Teil see Gewerblicher Rechtsschutz und Urheberrecht

Gewerblicher Rechtsschutz und Urheberrecht. Internationaler Teil. -- Weinheim, 1967-
Continues: Gewerblicher Rechtsschutz und Urheberrecht. Auslands- und internationaler Teil, 1952-1966, which formed part of Gewerblicher Rechtsschutz und Urheberrecht, together with Deutscher Teil, 1936-1951
ISSN 0435-8600

LO/N14
LO/U-3 1956-
LO/U24 1960-
OX/U15 1959-
XY/N-1 1969-

Gibson's law notes see Law notes (London)

Giornale di giurisprudenza practica. -- Milan; Venice, 1846-1862

LO/N-1 1851-62

Giornale di giurisprudenza universale. -- Milan, 1811-1814?

LO/N-1

Giornale per le scienze politico-legali teorico-pratico. -- Milan, 1850.

LO/N-1

Giurisprudenza commerciale: società e fallimento. -- Milan, 1974-

No holdings notified

Giurisprudenza comparata di diritto civile. -- Rome, 1938-

LO/U24 1938 (v.1-2);
1946-48 (v.10-11)

Giurisprudenza costituzionale. -- Milan, 1956-
ISSN 0436-0222

LO-MT 1958-
LO/U24 1965 (v.10)-
MA/U-1 1962 (v.7)-

Giurisprudenza delle imposte... -- Milan, 1953-

LO/U-3 1955-

Giurisprudenza italiana. -- Turin, 1848-
ISSN 0017-0623

BL/U-1 1972-
CA/U13 (w.1940-43, 1946)
EX/U-1 1974-
GL/U-1 1973-
HL/U-1 1972-75 (v.124-127)
LO-MT 1970-
LO/U24 1917 (anno 69)- (w.1919,1944-47)
XY/N-1 1931-39;1968 (anno 120)-

La Giustizia amministrativa: raccolta periodica mensile di giurisprudenza, dottrina e legislazione in materia di diritto amministrativo e finanziario. -- Città di Castello, 1890-1923
Merged with Rivista di diritto pubblico e della pubblica amministrazione in Italia, q.v.

Not on checklist circulated, so some holdings possible

Giustizia penale: rivista critica di dottrina, giurisprudenza, legislazione...-- Rome, 1895-
Title varies: Vol.1-20 as Giustizia penale: rivista critica settimanale;
vol.21-35 as Giustizia penale e la procedura penale italiana (vol.1-15 of Procedura)
1944 not published
ISSN 0017-0658

CA/U37 1895-1965	OX/U15 1936-37, 1939-41	XY/N-1 1970 (anno 75)-

Giustizia penale: rivista critica settimanale <u>see</u> previous entry

Giustizia penale e la procedura penale italiana <u>see</u> Giustizia penale: rivista critica di dottrina, giurisprudenza, legislazione...

Giustizia sociale. -- Naples, 1960-

XY/N-1 1967 (anno 8 no.1/3).

La Giustizia tributaria <u>see</u> next entry

La Giustizia tributaria e le imposte dirette: rivista mensile di dottrina, giurisprudenza e legislazione. -- Rome, 1928-
Continues: La Giustizia tributaria, 1924-1927
Absorbed Imposte dirette in 1928

No holdings notified

Glasnik Advokatske komore u A.P. Vojvodini. -- Novi Sad, 1952-
ISSN 0017-0933

LO/N-1 1958.

Glim/Inns of Court Students' Union. -- London, 1947/48-1964

AB/N-1 1947-56	LO/N-1	QS/S-6 1947-62
ED/S11	OX/U15	QS/S-7 1948-64
LO-MT	QS/S-4	

Glos prawniczy. -- London, 1944-

LO/N-1 1944-45

Godishnik na Sofiiskija Universitet <u>see</u> Annuaire de l'Université de Sofia. Faculté de Droit

Godishnik na Sofiiskija Universitet. Juridicheski Fakultet <u>see</u> Annuaire de l'Université de Sofia. Faculté de Droit

Godishnjak Pravnog fakulteta u Sarajevu = Annuaire de la Faculté de Droit de Sarajevo, 1953-
With summaries in French

LO/N-1	LO/U11 1956-58; 1960-	OX/U15 (w.1956,nos. 5,7;1962)

Golden Gate law review _see_ next entry

Golden Gate University law review. -- San Francisco, 1975 (vol.6)-
Continues: Cal law, trends and developments, 1967-1970 (ISSN 0068-5348) and: Golden Gate law review, 1971-1975 (vol.5)

No holdings notified

Goltdammer's Archiv für Strafrecht. -- Hamburg, 1953-
Continues: Archiv für preussisches Strafrecht, 1853-1870; Archiv für gemeines deutsches und für preussisches Strafrecht, 1871-1879; Archiv für Strafrecht, 1880-1899; Archiv für Strafrecht und Strafprozess, 1900-1920;1925-1933; and: Deutsches Strafrecht: Strafrecht, Strafrechtspolitik, Strafprozess..., 1934-1944 (n.f.)
ISSN 0017-1956

LO/N-1 1853-1925; Nov.1942-Oct.1943	LO/U24 1953-	XY/N-1 1968 (Feb.)-
	OX/U15 1965-	

Gonzaga law review. -- Spokane, Wash., 1966-
ISSN 0046-6115

LO/U24

Gospodarka i administracja terenowa. -- Warsaw, 1961-1972
Absorbed by: Rada narodowa, which then became: Rada narodowa, gospodarka, administracja, q.v.
ISSN 0434-2151

XY/N-1

Graya/Gray's Inn. -- London, Sept. 1927-

AB/N-1 1947-65	LO-MT	QS/Q13 1928-
BH/U-1	LO/N-1	QS/S-4
BL/U-1 1965-	LO/U24	QS/S-6
CA/U-1	LV/U-1 1928-37 imp.	QS/S-7
ED/N-1	OX/U15	

The Green bag. -- Boston, Mass., 1889-1914

ED/S10 1889-98	LO/U24 1889-1914 imp.	OX/U15 1889-1901
LO-MT 1889-93 imp.		

Grotius. Annuaire international = (Grotius) International yearbook. -- The Hague, 1913-1946
Title varies slightly

AB/N-1 1927-46	LO/N-1	LO/U24
CA/U-1 1927-46	LO/N17 1913-24	LV/P-1 imp.
ED/U-1 1940-46	LO/S14 1940-46	OX/U15
HL/U-1 1917·	LO/U-3	

Guardian gazette _see_ Law Society's gazette

Guild practitioner. -- Berkeley, Cal., 1965 (vol.24)-
Continues: Lawyers' Guild review, 1940-1960 (vol.20) and: Law in transition, 1961-1963 (vol.23).
None published in 1964
ISSN 0017-5390

CB/U-1 1973 (v.31)- LO/U24 1970 (v.29)- XY/N-1 1965 (v.24)-

Gujarat law reporter. -- Ahmedabad, 1960-
ISSN 0017-551X

CA/U13 1963-67 imp. LO/U14 1960;1963- QS/S-6 1962- imp.
LO-MT 1963- OX/U15 1962-67 QS/S-7 1963-67

Gujarat law times. -- Ahmedabad, 1964-
ISSN 0017-5528

LO/U14 QS/S-6 imp. QS/S-7 1964-65 imp.
OX/U15

Haengjong nonch'ong (Korean journal of Public Administration). -- Seoul National University School of Public Administration, 1962-
ISSN 0438-3486

LO/N-1 imp.

Haenjong yon'gu (Public administrative review)/ Republic of Korea Research Institute of Public Administration, Chung-Gu College. -- Seoul, 1963-
ISSN 0438-3494

LO/N-1 1966 (v.3).

Hamburgische Gerichtszeitung <u>see</u> Hanseatische Gerichtszeitung

Hamburgische Handelsgerichtszeitung <u>see</u> Hanseatische Gerichtszeitung

Hamburgische Monatsschrift für Politik und Handel <u>see</u> next entry

Hamburgische Zeitschrift für Politik, Handel und Handelsrecht. -- Hamburg, 1834-1836
1834 entitled: Hamburgische Monatsschrift für Politik und Handel

LO/N-1

Handai hōgaku = Osaka law review. -- Toyonaka City, 1951-
ISSN 0438-4997

XY/N-1 1966 (no.57)-

Handbook - Association of American Law Schools see Proceedings - Association...

Handbook and proceedings - Association of American Law Schools see Proceedings - Association...

Hanseatische Gerichtszeitung. -- Hamburg, 1880-1927 (vol.48)
Continues: Hamburgische Gerichtszeitung, 1861-1868 (vol.8) and: Hamburgische Handelsgerichtszeitung, 1868 (vol.1)- 1880 (vol.12)

LO/N-1 1868-1901

Hanzaigaku zasshi see Nippon hoigaku zasshi

Hapraklit/ Israel Bar Association. -- Tel Aviv, 1942-
ISSN 0017-7571

LO/U14 1952- imp. XY/N-1 1966 (v.23)-

Harvard civil rights - civil liberties law review. -- Cambridge, Mass., 1966-
ISSN 0017-8039

BH/U-1 1967/68 (v.3)-	LO/U24	SO/U-1 1974-
CR/U-1	NO/U-1	XY/N-1 1970 (v.5)-
LO/U-3		

Harvard International Law Club bulletin see Harvard international law journal

Harvard International Law Club journal see next entry

Harvard international law journal. -- Cambridge, Mass., 1967 (vol.8)-
Continues: Bulletin of the Harvard International Law Club, 1959-1960 (vol.2), Harvard International Law Club bulletin, 1961/62 (vol.3) and: Harvard International Law Club journal, 1962 (vol.4) -1966 (vol.7)
ISSN 0017-8063

AD/U-6	LO-MT 1973 (v.14)-	NO/U-1
BH/U-1	LO/N17 1971-	OX/U15
CA/U13 (w 1971 v.12)	LO/U11 1972-	SO/U-1 1971-
ED/U-1 1967 (v.8)-	LO/U24	XY/N-1 1967 (v.8)-
LO/C15 1968-	MA/U-1 imp.	

Harvard journal on legislation. -- Cambridge, Mass., 1964-
ISSN 0017-808X

CA/U13 1966-	LO/U24	QN/C70 1971-73 (v.9-10)
CV/U-1	OX/U15	XY/N-1
LO/N-1		

Harvard law review. -- Cambridge, Mass., 1887-
ISSN 0017-811X

AB/N-1
AB/U-1
AD/U-6
BC-UC 1966-70 imp.
BH/U-1
BL/U-1
BR/U-1
BT/U-1
CA/U-1 1887-1933
CA/U13
CB/U-1
CH-CI
CR/U-1
CV/U-1
DN/U-1
DR/U-1
ED/S11 1916- imp.
ED/U-1
EX/U-1
GL/U-1
GL/U-2 1965-
HL/U-1
KL/U-1
LC/C-1 1920-
LC/U-1
LD/C-1
LD/U-1
LO/C-3
LO/C10 1944 (v.58)-
LO/C14 1955-64;1969-
LO/C15 1945-
LO/C25 1959-
LO/C27 1971-
LO/C47 1970-
LO-MT
LO/N-1
LO/N46
LO/R74 1965-
LO/U-1 1947-
LO/U-2
LO/U-3
LO/U11
LO/U12
LO/U24
LO/U28 1966-
LV-LP 1972-
LV/U-1
MA/U-1
NO/U-1
NW/U-1 1924 (v.38)- (w.v.71)
OX/U15
OX/U25
QE/C76
QL/D15 1973/74-
QM/C48 1969/70-
QM/C68 1946/47-
QN/C70
QS/Q12 1888- 1949 imp., 1953-
QS/S-4
QS/S-6
QS/S-7
QW/D12
RE/U-1
SH/U-1
SO/U-1
XM/C10
XY/N-1 1931 (v.45)-
YK/U-1 1962-76

Harvard Law School bulletin. -- Cambridge, Mass., 1948-
ISSN 0017-8128

CV/U-1 1966 (v.18)- (w.v.20 no.1)
LO/U24 imp.
XY/N-1 1973 (v.24 no.5)-

Hastings constitutional law quarterly. -- San Francisco, 1974-
ISSN 0094-5617

BH/U-1
OX/U15
XY/N-1 1975 (v.2)-

Hastings law journal. -- San Francisco, 1949-
ISSN 0017-8322

BL/U-1 1965
LO/U24 1967 (v.19)-
OX/U15
XY/N-1 1969 (v.21)-

Hawaii Bar journal. -- Honolulu, 1963 (vol.1)-
Continues: a journal with the same title, 1959 (vol.1 no.1), (ISSN 0438-8054), and: Hawaii Bar news, 1961 (vol.1)-1962 (vol.2) (ISSN 0438-8062)
ISSN 0440-5048

LO/U24 1971 (v.8)-

Hawaii Bar news <u>see</u> previous entry

Highlights of current legislation and activities in Mid-Europe. -- Washington, 1953-1960 (vol.8 no.2)
ISSN 0439-1241

LO/S14 imp.
LO/U-3 1955-60 (w.v.3 no.7)
LO/U24 (w.v.2 nos.6-12)

Hikakuhō kenkyū (Comparative law review). -- Tokyo, 1951-
ISSN 0439-1365

No holdings notified

Hikakuhō zasshi (Comparative law review). -- Tokyo,

LO/U14 1971 (v.6 no.4)-

Hindu law journal. -- Coimbatore, Bombay, 1918-1925 (vol.7)

LO/N-1

Hitosubashi journal of law and politics. -- Tokyo, 1960-
ISSN 0073-2796

HL/U-1
LO/N-1
LO/U-3
LO/U14
LV/U-1 1964-
OX/U15
XY/N-1 1965 (v.4)-

Ho shakai-gaku (Sociology of law). -- Tokyo, 1951-
ISSN 0437-6161

LO/N-1 19?? (v.11); 1961 (v.16)-
LO/U14 1951-54 imp.

Hō to seiji (The journal of law and politics). -- Nishinomiya,

LO/U14 1950-55 (v.1 no.3- v.6 no.2)

Hofstra law review. -- Hempstead, N.Y., 1973-
ISSN 0091-4029

LO/C47 1975-
OX/U15
XY/N-1

Hōgaku see Kindai hogaku: the law review of Kinki University

Hōgaku kenkyū. Hitotsubashi daigaku kenkyū nempō (Studies in jurisprudence. Annual review of Hitotsubashi University). -- Tokyo, 1958-
ISSN 0439-3260

LO/N-1

Hōgaku Kyōkai zasshi (Journal of the jurisprudence Association). -- Tokyo, 1853-
ISSN 0022-6815

LO/U14 1960 (v.76 no.3)-

Hōgaku ronshū see Kansai Daigaku hōgaku ronshū

Hōgaku ronsō (Kyoto law review). -- Kyoto, 1905-

LO/N-1 1919-
XY/N-1 1966 (v.78)-

Hōgaku shimpō (The Chuo law review). -- Tokyo, 1891-
ISSN 0009-6292

LO/U14 1971-

Hōgaku shirin (Review of law and political sciences). -- Tokyo,

LO/U14 1971-75 (v.68-72)

Hōgaku zasshi (Journal of law and politics of Osaka City University). -- Osaka, 1954-
ISSN 0441-0351

LO/N-1
XY/N-1 1965 (v.12)-

Hong Kong law journal. -- Hong Kong, 1971-

BH/U-1
CA/U13
CB/U-1
LO/N-1
LO/N17
LO/U-3
LO/U14
LO/U24
OX/U15
XY/N-1

Honorary magistrate/ Justices' Association of South Australia. -- Adelaide, 1904-

LO/U24 1932 imp., 1941-

Hōritsu jihō (Law review). -- Tokyo, 1929-

LO/U14 1959-66 imp.
XY/N-1 1966 (v.38)-

Hōsei-kenkyū = Journal of law and politics/ Kyushu University Institute for law and politics. -- Fakuoka,

XY/N-1 1966 (v.32)-

Hōsei-shi kenkyū (Legal history review). -- Tokyo, 1952-
ISSN 0441-2508

LO/N-1 1961 (v.12)-
LO/U14 1952 (v.1).

Houston law review. -- Houston, Tex., 1963-
ISSN 0018-6694

LO/U24 (w.v.5 no.4; v.6)
OX/U15
XY/N-1 1969 (v.7)-

Howard journal *see* next entry

Howard journal of penology and crime prevention. -- London, 1921-
1921-1964 (vol.11 no.3) entitled: Howard journal
ISSN 0073-3741

AB/N-1
AB/U-1 1976-
AD/U-6 1966-
BH/P-1
BH/U-1 1938-
BL/U-1 1958- imp.
BR/U-1 1966-
BT/U-1 1949-71
CA/U-1
CA/U13 1924-
CA/U37
CB/U-1 1948
CH-CI
CR/U-1 1945 (v.7)-
CV/U-1 1970 (v.13)-
DN/U-1 1970-
DR/U-1 1966-
ED/N-1
EX/U-1 1962-
GL/U-2 1961 (v.10)- imp.
HL/U-1 1958/61 (v.10)-
KL/U-1 1922-52 imp.
LA/U-1 1967.
LC/U-1
LD/C-1 1971 (v.13)-
LO/C-3 1968-
LO/C-5 1970 (v.13)-
LO/C14 1962/65 (v.11)-
LO/C15 1970-
LO/C47 1960-61;1969-
LO/M32 1934-54 imp.
LO-MT
LO/N-1
LO/N26 1957 (v.9 no.4)-

(cont'd)

Howard journal of penology and crime prevention (cont'd).

LO/N27
LO/U-1
LO/U-2 1975-
LO/U-3 (w.v.12 no.2)
LO/U11 1974-
LO/U24
LO/U28 1971 (v.13)-
LV-LP 1968 (v.12)- (v.12-14 imp.)
LV/U-1 1938- imp.
MA/U-1 1924 (v.1 no.3)-
NW/U-1 1970 (v.13)-
OX/U15
QE/C76 1972-
QL/D15 1968 imp., 1970-
QN/C70 1969-
QW/C73
QW/D12 1968 (v.12)-
RE/U-1 1966-
SH/U-1 1941-
SO/U-1 1934-
SW/U-1 1943- imp.
XM/C10 1974-
XY/N-1 1935-58 imp., 1960 (v.10 no.3)-
YK/U-1 1966-

Howard law journal/ Howard University School of Law. -- Washington D.C., 1955-
ISSN 0018-6813

CA/U13 1958-
LO/U24
OX/U15
XY/N-1 1967 (v.13)-

Hsien-cheng shih-tai/ Society of Chinese Constitutional Law. -- Taipei,

LO/U14 1974-

Hukum dan masjarakat: madjallah Perhimpunan sardjana-hukum Indonesia. -- Djakarta, 1960-
Continues: Regt (Recht) in Nederlandsch-Indië, 1849-1914· Indisch tijdschrift van het recht, 1915-1947: Tijdschrift van het recht, 1947-1950 and: Hukum madjallah Perhimpunam ahlihukum Indonesia, 1951-1959

LO/N-1 1849-1950

Hukum madjallah Perhimpunam ahlihukum Indonesia <u>see</u> previous entry

Human rights/ American Bar Association Section of Individual Rights and Responsibilities. -- Chicago, 1971-
ISSN 0046-8185

LO/N-1
LO/U24

Human rights journal: international and comparative law <u>see</u> Revue des droits de l'homme: droit international et droit comparé

Human rights review. -- London, 1976-
ISSN 0308-0765

AB/N-1
AB/U-1
BL/U-1
CA/U-1
CA/U13
DR/U-1
ED/N-1
EX/U-1
LO/C-3
LO/C14
LO/C15
LO/C25
LO/N-1
LO/N17
LO/N26 last 5 years
LO/S14
LO-SC
LO-TS
LO/U-3
LO/U11
LO/U24
LV-LP
LV/U-1
NO/U-1
OX/U15
QE/C76
QG/C25 (cont'd)

Human rights review (cont'd).

QL/D15	QS/S-4	SH/U-1
QM/C68	QW/D12	SO/U-1
QN/C70	RE/U-1	XY/N-1

Hungarian Bar review see Ügyvédszövetséti közlöny

Hungarian law review. -- Budapest, 1961-
Continues: Review of Hungarian legislation, 1958-1960?
For edition in French see Revue de droit hongrois
ISSN 0441-4411

CA/U13 imp.	LO/U-3 1961-(w.1964 no.2)	OX/U15
LO-MT 1968-73	LO/U24 1961-	XY/N-1 1968-
LO/N-1 1964-		

IATA annual general meeting reports and proceedings. -- Montreal, 1972-
Continues: IATA bulletin, 1945-1971 (ISSN 0074-1329)

BH/U-1 1947-71	LO/U-1 1946 (no.3)- (w.1968-69 (nos.36-37))	LO/U24
BR/U-1 1947-66 imp.	LO/U-2 1954-	MA/P-1 June 1951-71; 1975-
GL/U-2 1972-	LO/U-3 1946- imp.	OX/U-1 1946 (no.3)-
LO/C47 1950-		XY/N-1 1967-71 (nos. 35-39)
LO/N26 last 10 years		

IATA bulletin see previous entry

ICAO bulletin. -- Montreal, International Civil Aviation Organization, Nov. 1946-
1946-May 1947 as PICAO monthly bulletin. June 1947-1952 as ICAO monthly bulletin
ISSN 0018-8778

BH/U-1 1947-	LO/N-1	LO/U24 1946-55 imp., 1956 (v.11)-
BL/U-1 1948-	LO/N-5 last 5 years	LV-LP last 5 years
BR/U-1 1947-	LO/N26 1960-	MA/P-1 1958 (v.13 no.2)-
CA/U-1 1960-	LO/S14 (w.Nov.1947-Feb.1948)	OX/U-1
CA/U13 1947-49 imp.	LO/U-1 1948	XY/N-1 1947-56; 1964 (v.19)-
ED/N-1	LO/U-2 1956-	
GL/U-1 Mar.1947-	LO/U11 1973-	
LO/C47 last 5 years		

The ISL law review. -- Washington, 1976-

Not included in check list circulated, so some holdings possible

ICAO monthly bulletin _see_ previous entry

ICC practitioners' journal. -- Washington, Nov. 1933-
ISSN 0018-8859

LO/U-3 1953-
LO/U24 1971 (v.39)-
XY/N-1 1976 (v.44)-

IIC: International review of industrial property and copyright law. -- Weinheim/Bergstr., 1970-
ISSN 0018-9855

CB/U-1 1973 (v.4)-
GL/U-1 1973-
LD/U-1 1970-74
LO/N-5
LO/N14
LO/U-2 1974-76 (v.5-7)
LO/U-3 1978-
LO/U24
SO/U-1 1974 (v.5)-
XY/N-1 1971 (v.2)-

Idaho law journal. -- Moscow, Idaho, Feb. 1931-Nov. 1933

LO/U24 1932-33 (v.2-3)
OX/U15

Idaho law review. -- Moscow, 1964-
ISSN 0019-1205

LO/U24
XY/N-1 1971 (v.8)-

Idea: the journal of law and technology. -- Concord, N.H., 1976 (vol.18 no.2)-
Continues: Patent, trademark and copyright journal of research and education, 1957-64 (vol.1-7) and: Idea: the patent, trademark and copyright journal of research and education, 1965-67 (vol.8-18 no.1) (ISSN 0019-1272)

LO/N14
LO/U-3
LO/U24 1971 (v.15)-
MA/P-1 1957-71
XY/N-1 1960-64 (v.4-8)

Idea: the patent, trademark and copyright journal of research and education _see_ previous entry

Illinois Bar journal. -- Springfield, 1931-
Continues: Illinois State Bar Association quarterly bulletin, 1912-July 1931
ISSN 0019-1876

LO/U24 1912-31;1932-55 imp.,1956-
OX/U15 1944 (v.33)-
XY/N-1 1966 (v.55)-

Illinois continuing legal education. -- Mundelein, Ill., 1963-
ISSN 0536-4841

No holdings notified

Illinois law bulletin _see_ next entry

Illinois law quarterly. -- Urbana, 1917-1924
Title varies: vol.1 - vol.2 no. 6 as Illinois law bulletin; vol.2 no. 7 - vol.3 as University of Illinois law bulletin.
Merged with Illinois law review; continued by Northwestern University law review q.v.

No holdings notified

Illinois law review <u>see</u> Northwestern University law review

Illinois State Bar Association quarterly bulletin <u>see</u> Illinois Bar journal

Index: quaderni camerti di studi romanistici: international survey of Roman law. -- Naples, 1970-

AD/U-6 LO/U-2 OX/U15

Index to Canadian legal periodical literature. -- Montreal, 1961-

BL/U-1 1968-72
LO/U24
OX/U15
SH/U-1 1974-

Index to current legal research in Canada. -- Ottawa, 1972-

LO/U24 OX/U15

Index to foreign legal periodicals. -- London, 1960-
Cumulates triennially
ISSN 0019-400X

AB/N-1
AB/U-1
AD/U-6
BC-UC 1963-74 imp.
BH/U-1
BL/U-1
BR/U-1
BT/U-1
CA/U-1
CA/U13
CA/U37
CB/U-1
CR/U-1
CV/U-1
DN/U-1
DR/U-1
ED/S11
ED-SLC
ED/U-1
EX/U-1 1969-
GL/U-1
GL/U-2
HL/U-1 1966-
KL/U-1
LC/U-1
LD/U-1
LO/C-3
LO/C14 1971-
LO/C15 1972-
LO/C25 1960-64;1966-
LO/C27
LO-MT
LO/N-1
LO/N-5
LO/N17
LO/N26 1963-76
LO/R74
LO/U-1
LO/U-2
LO/U-3
LO/U11
LO/U12
LO/U14
LO/U24
LO/U28
LV/P-1 1960-64; 1966-74
LV/U-1
MA/U-1
NO/U-1
OX/U15
QL/D15 1968-
QM/C48 1975-
QN/C70 1971-72
QS/Q12
QW/D12
SH/U-1 1965-
SO/U-1
XM/C10 1972-
XY/N-1 1963-

Index to Indian legal periodicals. -- New Dehli, 1963-
ISSN 0019-4034

BL/U-1
CA/U13
LO/U14
LO/U24 1963-68
OX/U15
XY/N-1 1971; 1974.

Index to legal periodical literature. -- Boston, Mass.; etc., 1887-1937

AB/U-1
BH/U-1
CA/U13 1887-1922
LO-MT 1887-1922
LO/U11 1887-1932
LO/U24
LV/P-1 1887-1932
OX/U15
QS/S-7 1888-1907
RE/U-1

Index to legal periodicals. -- New York, 1908-
Cumulates triennially from 1926/28
ISSN 0019-4077

AB/U-1 1926-
AD/U-6 1955-
BC-UC 1968;1970-71
BH/U-1 1926-
BL/U-1 1926-
BR/U-1 1961-
BT/U-1 1952-
CA/U-1 1926-32
CA/U13 1923-
CA/U37
CB/U-1 1955/6 (v.49)-
CR/U-1 1952-
CV/C-1 1952-
CV/U-1 1926-
DN/U-1 1958-
DR/U-1 1961-
ED/U-1
EX/U-1
GL/U-1 Aug. 1958-
GL/U-2 1964-
KL/U-1 1952-
LC/C-1 1973-
LC/U-1 1952
LD/C-1 1960 (v.14)-
LD/U-1
LO/C-3 1952-
LO/C14 1970-
LO/C15 1970-
LO/C25 1970-
LO/C27 1970-
LO/C47 1952-
LO-MT
LO/N-1 1915-
LO/N-5 1958-
LO/N26 1964-73
LO/N27 1964-
LO/R74 1929-
LO/U-2 1943-
LO/U-3 1926-
LO/U11 1931-
LO/U12 1926-
LO/U24
LO/U28 1926-
LV-LP 1974-
LV/P-1 1926-
LV/U-1 1961-
MA/U-1 1947-
NO/U-1 1926-
NW/U-1 1964-
OX/U15 1908-10;1913-14;1923-
QE/C76 1952-
QL/D15 1958/61-
QM/C48 1970-
QM/C68 Sept. 1974-
QN/C70 1952-
QS/S-4 1967-
QS/S-6 1926-
QS/S-7 1947-
QW/D12 1952-
RE/U-1 1926-
SH/U-1
SO/U-1 1952-
SW/U-1 1964-
XM/C10 1971-
XY/N-1 1967-

Index to periodical articles related to law selected from articles not included in the Index to Legal Periodicals. -- Stanford, etc., 1958-
ISSN 0019-4093

BL/U-1
CA/U13
CA/U37
CB/U-1 1973-
CR/U-1
CV/U-1 1969-
DN/U-1
GL/U-2
HL/U-1 1969-73 (v.15)
LO/C-3
LO/C15
LO/R74
LO/U-2 1958-76
LO/U24
LV/U-1
NO/U-1
OX/U15 1964 (v.6)-
QE/C76 1960-
QL/D15 1958-73;1976-
QM/C48 1975-
QN/C70 1976-
QS/S-6
QW/D12 1959-
SO/U-1 1958-64
XY/N-1 1969-

Indian Advocate/ Bar Association of India. -- Bombay, 1961-
ISSN 0019-4301

LO/U14 1964 (v.4)-
XY/N-1 1968 (v.8)-

Indian journal of international law. -- Bombay, 1960-
ISSN 0019-5294

BH/U-1
BL/U-1
CA/U13
CR/U-1 1960-74
ED/U-1 1967 (v.7)-
LO/N-1 1960-
LO/S55 imp.
LO/U-2
LO/U-3
LO/U14 (w.1968, v.8 no.1)
LO/U24
LV/U-1 1960-74
MA/U-1 1962 (v.2)-
NO/U-1
OX/U15
SH/U-1 1960-73 (v.13)
XY/N-1

Indian journal of public administration. -- New Delhi, 1955-
ISSN 0019-5561

BR/U-1 1966 (v.12)-
BT/U-1 1955/56;1958/59;1966-
DR/U-1 1971
LD/U-1 1964-
LO/N-1
LO/S55 imp.
LO/U-3 (v.8;20 imp., w.v.21)
LO/U14 (w.1961 v.7 no.1)
OX/U13
XY/N-1 1966 (v.12)-

Indian jurist. -- Madras, 1877-1893
Continues: Madras jurist, 1866-1876

LO/N-1 1868-74 imp., 1890-91 imp.
OX/U13 1881-85 imp.

Indian law journal. -- Lucknow, 1957-
ISSN 0442-7033

LO/U14 1957 (v.1 no.1)

Indian law magazine. -- Bombay, 1878.

LO/N-1

Indian law magazine. -- Calcutta, 1895.

LO/N-1

Indian law quarterly review. -- New Dehli, 1956- [ca 1963]
ISSN 0445-7773

CA/U13 1956-61 imp.
LO/S55 1956 (v.1 no.1).
LO/U14 1956-63
OX/U13

Indian law review. -- Calcutta, 1947-54; 1957 (i-iv)

CA/U13 1947-50
DR/U-4 1952-53 imp.
LO-MT 1947;1950-52; 1954-57
LO/S65 imp.
LO/U14 imp.
LO/U24 1947-52; 1953-57 imp.
OX/U13 1947 (no.2)-1957 (no.4)
QS/S-7 1947-49 imp.

Indian yearbook of international affairs. -- Madras, 1952-
ISSN 0537-2704

BL/U-1 1963-
BR/U-1 1952;1956.
BT/U-1 1955,1957; 1959-67
CA/U-1 1954;1956.
CA/U13 1952;1955-
CR/U-1 1959-66
ED/N-1 1957.
ED/U-1 1963.
EX/U-1 1952-3;1956.
GL/U-1
HL/U-1 1964-74
LC/U-1 1956- (w.1959)
LD/U-1 1955-
LO/N-1 1952-3;1959-66/7;1974-
LO/N17
LO/S14 1952-66/67; 1974-
LO/S55 (w.v.9-10)
LO/U-1
LO/U-2
LO/U-3
LO/U14
LO/U24
LV/P-1 1952;1958-64
LV/U-1 1953;1956.
MA/U-1 1957 (v.6)-
OX/U13
OX/U15 1952;1955-
XY/N-1 1966 (v.15)-

Indiana law journal. -- Bloomington, June 1925-
ISSN 0019-6665

BL/U-1 1969-
CH-CI
LO/U24
OX/U15
XY/N-1 1969 (v.45)-

Indiana law journal. -- Indianapolis, 1898-June 1899

LO/U24 imp.

Indiana law review. -- Indianapolis, 1972 (vol.6)-
Continues: Indiana legal forum, 1967-1971 (ISSN 0537-3344)
ISSN 0046-9106

LO/U24
XY/N-1 1968 (v.2)-

Indiana legal forum <u>see</u> previous entry

Indisch tijdschrift van het recht <u>see</u> Hukum dan masjarakat

Indisch weekblad van het recht. -- Batavia, 1863-1914

LO/U24 1891-96 (v.29-34)

Industrial and intellectual property in Australia: journal of the Australian Patent Office Society. -- Canberra, 1961-
ISSN 0587-4936

LO/N14 1961-69
ED/N-1 1965-69
OX/U15 1961-62;1965 (Mar.)-1969 (Jun.)

Industrial and labor relations review. -- Ithaca, N.Y. 1947-
ISSN 0019-7939

AB/U-1 1966-
AD/U-6 1957-
BH/U-1 1953-
BL/U-1 1962-
BR/U-1 1962-
BT/U-1 1947-59;1964-
CB/U-1 (1964 and 1966 imp.)
CR/U-1 1953-
DR/U-1
ED/U-1 1951- imp.
GL/U-2 1961-
HL/U-1 1960-
LA/U-1
LC/U-1 1960-
LD/C-1 1966 (v.20)-
LD/U-1 1947-73
LO/C-3 1970-
LO/C14 1972-
LO/N-1 1956-
LO/U-3 (w.v.18 no.3)
LO/U24
LO/U28 1968 (v.22)-
LV/P-1 Oct.1956-74
LV/U-1 1949-
MA/P-1 1961-
NW/U-1 1962 (v.16)-
QE/C76 1972-
QM/C68 1977-
QN/C70 1966 (v.20)-
SO/U-1 1963-
SW/U-1 1963-
XM/C10 1972-
XY/N-1 1960 (v.13 no.2)-
YK/U-1 1965-

Industrial law journal. -- London, 1972-
Continues: Bulletin - Industrial Law Society, 1968-1972 (no.12)

AB/N-1 1972-
AB/U-1 1970 (no.8)-
AD/U-6
BH/P-1 1972-
BH/U-1
BL/U-1 1972-
BR/U-1
BT/U-1 1975-
CA/U-1 1972-
CA/U13
CB/U-1 1973 (v.2)-
CH-CI
CR/U-1 1972-
CV/C-1 1972-
DN/U-1 1972-
DR/U-1 1972-
ED/S11 1972-
ED/U-1
EX/U-1
GL/U-1 1972-
GL/U-2 1973 (v.2)-
HL/U-1 1968-69 (no.6);1972-
KL/U-1 1972-

(cont'd)

Industrial law journal (cont'd).

LC/C-1
LC/U-1 1972-
LD/C-1 1972-
LD/U-1 1972-
LO/C-3 1972-
LO/C-5
LO/C10
LO/C14
LO/C15
LO/C18
LO/C25
LO/C27 1972-
LO/C47
LO-MT
LO/N-1
LO/N14
LO/N26 1972-
LO-SC 1972-
LO/U-2
LO/U-3
LO/U11
LO/U12
LO/U24 1968-70;1972-
LO/U28 1972-
LV-LP
LV/P-1
LV/U-1 1972-
MA/P-1 1972-
MA/U-1 1972-
OX/U15
OX/U25
QE/C76 1972-
QG/C25 1973-
QL/D15 1972-
QM/C48 1972-
QM/C68 1972-
QN/C70 1972-
QS/S-6 1972-
QS/S-8
QW/D12
RE/U-1
SH/U-1
SO/U-1 1972-
XM/C10
XY/N-1 1972-

Industrial law review. -- Leigh-on-Sea, 1946-1959/60

AB/N-1 1946-50
BH/U-1
CA/U-1
CA/U13
ED/S11
EX/U-1
GL/U-2 1946-48 (v.1-2)
HL/U-1
LO/N-1
LO/U-2 1950-59 imp.
LO/U-3
LO/U24
OX/U15
XY/N-1 1947-57

Industrial property. -- Geneva, 1962-
For ed. in French see Propriété industrielle
Continues: Industrial property quarterly, 1956-1961
ISSN 0019-8625

ED/U-1
LO/N14
LO/U-3
LO/U24
SO/U-1
XY/N-1 1973 (v.12)-

Industrial property quarterly see previous entry

Industrial relations law journal. -- Berkeley, California, 1976-

SH/U-1

Inequality in education/ Harvard Center for law and education. -- Cambridge, Mass., 1969-
ISSN 0579-3475

XY/N-1

Información jurídica see Documentación jurídica

Information bulletin: legislation - court decisions - doctrine, in the field of industrial property. -- Paris, 1962-65

LO/N14

Informations constitutionelles et parlementaires see Constitutional and parliamentary information

Informationsbrief des Untersuchungsausschusses freiheitlicher Juristen. -- Berlin, 1950-1969

LO/U-3

L'Ingénieur-conseil see Revue de droit intellectual: l'Ingénieur-conseil

Ingwōn yōnbo (Yearbook on human rights). -- Korea (Rep.) Min. of Justice

LO/N-1 1965.

Institute on Federal Taxation, New York University see Proceedings - New York University Institute...

Insurance counsel journal. -- Birmingham, Ala., 1934-
ISSN 0020 465X

LO/U24 1971 (v.38)-

Insurance law journal. -- Chicago, 1939-
Supersedes an earlier publication with the same title issued 1871-1938
ISSN 0020-4722

LO/U24 1971-   XY/N-1 1965-

Inter-American juridical yearbook see Anuario jurídico interamericano

Inter-American law review = Revista jurídica interamericano. -- New Orleans, 1959-1966 (vol.8)
ISSN 0020-4951

BL/U-1   LO/U24   XY/N-1 1963 (v.5)-1966
CA/U13 (w.1960(v.2))   OX/U15

Inter-American yearbook on human rights see Anuario interamericano de derechos humanos

Intercollegiate law journal see University law review

Interlex: revue internationale de droit comparé général et spécial. -- Montreal, 1971-1972 (vol.2 no.1)
No more published?
ISSN 0315-3541

LO/U24 imp.   OX/U15

International Air Transport Association annual general meeting reports and proceedings see IATA annual general meeting reports and proceedings

International and comparative law bulletin see International lawyer

International and comparative law quarterly. -- London, 1952-
Merger of: International law quarterly, q.v., and: Journal of comparative legislation and international law, q.v.
ISSN 0020-5893

AB/U-1
AD-A
AD/U-6
BC-UC
BH-LS
BH/U-1
BL/U-1
BR/U-1
BT/U-1 1952-64;1967-
CA/U-1
CA/U13
CB/U-1
CH-CI
CR/U-1
CV/C-1 1970 (v.19)-
CV/U-1 (w.v.12 no.1)
DN/U-1
DR/U-1
ED/S10 1952-58; 1966-69
ED/S11
ED-SLC
ED/U-1
EX/U-1
GL/U-1
GL/U-2
HL/U-1
KL/U-1
LA/U-1 1952-76
LC/U-1
LD/C-1 1967-
LD/U-1
LO/C-3
LO/C-5
LO/C10
LO/C14 1967-
LO/C15
LO/C18 1965 (v.14)-
LO/C25 1960-
LO/C47
LO-CBL last 10 years
LO-MT
LO/N-1
LO/N-5
LO/N17
LO/N26
LO/N46
LO/R74
LO/S14
LO/S55 1952-66 imp.
LO-SC
LO-TS
LO/U-1
LO/U-2
LO/U-3
LO/U11
LO/U12
LO/U14
LO/U24
LO/U28 1952-63
LV-LP 1973 (v.22)-
LV/P-1 1952-74
LV/U-1
MA/P-1
MA/U-1
NO/U-1
NW/U-1
OX/U15
OX/U25
QE/C76
QG/C25 1976-
QL/D15
QM/C48
QM/C68
QN/C70 1952-
QS/Q12
QS/S-4
QS/S-6
QS/S-7
QS/S-8
QW/D12
RE/U-1
SO/U-1
XY/N-1

International Arbitration and Peace Association monthly journal see Concord: journal of the International Arbitration and Peace Association

International arbitration journal see Arbitration journal

International Bar Association conference. Summary of proceedings see Summary of proceedings [etc.]- ... conference of the International Bar Association

International Bar journal. -- London, 1970-
ISSN 0047-0589

BH/U-1 1970 (no.2); 1971-
CA/U-1 1970-73
ED/S11
GL/U-2 1976 (no.2)-
LO-MT
LO/N-1
LO/U24
MA/U-1 1971-
OX/U15 1970 (no.2)-
XY/N-1 1970 (no.2)-

International bibliography on crime and delinquency see Crime and delinquency abstracts

International bulletin for research on law in eastern Europe = Bulletin international de recherches sur le droit en Europe de l'est = Internationales Bulletin zur Ostrechtsforschung. -- Stuttgart, 1972 (vol.5)-
Continues: Bulletin zur Ostrechtsforschung in den Ländern des Europarates, 1968-1971 (vol.4)

GL/U-1
LO/U-2
LO/U24
OX/U15
XY/N-1

International bulletin of agricultural law see International journal of law and legislation relating to food and agriculture

International bulletin of industrial property see Research, patents and trademarks

International business lawyer/ International Bar Association. Section on Business Law. -- London, 1973-

CA/U37
GL/U-2 1976 (v.4)-
LO-MT 1974 (v.2)-
LO/N-1
LO/U24
OX/U15 (w.1973 (v.1, nos.2-4))
XY/N-1

International Civil Aviation Organization bulletin see ICAO bulletin

International conciliation. -- New York, 1907-1972

AB/N-1 1911- imp.
AB/U-1 1946-1972 imp.
AD/U-6 1917-1925; 1925-1972
BH/P-1 1923-72
BL/U-1 1917-57
BT/U-1 1911-13;1915-51;1954-72
CA/U-1 1918-57
CA/U13 imp.
CR/U-1 1917-57
CV/C-1 1966-72
DN/U-1 1917-21; 1924-72
DR/U-1 1930- imp.
ED/S10 1910-19; 1933-48 imp.
ED/S11 1917-1972
ED/U-1 1917-71 imp.
GL/U-1 1917-72
HL/U-1 1922;1925-72
KL/U-1 1919-72 imp.
LC/U-1 1945-71
LD/P-1 1919-72
LO-MT 1922-57; 1967-71
LO/N-1 1921-1972
LO/N17 1917-49; 1952;1961-
LO/N26 1925-
LO/S14 1912;1914-72
LO/S65 1910-72 imp.
LO/U-1 1917-72
LO/U-2 1919-72 imp.
LO/U-3
LV/P-1 1938-57
LV/U-1 1917-71
MA/P-1 1912-57 (w.1922-Apr. 1924,Jan.1949. 1953-54 imp.)
NW/U-1 1924-70 imp.
OX/U-1 1912-72
OX/U15 1920-72 imp.
QS/Q29 1927-52 imp., 1953-72
QS/S-7 1921-57
RE/U-1 1929-72 imp.
SO/U-1 1924-71
SW/U-1 1918-57 imp., 1967-72
XY/N-1 1911-59 imp., 1960-72
YK/U-1 1964-72

International exchange of information on bills and draft regulations on penal matters/ Council of Europe, Committee on Crime Problems. -- Strasbourg, 1964-1966 (vol.3)
1966 incorporated in: Exchange of information between the member states on their legislative activity and regulations, q.v.
ISSN 0590-7136

BR/U-1
LC/U-1
LO/N-1
LO/U24
OX/U15

International exchange of information on current criminological research projects in member states/ Council of Europe, Committee on crime problems.-- Strasbourg, 1966-

AD/U-6 1966-	LC/U-1	LO/U-1
CA/U37		

International journal of criminology and penology. -- London; New York, 1973-
ISSN 0306-3208

AB/N-1	LC/C-1	QL/D15
AD/U-6	LO/C10	QN/C70
CA/U-1	LO/N-5	QW/C73
CB/U-1	LO/N27	QW/D12 1975 (v.3)-
DN/U-1 1974-	LO/U-2	SH/U-1
ED/N-1	LO/U-3	SW/U-1
EX/U-1	LV-LP	XY/N-1
HL/U-1	OX/U15	

International journal of law and legislation relating to food and agriculture. -- F.A.O., Rome, 1947-48
1947 as Food and agriculture: international law journal
Continues: International bulletin of agricultural law, 1940-46

CA/U-1 1940-47	LO/U-3	OX/U15 1947-48
LO/N-1		

International journal of law libraries. -- Marburg, 1973-
Continues: Bulletin - International Association of Law Libraries, 1960-1972
ISSN 0340-045X

AB/U-1 1973-	LO/N-1	LO/U24
BH/U-1 1964-	LO/N-5 1966 (no.16)-	LV/U-1 1960-72
BL/U-1	LO/N17 1973-	NO/U-1
CA/U13	LO/U-2 1966-	OX/U15
CA/U37	LO/U-3 1966-	QM/C48 1975-
CB/U-1 1974 (v.2)-	LO/U11 1966-	QS/S-7 1966-
GL/U-2 1973-	LO/U12 1966-	SO/U-1 1973-
LO-MT	LO/U14 1962-	XY/N-1 1975 (v.3)-

International journal of legal research. -- Meerut, 1966-
ISSN 0020-7330

XY/N-1 1966-72 (v.7 no.2)

International journal of offender therapy <u>see</u> next entry

International journal of offender therapy and comparative criminology. -- London, 1972 (vol.16)-
Continues: APTO, 1957-1960 (vol.4); Journal of offender therapy, 1961-1966 (vol.10), and: International journal of offender therapy, 1967-1971 (vol.15) (ISSN 0020-7497)
ISSN 0306-624X

CA/U37	LO/U11 1976 (v.20)-	OX/U15 1968 (v.12).
LO/C15 1969 (v.13)-		

International labour review. -- I.L.O., Geneva, 1921-

AB/U-1 (w.1965-72)
AD/U-6 1927-
BH/P-1
BL/U-1 1933-
BR/U-1 imp.
BT/U-1 1924-44 imp.; 1949 imp.; 1951-
CA/U-1
CA/U13 1936- imp.
CB/U-1 1945-
CC/U-1 1947-
CR/U-1 1923 (v.7)-
DN/U-1 1964-
DR/U-1 imp.
ED/N-1 1922-
EX/U-1 1921-33;1944-
GL/U-1 1922-
GL/U-2 1957-
HL/U-1 1930 (v.21)-
KL/U-1 1922 (v.5)- imp.
LA/U-1 1967-
LC/U-1
LD/C-1 1966 (v.93)-
LD/P-1 1923 (v.7-9); 1925 (v.11)-
LD/U-1
LO/C-3 1971-
LO/C-5 1964 (v.89)-
LO/C25 1972-
LO/C27 1969 (v.99)-
LO/M32 1946-69
LO-MT 1955-56 imp.
LO/N-1
LO/N17 1936-
LO/N26
LO/S14 1945-
LO/S28 1938-
LO/U-1
LO/U-2 1923-34;1974-
LO/U-3
LO/U24 1952-57 imp.; 1958 (v.77)-
LO/U28 1969 (v.99)-
LV/P-1
LV/U-1 1924-
MA/P-1
NW/U-1 1928-
OX/U-1 1921 (v.4 no.2)-
QN/C70 1973-
QS/Q29 1921-26 imp.; 1927-31;1938-
RE/U-1 1947 (v.55)-
SH/U-1 1949-
SO/U-1 1926-
SW/U-1 1921-23;1942-
XM/C10 1971-
XY/N-1 1925 (v.12)-
YK/U-1 1963-

International Law Association conference reports <u>see</u> Report of the ... conference/ International Law Association

International law bulletin <u>see</u> Columbia journal of transnational law

International law notes. -- London, 1916-1919

AB/N-1
CA/U-1
ED/S11
LO/N-1
LO/N17 1916-17
LO/U-3
LO/U24
OX/U15
QS/S-6

International law quarterly. -- London, 1947-1951 (vol.4)
Merged with: Journal of comparative legislation and international law, q.v., to become: International and comparative law quarterly, q.v.

AB/N-1
AB/U-1
AD/U-6
BC-UC
BH/U-1
BL/U-1
BR/U-1
CA/U-1
CA/U13
CH-CI
DN/U-1
ED/S10 1947-48
ED/S11
ED/U-1
EX/U-1
GL/U-1
HL/U-1
LC/U-1
LD/U-1
LO-MT
LO/N-1
LO/N17
LO/N26
LO/N46
LO/S14
LO-TS
LO/U-1
LO/U-2 1947;1950-51
LO/U-3
LO/U11
LO/U14
LO/U24
LO/U28 1947-50 (v.3)
LV/P-1 1948-51
LV/U-1
NO/U-1
OX/U15
OX/U25
QL/D15
QS/S-4
QS/S-6
QS/S-7
QS/S-8
QW/D12
RE/U-1
SH/U-1
XY/N-1 1947 (v.1 no.1).

International law review <u>see</u> Revue de droit international de sciences diplomatiques et politiques

International lawyer/ American Bar Association, Section of International Law. -- Chicago, 1966/67-
Merger of: Bulletin- American Bar Association. Section of International and Comparative Law, 1957-1966 and: Proceedings- American Bar Association. Section of International and Comparative Law, 1942/43-1965
ISSN 0020-7810

CA/U13 1966- imp.
DN/U-1 1968-
ED/U-1 1974 (v.8)-
LO/U24
LV-LP 1967- imp.
NO/U-1
OX/U15 1957-
XY/N-1 1967 (v.1 no.2)-

International legal education newsletter/ Association of American Law Schools. Section on Foreign Exchanges of Law Teachers and Students. -- St. Louis, 1973-
Continues: Foreign exchange bulletin, 1958-1972 (ISSN 0571-5989)

No holdings notified

The international mind <u>see</u> Esprit international

International organization. -- Boston, Mass., Feb. 1947-
ISSN 0020-7829

AB/N-1 1948-
AB/U-1
AD/U-6
BH/U-1
BL/U-1 1948-55
BR/U-1
BT/U-1 1947-53; 1956-62;1963-
CA/U-1 1962;1964-
CA/U13 1947;1949- imp.
CB/U-1 1970 (v.24)-
CR/U-1 1965-
CV/C-1 1961 (v.15)-
CV/U-1
DN/U-1
DR/U-1 (w.1963)
ED/N-1 1948-55
ED/U-1 1948-
EX/U-1 1966-76
GL/U-1
HL/U-1
KL/U-1 1960 (v.14)-
LA/U-1 imp.
LC/U-1 (w.v.8-9)
LD/U-1 1948-
LO/MT 1947-62
LO/N-1
LO/N17
LO/N26 last 10 years
LO/S14
LO/U-1
LO/U-2
LO/U-3
LO/U11 1972-
LO/U24
LO/U28 1973 (v.27)-
LV-LP 1973-
LV/P-1 1948-75
LV/U-1 1948-
MA/P-1
OX/U-1
OX/U15
QN/C70 1973-
QS/Q29 1947-64
QW/D12 1960 (v.14)-
RE/U-1
SH/U-1 1964-
SO/U-1 1966-
SW/U-1 1947;1949-53; 1957-
XM/C10 1972-
XY/N-1
YK/U-1

International relations/ David Davies Memorial Institute of International Studies. -- London, 1954-
ISSN 0047-1178

AB/N-1
AB/U-1 imp.
AD/U-6
BT/U-1 1960 (no.2)-
CA/U-1
DR/U-1 1954-56 imp.
ED/N-1
ED/U-1
GL/U-1
KL/U-1 1960 (v.2)- imp.
LC/U-1
LO/N-1
LO/N17
LO/N26
LO/S14
LO/U-1 1954-65 imp.
LO/U-3
LO/U24 1966- imp.
LV-LP 1957 (v.1 no.8)- imp.
NO/U-1 1955 (v.1 no.4)-
OX/U-1
QM/C68 1973-
QS/S-6 imp.
QW/D12 1973 (v.4 no.3)-
RE/U-1 1957 (v.1 no.8); 1960-
SO/U-1 1975-
SW/U-1 1963-
XY/N-1 1962 (v.2 no.5)-
YK/U-1 1965-

International review of administrative sciences. -- Brussels, 1957 (vol.23)-
Numbering continued from French ed., for which, see: Revue Internationale des sciences administratives
ISSN 0020-8523

AB/U-1 1965-	LD/U-1 1964-	NW/U-1 1967 (v.33)-
BH/U-1 1959-	LO/C-3 1970-	OX/U-1
CC/U-1	LO/N-1	QE/C76 1973-
CV/U-1 1963 (v.29)-	LO/N17 1971-	QN/C70 1971-
DR/U-1	LO/U-3	RE/U-1 1967 (v.33)-
ED/U-1 1964-	LO/U24 1962 (v.28)-	SH/U-1 1961-
EX/U-1 1962-	LO/U28 1970-	SW/U-1 1963-73
LC/C-1 1970-	LV/P-1 1958-74	XY/N-1 1964 (v.30)-
LC/U-1 1963-	LV/U-1 1962-	YK/U-1 1965-

International review of criminal policy/ United Nations. -- New York, 1952-
ISSN 0074 7688

AB/N-1	KL/U-1 1954 (no.5)-	MA/P-1
BH/P-1	LC/U-1 1962-	OX/U15
BH/U-1	LO/N-1	QS/Q29
BL/U-1	LO/N26	RE/U-1 1965 (v.23)-
CA/U-1	LO/N27	SH/U-1
CA/U37	LO/U-3	SO/U-1 1964-
DR/U-1 1960-68	LO/U11	SW/U-1 imp.
ED/U-1	LO/U24	XY/N-1 1954-59;
HL/U-1	LV/P-1 1962-	1966 (v.24)-

International review of industrial property and copyright law
<u>see</u> IIC

International review of the Red Cross. -- Geneva, 1961-
Supersedes the English supplement to Revue Internationale de la Croix-Rouge q.v.
ISSN 0020-8604

CA/U-1	LO/N26 last 2 years	LO/U24
LO/N17	LO/U-3	

International survey of legal decisions on labour law. -- Geneva, 1925-1937/38

HL/U-1 1930-36/37 (v.12)	LO/U-3	OX/U15
KL/U-1 1936-38 (v.12-13)	LO/U24	

International trade law and practice <u>see</u> Droit et pratique du commerce international

International trade law journal. -- Baltimore, 1975-

No holdings notified

Internationale Zeitschrift für Theorie des Rechts <u>see</u> Revue internationale de la théorie du droit

Internationales Bulletin zur Ostrechtsforschung see International bulletin for research on law in eastern Europe

Internationales Jahrbuch für Schiedsgerichtswesen in Zivil und Handelssachen. -- Berlin, 1926; 1928-34

LO/U-3	LO/U24	OX/U15

Internationales Recht und Diplomatie. -- Hamburg, 1956-
ISSN 0020-9503

LO/N-1	LO/U-3	OX/U15
LO/U-2 1956-74	LO/U24	XY/N-1 1962-

Interstate Commerce Commission practitioners' journal see ICC practitioners' journal

Intertax: European tax review = [Intertax] La Fiscalité du Marché Commun = [Intertax] Europäische Steuer-Zeitung. -- Deventer, 1973-
Order of sub-titles varies.
Text in English, French and German.
Continues: La Fiscalité du Marché Commun, 1962-1972 (Text in French and German; summaries in Italian, Dutch and English. ISSN 0015-282X)
Intertax: (Dutch edition) published by same publisher, continues: Fiscaal tijdschrift voor de Euromarkt, 1962-1972 (ISSN 0015-2811)
German edition published in Bonn: Intertax: Europäische Steuer-Zeitung (Text in French and German; summaries in Dutch and Italian)
Continues: Europäische Steuer Zeitung, 1962-1972 (ISSN 0014-2689)

EX/U-1 1974-	LO/U-2 1968-72 (Fr. ed.);1973-76 (no.6)	LO/U24 1962-72 (Fr. ed.);1973-
GL/U-1 1970-72 (Fr. ed.);1973-	LO/U-3 1962-72 (Fr. ed.);1973-77	SO/U-1 1974-76
KL/U-1 1973-		XY/N-1 1966 (no.17 Fr.ed.)-
LO-MT 1962-72 (Fr. ed.);1973-		

Intramural law review [Saint Louis University] see Saint Louis University law journal

Intramural law review/ New York University School of Law. -- New York, 1945-1968 (vol.23)
Ceased publication

BL/U-1 1958-68	ED/U-1 1958-68	OX/U15
LO/U24		

Intramural law review of Wake Forest College see Wake Forest law review

Iowa Bar review. -- Iowa City, 1934/35-1939/40
Issued as a supplement to Iowa law review, vols 20-25

No holdings notified

Iowa law bulletin see next entry

Iowa law review. -- Iowa City, 1925 (vol.11)-
Continues: Iowa law bulletin 1915-1925 (vol.10)
ISSN 0021-0560

CA/U13 1932-
LO-MT 1915-41;1946-
LO/U-1 1932-1954/55
LO/U24
OX/U15
XY/N-1 1971 (v.57)-

Irish jurist. -- Dublin, 1849-1867

BL/U-1 (w.1858/59 (v.11))
HL/U-1 1849-66 (v.18)
LO-MT
LO/N-1
LO/N46
LO/U24 1849-61 (v.13)
QS/S-7

Irish jurist. -- Dublin, 1935-1966; N.S. 1966-
ISSN 0021-1273

AB/N-1
AB/U-1
AD/U-6 1966-
BH/U-1 1966-
BL/U-1
BR/U-1 1966-
CA/U-1 1966-
CA/U13
CB/U-1 1966-
CR/U-1
CV/U-1 1966-
DN/U-1 1966-
DR/U-1 1973-
ED/S10 1935-47
ED/S11
ED-SLC 1966-
ED/U-1 1966-
EX/U-1 1973-
GL/U-1
HL/U-1 1966-
KL/U-1 1966-
LC/U-1
LD/U-1 1966-
LO/MT
LO/N-1
LO/N26
LO/N46
LO/R74
LO/U-2 1966-
LO/U11 1966-
LO/U12 1966-
LO/U24
LV/U-1 1966-
MA/U-1 1966-
NO/U-1 1966-
OX/U15
OX/U25 1968-
QN/C70 1935-65;1970-
RE/U-1 1966 (n.s.v.1)-
SH/U-1 1966-
SO/U-1 1966-
SW/U-1 1966-
XY/N-1 1966-

Irish jurist and local government review. -- Dublin, 1900-1905
Vols 1-4 entitled New Irish jurist and local government review

BL/U-1
LO/U-2

Irish law recorder see Law recorder

Irish law times and solicitors' journal. -- Dublin, 1867-
ISSN 0021-1281

AB/N-1 1928-36 imp.; 1937-
BL/LS
BL/U-1
BR/U-1 1977 (v.111)-
CA/U-1 1971-
CA/U13 1874-75;1879-
CB/U-1 1975 (v.109)-
CR/U-1 1972-
ED/S11 1908-
LO-MT
LO/N-1 1871-
LO-TS 1932-
LO/U-2 1885-1926; 1974-
LO/U24
LV/P-1 1956-
MA/U-1 1959 (v.93)-
NO/U-1 1969 (v.103)-
OX/U15 1908-
QN/C70 1970 (v.104)-
QS/S-4
QS/S-6 1882-
QS/S-8
RE/U-1 1974 (v.108)-
SH/U-1 1958 (v.92)-
XY/N-1 1967 (vol.101)-

Israel annual of public administation and public policy/ Israel Institute of Public Administration. -- Jerusalem, 1976 (vol.15)-
Continues: Public administration in Israel and abroad, 1960-1975 (ISSN 0079-7499)

AD/U-6 1960-73
CA/U-1
HL/U-1 1964-
LO/N-1 1960-72
LO/N17
XY/N-1 1960-73

Israel law review. -- Hebrew University of Jerusalem, 1966-
ISSN 0021-2237

AB/N-1 1966.
AD/U-6
BC-UC
BH/U-1
BL/U-1
CA/U13
CB/U-1
CR/U-1
ED/U-1
EX/U-1
HL/U-1 1966-72 (v.7)
LO/C-3
LO/C47 1966.
LO/R74
LO/U-2
LO/U-3
LO/U11 1971-
LO/U12
LO/U14
LO/U24
LV-LP
LV/U-1 1966-76
MA/U-1
OX/U15
QS/S-7 1966-67
SH/U-1
SO/U-1 1972-
XY/N-1

Israel studies in criminology. -- Tel Aviv, 1970-
ISSN 0075-1391

LO/N-1
LO/U14 1973 (v.2)-
OX/U15
XY/N-1 1973 (v.2)-

Israel yearbook on human rights. -- Tel Aviv, 1971-

AB/N-1 1973 (v.3).
BL/U-1 1973-
CR/U-1
ED/N-1 1973 (v.3).
ED/U-1 1973 (v.3).
HL/U-1 1973 (v.3).
LO/N-1
LO/N17
LO/S14 1971.
LO/U-2
LO/U14
LV/U-1 1973 (v.3).
OX/U15
XY/N-1

Issues in criminology. -- Berkeley, Cal., 1965-1975 (vol.10 no.1)
Absorbed by: Crime and social justice, q.v.
ISSN 0021-2385

BH/U-1 1967 (v.3)-1975
BL/U-1 1975 (v.10 no.1).
CA/U37
CB/U-1 1970 (v.5)-75
CH-CI 1965 (v.1).
LO/C10 1965-72, m/film 1973-
LO/C27 1975 (v.10 no.1).
LO/U-2 1975 (v.10 no.1).
LO/U24
LO/U28 1971-75
QL/D15 1974(v.9)-1975
QW/C73
QW/D12
SH/U-1
XY/N-1

Istanbul Universitesi Hukuk facültesi mecmuasi. -- Istanbul, 1935-

CA/U-1 1944-47
DR/U-4 1953/4 (no.19).
LO/U14

Istorisko-pravni zbornik. -- Sarajevo, 1949-53

OX/U15 1949-50 (no.4)

Iura: rivista internazionale di diritto romano e antico. -- Naples, 1950-
ISSN 0021-3241

AD/U-6	LO/U-2	OX/U15
CA/U-1	LO/U11 1964-	OX/U25
ED/U-1	LO/U24	XY/N-1 1969 (v.20)-
GL/U-1		

Ius canonicum: revista del Instituto Martín de Azpilcueta de la Universidad de Navarra. -- Pamplona, 1961-
ISSN 0021-325X

LO/N-1 1973-

Iustitia. -- Bloomington, Ind., 1973-
ISSN 0092-3524

XY/N-1 1974 (v.2)-

Iustitia. -- Milan, 1948-
ISSN 0021-3268

No holdings notified

Iyunei mishpat <u>see</u> Tel-Aviv University law review

Izvestija Akademii nauk Azerbajdzhanskoj SSR: serija istorii, filosofii i prava. -- Baku,

GL/U-1 Soviet Studies Branch Library 1967-	LO/U14 1966-
	XY/N-1 1966-

Izvestija Adademii nauk SSSR. Otdelenie ekonomiki i prava. -- Moscow,

GL/U-1 Soviet Studies Branch Library 1945-52

Izvestija na Ikonomicheskija i pravnija institut <u>see</u> Izvestija na Instituta za pravni nauki..Bŭlgarska Akademija na naukite

Izvestija na Ikonomicheskija i pravnija institut: serija pravi nauki <u>see</u> next entry

Izvestija na Instituta za pravni nauki... Bŭlgarska Akademija na naukite. -- Sofia, 1954-1974?
Transliterations vary.
Continues: Izvestija na Ikonomicheskija i pravnija Institut, 1950-51, and: Izvestija na Ikonomicheskija i pravnija institut: serija pravni nauki, 1952-53
ISSN 0068-3884

CA/U-1 1950-55;1956-59 imp.;1960-	LO/U-3 imp.	XY/N-1 1950-52 (no.1/2)
LO/N-1	OX/U15 1952-	

Izvestiya vysshikh uchebnikh zavedenii: Pravovedenie. -- Leningrad, 1957-

LO/U-2 1957-69	OX/U15	XY/N-1

JAG bulletin <u>see</u> Air Force law review

JAG journal/ Judge Advocate General of the U.S. Navy. -- Washington, 1947-
ISSN 0021-3519

LO/U-3 1948- LO/U11 1971/72- imp. LO/U24 XY/N-1 1962 (v.16)-

J.P.W.A.: the official organ of the Justices' Association of Western Australia. -- 1957 (vol.1)-
Continues: Magistrate: the official organ of the Justices' Association of Western Australia, 1916-1957 (vol.43 no.7)
ISSN 0447-2314

OX/U15 1961 (v.5)-

Jaarboek - Vereniging voor de vergelijkende studie van het recht van België en Nederland. -- Antwerp, 1947-1970 (vol.12)

LO/N-1 LO/U24 OX/U15 XY/N-1 1969/70 (v.12).

Jahrbuch - Internationale Gesellschaft für Urheberrecht. -- Berlin; Vienna, 1964-
Parallel texts in various languages
ISSN 0539-1512

LO/U24 OX/U15

Jahrbuch - Internationale Vereinigung für Gewerblichen Rechtsschutz = Yearbook - International Association for the Protection of Industrial Property. -- Berlin, 1897-1912?

LO/N-1 1904.

Jahrbuch der Akademie für Deutsches Recht. -- Munich, 1933-1940 (Bd.7)

LO/U24 (w.Bd.3;4) OX/U15 1933-38

Jahrbuch der Basler Juristenfakultät. -- Basle, 1924-

LO/N-1 32 (1953)- OX/U15

Jahrbuch der Internationalen Vereinigung für Vergleichende Rechtswissenschaft und Volkswirtschaftslehre zu Berlin. -- Berlin, 1895-1914 (vol.9)

AD/U-6 CA/U13 1898-1914 imp. LO/N-1 LO/U-3 1896-1914 imp.

Jahrbuch der preussischen Forst- und Jagd- Gesetzgebung und Verwaltung. -- Berlin, 1869-1905 (Bd.37)

LO/N-1

Jahrbuch des Arbeitsrechts und der damit zusammenhängenden Teile der Sozialökonomik. -- Mannheim, 1919-1931 (Bd.12)

LO/U-3 1918-25

Jahrbuch des deutschen Rechtes. -- Berlin, 1903-1942 (N.F. Bd.9)

LO/U24 1903-22; 1940-42

Jahrbuch des gemeinen deutschen Rechts. -- Leipzig, 1857-1863 (Bd.6)

LO/N-1

Jahrbuch des öffentlichen Rechts der Gegenwart. -- Tübingen, 1907-1914, 1920-1939 (Bd.25), 1951 (Bd.1 N.F.)-

BL/U-1 1966-75
CA/U-1
CA/U13 1951-
ED/U-1 1951-
EX/U-1 1974-
LC/U-1 1951-
LO/N-1
LO/U-3
LO/U24 1925-32;1961-
LV/U-1 1926 imp.,1927.
OX/U15
OX/U25
XY/N-1 1966 (Bd.15)-

Jahrbuch des Steuerrechts. -- Berlin, 1920-1931 (Bd.12)

LO/U-3 1925-31 imp.
LO/U24 1920-25 (Bd.6)

Jahrbuch des Strafrechts und Strafprozesses. -- Hannover, 1906-1921 (Bd.15)

LO/U24 1906-16 (Bd.11) (w.Bd.9)

Jahrbuch des Völkerrechts. -- Munich, 1913-1926 (Bd.9)

AD/U-6 1913-14
BL/U-1 1913-14
CA/U13 1913-14
GL/U-1
LO/N-1
LO/U-3
LO/U24
QS/S-7 1913.

Jahrbuch für den internationalen Rechtsverkehr. -- Munich, 1912-1913 (Bd.1)

LO/U-3

Jahrbuch für Gesetzgebung, Verwaltung und Rechtspflege des Deutschen Reiches <u>see</u> Zeitschrift für Wirtschafts- und Sozialwissenschaften

Jahrbuch für Gesetzgebung, Verwaltung und Volkswirtschaft im Deutschen Reiche <u>see</u> Zeitschrift für Wirtschafts- und Sozialwissenschaften

Jahrbuch für internationales Recht <u>see</u> German yearbook of international law...

Jahrbuch für internationales und ausländisches öffentliches Recht <u>see</u> German yearbook of international law...

Jahrbuch für Ostrecht. -- Munich, 1960-
ISSN 0075-2746

GL/U-1 Soviet Studies Branch Library
LO/N-1 1960.
LO/U-3
LO/U11
LO/U24 1962 (Bd.3)-
OX/U15
XY/N-1 1969 (Bd.10)-

Jahrbuch für Rechtssoziologie und Rechtstheorie. -- Bielefeld, 1970-

LO/N-1
OX/U15

Jahrbücher der deutschen Rechtswissenschaft und Gesetzgebung. -- Erlangen, 1855-1873 (Bd.14)

GL/U-1 1855-67
LO/N-1
LO/U24

Jahrbücher der gesammten deutschen juristischen Literatur. -- Erlangen, 1826-1836 (Bd.27)

CA/U-1
LO/N-1

Jahrbücher der Gesetzgebung und Rechtspflege im Königreiche Baiern. -- Erlangen, 1810-1820 (Bd.3)

LO/N-1

Jahrbücher der Gesetzgebung und Rechtspflege im Königreiche Würtemberg. -- Stuttgart, 1824-1834 (Bd.4)

LO/N-1

Jahrbücher der Gesetzgebung und Rechtspflege in Sachsen. -- Neustadt, 1829-1831 (Bd.3)

LO/N-1

Jahrbücher der Württembergischen Rechtspflege. -- Tübingen, 1888-1920 (Bd.29)
Absorbed by: Zeitschrift für die freiwillige Gerichtsbarkeit und die Gemeindeverwaltung in Württemberg, q.v.

LO/U11

Jahrbücher für die Dogmatik des heutigen römischen und deutschen Privatrechts see Jherings Jahrbücher für die Dogmatik des bürgerlichen Rechts

Jahrbücher für die preussische Gesetzgebung, Rechtswissenschaft und Rechtsverwaltung. -- Berlin, 1814-1845 (Bd.66)

LO/N-1

Jahrbücher für historische und dogmatische Bearbeitung des römischen Rechts. -- Brunswick, 1841-1844 (Bd.3)

LO/N-1

Jahresbericht über Schrifttum und Rechtsprechung zum gewerblichen Rechtsschutz,Urheber-, Wettbewerbs- und Kartellrecht. -- Berlin, 1933-1962
Title varies slightly
ISSN 0447-2780

LO/N14 1933-61 LO/U24 1933-40

Jaipur law journal. -- Jaipur, 1961-
ISSN 0448-1755

BL/U-1 1965- LO/U14 1962-

Jamaica law journal see West Indian law journal

Japan annual of law and politics. -- Tokyo, 1952-
ISSN 0075-3157

CA/U-1	LO/N-1	OX/U-1
DR/U-4 1953.	LO/U-3	SH/U-1 1962-
GL/U-1	LO/U14 1953;1957-	XY/N-1 1967 (no.15)-
LO/U-2 1952-53;1957-64;1970-	LV/U-1	

Japan science review: law and politics. -- Tokyo, 1950-1962 (no.12)
ISSN 0448-8725

CA/U-1 1950-59	LO/U-3 1950-59 (no. 10) (w.no.9)	LV/U-1 1952-62
DR/U-4 1953.		OX/U-1 1950-60
LO/U-2 1950-54; 1956-60	LO/U14	

Japanese annual of international law. -- Tokyo, 1957-
ISSN 0448-8806

BH/U-1	LO/U-2	LO/U24
CA/U13	LO/U-3	OX/U15
LD/U-1 1960 (no.4).	LO/U14	XY/N-1 1966 (no.10)-

Japanese journal of legal medicine see Nippon hoigaku zasshi

Javna uprava/ Sekretariat izvrsnega sveta za obco upravo v ljubljani. -- Ljubljana, 1959-
Continues: Ljudska uprava, 1948-1958
ISSN 0446-687X

LO/N-1 1957-

Jernal undang undang see Journal of Malaysian and comparative law

Jewish yearbook of international law. -- Jerusalem, 1949 (1948).
No more published

CA/U13	LO/U-3	LO/U24
LO/N-1	LO/U14	OX/U15
LO/U-2		

Jherings Jahrbücher für die Dogmatik des bürgerlichen Rechts. -- Jena, 1897 [Bd.37]-1943 (Bd.90)
Continues: Jahrbücher für die Dogmatik des heutigen römischen und deutschen Privatrechts, 1857-1892, and: Jherings Jahrbücher für die Dogmatik des heutigen römischen und deutschen Privatrechts, 1893 (Bd.32)-1896

LO/N-1 LO/U-2 OX/U15

Jherings Jahrbücher für die Dogmatik des heutigen römischen und deutschen Privatrechts see previous entry

Jogtudományi közlöny. -- Budapest, 1946-
ISSN 0021-7166

LO/N-1 1950- LO/U-3 1953-77 imp. XY/N-1 1953-58 imp., 1961-

John Marshall journal of practice and procedure. -- Chicago, 1967-
ISSN 0021-7212

LO/U24 1971 (v.5)- XY/N-1 1977 (v.10 no.2)-

John Marshall law quarterly. -- Chicago, 1935-1943 (vol.8)

LO/U24 imp. OX/U15

Jornal de direito comparativo e internacional para os países do sul da Africa see Comparative and international law journal of southern Africa

Jornal do fôro: revista trimestral de estudos jurídicos. -- Lisbon, 1937-

LO/U24 1960-66

Journal - American Academy of Matrimonial Lawyers. -- Chicago, 1970-

No holdings notified

Journal - Bar Association of the District of Columbia. -- Washington D.C., 1974 (vol.41).
Continues: Journal of the Bar Association of the District of Columbia, 1934-1966, and: D.C. Bar journal, 1967-1973
Ceased publication
ISSN 0012-4052

LO/U24 1972-74 XY/N-1 1974 (v.41).

Journal - Canadian Bar Association see National/ Canadian Bar Association

Journal - Cincinnati Bar Association. -- Cincinnati, Ohio, 1973-
ISSN 0094-2243

No holdings notified

Journal - Forensic Science Society. -- Harrogate, Sept. 1960-1966 (vol.6)

XY/N-1

Journal - Oklahoma Bar Association. -- Oklahoma City, 1930-
ISSN 0030-1655

No holdings notified

Journal de droit comparé et international des pays de l'Afrique australe see Comparative and international law journal of southern Africa

Journal de jurisprudence. -- Paris, (1800?)-1806

LO/N-1

Journal de jurisprudence hellénique et étrangère see Ephemeris hellenikes kai allodapes nomologias

Journal des avoués ou recueil général des lois. -- Paris, 1812-1906 (vol.47 3rd series)

LO/N-1

Journal des notaires et des avocats. -- Paris, 1808-

LO/N-1 1808-1925 (1-121)

Journal des sociétés civiles et commerciales: revue pratique de jurisprudence, de doctrine et de législation, 1880-1974 (vol.95)
Absorbed by: Revue des sociétés: jurisprudence, doctrine, législation française et étrangère, q.v.

LO/U-3 1947-   LO/U24 1935-74

Journal des tribunaux. -- Brussels, 1881-
ISSN 0021-812X

ED/U-1 1952-   SO/U-1 1970-76   XY/N-1 1966 (v.81)-
LO/U24 1960-

Journal des tribunaux d'outre-mer: périodique judiciaire du Congo et du Ruanda-Urundi. -- Brussels, 1950-1960 (vol.11)
ISSN 0446-9712

LO/U24

Journal des tribunaux de commerce. -- Paris, 1852-(1938 (v.84)?)

LO/N-1

Journal du droit criminel, ou Jurisprudence criminelle du royaume de la France. -- Paris, 1833-1889 (vol.60)
Continues: Jurisprudence criminelle du royaume, 1829-1832 (vol.4).
Absorbed by: Journal du ministère public et du droit criminel,q.v.

LO/N-1 1833-89

Journal du droit international. -- Paris, 1915 (vol.42)-
Continues: Journal du droit international privé, 1874-1914
ISSN 0021-8170

AB/N-1 1874-1945; 1950-54;1960-	HL/U-1 1874-1939	LO/U12 1967-
AD/U-6	LC/U-1 1969 (v.96)-	LO/U24
BH/U-1	LD/C-1 1967-	LV/U-1 1874/75;1880-1945;1950-
BL/U-1 1920- imp.	LD/U-1 1921-	MA/U-1
CA/U13	LO-MT	NO/U-1 1960,1963,1966-
ED/S11	LO/N-1 1874-1939	OX/U15
ED/U-1 1874;1886-1953(1-2);1954-	LO/N17 1874-1926;1940-45	OX/U25
GL/U-1 1940- imp.	LO/U-2 1940-	QS/S-4
	LO/U-3 imp.	QS/S-6 1940-
	LO/U11 1963-	XY/N-1 1940 (v.67)-

Journal du droit international privé <u>see</u> previous entry

Journal du ministère public et du droit criminel. -- Paris, 1858-1914 (vol.56)
Absorbed: Journal du droit criminel ou Jurisprudence criminelle du royaume de la France, q.v.

LO/N-1

Journal du Palais, 1791-1924 <u>see</u> Recueil Sirey

Journal of administration overseas. -- London, 1966 (vol.5 no.2)-
Continues: Journal of African administration, 1949-1961 (vol.13), and: Journal of local administration overseas, 1962 (vol.1)-1966
ISSN 0021-8472

AB/N-1 1949-61	HL/U-1 1961-76	LV/U-1 1958-
AB/U-1 1965-	LD/U-1 1966-	MA/P-1
AD/U-6 1974-	LO/C-3 1973-	OX/U-9
BH/U-1	LO/N-1	QS/Q12 1969-
BR/U-1	LO/N17 1949-61;1965-	QS/Q29
BT/U-1 1949-61;1966-	LO/N26	QW/C73
CA/U-1	LO/S14 1949-61	RE/U-1 1949-50 imp., 1952-61 imp., 1962-
CB/U-1 1966-	LO/S65	SW/U-1 1950-55 imp., 1962-
CV/U-1 1964 (v.3)-	LO/U-2 1953-	XY/N-1
DR/U-1	LO/U-3	
ED/N-1	LO/U14	
EX/U-1 1958-61	LO/U24	
GL/U-1	LV-LP 1972- (w.1972 v.11 no.2)	
GL/U-2 1956 (v.8)-		

Journal of African administration <u>see</u> previous entry

Journal of African law. -- London, 1957-
ISSN 0021-8553

AB/N-1 1957-74	CA/U-1 1971-	HL/U-1 1960-
AD/U-6 1970-	CA/U13	KL/U-1 1957-73 (v.17)
BH/U-1	CR/U-1	LA/U-1 1957-73
BL/U-1	ED/S11	LD/U-1 1966-
BT/U-1 1957-76 (w.v.8 no.1)	ED/U-1	LO/C15
	EX/U-1	LO-MT

(cont'd)

Journal of African law (cont'd).

LO/N-1
LO/N17
LO/U-2 1957-58
LO/U-3
LO/U11 1960-
LO/U14
LO/U24
LV/U-1 1957-75
MA/U-1
OX/U15
QS/S-4
QS/S-6
QS/S-7
RE/U-1
SH/U-1
SO/U-1
XY/N-1

Journal of air law and commerce. -- Dallas, 1930-
ISSN 0021-8642

AD/U-6 1961 (v.28)-
BH/U-1 1974-
CA/U13
ED/U-1
LO/C-5 1947 (v.14)- imp.
LO/C47 1958-
LO/U-2
LO/U-3
LO/U11
LO/U24
OX/U15
XY/N-1 1930-59 imp., 1960 (v.27)-

Journal of business law. -- London, 1957-
ISSN 0021-9460

AB/N-1
AB/U-1
AD/U-6 1957-60;1962-63;1967-
BC-UC 1961-
BH-LS
BH/U-1
BL-LS
BL/U-1
BR/U-1
BT/U-1 1967-
CA/U-1
CA/U13
CB/U-1
CH-CI 1962-
CR/U-1 1963-
CV/C-1
CV/U-1
DN/U-1 1957-67 imp., 1970-
DR/U-1
ED/S11
ED-SLC 1966-71
ED/U-1 1958; 1961-
EX/U-1
GL/U-1
GL/U-2
HL/U-1
KL/U-1 1961-
LC/C-1
LC/U-1
LD/C-1 1957-58;1961-62;1964-
LD/U-1
LO/C-3 1960-
LO/C-5
LO/C10 1957-69;1971-
LO/C14 1958-
LO/C15
LO/C18 1966-
LO/C25 1966-
LO/C27
LO/C47
LO-CBL*
LO-MT
LO/N-1
LO/N-5 1961-
LO/N26 last 10 years
LO/P-6
LO/R74
LO/S28 1957-
LO-TS 1966-
LO/U-2
LO/U-3
LO/U11
LO/U12 (w.1965)
LO/U24
LO/U28 1961;1963-
LV-LP 1963-
LV/P-1 (w.1962;1966)
LV/U-1
MA/P-1 (w. Oct.1965)
MA/U-1
NO/U-1
NW/U-1 1961-72
OX/U15
QE/C76 1961-
QG/C25 1964-
QL/D15 1960-
QM/C48 1963-
QM/C68 1966-
QN/C70
QS/Q12 1958-
QS/Q13 1973-
QS/S-4 1968-
QS/S-6 1961;1968-
QS/S-7
QW/D12
RE/U-1
SH/U-1
SO/U-1
XM/C10 1961-68;1970-
XY/N-1

Journal of Ceylon law. -- Colombo, 1970-

LO/N-1
LO/U24 1970-71
OX/U15 1970 (v.1 nos.1-2).
XY/N-1 1970-71

Journal of church and state. -- Waco, Tex., 1959-
ISSN 0021-969X

CA/U-1
HL/U-1 1969 (v.11)-
LO/U24
OX/U-1 1966-
XY/N-1 1967 (v.9)-

Journal of college and university law. -- Washington D.C., 1973-
ISSN 0093-8688

No holdings notified

Journal of Common Market studies. -- Oxford, 1962-
ISSN 0021-9886

AB/U-1
AD/U-6
BC-UC 1977-
BH/P-1
BL/U-1
BR/U-1
BT/U-1
CA/U-1
CA/U13
CB/U-1
CC/U-1
CR/U-1
DN/U-1
DR/U-1
ED/N-1
ED/U-1
EX/U-1
GL/U-1
GL/U-2
HL/U-1
KL/U-1
LA/U-1
LC/C-1
LC/U-1
LD/C-1 1966/67 (v.5)-
LD/P-1 1963-
LD/U-1 1963-
LO/C-3 1970 (v.9)-
LO/C-5 1966 (v.5)- imp.
LO/C10
LO/C14 1971/72 (v.10)-
LO/C15 1970-
LO/C25 1970-
LO/C27 1968-
LO/C47
LO-CBL*
LO/N-1
LO/N-5
LO/N17
LO/N26
LO/N46 1969-
LO/P-6
LO/S14
LO/U-1
LO/U-2
LO/U-3
LO/U24
LO/U28
LV-LP
LV/P-1
LV/U-1
MA/P-1
NW/U-1 1968-
OX/U-1
OX/U15
QM/C68 1974-
QN/C70 1966 (v.5)-
QS/S-6
QW/C73 1975- imp.
QW/D12
RE/U-1
SH/U-1
SO/U-1
SW/U-1
XM/C10
XY/N-1
YK/U-1 1964-

Journal of comparative legislation and international law. -- London, 1918 (vol.18, 2nd series)-1951 (vol.33, 3rd series)
Continues: Journal of the Society of Comparative Legislation, 1896-1917 (vol.17, 2nd series)
Merged with: International law quarterly, q.v., to become: International and comparative law quarterly, q.v.

AB/N-1
AB/U-1 1896-1951 imp.
AD/U-6
BH-LS 1899-1951
BH/P-1 1907-17; 1919-51
BH/U-1
BL/U-1
BR/U-1 1910-51
CA/U-1
CA/U13
CB/U-1
CR/U-1 1940-51
DN/U-1
DR/U-1 1904-13;1918.
ED/S10
ED/S11
ED/U-1
GL/U-1
HL/U-1 1896-1951
LA/U-1 1900-51 imp.
LC/U-1 1920-51 (ser. 3, v.2-33)
LD/U-1 1921-51
LO-MT
LO/N-1
LO/N-5 1929-51
LO/N14 1919-31
LO/N17
LO/N26 1919-51
LO/N46
LO-PC imp.
LO/S14 1945-51
LO/S55 1922 (3rd series v.4 no.2) -1951 (w.1942 nos.3-4)
LO/S65 1921-51
LO-SC 1896-1936
LO-TS 1901-50
LO/U-1
LO/U-2 1896-7;1907-51
LO/U-3 1897-1951
LO/U11 1899-1951
LO/U14 1921-51 imp.
LO/U24

(cont'd)

Journal of comparative legislation and international law (cont'd).

LV/P-1 imp.
LV/U-1 1919-51 (1920 imp.)
MA/P-1 1916-51
OX/U15
OX/U25
QS/Q12 1911-48 imp.
QS/S-4 1903/04;1907-16;1922-40; 1946-51
QS/S-6
QS/S-7
QS/S-8
RE/U-1
SO/U-1 1919-51
XY/N-1 1899-1951

Journal of conflict resolution: research on war and peace between and within nations. -- Beverly Hills, Cal., 1957-
ISSN 0022-0027

AB/U-1 imp.
BL/U-1 1968-
BR/U-1
BT/U-1
CB/U-1
CV/U-1 1967-
GL/U-1
HL/U-1 1964-
LC/U-1 1961 (v.5)-
LO/C14 1968-75
LO/N-1 Mar.1958 (v.2)-
LO/S14 1966 (v.10)-
LO/U-1 1963- (w.1974 (v.18 nos.1-2))
LO/U-2
LO/U-3
LO/U14 1964-
LO/U28 1969 (v.13)-
LV-LP (w.1957 v.1 no.3;1959,v.3 no.3;1961 v.5 no.1)
QM/C48 1970-76
QM/C68 1974-
QN/C70 1973-
QW/D12
RE/U-1
SH/U-1 1974-
SO/U-1
SW/U-1 1965 (v.9)-
XY/N-1 1960 (v.4)-
YK/U-1 1964-

Journal of contemporary law. -- Salt Lake City, Utah, 1974-

XY/N-1

Journal of contemporary Roman-Dutch law <u>see</u> Tydskrif vir hedendaagse romeins-hollandse reg

Journal of corporation law. -- Iowa City, Iowa, 1975-

No holdings notified

Journal of criminal justice. -- New York, 1973-
ISSN 0047-2352

AB/N-1
CA/U-1
CA/U37
ED/N-1
HL/U-1 1973-74 (v.2)
LO/C15
LO/N27
LO-SC 1977 (v.5)-
LO/U24
OX/U15
QN/C70
SH/U-1
XY/N-1

Journal of criminal law. -- Hertford, 1937-
ISSN 0022-0183

AB/N-1
AB/U-1
AD/U-6 1939-
BH-LS
BL/U-1 1953-55
CA/U-1
CA/U13
CA/U37 1960-71 (v.27-35)
CB/U-1 1961 (v.25)-
CH-CI 1974-
CR/U-1 1971-
ED/S10 1937-56
ED/S11
ED/U-1 1965-
EX/U-1 1948-
GL/U-1 1937-56
GL/U-2 1967-
HL/U-1
KL/U-1 1949 (v.13)-
LC/C-1 1938-
LC/U-1
LD/C-1 1970 (v.34)-
LD/U-1 1969-
LO/C-3
LO/C15 1974-
LO/C25 1973- (cont'd)

Journal of criminal law (cont'd).

LO-MT	LV/U-1 1937-41;1961; 1964-	QS/Q12 1971-
LO/N-1	MA/U-1 1962 (v.26)-	QS/S-4
LO/N-5 1937-	NO/U-1 1960 (v.24)-	QS/S-6
LO/N27	NW/U-1 1971-75	QW/C73
LO-TS 1973-	OX/U15	QW/D12
LO/U-2 1937-76	QG/C25 1976-	RE/U-1 1937-47;1965; 1974-
LO/U-3 1940-47; 1949-	QL/D15 1975-	SH/U-1 1937-74
LO/U11	QM/C48 1964 (v.28)-	SO/U-1 1954-
LO/U24	QN/C70 1973-	XY/N-1 1968-
LO/U28 1965- imp.		

Journal of criminal law = Keiho zasshi. -- Tokyo, 1949-
Title and contents page in English, text in Japanese
ISSN 0022-0191

XY/N-1 1966 (v.15)-

Journal of criminal law and criminology. -- Baltimore, Md., 1941 (vol.32)-1951 (vol.41), 1973 (vol.64)-
Continues: Journal of the American Institute of Criminal Law and Criminology, 1910-1941 (vol.31); and: Journal of criminal law, criminology and police science, 1951 (vol.42)-1972 (vol.63)
Absorbed: American journal of police science, 1930-1932, q.v.
In 1973 police science section became separate publication: Journal of police science and administration, q.v.
ISSN 0091-4169

AB/U-1 1960-	LC/U-1 1960-	LO/U24
AD/U-6 1970-	LO/C-3 1968-	LO/U28 1971-
BH/U-1 1945-	LO/C15 1972-	MA/U-1 1968-
BL/U-1 1966-	LO/C27 1973-	NO/U-1
BT/U-1 1960-	LO/C47 1973-	OX/U15
CA/U13 imp.	LO/M32 1950-51 imp., 1956-65; 1968-70	QN/C70 1965-
CA/U37 1910-72	LO-MT 1944-56	QW/C73 1950-
CB/U-1 1961-	LO/N-1 1910-21;1964-	RE/U-1 1960-
CR/U-1 1949-	LO/N27 1935-	SH/U-1 1955-
DR/U-1 1963-	LO/U-2 1974-	SO/U-1 1967-
ED/U-1 1932-	LO/U-3 1921-	SW/U-1 1959-
EX/U-1 1966-	LO/U11 1976-	XY/N-1
HL/U-1 1910-72		YK/U-1 1960-
KL/U-1 1910-72		

Journal of criminal law, criminology and police science <u>see</u> previous entry

Journal of criminal science. -- London, 1948, 1950 (vol.2).
Ceased publication

BH/U-1	LO/N-1	OX/U25
BL/U-1 1950.	LO/U-1	QS/S-4 1948.
CA/U13	LO/U-2	RE/U-1
ED/S11	LO/U-3	SH/U-1
ED/U-1	LO/U24	SO/U-1
GL/U-1	LV/P-1	SW/U-1 1948.
HL/U-1	LV/U-1	
LO-MT	OX/U15	

Journal of Ethiopian law. -- Addis Ababa, 1964-
ISSN 0022-0914

BL/U-1	LO/U14	OX/U15
CA/U13	LO/U24 1964-73 (v.9 no.1)	XY/N-1 1966 (v.3)-

Journal of family law. -- Louisville, Ky., 1961-
ISSN 0022-1066

AD/U-6 1973/74 (v.13 no.4).	ED/U-1	LO/U24
BH/U-1 1967-	HL/U-1	OX/U15
BL/U-1 1966-	KL/U-1 1961-73 (v.12)	SO/U-1 1969-
CA/U13	LO/C14	XY/N-1 1966 (v.6 no.2)-
CR/U-1	LO/C15 1972-	
	LO/U-3	

Journal of forensic medicine <u>see</u> Forensic science

Journal of forensic sciences: the official publication of the American Academy of Forensic Sciences. -- Chicago, Ill., 1956-
ISSN 0022-1198

AD/U-6	LD/U-1	LO/U24 1972-
GL/U-2	LO/M32 1966-	XY/N-1

Journal of health politics, policy and law. -- Durham, N.C., 1975-

XY/N-1

Journal of international law and diplomacy <u>see</u> Kokusaihō gaikō zasshi

Journal of international law and economics. -- Washington D.C., 1970 (vol.5 no.2)-
Continues: Studies in law and economic development, 1966-1967, and: Journal of law and economic development, 1968-1970
ISSN 0022-2003

CV/U-1 1970 (v.5 no.2)-	LO/U14	OX/U15
	LO/U24	XY/N-1 1968 (v.3 no.2)-

Journal of Islamic and comparative law. -- Zaria, Nigeria, 1968 (vol.2)-
Continues: Journal of the Centre of Islamic Legal Studies, (1966)

BL/U-1	LO/U14	OX/U15
CA/U13 1966-69	LO/U24	

Journal of jurisprudence: a new series of the American law journal [q.v.]. -- Philadelphia, 1821 (vol.1).
Cited as vol.7 of the American law journal

ED/S11	LO/N-1

Journal of jurisprudence and Scottish law magazine. -- Edinburgh, 1857-1891 (vol.35)
Absorbed: Scottish law magazine and Sheriff Court reporter, q.v.

AD/U-6
CA/U-1 1863-91
ED/S10
ED/S11
ED/U-1
GL/U-1
GL/U-2
LO-MT
LO/N-1
LO/U24
OX/U15 1863 (Nov.)-1891
QS/S-7 1865-91

Journal of juristic papyrology. -- Warsaw, 1946-

AB/N-1
BL/U-1 1950- imp.
CA/U-1
ED/U-1
KL/U-1 1946-56 (v.10) imp.
LO/U-1
LO/U-2
LO/U24
OX/U15
XY/N-1 1953/4 (v.7/8); 1971 (v.16/17)-

Journal of law. -- Philadelphia, 1830-1831 (no.24)
Ceased publication

LO/N-1
QS/S-7 1830.

Journal of law and commerce <u>see</u> Journal of the Law and Commerce Society

Journal of law and economic development <u>see</u> Journal of international law and economics

Journal of law and economics. -- Chicago, 1958-
ISSN 0022-2186

AB/U-1
AD/U-1
BC-UC 1958-68;1974-
BH/U-1
BL/U-1
BR/U-1
BT/U-1 1968-
CA/U13
CB/U-1
CC/U-1
CR/U-1
CV/U-1
DN/U-1
DR/U-1
ED/U-1
EX/U-1 1958-72
GL/U-1 1960-
HL/U-1
KL/U-1
LC/C-1 1973-
LC/U-1
LD/C-1 1973-
LO/C-3 1965-
LO/C-5 1974-
LO/C10
LO/C18
LO/C25 1971-
LO/C27 1972-
LO/N-1 1968-
LO/N-5
LO/U-2 1969-
LO/U-3
LO/U24
LO/U28 1967 (v.10)-
LV-LP 1974-
LV/U-1 1973-
MA/P-1 1966-
NW/U-1 1961-
OX/U15
QE/C76 1959;1961-62; 1964-72
QL/D15 1970-
QM/C48 1972-
QM/C68 1970-
QN/C70 1968-
QW/D12 1974 (v.16)-
RE/U-1
SH/U-1 1975 (v.18)-
SO/U-1 1964-
SW/U-1 1963;1965-
XY/N-1
YK/U-1 1962-

Journal of law and education. -- Silver Spring, Md., 1972-

No holdings notified

Journal of law and politics <u>see</u> Hōsei-kenkyū

Journal of law reform <u>see</u> University of Michigan journal of law reform

Journal of legal and political sociology. -- New York, 1942-1947 (vol.4)

LC/U-1 1943-47 imp.	LO/U-3	LO/U24 imp.

Journal of legal education. -- Lexington, Ky., 1948-
Continues: American law school review, 1903-1947 (vol.10)
ISSN 0022-2208

AB/U-1 1959-61 imp.	GL/U-1	LO/U24 1903-47 imp., 1948-
AD/U-6 1969-	HL/U-1 1948-	LO/U28
BC-UC 1957-75	LC/U-1 (w.v.17-19 no.2)	LV/U-1 1961-76
BH/U-1 1948-	LD/U-1 1948-	MA/U-1 1948-
BL/U-1 1948-	LO/C-3 1976-	NO/U-1 1948-
BR/U-1 1965-	LO/C10 1973 (v.25)-	OX/U15 1948-
CA/U13 1948-	LO/C15 1971-	QL/D15 1971/72-
CH-CI 1948-71 (v.23)	LO/C25 1971-	RE/U-1 1974 (v.26)-
CR/U-1	LO/C47 1952-63	SH/U-1
CV/C-1 1968 (v.21)-	LO/U12 1962-	XY/N-1 1966 (v.19)-
CV/U-1 1948-		
ED/U-1 1948-		

Journal of legal medicine (Berlin) <u>see</u> Zeitschrift für Rechtsmedizin

Journal of legal medicine. -- Chicago, 1973-
ISSN 0093-1748

XY/N-1 1977 (v.5)-

Journal of legal studies. -- Chicago, 1972-
ISSN 0047-2530

BL/U-1	LO-MT	OX/U15
CA/U13	LO/N-1	QL/D15 1974-
CB/U-1 1974 (v.3)-	LO/U-3 1974 (v.3)-	QW/C73
CR/U-1	LO/U12	SH/U-1 1974 (v.3)-
CV/U-1 (w.v.2)	LO/U24	XY/N-1 1972 (v.1 no.2)-
LO/C15	LV/U-1 1972-76	
LO/C25 1973-		

Journal of local administration overseas <u>see</u> Journal of administration overseas

Journal of Malaysian and comparative law = Jernal undang undang. -- Kuala Lumpur, 1974-

CA/U13	LO/U24	OX/U15
LO/U14		

Journal of maritime law and commerce. -- Cincinnati, Ohio, 1969-
ISSN 0022-2410

AD/U-6 1976-
BH/U-1
CA/U13
LO/C47
LO-MT
LO/N-5
LO/N17 1974 (v.6)-
LO/U-2
LO/U-3
LO/U24
OX/U15
SO/U-1
XY/N-1

Journal of offender therapy <u>see</u> International journal of offender therapy and comparative criminology

Journal of peace research. -- Oslo, 1964-
ISSN 0022-3433

AB/U-1
BL/U-1 1974-
BT/U-1
CA/U13
CB/U-1 1970-
GL/U-1 1967-
HL/U-1
LD/U-1 1965-
LO/U-3
LO/U28 1969-
LV-LP 1969- (w.1971, v.8)
SO/U-1 1968-
XY/N-1
YK/U-1 1970-

Journal of planning and environment law. -- London, 1973-
Continues: Journal of planning law, 1948-1953 and: Journal of planning and property law, 1954-1972 (ISSN 0022-376X)
1953 absorbed: Current property law, q.v.
ISSN 0307-4870

AB/N-1
AB/U-1
AD/U-6 1967-
BH-LS 1948-70
BH/U-1
BL/U-1 1966-
BR/U-1 1966-
BT/U-1 1954-
CA/U-1
CA/U13
CB/U-1 (w.1953-56)
CH-CI 1973-
CV/C-1 1973-
CV/U-1 1973-
DN/U-1 1968-
DR/U-1
ED/S10
ED/S11
ED-SLC 1957-65
ED/U-1
EX/U-1
GL/U-1 (w.1957-63)
GL/U-2 1963-
HL/U-1
LC/C-1
LC/U-1 1954-
LD/C-1
LD/U-1
LO/C-5 1974-
LO/C10
LO/C15
LO/C25 1966-
LO/C47 1972-
LO-CBL last 5 years
LO-MT 1954-72
LO/N-1
LO/N-5
LO/N26
LO/R74
LO/S28
LO-SC
LO-TS
LO/U-1
LO/U-2
LO/U-3
LO/U11
LO/U12 1948-72 (w.Jan.-Mar. 1948)
LO/U24
LO/U28
LV/U-1
MA/U-1
NO/U-1
NW/U-1 1948-72
OX/U15
QE/C76
QG/C25 1974-
QL/D15
QM/C48 1973-
QM/C68
QN/C70
QS/Q12 1958-
QS/S-4
QS/S-6
QS/S-7
QS/S-8
QW/D12 1959-
RE/U-1
SH/U-1
SO/U-1
XM/C10
XY/N-1

Journal of planning and property law <u>see</u> previous entry

Journal of planning law <u>see</u> Journal of planning and environment law

Journal of police science and administration. -- Gaithersburg, Md., 1973-
Continues in part: Journal of criminal law, criminology and police science, afterwards Journal of criminal law and criminology, q.v.
ISSN 0090-9084

AD/U-6	LO/N-1	QW/C73
BH/U-1	LO/N27 1973-	RE/U-1
CA/U37	LO/U-3	SH/U-1
HL/U-1	LO/U24	SO/U-1
LO/C-3	MA/U-1	XY/N-1

Journal of products liability. -- Oxford, 1977-

OX/U15

Not on checklist circulated, so other holdings possible

Journal of psychiatry and law. -- New York, 1973-
ISSN 0093-1853

CA/U37 1976 (v.4)-   XY/N-1 1974 (v.2)-

Journal of public administration (London) see Public administration

Journal of public administration (Wellington) see New Zealand journal of public administration

Journal of public law see Emory law journal

Journal of radio law. -- Chicago, 1931-1932 (vol.2)

AD/U-6	CA/U13	LO/U24

Journal of reprints for antitrust law and economics. -- New York, 1969-
ISSN 0022-4243

BH/U-1	LO/U-2 1969-73 (v.5)	LO/U24
LO/N-5	LO/U-3 1969-73 (v.5)	XY/N-1

Journal of research in crime and delinquency. -- New York, 1964-
ISSN 0022-4278

AB/U-1	LD/U-1 1965-	OX/U15
BH/U-1 1965-	LO/N-1	QW/C73 1973 (July)-
CA/U37	LO/N27	RE/U-1 1966 (v.3) imp., 1967-
CB/U-1	LO/U-3	SH/U-1
CR/U-1 1971.	LO/U24 1964-69; 1970-72 imp.	SW/U-1 1968-
ED/U-1	MA/U-1	XY/N-1
HL/U-1		
KL/U-1 1972 (v.9)-		

Journal of social philosophy see next entry

Journal of social philosophy and jurisprudence. -- New York, 1942 (vol.7).
Continues: Journal of social philosophy, 1935-1941 (vol.6)

EX/U-1 1935-38 LO/N-1 LO/U-3 imp.

Journal of South African law see Tydskrif vir die Suid-Afrikaanse reg

Journal of space law. -- University, Miss., 1973-

CA/U13 1975 (v.3)- XY/N-1 1973 (v.1 no.2)-

Journal of taxation: a national journal of current news and comment for professional tax men. -- New York, 1954-
ISSN 0022-4863

LO/U24 1972 (v.36)- XY/N-1 1966 (v.24)-

Journal of the American Institute of Criminal Law and Criminology see Journal of criminal law and criminology

Journal of the American Judicature Society see Judicature

Journal of the American Trial Lawyers' Association. -- Cambridge, Mass., 1965 (vol.31)-
Continues: NACCA law journal, 1948-1964 (vol.30)

LO-MT
LO/U24
OX/U15
QS/S-6
QS/S-7 1948-72
XY/N-1 1965-70 (v.31-34)

Journal of the Association of Law Teachers see Law teacher: journal of the Association of Law Teachers

Journal of the Bar Association of the District of Columbia see Journal - Bar Association of the District of Columbia

Journal of the Bar Association of the State of Kansas see Journal of the Kansas Bar Association

Journal of the Beverly Hills Bar Association. -- Beverly Hills, Cal., 1967-
ISSN 0045-1827

LO/U24 1971 imp., 1972-

Journal of the Centre of Islamic Legal Studies see Journal of Islamic and comparative law

Journal of the Denning Law Society see Dar es Salaam University law journal

Journal of the Forensic Science Society. -- Harrogate, 1960-
ISSN 0015-7368

AB/N-1
AB/U-1
AD/U-6
CA/U-1
DN/U-1 1967-
ED/S11
GL/U-2
HL/U-1 1960-75
LD/P-1
LO/M32
LO-MT
LO/N-1
LO/N27 1962-
LO/U24
LV/U-1
NO/U-1
QW/C73 1970-
XY/N-1

Journal of the Indian Law Institute. -- New Delhi, 1958-
ISSN 0019-5731

BH/U-1 1958-74
BL/U-1 1961-
CA/U13
CR/U-1 1961-
LO/C47 1963-70
LO/S55 (w.v.14-15 1972-73)
LO/U14
LO/U24
OX/U13
OX/U15
XY/N-1 1965 (v.5 no.3)-

Journal of the Indian Law Teachers Association. -- Madras, 1958-
ISSN 0445-782X

LO/U24 1958-60;1968.

Journal of the Institute of Arbitrators <u>see</u> Arbitration

Journal of the International Commission of Jurists. -- Geneva, 1957-1968 (vol.9)
Merged with: Bulletin of the International Commission of Jurists, q.v., to become: Review - International Commission of Jurists, q.v.
Editions also in French, German and Spanish
ISSN 0047-0678

AB/U-1
AD/U-6 1957-67
BH/U-1
BL-LS
BL/U-1
CA/U13 imp.
CB/U-1
ED/S10
ED/S11
ED/U-1
EX/U-1 1961-68
GL/U-1
LA/U-1 1957-64
LD/U-1 1958 (v.1 no.2)-1968
LO/C25 1961-68
LO-MT
LO/N17
LO/R74 1967-68
LO/U-2 1957-60; 1962-65
LO/U12
LO/U14
LO/U24
LV/U-1 1964-68
NO/U-1 (w.v.8 no.2)
OX/U15
OX/U25
QS/Q29 1957-61
QS/S-6
QS/S-7 1957-60
RE/U-1 1959 (v.2 no.2)-1968
SH/U-1
SO/U-1
XY/N-1 1959 (v.2 no.2)-1968

Journal of the John Bassett Moore Society of International Law <u>see</u> Virginia journal of international law

Journal of the Kansas Bar Association. -- Topeka, Kan.,
Continues: Journal of the Bar Association of the State of Kansas, 1932-
ISSN 0022-8486

LO/U24 1971 (v.40)-

Journal of the Law and Commerce Society. -- Hong Kong, 1936-1937; 1940.
Continues: Journal of law and commerce, 1928-1929 (vol.2 no.1)

OX/U15

Journal of the Law Society of Scotland. -- Edinburgh, 1956-
Absorbed: Conveyancing review, q.v.
ISSN 0458-8711

AB/N-1	ED/S11	LO/U24
AD/U-6	ED-SLC	OX/U15
CA/U-1 1971-	ED/U-1	QS/S-6
CA/U13	GL/U-1	XY/N-1 1971 (v.16)-
DN/U-1	GL/U-2	
ED/S10	LO/N-1	

Journal of the Missouri Bar. -- Jefferson City, 1945-
Continues: Missouri Bar journal, 1930-1944 (vol.15)
ISSN 0026-6485

LO/U24 1971 (v.27)-

Journal of the National Association of Referees in Bankruptcy <u>see</u> American bankruptcy law journal

Journal of the National Conference of Referees in Bankruptcy <u>see</u> American bankruptcy law journal

Journal of the Patent Office Society. -- Arlington, Va., 1918-
ISSN 0031-2886

LO/N14	LO/U24 1972 (v.54)-	XY/N-1 1964 (v.46 no.2)-

Journal of the Patent Office Society. -- Canberra, Australia, 1961-

OX/U15 1961-69 (v.6 no.2)

Journal of the Society of Clerks-at-the-Table in Empire Parliaments <u>see</u> Table

Journal of the Society of Commercial and Industrial Law. -- London, 1926-

CA/U-1 1926.	LO/N-1	OX/U15

Journal of the Society of Comparative Legislation <u>see</u> Journal of comparative legislation and international law

Journal of the Society of Public Teachers of Law. -- London, 1924-1938, 1947 (vol.1 n.s.)-
ISSN 0038-0016

AB/N-1	BH/U-1	BT/U-1 1975-
AB/U-1 1952-	BL/U-1	CA/U-1 1970-
AD/U-6 1947-	BR/U-1 1924-38 imp., 1947-	CA/U13 (w.1936-38)

(cont'd)

Journal of the Society of Public Teachers of Law (cont'd).

CB/U-1 1947-
CC/U-1 1959-75
CH-CI 1966 (v.9)-
CR/U-1 1964-
CV/C-1 1970 (v.11)-
CV/U-1 1960 (v.5 no.4)-
DN/U-1 1952-
DR/U-1 1926-
ED/S10 1956-67
ED-SLC 1949-54
ED/U-1 1953- imp.
EX/U-1
GL/U-1
GL/U-2 1964-
HL/U-1 1925-36;1938; 1952/54-
LA/U-1 1924-76
LC/U-1 (w.1924)
LD/U-1
LO/C-3 1947-
LO/C10 1947-72
LO/C15 1952-
LO/C25 1965- imp.
LO-MT
LO/N-1
LO/N26 last 10 years
LO/R74 1964-
LO/U-1 imp.
LO/U-2
LO/U-3
LO/U11 1925-
LO/U12
LO/U24
LO/U28 1974 (v.13)-
LV/U-1 1924-37;1947-
MA/U-1 1947-
NO/U-1 1927-38 (w.v. 6);1947-
NW/U-1 1928-38;1947-
OX/U15
OX/U25
QE/C76 1968-
QG/C25 1968-
QL/D15 1931- (w.1961)
QM/C48 1957/58-
QM/C68 1973- imp.
QN/C70 1952/54 (v.2)- imp.
QS/Q12 1957-
QS/S-4 1931-
QS/S-6 1970-
QS/S-7
QW/D12 1947-
RE/U-1
SH/U-1 1928;1931-38; 1947-
SO/U-1 1931-38;1947-
XY/N-1 1936;1952 (n.s.v.2)-

Journal of the State Bar of California <u>see</u> California State Bar journal

Journal of the University of Texas International Law Society <u>see</u> Texas international law journal

Journal of urban law <u>see</u> University of Detroit journal of urban law

Journal of world trade law. -- Twickenham, Middx., 1967-
ISSN 0022-5444

AB/N-1 1970-
AB/U-1
AD/U-6
BH/U-1
BL/U-1
CA/U-1
CA/U13
CR/U-1
CV/C-1
CV/U-1
DN/U-1
ED/S11
ED/U-1
EX/U-1 1971-
GL/U-2
HL/U-1
KL/U-1 1969 (v.3)-
LO/C-5 1974-
LO/C25 1975-
LO/C47
LO-CBL*
LO-MT
LO/N-1
LO/N-5
LO/N17
LO/N26
LO/S14
LO-SC 1977-
LO/U-2
LO/U-3
LO/U12
LO/U24
LV/U-1 1967-76
MA/P-1
NO/U-1 1970 (v.4)-
OX/U15
QL/D15 1973 imp., 1974-
QM/C68
QN/C70 1972-
QS/S-4
QS/S-6
QS/S-7
QW/D12
RE/U-1
SH/U-1
SO/U-1
XY/N-1

Journées juridiques - Société de Législation Comparé. -- Paris, 1965 (1960/61)-
ISSN 0449-3443

CA/U13
OX/U15

Judge Advocate General journal <u>see</u> JAG journal

Judge Advocate journal. -- Washington, 1944-1945; 1949-

LO/U24 1944-45 imp., 1949 (no.3)-

Judges' journal. -- Chicago, 1971 (vol.10 no.2)-
Continues: Trial judges' journal, 1962-1971
ISSN 0047-2972

LO/U24

Judicature. -- Chicago, 1966 (vol.50)-
Continues: Journal of the American Judicature Society, 1917-1966 (vol.49)
ISSN 0022-5800

BH/U-1
BL/U-1 1970- imp.
LO/U24
OX/U15
XY/N-1 1966 (v.50)-

Judicature quarterly review. -- London, 1896.
No more published.

LO/N-1
OX/U15

Judicial settlement of international disputes. -- Baltimore, Md., 1910-1917(?)

LO/U-2 1914-15;1917

Jugoslovenska advokatura. -- Belgrade, 1954-
ISSN 0022-6017

LO/N-1

Jugoslovenska revija za medjunarodno pravo. -- Belgrade, 1954-
ISSN 0022-6084

AD/U-6 1962- imp.
CA/U13 (w.1968-69, 1971)
CA/U37
GL/U-1 1960-
LO/N-1
LO/S14 1958-61; 1967 (v.13)-
LO/U-3 1954-72 (v.19)
LO/U24 1958 imp., 1959 (v.6)- (w.v.13)
OX/U15

Juridica. -- Rio de Janeiro, 1955-
ISSN 0022-6777

LO/N-1 1972 (Año 17 no.16)-
XY/N-1 1966 (v.31)-

Juridical review: the law journal of the Scottish universities. -- Edinburgh, 1889-1955 (vol.67); new series 1956-
Subtitle added with first vol. of new series

AB/N-1 1912-
AB/U-1
AD-A
AD/U-6
BH/U-1
BL/U-1 1956-
BR/U-1
CA/U-1
CA/U13
CB/U-1
CR/U-1
CV/U-1 1956- (cont'd)

Juridical review: the law journal of the Scottish universities (cont'd)

DN/U-1	LO/N-1	OX/U15
DR/U-1 1958-	LO/R74 1967-	OX/U25
ED/S10	LO/U-1 1951-	QE/C76 1975-
ED/S11	LO/U-2	QN/C70
ED-SLC	LO/U-3	QS/S-4 1956-
ED/U-1	LO/U11 1957-	QS/S-7
EX/U-1 1958-	LO/U12 1950-	QS/S-8 1889-1965
GL/U-1	LO/U24	QW/D12
GL/U-2	LO/U28	RE/U-1
HL/U-1 1956-	LV/U-1 1889-1912; 1966-	SH/U-1 1958-
LC/U-1		SO/U-1 1956-
LD/U-1 1956-	MA/U-1	XM/C10 1972-
LO/C-5 1956-70;1973-	NO/U-1 1955-	XY/N-1 1954;1960-
LO/C15 1970-	NW/U-1 1962-	

Juridisk arkiv <u>see</u> Nyt juridisk arkiv

Juridisk tidsskrift. -- Copenhagen, 1820-1840

LO/N-1

Juridisk ugeskrift <u>see</u> Nyt juridisk ugeskrift

Juridiska föreningen tidskrift. -- Stockholm, 1850-1861 (vol.23)

LO/N-1

Juridiskt arkif <u>see</u> Nytt juridiskt arkif

Jurimetrics journal. -- Chicago, 1966 (vol.8)-
Continues: M.U.L.L.: modern uses of logic in law, 1959-1966 (vol.7)
ISSN 0022-6793

BL/U-1 1964-	LO/N-1	OX/U15
CB/U-1 1970 (v.11)-	LO/U-3 1960-	QM/C48 1975 (v.15 no.4)-
CR/U-1 1971-	LO/U24	
ED/U-1	NO/U-1 1962- (w.1962 no.1; 1964 no.3)	SH/U-1 1964-
LD/U-1 1962 (June)-		XY/N-1 1960 (March)-

Juris-classeur périodique <u>see</u> La semaine juridique

Jurisprudence commerciale de Belgique. -- Brussels, 1968-
ISSN 0449-4296

No holdings notified

Jurisprudence criminelle du royaume <u>see</u> Journal du droit criminel, ou jurisprudence...

Jurisprudence criminelle du royaume de la France <u>see</u> Journal du droit criminel, ou Jurisprudence...

Jurisprudence du louage d'ouvrage: revue des conseils de prud' hommes see Revue de droit social

Jurisprudence générale. Recueil périodique et critique de jurisprudence, de législation et de doctrine see Recueil Dalloz de doctrine, de jurisprudence et de législation

Jurisprudencia argentina. -- Buenos Aires, 1918-

LO/U24 1960- imp. XY/N-1 1969-

Jurist (Washington) see Jurist: studies in church law and ministry

Jurist/ ed. R.M. Stephenson. -- London, 1887- 1890 (vol.4)
Absorbed by: Law students' journal, q.v.

ED/S11 LO/N-1 OX/U15

Jurist: or, quarterly journal of jurisprudence and legislation. -- London, 1827-1833 (vol.4)

CA/U13
ED/S10 1827-28
ED/S11
ED/U-1 1827-32
LO/N-1
OX/U15 1827 (March).
QS/S-6
QS/S-7

Jurist: studies in church law and ministry. -- Washington D.C., 1941-
Subtitle added with vol.34, 1974. See also: Seminar: Annual extraordinary number of 'The Jurist'
ISSN 0022-6858

CA/U13 1971 (v.31 no.3)-
LO/N-1 Oct.1961 (v.21)-
LO/U24
OX/U15
XY/N-1 1973 (v.33)-

Juristen. -- Copenhagen, 1919-1973
Merged with: Oekonomen, to become: Juristen og oekonomen, q.v.
ISSN 0022-6874

LO/U24 1938-46 imp., 1957-73
XY/N-1 1966-73

Juristen og oekonomen. -- Copenhagen, 1974-
Merger of: Juristen, q.v., and: Oekonomen

LO/U24 XY/N-1

Juristenblad. -- Antwerp, 1941-1944 (vol.4)
Between 1941 and 1944, replaced: Rechtskundig weekblad, q.v.

LO/U24

Juristen-Jahrbuch. -- Köln-Marienburg, 1960-1970 (Bd.10)
Ceased publication
ISSN 0449-4334

LO/U24 OX/U15

Juristenzeitung. -- Tübingen, 1951 (Bd.6)-
Merger of: Deutsche Rechtszeitschrift, q.v., and: Süddeutsche Juristenzeitung, q.v.
ISSN 0022-6882

CA/U13
ED/U-1
EX/U-1 1951-
GL/U-1 1968-
LO/U-3 1951-62 imp.
LO/U11 1963-
LO/U12
LO/U24
OX/U15
QE/C76 1975-
QL/D15 1974-
SO/U-1 1974-76
XY/N-1 1966 (Bd.21)-

Juristische Blätter. -- Vienna, 1872-
ISSN 0022-6912

LO/U24 1947 (Jg.69)-
XY/N-1 1963 (Jg.85)-

Juristische Rundschau. -- Berlin, 1947-
ISSN 0022-6920

EX/U-1 1972-
LO/U24 1947-51;1959 imp.,1960-
OX/U15
XY/N-1 1969-

Juristische Schulung. -- Munich, 1961-
ISSN 0022-6939

LO/U24 1969 (Bd.9)-

Juristische Wochenschrift. -- Leipzig, 1872-1939 (Jg.68)
Absorbed: Friedensvertrag: Zeitschrift für Rechts- und Wirtschaftsfragen, 1923
Merged with: Deutsches Recht, to become: Deutsches Recht, Ausgabe A, q.v.

CA/U13 1919-39
LO/N-1 1904-32 imp.
LO/U11 imp.
LO/U24 1898-1939 imp.
XY/N-1 1925-26 (Jg. 54-55);1930 (Jg.59).

Jurisuto. -- Tokyo, 1952-
ISSN 0448-0791

LO/N-1

Jus: rivista di scienze giuridiche. -- Milan, 1950-
ISSN 0022-6955

AD/U-6 1959 and 1967, imp.
BH/U-1
CA/U13 1953-
ED/U-1 1960-
LC/U-1 1965 (v.16)-
LO/N-1
LO/U24
OX/U15
XY/N-1 1967 (anno.18)-

Jus gentium: diritto delle relazioni internazionali. -- Rome, 1949-
Sub-title varies
ISSN 0022-6963

CA/U13 1960 (v.6 no.5)-
LO/U-3 1949-74 (v.9)
LO/U24
XY/N-1 1967 (v.8)-

Jus gentium: Nordisk tidsskrift for folkeret og international privatret. -- Copenhagen, 1949-1951 (Bd.2)
Absorbed by: Nordisk tidsskrift for international ret, now entitled: Nordisk tidsskrift for international ret: Acta Scandinavica juris gentium, q.v.

LO/N-1 LO/U-3 OX/U15

Justiça portuguesa: revista de direito. -- Porto, 1933-1967 (ano 34)
Ceased publication

LO/N-1 1954-64 LO/U24 1961-67

The Justice (Seoul) see Chŏsut'isŭ

Justice: Irish student law review. -- Dublin, (ca 1964)-
ISSN 0449-4466

AB/N-1 1965-66 CA/U-1 1964-65 imp. OX/U15 1965-66

Justice: journal of the International Commission of Jurists, Australian section. -- Sydney, 1968-

OX/U15 1968-69 (no.2)

Justice internationale. -- Paris, 1903-1905

LO/N-1

Justice of the Peace. -- London, 1971 (vol.135 no.47)-
Continues in part: Justice of the Peace and local government review, 1837-1971, q.v.

AB/U-1
BH-LS
BH/U-1
BL/U-1
BR/U-1
CA/U-1
CA/U13
CA/U37
CB/U-1
CH-CI
CR/U-1
CV/C-1 1972-
DG-LS 1973-74
DR/U-1
ED/S11
EX/U-1
GL/U-2
HL/U-1
LC/U-1
LD/P-1
LD/U-1
LO/C-3 1973-
LO/C-5 1974 (July)-
LO/C14 1973-
LO/C15
LO/C25 1976-
LO-MT
LO/N-1
LO/N-5
LO/N26 1974-76 (v.138 no.32-v.140)
LO/N27
LO/N46
LO/R74
LO-SC
LO-TS
LO/U-2 1972-
LO/U-3
LO/U12
LO/U24
LO/U28
LV/P-1
LV/U-1 1971-76
MA/P-1
NO/U-1
NW/U-1
OX/U15
QE/C76 1972-
QL/D15 1972 (v.136)-
QM/C48 1972 (v.136)-
QM/C68 1971-74 (v.138)
QN/C70
QS/Q12
QS/Q13
QS/S-4
QS/S-6
QS/S-7
QS/S-8
QW/C73
QW/D12
RE/U-1
SH/U-1
SO/U-1
XY/N-1
YK/U-1

Justice of the Peace. -- Melbourne, 1911-

LO/U24 1958 (v.48)-

Justice of the Peace and local government review. -- London, 1837-1971
Continued by: Justice of the Peace, q.v., and: Local government review, q.v.

AB/N-1 1838-42;1844-48 imp.,1857-1971
AB/U-1 1842-1971
BH-LS 1927-71
BH/U-1
BL/U-1 1844-1971
BR/U-1 1837-1932 (w.1910);1951;1953;1970-71
CA/U-1 1870 (v.34)-1971
CA/U13
CA/U37
CB/U-1 1848-1917;1932-71
CH-CI 1862-1971
CR/U-1 1839-71;1880-1971 imp.
DG-LS
DR/U-1 1895-1971 imp.
ED/S11
EX/U-1
GL/U-2 1963 (v.127)-1971
HL/U-1 1842-59 imp., 1862-1971
LC/U-1 1839-1971
LD/P-1 1841-1971
LD/U-1 1956-71
LO/C-3 1960-67
LO/C15 1879-1970 imp.
LO-MT
LO/N-1
LO/N-5 1932-71
LO/N27
LO/N46
LO/R74
LO-SC (w.1838;1847;1849-51)
LO-TS 1863-1971
LO/U-2 1840-41;1843;1885-1953;1955-58
LO/U-3 1896-1923 imp. 1949-71
LO/U12 1839-1971 (w.1870,1966,1968;1963-64 imp.)
LO/U24
LO/U28 1851-1971
LV/P-1 1955-71
LV/U-1 1957-71
MA/P-1 1846-1971 (w.1849)
NO/U-1 1861-1971
NW/U-1 1937-61;1963-71
OX/U15 1839 (v.3)-1971
QE/C76 1903-71 imp.
QL/D15 1901;1904-12;1919-49;1951;1968-71
QM/C68 1950-71
QN/C70 1866-1971
QS/Q12 1866-1971
QS/Q13 1869-1919 imp., 1922-55;1966-71
QS/Q29 1837-1929
QS/S-4
QS/S-6
QS/S-7
QS/S-8
QW/C73 1902-05; 1920-71
QW/D12
RE/U-1
SH/U-1
SO/U-1 1871-1971
XY/N-1 1846 (v.10)-1971 imp.
YK/U-1 1969-71

Justice system journal. -- Denver, Colo., 1974-

No holdings notified

Justicia: revista mensual. -- Mexico City, 1931-

LO/U24 1963 (v.23)- XY/N-1 1966-

Justicia: revista peninsular y ultramarina de legislación, jurisprudencia y administración pública. -- Madrid, 1866 (tom.1-2)

LO/N-1

Justinien: revue annuelle publiée par la Section de Droit Civil de la Faculté de Droit de l'Université d'Ottawa <u>see</u> Revue générale de droit

Justitia: journal of the students/ Osmania university law college. -- Hyderabad, 1953-
ISSN 0447-1954

LO/S55 1956 (v.2-3). LO/U14 1960 (v.7 no.7). OX/U15 1957.

Justiţia nouǎ <u>see</u> Revista românǎ de drept

Justiz: Zeitschrift für Erneuerung des deutschen Rechtswesens. -- Berlin, 1925-1933 (Bd.8)

LO/U-3

Justizministerial-Blatt für die preussische Gesetzgebung und Rechtspolitik <u>see</u> Deutsche Justiz: Rechtspflege und Rechtspolitik

Juvenile court judges journal <u>see</u> next entry

Juvenile justice. -- Reno, 1972 (vol.23 no.2)-
Continues: Juvenile court judges journal, 1949-1972, (ISSN 0022-7153)
ISSN 0093-7231

LO/U24 1972 (v.23)-   XY/N-1 1972 (v.23 no.2)-

Kansai Daigaku hogaku ronshu = Law review of Kansai University. -- Suita-shi, Osaka, 1951-
ISSN 0451-3398

LO/U14   XY/N-1 1966 (v.15 pt.4)-

Kansas City law review <u>see</u> U.M.K.C. law review

Kanūn-e Vokalā = Law review/ Iranian Bar Association. -- Tehran, 19(?)-
Text in Persian

CA/U-1 1953 (no.32)-   OX/U-1 1953-60,1961-73 (nos.32-73, 76-121)   XY/N-1 1969 imp., 1971 imp.
LO/U14 1955-

Karachi law journal/ Sind Muslim Law College. -- Karachi, 1964-
ISSN 0075-5095

LO/U14 1967-   OX/U15   XY/N-1 1968 imp., 1970 imp.
LO/U24 1964-71

Karlsruher juristische Bibliographie. -- Munich, 1965-
ISSN 0453-3283

ED/U-1   LO/U12 1974-   LO/U24

Kashmir law journal. -- Jammu, 1962-
ISSN 0451-4823

LO-MT 1962-69 imp.   QS/S-6 imp.   QS/S-7 1962-67 imp.

Keihō zasshi <u>see</u> Journal of criminal law

Kentucky Bar journal <u>see</u> next entry

Kentucky Bench and Bar. -- Frankfort, Ky., 1975 (vol.39)-
Continues: Kentucky State Bar journal, 1936-1971 (vol.35 no.3) (ISSN 0023-0367), and: Kentucky Bar journal, 1971 (vol.35 no.4)-1974 (vol.38)

No holdings notified

Kentucky law journal. -- Lexington, 1912-
ISSN 0023-026X

LO/C10 1968 (v.57)- OX/U15 1936-39 imp. XY/N-1 1969 (v.58)-
LO/U24

Kentucky State Bar journal <u>see</u> Kentucky Bench and Bar

Kikan horitsugaku = Quarterly law review. -- Osaka, Tokyo, 1949-
Text in Japanese, title and contents page in English
ISSN 0033-5673

LO/N-1

Kindai hogaku: the law review of Kinki University. -- Osaka, 1969 (vol.17)-
Continues: Hogaku, 1953?-1968 (vol.16)

XY/N-1 1966 (v.15)-

King's counsel/King's College London Law Society. -- London, 1936-1939; 1948; 1950-

AB/U-1 1973 (no.26)-	LD/U-1 1973-	OX/U15 1936-39; 1951-73
BL/U-1 1974/75 (no.27)-	LO/C15 1973-	QE/C76 1969-
CA/U-1 1937-39;1951-	LO/N-1	QM/C68 1975-
CR/U-1	LO/U11	QN/C70 1977-
ED/S11 1938- imp.	LO/U24	SO/U-1 1974-

Kingston law review. -- Kingston, Surrey, 1968-
ISSN 0453-8854

BL/U-1 1968-75 imp.	LO/C10	OX/U15 1970-74 (v.2-4 no.1); 1975 (v.5)-
CA/U-1 1971 (v.3)-	LO-MT 1973 (v.3 no.2)-	QL/C48 1973-
CA/U13	LO/N-1	QN/C70 1971-
CR/U-1	LO/U24	
LO/C-5	LV/U-1 1970-75	

Kobe University law review. International edition/ Faculty of Law, Kobe University. -- Kobe, 1961-
ISSN 0075-6423

BL/U-1 LV/U-1 XY/N-1

Kokugakuin hōgaku (Kokugakuin journal of law and politics). --
Tokyo, 1963-

LO/U14 imp.

Kokusaihō gaikō zasshi = Journal of international law and
diplomacy = Revue de droit international. -- Tokyo, 1902-
ISSN 0023-2866

LO/U14 1921- XY/N-1 1966 (v.64)-

Kommentariĭ sudebnoĭ praktiki. -- Moscow,

GL/U-1 Soviet Studies Branch Library 1973-

Komuna: časopis za pitanja teorije i prakse komunalnih zajednica.
-- Belgrade, 1954-
ISSN 0023-3161

LO/N-1 XY/N-1 1973 (v.20)-

Korean journal of comparative law. -- Seoul, 1973-

No holdings notified

Korean journal of international law = Kukche pophakhoe nonch'ong.
-- Seoul, 1956-
Title page in Korean and English; text in Korean or English
ISSN 0023-3994

LO/U14 1962-69 imp.

Kredit i khozraschet see Den'gi i kredit

Kriminalistik. -- Hamburg, 1949 (vol.3)-
Continues: Kriminalistische Rundschau, 1947-1948
ISSN 0023-4699

XY/N-1 1967 (Bd.21)-

Kriminalistische Rundschau see previous entry

Kriminologisches journal. -- Munich, 1969-

CA/U37

Kritische Jahrbücher für deutsche Rechtswissenschaft. -- Leipzig,
1837-1848

LO/N-1

Kritische Justiz. -- Frankfurt am Main, 1968-
ISSN 0023-4834

LO/U24 imp. XY/N-1 1972-

Kritische Überschau der deutschen Gesetzgebung und Rechtswissen-
schaft see next entry

Kritische Vierteljahresschrift für Gesetzgebung und Rechtswissenschaft. -- Munich, 1859-1944
1920/1921 never published
Continues: Kritische Überschau der deutschen Gesetzgebung und Rechtswissenschaft, 1853-1859

CA/U-1 1853-1941
ED/S11 1876-1914
LO/N-1 1853-1939
LV/U-1 1914-44 (w.Bd.33-51)
OX/U15 1853-1939;1944.
OX/U25 1878-1939

Kritische Zeitschrift für die gesammte Rechtswissenschaft. -- Heidelberg, 1852-1859

LO/N-1

Kritische Zeitschrift für Rechtswissenschaft. -- Tübingen, 1826-1829

ED/S11

Kritische Zeitschrift für Rechtswissenschaft und Gesetzgebung des Auslandes. -- Heidelberg, 1829-1856

LO/N-1
OX/U15

Kritisches Literaturblatt für Rechts- und Staatswissenschaft <u>see</u> Carl Heymann's kritisches Literaturblatt für Rechts- und Staatswissenschaft

Kritisches Repertorium für die gesammte Heilkunde <u>see</u> Zeitschrift für Rechtsmedizin

Kukche pophakhoe nonch'ong <u>see</u> Korean journal of international law

Kwansei Gakuin law review/ Faculty of Law, Kwansei Gakuin University. -- Nishinomiya, 1962-

LV/U-1

Kybernetik - Datenverarbeitung - Recht. -- Frankfurt a.M., 1971-

XY/N-1 1973 (Bd.2).

Kybernetika a pravo. -- Prague, 1967-1972 (vol.4)

OX/U15

LAG bulletin/ Legal Action Group. -- London, 1972-

AB/U-1 1974-
BH/P-1 1975-
BH/U-1 1972-73 imp., 1974-
BL-LS
BL/U-1 1974-
BR/U-1 1973- imp.
BT/U-1 1972 (no.4)-1975
CA/U-1 1973-
CA/U13 1973-
CB/U-1 1974-
CH-CI 1975-
CR/U-1
CV/C-1 1973-76
CV/U-1 1972-74 imp.
DN/U-1 1972-75 imp., 1976-
ED/N-1 Feb. 1973-
ED/U-1 1974-
EX/U-1 1973-
GL/U-2
HL/U-1
KL/U-1 imp.
LA/U-1 1975-
LC/C-1 1973-
LC/U-1 1973-
LD/C-1 1975-
LD/U-1 1972-74 imp., 1975-
LO/C-3 May 1973-
LO/C-5 1974-
LO/C10 1973-
LO/C14 Feb.1973-
LO/C15
LO/C25 1973- imp.
LO-MT
LO/N-1
LO/N26 last 2 years
LO/N27
LO/R74 July 1973-
LO-SC 1975-
LO/U-2
LO/U-3 1974-
LO/U12 1973-
LO/U24
LO/U28 1976-
LV-LP (w.Jan.1973; Sept.1974)
LV/U-1 1974-
MA/U-1 1974-
NO/U-1 1972 (no.5)-(1973 imp.)
OX/U15 Dec.1972-
QE/C76
QL/D15 1973-74 imp., 1975-
QM/C48 1975-
QM/C68 1976-
QN/C70 1972 (no.3)-
QS/Q13 1977-
QS/S-8
QW/D12
SH/U-1 1973-
SO/U-1
XM/C10 1973-
XY/N-1 1973-
YK/U-1 1975-

Labeo: rassegna di diritto romano. -- Naples, 1955-
ISSN 0023-6462

AD/U-6
CA/U-1
ED/U-1
GL/U-1
LO/U-2
LO/U24
OX/U15
XY/N-1 1969 (v.15)-

Labor law journal. -- Chicago, 1949-
ISSN 0023-6586

BL/U-1 1962-
CA/U13 1962-66;1968-
CB/U-1 1975 (v.26)-
CR/U-1 1972-
CV/U-1
DN/U-1 1969-75
HL/U-1 1971 (v.22)-
LC/U-1 1949-61 (v.12);1969 (v.20)- imp.
LO/U-3 1957-
LO/U24 1972 (v.23)-
OX/U15
XY/N-1 1964 (v.15)-

Labour law journal. -- Madras, 1949-
ISSN 0023-6977

LO/U14 1959-
MA/U-1 1972 (v.23)-

Lahore law times. -- Lahore, 1922-

LO/N-1 1935-39
LO/U14

Lakimies. -- Helsinki, 1903-
ISSN 0023-7353

LO/N-1 1964-
LO/U24 1962 (v.60)-
XY/N-1 1966 (v.64)-

Land and water law review. -- Laramie, 1966 (vol.1)-
Continues in part: Wyoming law journal, 1946-1965 (vol.19)-
ISSN 0023-7612

BL/U-1 1966-	LO/U24 1946-48 (v.2) imp., 1948 (v.3)-	OX/U15
CR/U-1 1970-74		XY/N-1

Lavoro e previdenzi oggi. -- Milan, 1974-

No holdings notified

Law. -- London, Nov. 1874-July 1875

ED/S11	OX/U15	QS/S-7
LO/N-1		

Law advertiser. -- London, Mar. 1823-1831

ED/S10 1823-28	LO/N-1	MA/P-1 1829-30

Law amendment journal. -- London, 1855-1858

LO-MT 1855-57	LO/N-1 1857-58	QS/S-7 1855-57

Law and computer technology. -- Washington D.C., 1968-
ISSN 0023-9178

BH/U-1	LO/U24	QS/S-6 1968 (v.1 nos.1-11).
DN/U-1 1968-75	OX/U15	XY/N-1

Law and contemporary problems. -- Durham, N.C., Dec. 1933-
ISSN 0023-9186

AD/U-6	HL/U-1	LV/U-1 1956.
BH/U-1 1937-46 imp., 1948-	KL/U-1	MA/U-1
	LC/U-1	NO/U-1
BL/U-1	LD/U-1	OX/U15
BT/U-1 1966-	LO/C15 1970-	QL/D15 1971-
CA/U13	LO/C47 1949-	QN/C70 1963- imp.
CB/U-1 1967 (v.32)-	LO/N-1 1933-63	SH/U-1 1961 (v.26)-
CV/C-1 1966 (v.31)-	LO/R74	SO/U-1 1957 imp., 1969-
CV/U-1	LO/U-2	
DN/U-1 1969-	LO/U-3	XY/N-1 1950 (v.15)-
DR/U-1	LO/U11	YK/U-1 1965-
ED/U-1	LO/U12	
GL/U-1 1963-	LO/U24	

Law and international affairs/ Bangladesh Institute of Law and International Affairs. -- Dacca, 1975-

LO/U14

Law and justice. -- London, 1974 (no.42)-
Continues: Quis custodiet? 1962-1973 (ISSN 0033-6610)

BL/U-1 1972 (no.34)-
CA/U-1 1969-
CB/U-1 1968 (no.18)-
ED/N-1 1974 (no.42)-
EX/U-1 1967-
LD/U-1 1969-73 imp., 1974 (nos.42, 43).
LO/N-1
LO/R74 1974-
LO/U24
OX/U15 1969 (no.22)-
XY/N-1 1969 (no.24)-

Law and labor. -- New York, 1919-May 1932

LO/U-3 1920-30 imp.
OX/U-9 1920-32 (v.2-14 no.3)

Law and land. -- London, 1903.

LO/N-1
OX/U15 1903 (v.1 no.1).

Law and legislation in the German Democratic Republic. -- Berlin-Ost, 1959-
ISSN 0458-8460

AD/U-6
BL/U-1 1960- imp.
CA/U37
EX/U-1 1968-
GL/U-1 1969-
HL/U-1 1967-
LO-MT
LO/U-2 1971-
LO/U-3 1965-
LO/U24 1965-
OX/U15 1963-
QS/S-6 1967-
QS/S-7 1966-71
XY/N-1 1967-

Law and liberty. -- Menlo Park, California, (1974?)-
ISSN 0094-0615

No holdings notified

Law and policy in international business. -- Washington D.C., 1969-
ISSN 0023-9208

CV/U-1
EX/U-1
LO/C15 1973-
LO/N17 1974-
LO/U24
OX/U15
XY/N-1 1970 (v.2)-

Law and psychology review. -- Alabama, 1975-

No holdings notified

Law and society review. -- Beverly Hills, Calif., 1966/67-
ISSN 0023-9216

AD/U-6
BH/U-1
BL/U-1 1967 (v.1 no.2)-
CA/U-1 1971-
CB/U-1
CC/U-1
CR/U-1
CV/U-1
DN/U-1
DR/U-1 1972-
ED/U-1 1967 (v.1 no.2 & v.2)-
GL/U-2
KL/U-1 1973 (v.8)-
LC/U-1
LO/C-3
LO/C25 1977-
LO/U-2
LO/U-3 1970 (v.5)-
LO/U24
LO/U28
OX/U15
QL/D15 1971/72-
SH/U-1
XY/N-1

Law and the social order <u>see</u> Arizona State law journal

Law bulletin/ University of Zambia. -- Lusaka, (ca 1970)-

LO/U14 1971 (v.2 no.1)-

Law chronicle. -- Dundee, Apr. 1856-Mar. 1860

ED/S11

Law chronicle: or, Journal of jurisprudence. -- Edinburgh, August 1829-1832
Continues: Scots law chronicle, April-July, 1829

BH-LS 1830-32
ED/S10
ED/S11
ED/U-1 1829-31
LO/N-1
OX/U15 1829 (v.1 no.1); 1830 (v.2 no.13).

Law chronicle (London) see Law students examination chronicle

Law chronicle and law students' magazine see Law students examination chronicle

Law clerk and municipal assistant. -- London, Mar. 1906-Jan.1913

LO-MT 1906-07
LO/N-1
OX/U15 (w.June 1911-Apr.1912)
QS/S-7 1906-07

Law clerks' magazine see Weekly law magazine

Law coach. -- Cambridge, 1920-1924; Oct.-Nov.1926; 1928.

AB/N-1 1920-24
CA/U-1 1920-24
ED/S11 1920-24
LO/N-1
NW/U-1 1920-22
OX/U15 1920-24

Law College magazine. -- Poona, 1939-

No holdings notified

Law Council newsletter see Australian law news

Law examination journal and law student's magazine. -- London, 1869-1885

CA/U-1
ED/S11 1869-73
LO/N-1
OX/U15

Law examination reporter. -- London, 1866-1869

ED/S11
LO/N-1
OX/U15

Law gazette. -- London, Aug. 1822-Dec.1847

LO/N-1

Law gazette. -- London, May 1890-Apr. 1894

LO-MT 1890.
LO/N-1
QS/S-8

Law gazette/ Queensland Law Students' Association. -- Brisbane, 1931-1932

LO/U24 imp.

Law guardian. -- London, 1965-1973 (no.87)
Continued by: Guardian gazette, 1973 (no.88)- which constitutes every 4th issue of Law Society's gazette, q.v.
ISSN 0023-9259

AB/N-1	LO/C-5 1970-72	OX/U15
AB/U-1	LO/C15 1966-73	QN/C70 1967-73 (nos. 22-87)
BH-LS	LO/C47 1968-73	
BH/U-1	LO-MT	QS/Q12
BL/U-1 1968-73 imp.	LO/N-1	QS/S-4
BR/U-1 imp.	LO/N-5	QS/S-6 imp.
CA/U-1	LO/N27 1965-71	QS/S-7 1965-72
CA/U13 1965-72	LO/R74	QS/S-8 1965-72
CB/U-1 1965-71	LO-SC	RE/U-1 1965-72 imp.
CR/U-1 1966-72	LO-TS	SO/U-1
ED/S11	LO/U-2	XY/N-1 1970-73 (nos. 55-87)
LA/U-1 1967-71	LO/U24	
LD/U-1	LV/U-1	
LO/C-3 1965-72	NO/U-1 (w.nos.56,82)	

Law in American society. -- Chicago, 1972-

No holdings notified

Law in Eastern Europe. -- Leyden, 1958-
ISSN 0075-823X

AB/U-1	EX/U-1	LV/U-1
AD/U-6	GL/U-1	OX/U15
BH/U-1	HL/U-1	QS/S-6
BL/U-1	LO/C10 1958-66	SH/U-1 1958;1964-66
CA/U13	LO/N-1	SO/U-1 1962-75
CC/U-1	LO/U-2	XY/N-1 1973 (no.18 v.1)-
CR/U-1 1963- imp.	LO/U24	

Law in Japan: an annual. -- Tokyo, 1967-
ISSN 0458-8584

BL/U-1 1968-	LO/U24	XY/N-1

Law in society: journal of the Law Society of Ahmadu Bello University. -- Zaria, 1964/65-
ISSN 0458-8592

BL/U-1	LO/U14	LO/U24 1964-67

Law in the service of peace <u>see</u> Review of contemporary law

Law in transition <u>see</u> Guild practitioner

Law in transition quarterly/ Institute of Modern Legal Thought. -- Los Angeles, Calif., 1964-Dec.1967
ISSN 0458-8606

LO/N-1 1965-67 (v.2 no.2)	OX/U15	XY/N-1

Law Institute journal/ Law Institute of Victoria. -- Melbourne, July 1927-
ISSN 0023-9267

ED/S10 1953-71	LO/U24	XY/N-1 1970 (v.44)-
LO/N-1 1963-	OX/U25 1930-33;1935; 1964-	

Law intelligencer. -- London, 1843.

LO/N-1

Law journal (London) <u>see</u> New law journal

Law journal. -- Valletta, Malta, Oct.1944-Dec.1957
Suspended 1953-1954

LO/S65 1946-52	LO/U24 1944-52 imp.

Law journal/ ed. Morgan and Williams. -- London, Mar.1803-Jan.1804

No holdings notified

Law journal/ ed. Smith. -- London, 1804-1806
Known as Smith's law journal
Vol.1 begun as vol.3 of Law journal (Morgan and Williams)

LO/N-1	QS/S-7 1804.

Law journal: Irish section. -- London, May 1931-December 1934

LO/N-1	LO/U24	OX/U15 1932-34 (v.2-4)

Law journal of the Student Bar Association of Ohio State University <u>see</u> Ohio State law journal

Law librarian. -- London, 1970-
ISSN 0023-9275

AB/U-1	CR/U-1	LC/C-1
AD/U-6	CV/C-1 1976 (v.7)-	LC/U-1
BC-UC	DN/U-1	LD/C-1
BH/U-1 1971-	DR/U-1 1971-	LD/U-1
BL/U-1	ED/S11	LO/C-3
BT/U-1 1970-72	EX/U-1 1971-	LO/C14 imp.
CA/U-1	GL/U-1 1973-	LO/C15
CA/U37	GL/U-2	LO/C25
CB/U-1	HL/U-1	LO/C27 1974-
CC/U-1	LA/U-1 1973-	LO/C47 1973-

(cont'd)

Law librarian (cont'd).

LO-MT	LV-LP	QS/Q12
LO/N-1	LV/U-1	QS/Q13 1976 (v.7 no.3)-
LO/N-5	MA/P-1	QS/S-4
LO/N17	NO/U-1	QS/S-6
LO/N26 last 5 years	NW/U-1	QS/S-7
LO/N27	OX/U15	QS/S-8
LO-SC 1974 (v.5)-	OX/U25	QW/D12
LO/U-2	QE/C76 1972-	RE/U-1
LO/U-3	QG/C25 1976-	SO/U-1
LO/U11	QL/D15	XM/C10
LO/U12	QM/C48 1974- (5-year file)	XY/N-1
LO/U14	QM/C68 1976-	
LO/U24	QN/C70	
LO/U28		

Law library. -- London, 1892-Mar.1893

LO/N-1

Law library journal. -- New York, 1936 (vol.29)-
Sept. 1937 absorbed Law library news
Vol.1-28, 1908-1935, as part of Index to legal periodicals and law library journal
ISSN 0023-9283

BH/U-1 1955-	LO/N-1 1915-	NO/U-1 1966 (v.59)-
BL/U-1 1939- imp.	LO/N-5 1963-	OX/U15
CA/U13 1956-67;1969-	LO/R74 1966-	QE/C76 1972-
CR/U-1 1972-	LO/U-2 1960-	QL/D15 1975-
HL/U-1 1968 (v.61)-	LO/U-3 1946-	QS/S-6 1966-
LC/U-1 1952 (v.45)-	LO/U11 1934-37	RE/U-1 1974 (v.67)-
LD/U-1 1909-26 imp.	LO/U12 1968-	SH/U-1
LO/C-5 1961-66 (microfilm)	LO/U24 1908-27 (microfilm) 1931-34 imp. 1935-	XY/N-1 1966 (v.59)-
LO-MT		

Law magazine: or Quarterly review of jurisprudence <u>see</u> Law magazine and review

Law magazine and law review: or Quarterly journal of jurisprudence <u>see</u> next entry

Law magazine and review. -- London, Feb.1872-Aug.1915
Absorbed Law review and quarterly journal of British and foreign jurisprudence, 1856, q.v.
Continues: Law magazine: or Quarterly review of jurisprudence, 1828-1856 and: Law magazine and law review: or Quarterly journal of jurisprudence, 1856-1871

AB/N-1 1831;1851-58 imp., 1860-68;1913-15	CA/U-1 1830-1915	GL/U-1 1828-35
	ED/S10 1828-98	HL/U-1 1828-39 imp.
	ED/S11	LO-MT
BH-LS 1856-1915	ED/U-1 1828-92	LO/N-1

(cont'd)

Law magazine and review (cont'd).

LO/N46
LO/U-2 1828-72
LO/U24 1845;1866 imp. 1902-15 imp.
NW/U-1 1828-41 (w.v.15)
OX/U15 1828;1837-1915
OX/U25 (w.1828-74)
QS/S-6
QS/S-7
QS/S-8 1828-1905
XY/N-1 1828-66 (v.20 n.s.)

Law notes. -- London, 1885 (vol.4)-
Continues: Gibson's law notes, 1882-1884 (vol.3)

AB/N-1 1887;1912-
AB/U-1
BC-UC 1951-71;1976-
BH-LS 1893- imp.
BH/U-1
BL/U-1 1969-
BR/U-1 1972-
CA/U-1
CA/U13
CB/U-1 1920 (v.39)-
CH-CI 1969-
CR/U-1 1905-55 imp.
CV/C-1 1968-73
DN/U-1 1977-
DR/U-1 1901-62 imp.
ED/S11 1882-1904; 1916-
EX/U-1 1904-13;1915; 1920;1923-
GL/U-2 1968 (v.87)-
HL/U-1 1897-1943; 1946-
LC/C-1 1970-
LC/U-1 1966-
LD/C-1 1950 (v.69)-
LD/P-1 1887-1927 (w. 1896); 1965-
LD/U-1 1888-94;1899-1907;1912-
LO/C-3 1975-
LO/C14 1949;1951-52; 1957-67
LO/C15 1895-1914; 1921-
LO/C18 1964 (v.83)-
LO/C27 1968-
LO/M32 1947-63 imp.
LO-MT 1894-1912;1913; 1919-
LO/N-1
LO/N17 last 2 years
LO/N26 1956 (v.75 no.11)-
LO/R74 1972-
LO-TS 1923-
LO/U-1 1890-1912; 1956-62;1964.
LO/U-2 1961-
LO/U11 1933-
LO/U12 1951-72 imp., 1973-
LO/U24 1890 (v.9)-
LV-LP 5 years held
LV/P-1 1956-
LV/U-1 1894- (w.1922)
MA/P-1 1924-49
NO/U-1
NW/U-1 1961-
OX/U15
QE/C76 1929-
QG/C25 1964-
QL/D15 1905-12 imp., 1971-
QM/C48 1955-
QM/C68 1925-39 imp., 1967-
QN/C70 1970-
QS/Q12 1921-44;1946-
QS/Q29 1926-
QS/S-4 1899-
QS/S-6 1895-
QS/S-7 1887;1903-
QS/S-8 1935-
QW/D12 1970 (v.89)-
RE/U-1 1888 (v.7)-
SH/U-1 1912-
SO/U-1 1937- imp.
XM/C10 1957-
XY/N-1 1899-1932 imp. 1944 (v.63)-

Law notes. -- Northport, N.Y., Apr.1897-May 1946
With Lawyer (Brooklyn) formed Lawyer and law notes q.v.

LO/U24 1898-1928 (v.31) imp., 1929 (v.32)-1946

Law notes/ American Bar Association Section of General Practice. -- Chicago, 1964-
Until 1973 issued also by the Young Lawyers' Section as Law notes for the young lawyer. From 1974 this edition incorporated as a supplement in: Barrister, q.v.
ISSN 0023-9305

LO/U24 (w.v.1)
SO/U-1 1939- imp.

Law of the sea: proceedings of the annual conference/ Rhode Island University Law of the Sea Institute. -- Kingston, R.I., 1966-
ISSN 0557-8620

AD/U-6 1968 and 1973
CA/U13
DR/U-1 1967-70
ED/U-1
HL/U-1 1973 (8th)-
1975 (9th)
LO/S14
LO/U-2 1967 (2nd)-
LO/U24
XY/N-1 1967 (2nd)-

Law office economics and management. -- Mundelein, Ill., 1960-
ISSN 0458-8630

No holdings notified

Law quarterly review. -- London, 1885-
ISSN 0023-933X

AB/N-1 1885-1906 imp.
1907-
AB/U-1
AD-A 1948-
AD/U-6
BC-UC
BH-LS
BH/U-1
BL-LS
BL/U-1
BR/U-1
BT/U-1 1934-
CA/U-1
CA/U13
CA/U37 1962-75
(v.78-91)
CB/U-1
CC/U-1 1967-76
(v.83-92)
CH-CI
CR/U-1
CV/C-1 1935 (v.51)-
CV/U-1 1885-1925 imp.
1926 (v.42)-
DN/U-1
DR/U-1
ED/S10
ED/S11
ED-SLC 1965-
ED/U-1
EX/U-1
GL/U-1
GL/U-2
HL/U-1
KL/U-1
LA/U-1 1948-77
LC/C-1
LC/U-1
LD/C-1 1902 (v.18)-
LD/P-1 1885-1919;
1926-
LD/U-1
LO/C-3
LO/C10
LO/C14 1970-
LO/C15
LO/C18 1940 (v.56)-
LO/C25 1952-
LO/C27
LO/C47 1945-
LO-CBL last 10 years
LO-MT
LO/N-1
LO/N-5 1948-
LO/N17 1938-
LO/N26 1938-
LO/N27 1938-
LO/N46
LO/R74
LO/S28 1935-
LO-SC
LO-TS 1919-
LO/U-1 (w.1896-1900;
1913-14)
LO/U-2
LO/U-3 imp.
LO/U11
LO/U12
LO/U14 1973-
LO/U19
LO/U24
LO/U28
LV-LP
LV/P-1 1954-
LV/U-1
MA/P-1
MA/U-1
NO/U-1
NW/U-1
OX/U15
OX/U25
QE/C76
QG/C25 1968-
QL/D15 1930-
QM/C48 (w.v.61-63,
67,70,79,81)
QM/C68 1948 (v.64)-
QN/C70
QS/Q12 1923-
QS/Q13 1959-
QS/Q29 1942-
QS/S-4
QS/S-6
QS/S-7
QS/S-8
QW/C73
QW/D12
RE/U-1
SH/U-1
SO/U-1
SW/U-1
XM/C10
XY/N-1 1950 (v.66)-
YK/U-1 1963-

Law recorder. -- Dublin, Nov.1828-1830/31; n.s. 1833-1837/38
Continues: Irish law recorder, Nov.1827-Oct.1828

BH-LS 1827-31
BL/U-1 1828-38
ED/U-1 1827-31
HL/U-1
LO-MT
LO/N-1
LO/U-2
QS/S-7

Law review/ International School of Law. -- Washington D.C., 1976-
ISSN 0364-8338

No holdings notified

Law review/ Iranian Bar Association <u>see</u> Kanūn-e Vokalā

Law review/ University of Connecticut School of Law <u>see</u> Connecticut law review

Law review: monthly journal of the Law Society, School of Oriental and African Studies. -- London, 1969.
No more published.

LO/N-1	QS/S-4	QS/S-6 imp.
LO/U24		

Law review and quarterly journal of British and foreign jurisprudence. -- London, Nov. 1844-Feb. 1856
Absorbed by Law magazine and review, May 1856.q.v.

AB/N-1 1851-56 imp.,	LO-MT	QS/S-6
BH-LS	LO/N-1	QS/S-7
BL/U-1 1845-54	LO/N46	QS/S-8
CA/U-1	LO/U-2	XY/N-1
ED/U-1 1845-56	OX/U15	

Law review of Kansai University <u>see</u> Kansai Daigaku hōgaku ronshu

Law School record/ University of Chicago Law School. -- Chicago, 1951-
ISSN 0529-097X

LO/U24 1951-64 (v.12); 1965-72 imp.

Law Society journal: the official journal of the Law Society of New South Wales. -- Sydney, 1963-
ISSN 0023-9372

BL-LS	LO/N-1 1963;1965-	OX/U15
CA/U-1	LO/U24	

Law Society of Scotland newsletter. -- Edinburgh, 1950
Absorbed by Scots law times, 1951 q.v.

No holdings notified

Law Society (of Upper Canada) gazette. -- Toronto, May 1967-
Title varies: Law Society gazette
ISSN 0023-9364

BL/U-1	LO/U24	OX/U15
LO-MT		

Law Society's gazette. -- London, 1903-
From 1973 (vol.70, no.13) every 4th issue entitled Guardian gazette, in continuation of Law guardian, q.v.
ISSN 0023-9380

AB/N-1 1965-
AB/U-1 1954-
AD-A
AD/U-6 1967-
BC-UC 1963-72;1976-
BH/U-1 1953-
BL/U-1 1964-
BR/U-1 1948- (w.1951-2;1966)
CA/U-1 1953-
CA/U13 1941-
CA/U37 last 2 years
CB/U-1 1966-
CR/U-1 1946- imp.
CV/U-1 1966- imp.
DR/U-1 1963-66 imp.
ED/S10 1911-
ED/S11 1953-
ED-SLC 1966-
ED/U-1 1966-
EX/U-1 1942-
GL/U-2 1973- Guardian gazette only
HL/U-1 1968- imp.
LC/U-1 1948-
LD/U-1 1950-51 imp., 1957-71
LO/C-3 1973-
LO/C-5 1974-
LO/C14 1970-
LO/C15 1925-
LO/C25 last 5 years
LO/C27 1976-
LO/C47 1972-
LO-CBL last 10 years
LO-MT 1942-
LO/N-1 1934-
LO/N-5 1938-46 imp., 1947-57;1966-
LO/N17 last 2 years
LO/N26 last 5 years (Guardian gazette last 2 years)
LO/N27 1970-
LO/R74 1965-
LO-SC 1963-71;1974-
LO-TS 1952-
LO/U-1 1933-40 imp., 1950-
LO/U-2 1966-
LO/U-3 1967-
LO/U11 1949-
LO/U12 1952-(w.1971-73)
LO/U24 1919 (v.17)-
LV-LP 3 years held
LV/U-1 1966-
MA/U-1 1966 (v.63)-
NO/U-1 1950 (v.47)-
OX/U15 1903-14;1953-
QE/C76 1935-
QL/D15 1960-66;1968 imp.,1971-73 imp.,1974-
QM/C48 1958- (Guardian gazette only 5 years kept)
QM/C68 1970 (v.67)-
QN/C70 1974-
QS/Q12 1951 imp.,1952-
QS/S-4 1939-
QS/S-6 1940-
QS/S-7 1929-71
QS/S-8
QW/D12 1975-
RE/U-1 1949-56;1961-
SH/U-1 1958-
SO/U-1 1957-
XY/N-1 1963 (v.60)-

Law student. -- London, 1947-1949

LO-MT
LO/N-1

Law students' debating society's journal and reporter. -- London, 1865-1866

LO/N-1

Law students examination chronicle. -- London, 1861-1868
Continues: Law students' magazine, Aug. 1844-June 1854; Law chronicle, June 1854-Dec. 1858; and: Law chronicle and law students' magazine, 1859-1860

CA/U-1
ED/S11 1844-59
LO/N-1
OX/U15
QS/S-7 1844-51

Law students' journal. -- London, 1879-1917
Absorbed: Jurist/ ed. R.M. Stephenson, 1890 q.v.

AB/N-1 1897-99; 1912-17
CA/U-1 1883-1917 (w.1887)
ED/S11 1883-1917
HL/U-1 1900.
LO-MT 1880-1917
LO/N-1
LO/U11 1898.
LO/U24 1901-17 (v.23-39)
NO/U-1 1883-84
OX/U15 1883-1912 (w.1887)
QS/S-7 1896-1917

Law students' magazine see Law students examination chronicle

Law teacher: journal of the Association of Law Teachers. -- London, 1971 (vol.5)-
Continues: Journal of the Association of Law Teachers, 1967-1970 (ISSN 0044-9628)
ISSN 0303-9400

AB/N-1 1969-
BH/U-1 1971-
CA/U-1
CA/U13
CB/U-1
CR/U-1 1967-70;1973-
DN/U-1 1971-75
ED/S11
EX/U-1 1971-
GL/U-2
LC/C-1 1971-
LC/U-1 1971-
LD/C-1
LO/C10 1971-
LO/C14
LO/C15 1967;1969; 1971 (v.5)-
LO/C25 1971;1973-
LO/C47 1972-
LO-MT 1971-
LO/N-1
LO/U-3
LO/U11
LO/U12
LO/U14 1971-76
LO/U24
LV-LP 1971 (v.5 no.3)- (w. v.6, no.1)
LV/U-1
NO/U-1
OX/U15
QE/C76 1971-
QG/C25 1969-
QL/D15 1973-
QM/C48 1971-
QM/C68 1974 (v.8 no.3)-
QN/C70 1972-
QW/D12 1975 (v.9)-
SH/U-1
SO/U-1 1967,1969,1971-
XY/N-1

Law times. -- London, Apr.1843-1965
1965 absorbed by Law journal to form New law journal, q.v.

AB/N-1 1843-85 imp., 1912-65
AB/U-1 1843-1963
BH-LS
BH/U-1
BL/U-1 1845-60; 1952-60
CA/U-1 1909-65
CA/U13
CB/U-1 1843-60 (v.2-34)
CR/U-1 1846-1964
DG-LS 1932-65
DR/U-1 1959-65
ED/S10 1881-1965
ED/S11
EX/U-1 1959-65
GL/U-1 1940-65
HL/U-1 1843-69 imp.
LC/U-1 1843-1952 imp.
LD/C-1 1906-07; 1911-37
LD/P-1 1867-1965 imp.
LD/U-1 (w.1860-62; 1869-80;1897-99)
LO/C15 1898-1917; 1964-65
LO-MT
LO/N-1
LO/N-5 1948-53; 1956-65
LO/N17 1925-65
LO/N27 1898-1965
LO/N46
LO/P-6 1843-52; 1891-1915
LO-SC 1889-1965
LO-TS 1918-65
LO/U-1 1900-06 imp.
LO/U-3 1949-65
LO/U11 1946-65
LO/U24
LO/U28 1893-1965
LV/P-1 1956-65
LV/U-1 1884-99; 1927-65
MA/P-1 May 1883-1965
NO/U-1
NW/U-1 1945-65
OX/U15
OX/U25 1882-96; 1912-65
QL/D15 1952-53; 1957-65
QN/C70 1844-47
QS/Q12 1866-1917; 1945-65
QS/Q13 1904-17
QS/Q29 1942-65
QS/S-4
QS/S-6
QS/S-7
QS/S-8
QW/D12
RE/U-1 imp.
SH/U-1 1878-80/81; 1912-65
SO/U-1 1848-76;1883-85;1925-65
SW/U-1 1932-65

Law weekly review see Fa lü p'ing-lun

Lawasia: journal of the Law Association for Asia and the Western Pacific. -- Sydney, 1969/70-
ISSN 0047-4207

CB/U-1
HL/U-1 1969-75 (v.6)
LO/U14
LO/U24 1969-73
OX/U15
XY/N-1

Lawyer. -- Brooklyn, Mar.1938 (vol.1 no.3)-June 1946
Continues: American lawyer, Sept.1937-Dec.1937 (vol.1 no.2)
With Law notes (Northport) formed Lawyer and law notes, q.v.

LO/U24 imp.

Lawyer. -- Lagos, 1965?-1974 (vol.6 no.1)
Ceased publication?
Issues notified in the returns numbered: 2:1(1966), 2:2, 3:1, 3:2, 4:1, 5:1, 6:1
ISSN 0023-9437

LO/U14
LO/U24 1967-74 (v.2 no.2 - v.6 no.1)
XY/N-1

Lawyer. -- London, Nov.-Dec. 1900.

LO/N-1
OX/U15 (w. v.1, nos.2-5)

Lawyer. -- Oxford; London, 1961-1965
Continues: Oxford lawyer, 1958-1961
ISSN 0458-8827

AB/N-1 imp.
AD/U-6
BH/U-1
BL/U-1 1961-65
BR/U-1 1961-65
CA/U-1
CR/U-1 1961-65
ED/S11
ED/U-1 1960-64
HL/U-1
KL/U-1 1958-60
LC/U-1
LD/U-1 1964-65
LO-MT
LO/N-1
LO/U-2 1963-65
LO/U24
NO/U-1 1959 (v.2)-1964 (w. v.4 no.2; v.7 no.1)
OX/U15
QS/Q12 1961-65
QS/Q29 1963-65 (v.6-8 no.1)
QS/S-6
QS/S-7
SH/U-1
SO/U-1

Lawyer/ Indian Law Institute. -- Madras, 1969-
Continues: Lawyer/ Provincial Bar Federation, 1955-1968 (ISSN 0458-8835)
ISSN 0460-1165

LO/U14

Lawyer/ Provincial Bar Federation <u>see</u> previous entry

Lawyer: or, Jurisprudential record. -- London, May-Nov. 1848.

CA/U-1
ED/S11
ED/U-1
LO/N-1
OX/U15

Lawyer and law notes. -- Brooklyn, 1946-1952
Formed by union of Law notes (Northport) and Lawyer (Brooklyn)

LO/N-1 1949-52
LO/U24
OX/U15 (w. v.1 no.1; v.2)

Lawyer of the Americas. -- Miami, Fla., 1969-
ISSN 0023-9445

LO/U24

Lawyer's and magistrate's magazine. -- London, 1790-Mar.1794

BH-LS 1790-93
LO-MT 1790-91 (Dublin ed.)
LO/N-1
OX/U15 1790-91
QS/S-7
QS/S-8

Lawyers' Guild review see Guild practitioner

Lawyers' magazine. -- London, 1761-1762

LO-MT 1761
LO/N-1
OX/U15 1761 (Easter term)

Lawyer's medical journal. -- Rochester, N.Y., 1st series 1965-1971; 2nd series, 1972-
ISSN 0023-947X

No holdings notified

Learning and the law/ American Bar Association Section of Legal Education. -- Chicago, 1974-
ISSN 0093-8696

LO/U24

Lecciones y ensayos - Facultad de Derecho y Ciencias Sociales, Universidad de Buenos Aires, 1957-196?
Suspended
ISSN 0024-0079

OX/U-1 1966-

Lecturas jurídicas. -- Chihuahua, 1959-
ISSN 0455-5104

OX/U15 1961 (no.6)- imp.

Legal advertiser. -- London, 1881-1887
Entitled Monthly legal advertiser, nos. 22-50, Aug.1883-Dec.1885

LO/N-1 1881-84 (1-36)

Legal aid brief case see NLADA briefcase

Legal aid review. -- New York, Apr.1903-1972 (vol.68)

LO/U24 imp.

Legal companion. -- Serampore; Konnagar, 1893-1896

LO/N-1 imp.

Legal economics/ American Bar Association Section of Economics of Law Practice. -- Chicago, 1975-
ISSN 0360-1439

LO/U24

Legal examiner. -- London, 1831-1833
With Law chronicle: or Journal of jurisprudence became Legal examiner and law chronicle, afterwards Westminster Hall chronicle and legal examiner, q.v.

CA/U-1
ED/S11
ED/U-1
GL/U-1
LO/N-1
LO/U11 1831/32 (v.1).
OX/U15 1832/33 (v.3).

Legal examiner. -- London, 1862-1868

LO/N-1
OX/U15

Legal examiner and law chronicle see Westminster Hall chronicle and legal examiner

Legal examiner and medical jurist. -- London, 1853.
Continues: Legal examiner, weekly reporter and journal of medical jurisprudence, 1852.

LO-MT
LO/N-1
QS/S-7 imp.

Legal examiner, weekly reporter and journal of medical jurisprudence see previous entry

Legal executive. -- London, 1963-
ISSN 0024-0362

AB/N-1
CA/U-1
ED/S11
LC/C-1 1973-
LO/C15 1968-
LO/N-1
LO/N26 last 2 years
LO/R74
LO/U24
LV-LP last 5 years
OX/U15
QL/D15 1 year kept
QM/C48 last 5 years
QN/C70
QW/D12 1964 (v.2 no.10)-
XY/N-1 1966 (v.4)-

Legal guide. -- London, Nov.1838-1843

CA/U-1 1839-42
ED/S11 1838-42
LO/N-1
OX/U15 1838-42 (Jan.)

Legal historian/ American Society of Legal History. -- Indianapolis, 1958-1961
ISSN 0457-3463

BL/U-1 1958.
LO-MT 1958-59
LO/N-1
OX/U15

Legal history. -- Calcutta, 1975-

LO/U14

Legal inquirer. -- London, 1869-1872

ED/S11
LO/N-1
OX/U15

Legal issues of European integration/ Europa Instituut, University of Amsterdam. -- Deventer, 1974-

AD/U-6
BC-UC
BH/U-1
BL/U-1
CR/U-1
CV/U-1
DR/U-1
ED/U-1
EX/U-1
GL/U-1
GL/U-2
HL/U-1 1974-75
LD/U-1
LO/C14
LO/C15 1976-
LO/C25
LO/C47 1975-
LO-MT
LO/N-5
LO-TS 1976-
LO/U-2
LO/U-3
LO/U11
LO/U12
LO/U24
LV-LP 1975-
LV/U-1
MA/U-1
NO/U-1 1974 (1-2).
OX/U15
OX/U25
QE/C76
QG/C25 1976-
QL/D15
QN/C70 1977-
QW/D12
RE/U-1
SO/U-1

Legal news. -- Montreal, 1878-1897

LO/U24 1878-95 (v.18)(w. v.10,14-17)
OX/U15

Legal observer: or Journal of jurisprudence <u>see</u> Solicitors' journal

Legal observer and solicitors' journal <u>see</u> Solicitors' journal

Legal observer digest: or Journal of jurisprudence <u>see</u> Solicitors' journal

Legal practitioner and solicitors' journal. -- London, Nov.1846-1847 (n.s. 1849-1851)
New series is identical with Law students' magazine

CA/U-1 1849-51
ED/S11 imp.
LO/N-1
OX/U15
QS/S-7 1846-47

Legal record. -- London, June 1844-1845 (no.9)

LO/N-1 Aug.1844-45 (3-9)
OX/U15 (w.1845(no.9))

Legal reformer. -- London, 1819-1820

LO/N-1

Legal reporter. -- Dublin, Nov.1840-Apr.1843 (no.6)

HL/U-1
LO-MT 1840-41 (no.2)
LO/N-1
LO/U-2

Legal research journal. -- Pasadena, 1976-

No holdings notified

Legal review. -- London, Nov.1812-July 1813

QS/S-7

Legal service bulletin/ Faculty of Law, Monash University. -- Clayton, Victoria, 1974-

LO/U24 1976 (v.1 no.13)-

Légalité yougoslave see Naša zakonitost

Legislative studies quarterly/ Comparative Legislative Research Center, University of Iowa. -- Iowa City, 1976-

CV/U-1

Leguleian. -- London, 1850-Oct.1851

CA/U-1 LO/N-1 imp. OX/U15

Leguleian. -- London, 1856 (no.23)-1865 (no.59)
Continues: Examination of articled clerks, 1851-1856 (no.22)

CA/U-1 1858-61 LO/N-1 OX/U15 1863-64;1865 (Easter)

Leipziger Zeitschrift für deutsches Recht. -- Munich, 1914 (vol.8)-1933 (vol.27)
Continues: Leipziger Zeitschrift für Handels- Konkurs- und Versicherungsrecht, 1907-1913 (vol.7)

LO/U24

Leipziger Zeitschrift für Handels- Konkurs- und Versicherungsrecht see previous entry

Lex et scientia: the international journal of law and science. -- New York, 1964-
ISSN 0024-1601

LO/U24 1971 (v.8)- XY/N-1 1965 (v.2)-

Lex mercatorum: legal notes for business men. -- London, 1866-1867 (no.12)

CA/U-1 LO/N-1 1866 (1-8) OX/U15
ED/S11

La Ley. -- Seville, 1853-1854 (tom.4)

LO/N-1

La Ley: revista jurídica argentina. -- Buenos Aires, 1936-

LO/U24 1959 (v.93)- XY/N-1 1969-73 (v.133-149)

Liberación y derecho. -- Buenos Aires, 1974-

No holdings notified

Liberian law journal/ University of Liberia. -- Monrovia, 1965-
ISSN 0024-1970

BL/U-1 1966-	LO/U24	XY/N-1 1966 (v.2)-
LO/U14		

Lincoln law review. -- San Francisco, 1965-
ISSN 0024-306X

BL/U-1

Literaturblatt für Rechts- und Staatswissenschaft <u>see</u> Carl Heymann's kritisches Literaturblatt für Rechts- und Staatswissenschaft

Litigation: the journal of the Section of Litigation, American Bar Association. -- Chicago, 1975-
ISSN 0097-9813

LO/U24

Livingston's monthly law magazine. -- New York, 1853-Jan.1856
Continues: United States monthly law magazine

LO/N-1 1853-54 (1-2)

Ljudska uprava <u>see</u> Javna uprava

Lloyds maritime and commercial law quarterly. -- London, 1974-
ISSN 0306-2945

AB/N-1	LD/C-1 Feb.1975-	LO/U24
AD/U-6	LO/C-3	LV/U-1
BH/U-1	LO/C14	OX/U15
BL/U-1	LO-CBL 10 years	QE/C76
CA/U-1	LO-MT	QL/D15
CA/U13	LO/N-1	QM/C68
CH-CI 1974 (pt.2)-	LO/N-5	QN/C70
CR/U-1	LO/N26 last 5 years	QS/S-4
CV/U-1	LO/R74	QS/S-6
DR/U-1	LO-SC	QW/D12
ED/S11	LO-TS	SH/U-1
EX/U-1	LO/U-2	SO/U-1
HL/U-1	LO/U12	XY/N-1

Local courts' and municipal gazette. -- Toronto, 1865-1872

ED/S11 1865-71	LO-MT	OX/U15

Local government review. -- London, 1971 (vol.136)-
Continues in part: Justice of the Peace and local government review, 1837-1971, q.v.

BH-LS	CV/U-1	LC/C-1 last 2 years only
BL/U-1	DR/U-1	
BR/U-1	ED/S11	LC/U-1
CA/U-1	EX/U-1	LD/C-1 1972-
CA/U13	HL/U-1	LD/P-1
CA/U37	KL/U-1 1973 (v.137)-	LD/U-1 (cont'd)

Local government review (cont'd).

LO/C-5 1974 (July)-
LO/C15
LO/C25 1976-
LO-MT
LO/N-1
LO/N26 last 5 years
LO/R74
LO-SC 1977 (v.141)-
LO-TS 1973-
LO/U-3
LO/U12
LO/U24
LO/U28
LV/P-1
LV/U-1
MA/P-1
NW/U-1
OX/U-1
QL/D15
QN/C70
QS/Q12
QS/Q13
QS/Q29 last 5 years
QS/S-4
QS/S-6
QS/S-7
QW/C73
SH/U-1
SO/U-1
XY/N-1
YK/U-1

Los Angeles Bar bulletin <u>see</u> next entry

Los Angeles Bar journal. -- Los Angeles, Cal., 1975 (vol.51)-
Continues: Los Angeles Bar bulletin, 1925-1975, (ISSN 0024-6530)
ISSN 0362-837X

LO-MT 1966 (v.41 no.7);1971-
LO/U24 1972 (v.48)-

The Louisiana Bar <u>see</u> next entry

Louisiana Bar journal. -- New Orleans, La., 1953-
Continues: The Louisiana Bar, 1942-1953
ISSN 0459-8881

LO/U24 1971 (v.19)-

Louisiana law journal. -- New Orleans, May 1841-Apr.1842

LO/N-1
LO/U24 nos.2 and 3

Louisiana law review/ Louisiana State University Law School. --
Baton Rouge, La., Nov.1938-
ISSN 0024-6859

BL/U-1 1956-
CA/U13 1958- imp.
ED-SLC 1958-70
ED/U-1
LC/U-1
LO/U24
OX/U15
XY/N-1 1969 (v.30)-

Lov og rett: norsk juridisk tidsskrift. -- Oslo, 1962-
ISSN 0024-6980

LO/U24
XY/N-1 1967-

Lower Canada law journal <u>see</u> Canada law journal (Montreal)

Loyola consumer protection journal. -- Los Angeles, 1972-
ISSN 0090-9505

No holdings notified

Loyola law journal. -- New Orleans, 1920-1932

OX/U15 1922-24 imp.

Loyola law review. -- New Orleans, May 1941-

LO/U24 OX/U15 XY/N-1 1968 (v.15)-

Loyola University law journal (Chicago). -- Chicago, Ill., 1970-
ISSN 0024-7081

LO/U24

Loyola University of Los Angeles law review. -- Los Angeles, 1968-
ISSN 0459-9381

LO/U24 1972 (v.5)-

M.U.L.L. <u>see</u> Jurimetrics journal

McGill law journal. -- Montreal, 1952-
ISSN 0024-9041

BL/U-1 1965-	LD/U-1 1952-60 imp., 1960 (v.7)-	LO/U24
CA/U13	LO/N17 1966-	NO/U-1
CV/U-1 1970 (v.16)-	LO/U-2	OX/U15
DN/U-1	LO/U-3 1968 (v.14)-	QN/C70 1971 (v.17)-
ED/U-1	LO/U12 1965-	XY/N-1 1967 (v.13)-

Madras jurist <u>see</u> Indian jurist

Madras law journal. -- Mylapore; Madras, 1891-

CA/U13 1891-1954 imp., 1956-66 (v.110-131); 1967 (v.133)-	LO-MT 1926-	QS/S-4 1938-47
	LO/N-1 1891-1946	QS/S-6 1891-1951 imp.
	LO/U14	QS/S-7 1891 imp.
	OX/U15	XY/N-1 1968 (v.134)-

Magazijn van handelsrecht <u>see</u> next entry

Magazijn van handelsregt. Nieuwe versameling. -- Amsterdam, 1889-1920 (vol.30)
Continues: Magazijn van handelsrecht, 1857-1875 (vol.17) and: Nieuw magazijn van handelsregt, 1882-1885

LO/N-1

Magazin für das Kirchenrecht, die Kirchen- und Gelehrtengeschichte. -- Göttingen, 1787-1793

LO/N-1

Magazin für die gerichtliche Arzeneikunde und medicinische Polizei <u>see</u> Repertorium für die öffentliche und gerichtliche Arzeneywissenschaft

Magazin für Geschichte, Statistik und Staatsrecht der österreichischen Monarchie. -- Göttingen, 1806-08 (vol.2)

LO/N-1

Magazin für Kirchengeschichte und Kirchenrecht des Nordens. -- Altona, 1792-1796 (vol.II)

LO/N-1

Magazin für Rechts- und Staatswissenschaft see Österreichische Vierteljahresschrift für Rechts- und Staatswissenschaft

The Magistrate (London 1848/49) see Magistrate and municipal and parochial lawyer

Magistrate. -- London, 1921-
ISSN 0024-9920

AD/U-6 1967-	EX/U-1	NO/U-1
BH/U-1 1947-	LD/U-1	OX/U15
BL/U-1 1967-	LO-MT 1964-	QW/C73 1955-
CA/U-1 1972-	LO/N-1 1929-	SH/U-1 1960 (v.16)-
CA/U13	LO/N26 last 2 years	SO/U-1 1950-
CA/U37	LO/N27	XY/N-1 1963 (v.19 no.7)-
CB/U-1 1967-	LO/R74 1966 (Oct.)-	YK/U-1 1970-
DR/U-1 1921-62	LO-SC 1975-	
ED/U-1 1960-	LO/U24	

Magistrate (Western Australia) see J.P.W.A.

Magistrate: or, Sessions and police review, critical, humorous and instructive. -- London, My.-Jl.1825 (3 nos.)

LO/N-1

Magistrate and municipal and parochial lawyer. -- London, 1848-1853 (vol.5)
Vol.1, 1848/49 entitled: The Magistrate

CA/U-1	LO/N-1	QS/S-7
ED/S11	OX/U15	

Magyar jog és külföldi jogi szemle = Review on Hungarian and foreign law. -- Budapest, 1954-
Title varies
ISSN 0025-0147

LO/N-1 1960- XY/N-1 1968-

Magyar jogi szemle = Revue hongroise de droit et de jurisprudence. -- Budapest, 1920-1944

OX/U15 1924-30 (v.5-11)

Maharashtra law journal. -- Nagpur, 1963-
ISSN 0025-0465

LO/U14

Maine law review/ University of Maine. -- Bangor; Portland, 1908-1920; 1962-
ISSN 0025-0651

CA/U13 1967 (v.19)-   LO/U24 1972 (v.24)-   XY/N-1 1970 (v.22)-

Majallat al-quada wa-'qanun (Revue de la jurisprudence et des lois). -- Morocco, 1957-

LO/N-1   LO/U14 1965- imp.

Majallat al-'ulum... see Revue "al-'ulum..."

Makerere law journal. -- Kampala, 1971-

No holdings notified

Malaya law review. -- Singapore, 1962 (vol.4)-
Continues: University of Malaya law review, 1959-1961 (vol.3)
ISSN 0542-335X

BH/U-1
BL/U-1
CA/U13
CR/U-1
EX/U-1
HL/U-1 1959-74
LO/N17 1969 (v.11)-
LO/U12
LO/U14 1963 (v.5 no.1); 1969 (v.11 no.1).
LO/U24
NO/U-1
OX/U15
SO/U-1
XY/N-1 1967 (v.9)-

Malayan law journal. -- Singapore, July 1932-
ISSN 0025-1283

BL/U-1 1956-58;1964-
CA/U13 imp.
CB/U-1 1973 (v.42)-
CR/U-1
LO-MT 1958 (v.24)-
LO/N-1
LO/N17 1955-
LO-PC 1950-
LO/U14 1958-
LO/U24
OX/U15
QS/S-7 1952-
SO/U-1 1970-73
XY/N-1 1970-

Manchester law students' chronicle. -- Manchester, 1901-

CA/U-1 1901-13   LO/N-1 imp.   OX/U15 1910-13;1947.

Manchester law students' journal. -- Manchester, 1926 (vol.1 no.1).

LO/N-1

Manitoba Bar news. -- Winnipeg, Oct. 1928-

LO/U24 1933-43 imp., 1944 (v.16)-

Manitoba law journal. -- Winnipeg, 1884-1885 (vol.2)

OX/U15

Manitoba law journal. -- Winnipeg, 1962-
Vol.1 1962/65 entitled: Manitoba Law School journal
ISSN 0076-3861

CA/U13
LO/C47 1963-70
LO/N-1 1962-71
LO/U24
OX/U15
XY/N-1 1963 (v.1 no.2)-

Manitoba Law School journal <u>see</u> previous entry

Marine marchande <u>see</u> Annuaire de la marine marchande

Maritime law review <u>see</u> Recht der Schiffahrt

Markenartikel: Monatsschrift zur Förderung der Qualitätsware.
-- Munich, 1934-1944;1950-

LO/N14 1953 (Jg.15 Hft.4)- XY/N-1 1962 (Jg.24)-

Marquette law review. -- Milwaukee, Dec. 1916-
ISSN 0025-3987

BL/U-1 1964- LO/U24 XY/N-1 1970 (v.55)-
CA/U13 1959- OX/U15

Maryland Bar journal. -- Baltimore, 1968-
ISSN 0025-4177

No holdings notified

Maryland law review. -- Baltimore, 1936-1951;1953-
ISSN 0025-4282

CA/U13 1967 (v.27)- OX/U15 XY/N-1 1971 (v.31)-
LO/U24

Massachusetts law quarterly <u>see</u> next entry

Massachusetts law review. -- Boston, 1978 (vol.63)-
Continues: Massachusetts law quarterly, 1915-1977 (vol.62)
(ISSN 0025-4835)

BL/U-1 1964 LO/U24 OX/U15
LO-MT 1915-71

Me judice <u>see</u> Singapore law review

Mecklenburgische Zeitschrift für Rechtspflege und Rechtswissenschaft. -- Wismar; Rostock, 1881-1939 (vol.56)

LO/N-1 1881-1901

Médecine légale et dommage corporel. -- Paris, 1968-1974
Continues: Annales de médecine légale, de criminologie et de police scientifique, 1921-1967
ISSN 0025-679X

ED/U-1 LD/U-1 1949-67 LO/M32 1954-61; 1964-67

Médecine légale et jurisprudence médicale <u>see</u> Revue de médecine légale

Mededelingen van de Nederlandse Vereniging voor Internationaal Recht. -- Amsterdam, 1911-
ISSN 0077-6440

CA/U13 1946-52 (nos.24-30);
1956 (no.36).
LO/U24 1936 (no.21)-
(w. nos.22,24,58)

Medical trial technique quarterly. -- Mundelein, Ill., 1954-
ISSN 0025-7591

XY/N-1 1962 (v.9)-

Medicine, law, and public policy. -- New York,

DR/U-1 1975.

Medicine, science and the law. -- London, 1960-
ISSN 0025-8024

AB/N-1
AB/U-1
AD/U-6
BH/U-1
BR/U-1
CA/U-1
CA/U-37
CB/U-1 1966-
CV/U-1 1971 (v.11)-
DN/U-1 1964-
DR/U-1
ED/S11
ED/U-1
GL/U-1
HL/U-1 1960-76
LC/U-1
LD/C-1 1971 (v.11)-
LD/P-1
LD/U-1
LO/C25 1975- imp.
LO/C47 1972-
LO/M32
LO-MT
LO/N-1
LO/N26 1961-
LO/N27
LO-SC
LO/U-1 1964-69 imp.
LO/U-2
LO/U12
LO/U24
LV/U-1 1962-
NO/U-1
NW/U-1
OX/U15
QL/D15 1968-
QM/C48 1976-
QN/C70
QS/S-6
QW/C73
SH/U-1
SO/U-1
XY/N-1

Medico-legal and criminological review <u>see</u> next entry

Medico-legal journal. -- London, 1933-
Continues: Transactions of the Medico-Legal Society, 1902-1932 (vol.26).
1933-1946 (vol.14) entitled: Medico-legal and criminological review
ISSN 0025-8172

AB/N-1 1904-32 imp.,
1933-
BH/U-1 1904-
BL/U-1 1953-
BR/U-1 1904-33 imp.
BT/U-1 1902-31;
1964-77
CA/U-1
CA/U37 1962-
CR/U-1 1971-
DN/U-1 1936-45 imp.,
1949-
ED/S11
ED/U-1 1933 (v.1
no.4)-
LD/U-1 1926-
LO/C25 1977-
LO/M32
LO-MT
LO/N-1
LO/N26 1960-
LO/U-1
LO/U-3 1902-13 imp.,
1939- imp.
LO/U24
NO/U-1 1969 (v.37)-
NW/U-1 1921-22;1939-
QS/S-4 1933-46 imp.,
1947-
QS/S-6
QS/S-7 1902-39
QS/S-8
QW/C73 1948-
SO/U-1 1958-63 imp.,
1966-
XY/N-1 1902-59 imp.,
1960 (v.28)-

Medico-legal journal. -- New York, 1883-1933 (vol.50 no.3)

AD/U-6 1895-1924
ED/U-1 1893-96 imp.
LO/N-1 1888-1914 imp.
LV/U-1 1902-20

Meditationes medii: Tydskrif van die regstudente van die Universiteit van die Oranje-Vrystaat. -- Bloemfontein, 1969-

LO/N-1 1969-73
LO/U24

Melanesian law journal. -- Sydney; Port Moresby, 1970-

CA/U13
LO/N-1 1970-
LO/U14
LO/U24
OX/U15
XY/N-1

Melbourne University law review. -- Melbourne, 1957 (vol.1)-
Continues: Res judicatae, 1935-1957 (vol.7)
ISSN 0025-8938

BH/U-1 1957-
BL/U-1 1952-57;1963-
BR/U-1 1965 (v.5)-
CA/U13
CV/U-1 1969-73 (v.7-9)
ED/U-1 1957-
LC/U-1
LD/U-1 1952- (w. 1958,v.1 no.4)
LO/N-1
LO/U11 1959-62; 1971- imp.
LO/U12 1961-64 imp., 1965-
LO/U24
MA/U-1 1955-
NO/U-1 1940-57 imp., 1957-
OX/U15 1935-40 (v.2); 1947 (v.3 no. 3); 1948-
SO/U-1 1961-
XY/N-1 1961 (v.3)-

Mémoires de l'Académie Internationale de Droit Comparé. <u>see</u> Acta Academiae Universalis Jurisprudentiae Comparativae

Mémoires de la Société pour l'histoire du droit et des institutions des anciens pays bourguignons, comtois et romands. -- Dijon, 1934 (1932/33)-

LO/N-1 1935-1973/74
OX/U-1 1935 (fasc.2); 1939 (fasc.6)-
XY/N-1 1968 (fasc. 29)-

Memorial book - Association of the Bar of the City of New York. 1948 (for 1940)-
Reprinted from the Yearbook of the Association, 1940-

CA/U-1 1958-72 (w.1962)

Memorie dell'Accademia delle scienze dell'Istituto di Bologna. Classe di scienze morali. -- Bologna, 1906/07-

LO/N-1 1906/07-1951/52
LO/U-2 1907/08.
OX/U15 1906/07-1919/20

Memorie dell'Istituto giuridico dell'Universita di Torino. Esercitazioni nelle scienze ... -- Turin, 1884-1900; 1928-

LO/N-1

Memphis State University law review. -- Memphis, Tenn., 1970-
ISSN 0047-6714

No holdings notified

Mercer law review. -- Macon, Ga., 1949-
ISSN 0025-987X

BL/U-1 1963- LO/U24 1972 (v.23)- XY/N-1 1971 (v.22)-

Metropolitan Police College journal. -- London, 1935-Mar.1939

HL/U-1 1938-39 (v.4-5) LO/N-1 OX/U15

Miami law quarterly see University of Miami law quarterly

Michigan law journal. -- Detroit, 1892-1898 (vol.7)

No holdings notified

Michigan law review. -- Ann Arbor, 1902-
ISSN 0026-2234

AB/U-1	ED/U-1	LO/U12 1964-
AD/U-6	KL/U-1 1905-75 (v.4-73)	LO/U24
BH/U-1 1959-		MA/U-1
BL/U-1 1940-	LC/U-1	NO/U-1
BR/U-1 1973 (v.72)-	LD/U-1	OX/U15
CA/U13	LO-MT	QN/C70
CB/U-1	LO/N-1 1964 (v.62 no.7)-	QW/D12
CR/U-1		SH/U-1 1957 (v.56)-
CV/U-1 1966 (v.65)-	LO/U-2	SO/U-1 1965-
DR/U-1 1951-	LO/U-3	XY/N-1 1964 (v.63)-

Michigan lawyer. -- Detroit, 1875-June 1879 (vol.4)

No holdings notified

Michigan State Bar journal. -- Lansing, Mich., 1921-
ISSN 0026-2447

LO/U24 1972 (v.51)-

Middle East law review. -- Beirut, 1958-1959 (vol.1 no.12)
ISSN 0539-9424

LO/U14 OX/U15 imp.

Militair-rechtelijk tijdschrift/ Ned. Ministerie van Marine. -- The Hague, 1905-

LO/N-1 1950 (43)-

The Military law journal see Chün-fa chuan-k'an

Military law review/ U.S. Department of the Army. -- Washington D.C., 1958-
ISSN 0026-4040

BH/U-1 1965-	LO/N-1 1958- imp.	LO/U24
BL/U-1 1970 (v.48)-	LO/U11 1958-60; 1967-71	XY/N-1 1967 (v.35)-
CA/U13 1972 (v.56)-		

Milwaukee Bar Association gavel. -- Milwaukee, Wis., 1938-

No holdings notified

Minnesota law review. -- Minneapolis, 1917-
ISSN 0026-5535

BL/U-1 1963-	LO/N-1	SO/U-1 1949/50-62/63
CA/U13 1956-	LO/U24	XY/N-1 1966 (v.51)-
LD/U-1 1945-	OX/U15	
LO-MT	QM/C48 1975-	

Minshōhō zasshi (Journal of the civil and commercial laws). -- Tokyo, 1935-

LO/U14 1963 (v.48 no.3-v.49 no.2)

Minutes of proceedings of the annual meeting - Canadian Bar Association see Yearbook of the Canadian Bar Association

Minutes of the annual meeting - Association of American Law Schools see Proceedings - Association ...

Misdaad, straf en hervorming see South African journal of criminal law and criminology

Mishpatim: the law review of the students/ Faculty of Law, Hebrew University of Jerusalem. -- Jerusalem, 1968-
ISSN 0581-1651

No holdings notified

Mississippi law journal. -- University, 1928-
ISSN 0026-6280

BL/U-1 1964-	LO/U-2 1946-76	OX/U15
CA/U13 1937-	LO/U24	XY/N-1 1969 (v.41)-

Mississippi law review. -- University, Nov. 1922-April 1923 (vol.1 nos.1-5)

OX/U15

Missouri Bar journal see Journal of the Missouri Bar

Missouri law review. -- Columbia, 1936-
ISSN 0026-6604

BH/U-1 1956 (v.20)-	LO/U24	XY/N-1 1968 (v.33)-
BL/U-1 1964-	OX/U15	

Mitteilungen - Verband Deutscher Patentanwälte see Mitteilungen der deutschen Patentanwälte

Mitteilungen der Arbeitsgemeinschaft für juristisches Bibliotheks- und Dokumentationswesen. -- Bonn, etc., 1971-
ISSN 0300-0990

LO/U24

Mitteilungen der Deutschen Gesellschaft für Völkerrecht. -- Berlin, 1918-1933 (Hft.33)

LO/U24 1918-32 (Hft.1-3;6-11)   OX/U15 1918-25 (Hft.1-3;5;6)

Mitteilungen der deutschen Patentanwälte. -- Berlin, 1901-
1901-1933 (vol.33) entitled: Mitteilungen - Verband Deutscher Patentanwälte
ISSN 0026-6884

LO/N14 1901-39;1954-   XY/N-1 1968 (Jg.59 Hft.8)-

Mitteilungen der Gesellschaft für Rechtsvergleichung: deutsche Landesgruppe des Internationalen Verbandes der Rechtswissenschaft. -- Tübingen, 1950-
ISSN 0433-8693

LO/U24   OX/U15

Mitteilungen der Internationalen kriminalistischen Vereinigung. -- Berlin, 1889-1914 (Bd.21); 1926 (N.F. Bd.1)-1933 (N.F. Bd.6).
First series also entitled: Bulletin de l'Union internationale de droit pénal

LO/N-1 1889-1914   LO/U-3 1889-1914

Mitteilungsblatt - Deutsche Arbeitsgemeinschaft ... <u>see</u> next entry

Mitteilungsblatt - Deutsche Vereinigung für Gewerblichen Rechtsschutz und Urheberrecht. -- Cologne, 1948-1969
1948-1949 called Deutsche Arbeitsgemeinschaft...

LO/N14

Modern law and society. -- Tübingen, 1968-
ISSN 0026-7953

BC-UC 1968-71	EX/U-1	LV/P-1
BL/U-1 1972-	GL/U-1 1972-	MA/U-1 1972 (v.5)-
CA/U-1 1972-	LO/U-1 1973-	SW/U-1 1972-
CV/U-1 1975 (v.8 no.2)-	LO/U-3 1968 (v.1 no.2)-	XY/N-1 1969 (v.2)-

Modern law review. -- London, 1937-
ISSN 0026-7961

AB/N-1	BL-LS	CA/U37 1962-76
AB/U-1	BL/U-1	CB/U-1
AD-A	BR/U-1	CC/U-1 1950-
AD/U-6	BT/U-1	CH-CI
BC-UC 1946-	CA/U-1 1971-	CR/U-1
BH/U-1	CA/U13	CV/C-1 (w. v.35 no.1)

(cont'd)

Modern law review (cont'd).

DN/U-1	LO/C47 1955-	NO/U-1
DR/U-1	LO-CBL last 10 years	NW/U-1
ED/S10 1949-	LO-MT	OX/U15
ED/S11	LO/N-1	OX/U25
ED-SLC	LO/N-5 1953-	QE/C76
ED/U-1	LO/N17 1946-	QG/C25 1968-
EX/U-1	LO/N26	QL/D15
GL/U-1	LO/N27 1962-	QM/C48 (w.1952 (v.15))
GL/U-2	LO/N46	QM/C68
HL/U-1	LO/R74	QN/C70
KL/U-1	LO/S28	QS/Q12 1946-
LA/U-1 1958-	LO-SC (w.1961-62)	QS/Q13 1964-
LC/C-1	LO-TS 1962-	QS/S-4
LC/U-1	LO/U-1	QS/S-6
LD/C-1	LO/U-2	QS/S-7
LD/P-1	LO/U-3	QS/S-8
LD/U-1	LO/U11	QW/C73 Sept.1974-1976
LO/C-3	LO/U12	QW/D12
LO/C-5 1954 (v.17)- imp.	LO/U14 1973-	RE/U-1
	LO/U24	SH/U-1
LO/C14	LO/U28	SO/U-1
LO/C15	LV-LP (w.1939 (v.3))	SW/U-1 1947-58
LO/C18	LV/U-1	XM/C10
LO/C25	MA/P-1 (w.May 1973)	XY/N-1
LO/C27	MA/U-1	

Monash University law review. -- Clayton, Vic., 1974-
ISSN 0311-3140

BR/U-1	OX/U15	XY/N-1
LO/U24	SO/U-1	

Monatsschrift für deutsches Recht. -- Hamburg, 1947-

EX/U-1	LO/U24 1947-59 imp., 1960 (Jg.14)-	OX/U15
GL/U-1		XY/N-1 1969 (Jg.23)-
LO/N-1		

Monatsschrift für die wilkürliche Gerichtsbarkeit und das Notariat in Württemberg <u>see</u> Zeitschrift für die freiwillige Gerichtsbarkeit und die Gemeindeverwaltung in Württemberg

Monatsschrift für Kriminalbiologie und Strafrechtsreform <u>see</u> Monatsschrift für Kriminologie und Strafrechtsreform

Monatsschrift für Kriminalpsychologie und Strafrechtsreform <u>see</u> next entry

Monatsschrift für Kriminologie und Strafrechtsreform. -- Cologne, etc., 1904-1944; 1953-
1904-1936 (Bd.27) entitled: Monatsschrift für Kriminalpsychologie und Strafrechtsreform; 1937 (Bd.28)-1944 (Bd.34) entitled: Monatsschrift für Kriminalbiologie und Strafrechtsreform
ISSN 0026-9301

CA/U-37 1965-
LO/U-3 1958-
OX/U15 1904-18 (Bd.1-11); 1924-35 (Bd.15-26); 1960 (Bd.43)-
XY/N-1 1960 (Bd.43)-

Monitor: a practical review for all in law offices and chambers. -- London, 1960-1970 (vol.10 no.1)
ISSN 0540-6498

AB/N-1
CA/U-1
ED/S11
LO/N-1
OX/U15

Montana law review. -- Missoula, 1940-
ISSN 0026-9972

BL/U-1 1963-
CA/U13
LO/U24
OX/U15
XY/N-1 1969 (v.31)-

Monthly jurist see Weekly jurist

Monthly law journal see Fides

Monthly law magazine. -- London, 1838-1841 (vol.10)
1838-1840 (vol.7) entitled: Monthly law magazine and political review

BH/LS
CA/U-1
ED/S11
LO-MT
LO/N-1
OX/U15
QS/S-6
QS/S-7
QS/S-8

Monthly law magazine and political review see previous entry

Monthly legal advertiser see Legal advertiser

Monthly western jurist see Weekly jurist

Munkajog: Munkaügyi döntőbizottsági tájékoztató. -- Budapest,

OX/U15 1971/72-

Musik und Dichtung: Organ für die Rechte der Urheber in aller Welt. -- Berlin, 1954-1955 (no.6)
ISSN 0464-0489

LO/N14

NACCA law journal see Journal of the American Trial Lawyers' Association

N.A.L.A.O. brief case see NLADA briefcase

NCCD news/ National Council on Crime and Delinquency. -- New York, 1960-1972 (vol.51)
Continues: Probation, 1922-Oct. 1947; Focus, Jan. 1948-Mar. 1955, and: NPPA news, Sept.1955-May 1960

LO/U24 1964-69 imp. OX/U15 1966-72 (v.45-51) XY/N-1 1966-72 (v.45-51)

NDAA see Prosecutor

NIR: Nordiskt immateriellt rättsskydd. -- Stockholm, 1932-
1932-1948 entitled: Nordiskt industriellt rättsskydd

LO/N14 1949- OX/U15 1965- XY/N-1 1969-
LO/U24 1965 (v.34)-

NLADA briefcase/ National Legal Aid and Defender Association. -- Washington D.C., 1971 (vol.30)-
Continues: N.A.L.A.O. brief case, 1943-1949 (vol.7 no.9); Brief case, 1949-1950 (vol.8) and: Legal aid brief case, 1950 (vol.9)-1970 (vol.29) (ISSN 0024-0338)

LO/U24 1943-52 imp., 1952 (v.11)-

NPPA journal see Crime and delinquency

NPPA news see NCCD news

Nachrichten der Studiengesellschaft für privatrechtliche Auslandsinteressen see Recht der internationalen Wirtschaft: Aussenwirtschaftsdienst des Betriebs-Beraters

Nagoya daigaku hōsei ronshū (Journal of law and political science). -- Nagoya,

LO/U14 1960 (v.15)-

Narodna uprava: časopis za pitanja izgradnje narodne vlasti. -- Sarajevo, 1950-
ISSN 0547-2512

LO/N-1 1954-57 imp., 1964-

Narodni odbor. -- Belgrade, 1948-
ISSN 0465-8906

LO/N-1 1956/57-

Naša zakonitost = Légalité yougoslave. -- Zagreb, 1950-
ISSN 0027-8165

LO/N-1 1958 (v.12)-

Natal law journal. -- Durban, 1905-1907 (vol.3)
Merged with: Natal law quarterly to form: Natal law magazine, q.v.

LO/U24 1905 (v.1 pts.1-6)

Natal law magazine. -- Durban, 1908-1909 (vol.2)
Merger of: Natal law journal and: Natal law quarterly, q.v.

LO/U24 1908 (v.1 no.2).

Natal law quarterly. -- Durban, 1902-1907 (vol.6)
Vol.3 not published.
Merged with: Natal law journal to form: Natal law magazine, q.v.

LO/U24

Natal University law review. -- Durban, 1972-

LO/U24

National/ Canadian Bar Association. -- Ottawa, 1974-
Continues: Canadian Bar journal, 1958-1969 (vol.12), (ISSN 0008-2996) and: Journal - Canadian Bar Association, 1970-1973 (vol.4)
ISSN 0315-2286

AB/U-1 1974- imp.
AD/U-6 1958-69
1974-
BH/U-1 1958-73
BL/U-1 1958-69
BR/U-1 imp.
CA/U13 1958-73
CB/U-1 1967-
CV/C-1 1974-75
CV/U-1 1974-
ED/S11 1958-72
ED/U-1
EX/U-1 1958-69
HL/U-1 1958-73
LC/U-1 1974-
LD/U-1 1958-69
LO-MT 1958-
LO/R74 1967-69
LO/S65 1958-73
LO/U-2 1958-73
LO/U11 1974-
LO/U24
LO/U28 1958-65
LV/U-1 1958-73
NO/U-1 1958-69
OX/U15 1958-73
QS/S-6 1958-73
QS/S-7 1958-69
RE/U-1 1974-
XY/N-1 1967-

National Bar bulletin. -- Kansas City, 1969?-

No holdings notified

National civic review. -- New York, 1912-
1912-1958 entitled: National municipal review
ISSN 0027-9013

NW/U-1 1927-28 imp.
LO/U-3 (w.1920 (v.9), and suppl. to no.8)
QS/Q12 1948-76
XY/N-1 1947;1966 (v.55)-

National journal of criminal defense/ National College of Criminal Defense Lawyers and Public Defenders, College of Law, University of Houston. -- Houston, 1975-

No holdings notified

National municipal review <u>see</u> National civic review

National tax journal/ National Tax Association. -- Chicago, etc., 1948-
Continues: the Association's Bulletin, 1907-1947
ISSN 0028-0283

BH/U-1 1948-	KL/U-1 1962 (v.15)-	OX/U-1 1948-
BL/U-1 1958-60;1968-	LO/C25 1974-	SH/U-1 1965-
BR/U-1 1966-	LO/U-3 imp.	SO/U-1 1956-
BT/U-1 1972-	LO/U24 1971 (v.24)-	XY/N-1 1948-
GL/U-1 1968-	LV/U-1 1955-68	

Natural law forum <u>see</u> American journal of jurisprudence

Natural resources journal/ University of New Mexico School of Law. -- Albuquerque, 1961-
ISSN 0028-0739

LD/C-1 1973 (v.13)-	LO/U-2	XY/N-1
LD/U-1 1970-	LO/U24	

Natural resources lawyer/ American Bar Association Section of Natural Resources Law. -- Chicago, 1968-
ISSN 0028-0747

CA/U13	OX/U15 (w.1968 (v.1 no.2); 1970 (v.3 no.1))	XY/N-1 1972 (v.5 no.4)-
LO/U24		

Nauchny kommentarii sudebnoi praktiki. -- Moscow,

GL/U-1 Soviet Studies Branch Library 1955-

Nebraska law bulletin <u>see</u> next entry

Nebraska law review. -- Lincoln, Neb., 1941 (vol.20)-
Continues: Nebraska law bulletin, 1922-1940 (vol.19)
ISSN 0047-9209

BL/U-1 1963-	EX/U-1 1970 (v.50)-	OX/U15
CA/U13 1959 (v.38)-	LO/U24	XY/N-1 1972 (v.52)-

Nebraska State Bar journal. -- Lincoln, Neb., 1952-1971 (vol.20)
ISSN 0548-0965

No holdings notified

Nederlands juristenblad. -- Zwolle, 1948 (Jg.23)-
1926-1947 (Jg.22) entitled: Nederlandsch juristenblad

LO/U24	OX/U15	XY/N-1 1967-

Nederlands tijdschrift voor criminologie. -- Meppel, 1959-

LO/U-3

Nederlands tijdschrift voor internationaal recht <u>see</u> Netherlands international law review

Nederlandsch juristenblad see Nederlands juristenblad

Nemzetközi jog tára. -- Budapest, 1920-1944

OX/U15 1927-30

Neon dikaion. -- Athens, 1945-

LO/U24 1960 (v.16)-

Netherlands international law review. -- Leyden, 1953-
1953-1974 (vol.21) also entitled: Nederlands tijdschrift voor internationaal recht.
1962 (vol.9)-1974 (vol.21) also entitled: Revue néerlandaise de droit international
ISSN 0028-2138

AD/U-6 1975-	LO/N-1 1953-58 imp.,	MA/U-1 1970-
BH/U-1 1974-	1959-	NO/U-1 1961 (v.8)-
BL/U-1 1967-	LO/U-2 1959-	OX/U15
CA/U13	LO/U-3	SO/U-1 1974-
ED/U-1 1970 (v.17)-	LO/U24	XY/N-1

Netherlands yearbook of international law. -- Leyden, 1970-

AD/U-6 1975-	LO/N-1	NO/U-1
BH/U-1	LO/N17 1976-	OX/U15
BL/U-1	LO/U-1 1974.	QE/C76 1975-
CA/U13	LO/U-2	SO/U-1 1974-
ED/U-1	LO/U24	XY/N-1

Neue juristische Wochenschrift. -- Munich; Berlin, 1947-

BL/U-1 1974-	LC/U-1 1953 (Jg.6)-	LO/U12 1950;1952-
CA/U13	LD/U-1 1953-	LO/U24
CV/U-1	LO-MT 1968-	OX/U15
ED/U-1	LO/U-2 1947-72	SH/U-1 1949-
EX/U-1 1950-	LO/U11	XY/N-1 1961 (Jg.14)-
GL/U-1		

Neue Justiz. -- Berlin, D.D.R., 1947-
ISSN 0028-3231

LO/U24	OX/U15	XY/N-1 1967 (Bd.21)-

Neue Zeitschrift für Wehrrecht. -- Berlin, B.R.D., 1959-
ISSN 0028-3525

LO/U-3 1959-77	OX/U15	XY/N-1 1972 (Bd.14)-

Neues Archiv der preussischen Gesetzgebung und Rechtsgelehrsamkeit. -- Berlin, 1800-1805 (vol.4)
Continues: Archiv des preussischen Rechts, 1799-1800 (vol.3)

LO/N-1

Neues Archiv des Criminalrechts see Archiv des Criminalrechts

Neues Archiv für preussisches Recht und Verfahren so wie für deutsches Privatrecht. -- Arnsberg, 1834-1854 (Jahrg.16)

LO/N-1

Neues Magazin für die gerichtliche Arzeneikunde see Repertorium für die öffentliche und gerichtliche Arzeneywissenschaft

Nevada State Bar journal. -- Reno, 1936-
ISSN 0028-4092

No holdings notified

New community: quarterly journal of the Community Relations Commission. -- London, 1971-
ISSN 0047-9586

AD/U-6	LO/C-3 1972 (v.2)-	OX/U-1
BH/P-1	LO/C14	QM/C68
BR/U-1	LO/N-1	QN/C70
BT/U-1	LO/N26 last 10 years	QS/Q12
CA/U-1	LO/N27	QW/C73
DN/U-1	LO/U-1	QW/D12
ED/N-1	LO/U-3	XY/N-1
LC/U-1	LV-LP	YK/U-1
LD/C-1	MA/P-1	

New dimensions in legislation see Notre Dame journal of legislation

New England journal on prison law. -- Boston, Mass., 1974-

CA/U37	XY/N-1 1972 (v.2)-

New England law review. -- Boston, Mass., 1969 (vol.4 no.2)-
Continues: Portia law journal, 1965-1968 (vol.4 no.1)
ISSN 0028-4823

AB/U-1 1976-	CA/U13	XY/N-1 1968 (v.4 no.1)-
BL/U-1 1971-	LO/U24	

New Hampshire Bar journal. -- Manchester, N.H., 1958-
ISSN 0548-4928

No holdings notified

New Irish jurist and local government review see Irish jurist and local government review

New law journal. -- London, 1965 (vol.116)-
Continues: Law journal, 1866-1965 (vol.115)
1965 absorbed: Law times, q.v.

AB/N-1 1912-	BH-LS 1868-	BR/U-1 1965-
AB/U-1 1934-	BH/U-1 1924-	BT/U-1 1973 (no.5597)-
AD/U-6 1952-	BL-LS 1965-	CA/U-1 1971-
BC-UC 1946-	BL/U-1 1935-	CA/U13 (w.1867)

(cont'd)

New law journal (cont'd).

CB/U-1 1930-63;1966-
CH-CI 1970-
CR/U-1 1933-
CV/C-1 1973-
CV/U-1 1968-
DG-LS 1933-
DN/U-1 1965-
DR/U-1 1965-
ED/S10 1938-
ED/S11 1888-1904; 1916-
ED-SLC 1965-
ED/U-1 1965-
EX/U-1 1924-
GL/U-1 1940-
GL/U-2 1965-
HL/U-1 1929-
JE-LS 1965-
KL/U-1 1965-
LC/C-1 1965-
LC/U-1 1945-
LD/P-1 1882-1910 (w. 1884;1909); 1915-
LD/U-1 1926-
LO/C-3 1965-
LO/C-5 1937-51;1965-
LO/C10 1968-
LO/C14 1966 (v.116)-
LO/C15 1950-
LO/C18 1971 (v.121)-
LO/C25 1970-
LO/C27 1969-
LO/C47 1965-
LO-CBL 1955-*
LO-MT
LO/N-1
LO/N-5 1946-
LO/N17 last 2 years
LO/N26 1975 (Oct.)-
LO/N27 1928-
LO/P-6 1955.
LO/R74 1965 (Oct.)-
LO-SC 1965-
LO-TS 1925-
LO/U-1 1970-
LO/U-2 1947-
LO/U-3 1932-
LO/U11 1965-
LO/U12 1965-
LO/U24 1925 (v.60)-
LO/U28 1967-72;1975-
LV-LP 1967- imp.
LV/P-1 1954 (v.104)-
LV/U-1 1930-
MA/P-1 1931 (July)-
MA/U-1 1965 (v.116)-
NO/U-1 1925 (v.60)-
NW/U-1 1965-
OX/U15
OX/U25 1873-
QE/C76 1965-
QG/C25 1973-
QL/D15 1941-63;1968-69 imp.,1971-
QM/C48 1965-
QM/C68 1973 (v.123 no.5578)-
QN/C70 1955-
QS/Q12 Dec.1954-62; 1965-
QS/Q13 1965-74;1975 (July)-
QS/Q29 1943-
QS/S-4 1868-1923 imp., 1925-
QS/S-6 1898-1906 imp., 1931-
QS/S-7
QS/S-8
QW/C73 1965 (Oct.)-
QW/D12 1930 (v.69)-
RE/U-1 1866-91;1926-
SH/U-1 1925-
SO/U-1 1949-
SW/U-1 1965-
XM/C10 1968-
XY/N-1 1950 (v.100)-

New Mexico law review. -- Albuquerque, 1971-
ISSN 0028-6214

LO/U24
XY/N-1 1974 (v.5)-

New York law forum <u>see</u> New York Law School law review

New York law review. -- New York, 1923-May 1929 (vol.7 no.5)
Absorbed by: American law review to become: United States law review, q.v.

LO/U24 1925 (v.3 no.11)
OX/U15

New York law review (1940) <u>see</u> United States law review

New York Law School law review. -- New York, 1976 (vol.22)-
Continues: New York law forum, 1955-1976 (vol.21)

CA/U13 1969 (v.15)-
DR/U-1
LO/U24 1971 (v.17)-
OX/U15
XY/N-1 1974 (v.20)-

New York State Bar journal. -- Albany, 1961 (vol.33)-
Continues: Bulletin - New York State Bar Association, 1928-1960 (vol.32)
ISSN 0028-7547

LO-MT
LO/U24 1962 (v.34)-
OX/U15 1965 (v.37 no.4)-
XY/N-1 1971 (v.43 no.3)-

New York University conference on charitable foundations see Proceedings of the... biennial conference...

New York University conference on labor see Proceedings - Conference on labor

New York University Institute on Federal Taxation see Proceedings - New York...

New York University journal of international law and politics. -- New York, 1968-
ISSN 0028-7873

BH/U-1	LO/C15 1969 (v.2)-	NO/U-1
BL/U-1 1968 (v.1 no.2)-	LO/N-1	OX/U15
	LO/U-3	SH/U-1
CA/U13	LO/U24	XY/N-1 1968 (v.1 no.2)-

New York University law quarterly review see next entry

New York University law review. -- New York, 1924-May 1942; June 1944-
1924 (vol.1) entitled: Annual review of the Law School of New York University.
1929 (vol.7)-1947 (vol.24) entitled: New York University law quarterly review
ISSN 0028-7881

AB/U-1	LC/U-1 1944 (v.20)-	NO/U-1 1961-72
BL/U-1 1951-	LO/C27 1974 (v.49)-	OX/U15
BR/U-1	LO/U-2	QN/C70 1960-
CA/U13	LO/U-3 1929-	QW/D12
CH-CI	LO/U12 1950-	SH/U-1 1960 (v.35)-
CR/U-1	LO/U24	SO/U-1 1973-
HL/U-1 1924-71	MA/U-1 1937 (v.14)-	XY/N-1 1950 (v.25)-

New York University review of law and social change. -- New York, 1971-
ISSN 0048-7481

XY/N-1 1972 (v.2)-

New Yugoslav law see Yugoslav law

New Zealand journal of public administration. -- Wellington, 1938-
1938-March 1949 entitled: Journal of public administration
ISSN 0028-8357

DR/U-1 1973 imp., 1974-	LO/N-1	XM/C10 1971-
	LO/U-3	XY/N-1 1963 (v.25 no.2)-
LD/U-1 1962-	MA/P-1	

New Zealand law journal. -- Wellington, Mar. 1928 (vol.4)-
Continues: Butterworths' fortnightly notes, 1925- Feb.1928 (vol.3)
ISSN 0028-8373

CA/U13 1926-32;1934-35;1951-	LO/N17 1966-72	QN/C70 1970-
CB/U-1 1966 imp., 1967-	LO/R74 1965-	QS/S-4 1957-
ED/U-1 1959-	LO/U24	SO/U-1 1964-
LO/N-1 1953-	NO/U-1 1965-	XM/C10 1972-
	OX/U15 1929 (v.5)-	XY/N-1 1962-

New Zealand Law Society newsletter. -- Wellington, 1965-

LO/U24 1965-67 (no.12)

New Zealand universities law review. -- Wellington, 1963-
ISSN 0549-0618

AD/U-6	HL/U-1 1970 (v.4)-	LO/U24
BH/U-1	LC/U-1	LO/U28
BL/U-1 1963-	LD/U-1	MA/U-1 1965-
BR/U-1	LO/C15 1974-	NO/U-1
CA/U13	LO-MT	OX/U15
DN/U-1 1963-69 imp., 1970-	LO/U-2 1963-73	SH/U-1
DR/U-1	LO/U-3 1966 (v.2)-	SO/U-1
GL/U-2 1970 (v.4)-	LO/U12	XY/N-1

Newsletter - International Society for Labor Law and Legislation
<u>see</u> Comparative labor law

Newsletter - Society for Computers and Law Ltd. <u>see</u> Computers and law

Newsletter of the International Commission of Jurists. -- Geneva; etc., 1957-1964 (no.15)
ISSN 0538-5733

LO/N-1	OX/U15	XY/N-1 1962-64 (nos.13-15)
LO/U-2	QS/S-6 1963-64	
LO/U24 (w. no.15)	SH/U-1	

Newsletter on legislative activities/ Council of Europe, Directorate of Legal Affairs. -- Strasbourg, 1972-

AB/U-1 1973 (no.10)- imp.	ED/U-1 (w.nos.14;22)	LO/U-3 current issues
AD/U-6	EX/U-1	LO/U24
BL/U-1	HL/U-1 1974 (no.13)-	LV/P-1
BR/U-1	LC/U-1	OX/U15
BT/U-1	LD/U-1	QM/C48 1975-
CA/U13	LO-MT	QS/Q12
CA/U37	LO/N-5	QS/S-6
CB/U-1 1974 (no.14)-	LO/R74	RE/U-1
DN/U-1	LO/U-2 1972-3;1974 (no.13)-	SO/U-1

Niemeyers Zeitschrift für internationales Recht. -- Erlangen, etc., 1915 (Bd.25)-1938 (Bd.52 Hft.3/4)
Continues: Zeitschrift für internationales Privat- und Strafrecht, 1890-1902 (Bd.11); Zeitschrift für internationales Privat- und öffentliches Recht, 1903 (Bd.12)-1909 (Bd.19) and: Zeitschrift für internationales Recht, 1910 (Bd.20)-1914 (Bd.24).
Absorbed by: Zeitschrift für Völkerrecht, q.v.

AD/U-6 1903.	LO/N-1	LV/U-1 1924-38 (w.Bd.35;41)
BH/U-1 1924-37	LO/U-1 1921-29	OX/U15
BL/U-1 1923-37	LO/U-3	OX/U25 1890-93
CA/U-1 1923-38	LO/U24 1890-1932 (Bd.46)	
CA/U13 1923-37		

Nieuw magazijn van handelsregt <u>see</u> Magazijn van handelsregt

Nieuwe bijdragen voor regtsgeleerdheid en wetgeving. -- Amsterdam, 1851-1884 (in 34 vols.)

LO/N-1 1853-65 (v.3-15)

Nigeria lawyers' quarterly. -- Lagos, 1964-
ISSN 0029-0025

LO/U14 v.4-6 (undated)	OX/U15 1964-[1973] (v.6)	XY/N-1 1968 (v.3)-19?? (v.5)

Nigerian Bar journal. -- Lagos, 1958-
ISSN 0549-2688

LO/U14 1973-	LO/U24 1957-67; 1973-74	OX/U15 1958-61 (v.1 no.2-v.3 no.1); 1963-

Nigerian journal of contemporary law. -- Lagos, 1970-
ISSN 0048-0401

BL/U-1	LO/U24 imp.	XY/N-1 1973 (v.3 no.2).
LO/U14		

Nigerian law journal. -- Lagos; London, 1964-
ISSN 0078-0774

AB/N-1	CR/U-1	LV/U-1 1964-74
BH/U-1	ED/S11	MA/U-1
BL/U-1	LO/N17 1964-70	NO/U-1 1969 (v.3)-(w.v.7)
BR/U-1 1975 (v.9)-	LO/U-3	OX/U15
CA/U-1 1971-	LO/U12 (w.1965)	QS/S-6
CA/U13	LO/U14	XY/N-1
CB/U-1	LO/U24	

Nigerian law quarterly review. -- Lagos, Apr. 1946-Jan. 1947 (vol.2 no.1)

LO/S65 1946.

Nippon hoigaku zasshi = Japanese journal of legal medicine. -- Tokyo, 1944 (vol.1)-
Continues: Hanzaigaku zasshi: Archiv für gerichtliche Medizin und Kriminologie, 1928-1943 (vol.17 no.5/6)
Both series also cited as: Acta criminologiae et medicinae legalis Japonica
ISSN 0047-1887

CA/U37 1960 (v.26)-

Nisi prius: journal of the law societies in the University of Oxford/ Keble College Law Society. -- Oxford, 1950-1951 (vol.2 no.3)
ISSN 0468-2882

LO/N-1
LO/U24

Nomos: journal of the American Association for Legal and Political Philosophy. -- Cambridge, Mass., 1958-
ISSN 0078-0979

CA/U-1
CR/U-1 1971-
DN/U-1 1971-
DR/U-1 1958;1960-
GL/U-1
HL/U-1
LO/U-2 1958;1963-
OX/U15 1967-
QE/C76 1963;1965;1967-
XY/N-1 (v.10;13;15; 17)-

Nordisk administrativt tidsskrift. -- Copenhagen, 1920-
ISSN 0029-1285

LO/N-1 1929- (v.10-27 imp; w. v.28-33)
LO/U-3 imp.
LO/U24 1960 (v.41)-
XY/N-1 1966 (v.47)-

Nordisk kriminalistisk årsbok. -- Stockholm, 1936-1963
From 1960 has subtitle: Nordiska Kriminalistföreningarnas årsbok
ISSN 0546-2886

LO/N-1 1946-63
LO/U-3
NW/U-1 1959.
OX/U15
XY/N-1 1963.

Nordisk tidsskrift for international ret: Acta Scandinavica juris gentium. -- Copenhagen, 1930-
With vol.21, 1951 absorbed: Jus gentium, q.v., and from then until 1964 (vol.34) entitled: Nordisk tidsskrift for international ret og jus gentium
ISSN 0029-151X

BL/U-1 1935-48
CA/U13 1930-38;1939-50 imp.;1951-
ED/U-1 1935-48;1952-
GL/U-1 (w.v.1 no.3)
LO/N-1 1949-
LO/U-1 1930-46 imp.
LO/U24
NO/U-1 1963 (v.33)- (w.v.34;36-40)
OX/U15 1930- (1947-48; 1952 imp.)
OX/U25 1931-
XY/N-1 1952-55 (v.22-25); 1969 (v.39)-

Nordisk tidsskrift for kriminalvidenskab. -- Copenhagen, 1913-
1913-1948 entitled: Nordisk tidsskrift for strafferet
ISSN 0029-1528

CA/U37
LO/U-3 1949-
XY/N-1 1963 (v.51)-

Nordisk tidsskrift for strafferet *see* previous entry

Nordiskt immateriellt rättsskydd *see* NIR

Nordiskt industriellt rättsskydd *see* NIR

Norsk retstidende. -- Oslo, 1836-
ISSN 0029-2060

LO/N-1 1901-1961/65   LO/U24 1950-65 (v.115-130) imp.

Norske tidende for industrielle rettsvern. -- Oslo, 1911-
Issued in 3 sections: Patenter, ISSN 0029-2206, Varemerker, ISSN 0029-2192, and Mønstre, ISSN 0029-2184

No holdings notified

North Carolina central law journal. -- Durham, N.C., 1970(vol.2)-
Continues: North Carolina College law journal, 1969 (vol.1)
ISSN 0549-7434

No holdings notified

North Carolina College law journal *see* previous entry

North Carolina law journal. -- Tarboro, 1900-1902 (vol.2 no.11)

LO/U24 imp.

North Carolina law review. -- Chapel Hill, 1922-
ISSN 0029-2524

BL/U-1	LO/U24	XY/N-1 1967 (v.45 no.2)-
CA/U13 1957-	OX/U15	

North Dakota Bar briefs *see* next entry

North Dakota law review. -- Grand Forks, etc., 1951 (vol.27)-
Continues: Bar briefs, 1924-1948 (vol.24 no.1) and: North Dakota Bar briefs, 1948 (vol.24 no.2)-1950 (vol.26)
ISSN 0029-2745

LO/U24	OX/U15	XY/N-1 1969 (v.46)-

Northern Ireland legal quarterly. -- Belfast, Nov. 1936-
New series commenced in 1964
ISSN 0029-3105

AB/N-1 1964-	CA/U-1	EX/U-1 1970-
AB/U-1	CA/U13	GL/U-1 1964-
AD/U-6	CB/U-1 1967-	GL/U-2
BH/U-1	CR/U-1	HL/U-1
BL-LS	DN/U-1	KL/U-1 1936-74 (v.25)
BL/U-1	DR/U-1 1964-	LC/U-1
BR/U-1	ED/S11 1942-	LD/C-1
BT/U-1 1936-74	ED/U-1	LD/U-1

(cont'd)

Northern Ireland legal quarterly (cont'd).

LO/C-3
LO/C-5 1974-
LO/C10 1968-
LO-MT
LO/N27 1970-
LO/R74 1964-
LO/U-2
LO/U-3 1977-
LO/U12
LO/U24
LO/U28
LV/U-1
MA/U-1
NO/U-1
NW/U-1
OX/U15
QE/C76 1975-
QM/C68 1975-
QN/C70
QS/S-4 1948-
QS/S-6
QS/S-8 1937-
QW/D12
RE/U-1
SH/U-1 1936-60;1964-
SO/U-1
XM/C10
XY/N-1 1967 (v.18)-

Northern Kentucky law review. -- Covington, Ky., 1976 (vol.3 no.2)-
Continues: Northern Kentucky State law forum, 1973-[1976]

No holdings notified

Northern Kentucky State law forum see previous entry

Northwestern University law review. -- Chicago, 1952 (vol.47)-
Continues: Illinois law review, 1906-1952 (vol.46)
ISSN 0029-3571

BL/U-1 1970-
CA/U13
CR/U-1
LO-MT 1913-
LO/U24
OX/U15
OX/U25 1918/19 imp.
XY/N-1 1964 (v.59)-

Notre Dame journal of legislation/ Notre Dame School of Law. -- Notre Dame, 1974 (vol.1)-
Continues: New dimensions in legislation, 1970-1972 (vol.3), (ISSN 0300-6018)

LO-MT 1970-72 (v.3 no.1)
XY/N-1 1974-75 (v.1-2)

Notre Dame lawyer. -- Notre Dame, Ind., 1925-
ISSN 0029-4535

CA/U13 1959 (v.35)-
LO-MT 1970 (v.46)-
LO/U24
OX/U15
XY/N-1 1969 (v.45)-

Nouvelle revue de droit international privé. -- Paris, 1934-1949 (vol.16)

LO/U-2 1946-47
LO/U-3 1946-48
LO/U24 (w.v.11;12)

Nouvelle revue historique de droit français et étranger see Revue historique de droit français et étranger

Nowe pravo. -- Warsaw, 1945-
1945-Sept. 1950 entitled: Demokratyczny przegląd prawniczy

LO/N-1
LO/U-3
XY/N-1 1955 imp; 1968-

Nuclear law bulletin/ Nuclear Energy Agency, O.E.C.D. -- Paris, 1972 (no.10)-
Continues: Nuclear law bulletin/ European Nuclear Energy Agency, O.E.C.D., 1968-1972 (no.9) (ISSN 0550-3132)
ISSN 0304-341X
For French edition, see: Bulletin de droit nucléaire

CA/U-1 LD/U-1 1968 (no.1). OX/U15
GL/U-2 1973- LO/U24 RE/U-1 1968-69
HL/U-1 1968-69 LV/U-1 1968-76 XY/N-1

Nuova rivista di diritto commerciale, diritto dell'economia, diritto sociale. -- Pisa, 1947-1957 (vol.10)

LO/U-3 OX/U15

Nyt juridisk arkiv. -- Copenhagen, 1812-1820 (Bd.30)
Continues: Juridisk arkiv, 1803-1812

LO/N-1

Nyt juridisk ugeskrift. -- Copenhagen, 1869-1875 (vol.7)
Continues: Juridisk ugeskrift, 1839-1868

LO/U24

Nytt juridiskt arkiv. -- Stockholm, 1874-
From 1876 issued in 2 parts: Avd.1: Tidskrift för lagskipning, 1874- Avd.2: Tidskrift för lagstiftning, 1876-
Continues: Juridiskt arkif, 1830-1862

LO/N-1 1830-62 LO/U24 1: 1874-1964
2: 1876-

Obiter/ London School of Economics Law Society. -- London, 1952-1964
ISSN 0473-7121

LO/N-1 LO/U-1 1953-57 imp. LO/U-3 imp.

Obiter/ Queen Mary College Law Society. -- London, 1976-

LO/U12

Obiter dicta/ Osgoode Hall Legal and Literary Society. -- Toronto, Ont., 1928-
Until 1963 semiannual, ISSN 0472-4143.
From 1963 monthly, ISSN 0029-7585.
Vol.21 never published

LO/U24 1943-63 imp. OX/U15 1960.

L'Observateur see The Examiner

Occasional newsletter - American Bar Association Special Committee on Environmental Law see Quarterly newsletter...

Ocean development and international law. -- New York, 1973-
ISSN 0090-8320

CA/U13 LO/U-2 LO/U24
ED/U-1 LO/U-3 1974 (v.2)- XY/N-1 1974 (v.2)-
LO/S14

Ocean management. -- Amsterdam, 1973-
ISSN 0302-184X

CA/U13 LO/U24

Offender rehabilitation. -- New York, 1976-

XY/N-1

Öffentliche Verwaltung. -- Stuttgart, 1948-
ISSN 0029-859X

ED/U-1 1966- LO/U24 1965 (Jg.18)- XY/N-1 1966 (Jg.19)-
LO/U-3 1951-62 imp. OX/U-1 1957-

Official journal of patents, trademarks, designs and copyright see Patent journal including Trademarks and models

Ohio Northern University intramural law review see next entry

Ohio Northern University law review. -- Ada, Ohio, 1973 (vol.1)-
Continues: Ohio Northern University intramural law review, 1970-1972?
ISSN 0094-534X

OX/U15 1973-

Ohio State law journal. -- Columbus, 1935-1941;1948-
1935-1937 entitled: Law journal of the Student Bar Association of Ohio State University
ISSN 0048-1572

BL/U-1 1964- OX/U15 XY/N-1 1970 (v.31)-
LO/U24

Oil and gas tax quarterly. -- Albany, N.Y., 1951-
ISSN 0030-1396

LO/U24 1971 (v.20)-

Oklahoma law review. -- Norman, Okla., May 1948-
ISSN 0030-1752

BL/U-1 1964- LO/C47 1976- OX/U15 1951-
CA/U13 1968- LO/U24 XY/N-1 1968 (v.21)-

Ophavsretlige perspektiver. -- Copenhagen, 1954/58-

No holdings notified

Oregon law review. -- Eugene, 1921-

BH/U-1 1964-	CA/U13 1936-	OX/U15
BL/U-1 1963-	LO/U24	XY/N-1 1969 (v.49)-

Oregon State Bar bulletin. -- Eugene; Portland, 1935-

OX/U15 1935-39 (v.4)

Osaka law review <u>see</u> Handai hōgaku

Osaka University law review. -- Osaka, 1952-
ISSN 0472-1381

BH/U-1	LD/U-1 imp.	LV/U-1 1963-
BL/U-1 1953-	LO/U24	OX/U15

Osgoode Hall law journal. -- Toronto, 1958-
ISSN 0030-6185

AB/U-1 1960-70 imp.	CV/U-1 1974 (v.12)-	NO/U-1 1975 (v.13)-
BL/U-1 1965-68 imp., 1973-	ED/U-1	OX/U15
	LO/U-3 1977-	SH/U-1
BR/U-1 1975 (v.13)-	LO/U12 1975-	XY/N-1 1973 (v.11)-
CA/U13	LO/U24	

Österreichische Blätter für gewerblichen Rechtsschutz. -- Vienna, 1933-1937 (Bd.4 Hft.2/3)

LO/N14

Österreichische Blätter für gewerblichen Rechtsschutz und Urheberrecht. -- Vienna, 1952-
Beilage zur Zeitschrift Die Industrie
ISSN 0029-8921

LO/N14

Österreichische Juristen-Zeitung. -- Vienna, 1946-
ISSN 0029-9251

LO/U24 1960 (Jg.15)-	OX/U15 1969 (Jg.24)-	XY/N-1 1964 (Jg.19)-

Österreichische Vierteljahresschrift für Rechts- und Staatswissenschaft. -- Vienna, 1858-1866 (Bd.18)
Continues: Magazin für Rechts- und Staatswissenschaft, 1850-1857 (Bd.16)

LO/N-1	LO/U-3 1850-57

Österreichische Zeitschrift für öffentliches Recht <u>see</u> next entry

Österreichische Zeitschrift für öffentliches Recht und Völkerrecht. -- Vienna, 1977 (N.F. Bd.28)-
Continues: Österreichische Zeitschrift für öffentliches Recht, 1914-1917 (Bd.3); Zeitschrift für öffentliches Recht, 1919 (Bd.1)-1942 (Bd.23) and: Österreichische Zeitschrift für öffentliches Recht, 1946 (N.F. Bd.1)-1976 (N.F. Bd.27)

ED/U-1 1929-33	LO/U-3 1919- (w.1920/21)	OX/U15 1946-
LO/N17 1916-18	LO/U24	XY/N-1 1966 (N.F. Bd.16)-

Österreichische Zeitschrift für Rechts- und Staatswissenschaft. -- Vienna, 1846-1849
Continues: Zeitschrift für österreichische Rechtsgelehrsamkeit und politische Gesetzkunde, 1825-1845

LO/N-1 (1846 imp.)

Österreichisches Archiv für Kirchenrecht. -- Vienna, 1950-
ISSN 0029-9820

XY/N-1 1972 (Jg.23)-

Osteuropa-Recht: Gegenwartsfragen aus den Rechten des Ostens. -- Stuttgart, 1955-
Sub-title varies
ISSN 0030-6444

CA/U13 1957-	LO/N-1	LO/U11 1956-
GL/U-1 Soviet Studies Branch Library	LO/S14	LO/U24 1960 (Jg.6)-
	LO/U-2 1960-	OX/U15
	LO/U-3	XY/N-1 1966 (Jg.12)-

Ostrecht. -- Berlin, 1925-1927 (Jg.3)
Merged with: Zeitschrift für osteuropäisches Recht to form: Zeitschrift für Ostrecht, q.v.

LO/U-3

Otago law review. -- Dunedin, N.Z., 1965-
ISSN 0078-6918

BL/U-1 1969-	OX/U15	SO/U-1 1973-
LO/U24		

Ottawa law review. -- Ottawa, 1966-
ISSN 0048-2331

BH/U-1	LO/U24	SO/U-1 1973-
BL/U-1	OX/U15	XY/N-1 1967 (v.2)-
CA/U13	SH/U-1 1967 (v.2)-	

Oudh law journal. -- Lucknow, 1914-1926

LO/U14	OX/U15

Oudh weekly notes. -- Lucknow; Allahabad, 1924-1948

OX/U15

Oxford lawyer see Lawyer (Oxford)

Oyez bulletin. -- London, 1937-1940

LO/N-1

Oyez! Oyez! Bulletin of the Judicial Administration Division, American Bar Association. -- Chicago, 1957-1974
ISSN 0569-3225

LO/U24 1962-68 imp., 1969-74

PICAO journal/ Provisional International Civil Aviation Organization. -- Montreal, 1945-Sept.1946/May 1947 (vol.1 no.8)
Ceased publication

CA/U13

PICAO monthly bulletin see ICAO bulletin

Pacific law journal. -- Sacramento, Cal., 1970-
ISSN 0030-8757

CA/U13 1971- LO/U24

Pakistan Bar journal. -- Lahore, 1956-1960 (vol.5 no.2)
ISSN 0479-2289

LO/U14 1958-60 imp.

Pakistan criminal law journal. -- Lahore, 1968-

OX/U15

Pakistan law review. -- Karachi, 1952 (vol.1 no.1)
ISSN 0479-2394

LO/U14

Palestra/ Naczelna Rada Adwokacka. -- Warsaw, 1957-
Continues its Biuletyn, 1956.
ISSN 0031-0344

LO/N-1 1957-
LO/U-3 1960-May 1976 imp.
OX/U15 (1957 imp.)
XY/N-1 1962 (Rok 6)-

Pandectes françaises périodiques see Recueil Sirey

Pánstwo i prawo. -- Warsaw, 1946-
From 1957 (vol.12) contains English summary entitled: State and law
ISSN 0031-0980

CA/U13 1956-63 imp.
LO/N-1
LO/U-3 imp.
OX/U15 1947-52 imp., 1953-
XY/N-1 (w.1960-65)

Papers of the annual conference of the Nigerian Society of International Law. -- Benin City, (ca 1969)-

LO/U14 1971 (3rd)-

Papers read before the Juridical Society, 1855-1873. -- London, 1858-1874 (vol.4 no.5)

AB/N-1 1855-71
CA/U-1
LO/N-1
LO/U-2 1857 (Oct.).
OX/U15
QS/S-7 1855-58

Papers read before the Medico-Legal Society of New York. -- New York, 1868-1878

LO/N-1 1874-78

Patent and trade mark review. -- New York, Oct. 1902-
ISSN 0031-2835

LO/N14
MA/P-1 1922/23-
LV/P-1 Oct.1953-
XY/N-1 1977 (v.75)-

Patent and trade mark review/ Patent Attorneys' Association, Japan. -- Tokyo, 1932-1941
In Japanese

LO/N14 (w.v.3 no.3)

Patent, design and trade mark review. -- Calcutta, 1944-

LO/N14 1944-54

Patent journal including Trademarks and models. -- Pretoria, 1961 (vol.1)-
Continues: Official journal of patents, trade marks, designs and copyright, 1948-1960
ISSN 0031-286X

LO/N-1
XY/N-1 1963 (v.3)-

Patent law annual: proceedings of the Annual Institute on Patent Law/ Southwestern Legal Foundation. -- Washington D.C., 1963-
Entitled Patent law annual from 1966.
Earlier vols. have distinctive titles
ISSN 0553-3864

LO/N14

Patent law review. -- Albany, N.Y., 1969-
ISSN 0079-0168

AB/U-1
BH/U-1 imp.
CA/U-1 1973-
ED/U-1
GL/U-2
HL/U-1 1973 (v.5).
LO/C47
LO/N14
LO-SC 1969-73 (v.5)
LO/U12
MA/U-1
OX/U15 1969;1973.
QS/Q12
QW/D12
SO/U-1
XM/C10 1970-73;1975.
XY/N-1

Patent Office journal. -- Calcutta,

LO/S55 1921-40;1946;1950-

Patent Office Society journal. -- Washington D.C., 1918-
ISSN 0031-2886

LV/P-1 1959-

Patent, trademark and copyright journal of research and education
see Idea: the journal of law and technology

Patna law journal. -- Bankipore, 1916-1921 (vol.6)

DR/U-4 1916;1918-21
LO-MT
LO/N-1
LO-PC
LO/U14
OX/U15
QS/S-6
QS/S-7

Penal Reform League monthly record see next entry

Penal Reform League quarterly record. -- London, 1909-1920 (vol.9)
1909-1912 (vol.4 no.8/9) entitled: Penal Reform League monthly
record

LO/N-1
LO/U-3 imp.

Penal reform news = Strafhervormingnuus. -- Pretoria, 1947-

OX/U-9 1947-64 (nos.2-65)

Penal reformer/ Howard League for Penal Reform. -- London, 1934-
1939 (vol.6)

LO/N-1
LO/U-3
OX/U15

Penant: revue de droit des pays d'Afrique. -- Paris, 1934-
Continues: Tribune des colonies et des protectorats, 1891-1899;
and: Recueil général de jurisprudence, de doctrine et de législation
coloniales et maritimes, 1899-1933. 1958-1960 entitled: Recueil
Penant. Subtitle varies
ISSN 0034-1894

BH/U-1 1963-
CA/U13 1963-
LO/U14 1967-
LO/U24 1955 (v.65)-
OX/U15 1949-
XY/N-1 1967 (no.715)-

Pennsylvania Bar Association quarterly. -- Harrisburg, 1929-

LO/U24

Pennsylvania law journal see American law journal

Peperdine law review. -- Anaheim, Cal., 1973-
ISSN 0092-430X

No holdings notified

Performing arts review: the journal of management and law of the arts. -- New York, 1969-
ISSN 0031-5249

XY/N-1 1972 (v.3)-

Performing right/ Performing Right Society. -- London, 1939-
Continues: Performing right gazette, 1922-1939
ISSN 0031-5257

CA/U-1 LO/N-1 LO/N14 1957 (v.29)-

Performing right gazette see previous entry

Persona y derecho: revista de fundamentación de las instituciones jurídicas y de cuestiones interdisciplinares/ Facultad de Derecho, Universidad de Navarra. -- Pamplona, 1975-

No holdings notified

Philippine international law journal. -- Manila, 1962-1966 (vol. 4 no.1/2)
ISSN 0031-7675

CA/U13 1962-65 imp. DR/U-1 1965. LO/U24

Philippine journal of public administration/ University of the Philippines, Institute of Public Administration. -- Manila, 1957-
ISSN 0031-7675

DR/U-1 1957-67 imp., 1968- GL/U-2 imp. LO/N-1 1957-67;1973- LO/U14 1973- XY/N-1 1966 (v.10)-

Philippine labour relations journal. -- Manila,

No holdings notified

Philippine law journal. -- Quezon City, 1914-
ISSN 0031-7721

LO/U24 1960 (v.35)- XY/N-1 1968 (v.43)-

Planning, zoning and eminent domain institute/ Southwestern Legal Foundation. -- New York, 1970-
Merger of: Proceedings - Institute on planning and zoning, 1960-1969, q.v. and: Proceedings - Institute on eminent domain, 1959-1969, q.v.

No holdings notified

Police Federation newsletter. -- London, 1957-

CA/U-1 1962- imp.	LO/N-1	OX/U15 (w.1961, 1962 (June),1963)

Police journal. -- London, 1928-
Last 10 years not available for public use
ISSN 0032-258X

BL/U-1 1967-76	LO/N-1	MA/P-1 1928-47 (w.Jan-Mar.1944)
CA/U-1	LO/N27	OX/U15
CA/U37	LO/U24 1928-35;1963 (v.36)-	XY/N-1 1947-60 imp., 1961 (v.34)-
ED/N-1		
HL/U-1 1932-39		

Police law quarterly. -- Chicago, 1971-

XY/N-1 1972 (v.2)-

Polish yearbook of international law. -- Wroclaw, 1968-

CA/U-1 1968/69 (v.2)-	LO/U-2 1968/69 (v.2)-	OX/U15
CA/U13 (w.1971 (v.4))	LO/U24 1970 (v.3)-	OX/U25 1970,1974-
HL/U-1 1974 (v.6).		XY/N-1 1970 (v.3)-

Poly law review/ Polytechnic of Central London School of Law. -- London, 1975-

AB/U-1	LO/C15	LO/U-3
BC-UC 1975.	LO/C25	OX/U15
CA/U-1	LO/C47	QE/C76
CA/U13	LO-MT	QL/D15
ED/S11	LO/N-1	QM/C48
HL/U-1	LO/N26 1976 (v.1 no.3)-	QN/C70
LO/C14		XY/N-1

Pomorsko pravo. -- Zagreb, 1951-

LO/N-1

Poor law and local government magazine. -- Edinburgh; Glasgow, 1858-1930
1st series 1858-1867, 9 vols., new series 1868-1872, 5 vols, 3rd series 1873-1890, 18 vols, new series 1891-1930, 40 vols.
To 1903 entitled: Poor law magazine

ED/S10	ED/S11 1891-1930	LO/N-1

Poor law magazine <u>see</u> previous entry

Pophak (The Seoul law journal). -- Seoul, Korea, 1959-

CA/U-1 1963- imp.	LO/U14	XY/N-1 1967 (v.9)-
LO/N-1 1959;1962-	OX/U-1 1959-68 imp.	

Popular monthly law tracts. -- London, 1877-1878

LO/N-1	OX/U15 (w.1877 (nos.2-4))

Portia law journal <u>see</u> New England law review

Practical lawyer. -- Philadelphia, 1955-
ISSN 0032-6429

BL/U-1 1964- LO/U24 XY/N-1 1970 (v.16)-

Pravna misăl. -- Sofia, 1935-1943

OX/U15 1935-41

Pravna misla: spisanie za pravni i opstestveni prasanja. -- Skopje, 1955?-
ISSN 0032-695X

LO/N-1 1960- OX/U15 1960 (no.10)-

Pravna misŭl. -- Sofia, 1957-
ISSN 0032-6968

LO/N-1 LO/U-3 OX/U15 1957;1960; 1962-

Právněhistorické studie. -- Prague, 1955-
ISSN 0079-4929

CA/U-1 1973- OX/U15 XY/N-1
LO/N-1

Pravni zbornik. -- Titograd, 1933-1940;1952-

LO/N-1 1960- OX/U15 1960 (n.s. no.9)-

Pravni život. -- Belgrade, 1952-1975

LO/N-1 1954-57 imp. LO/U-3 1953-75 imp.

Právnické štúdie. -- Bratislava, 1953-

LO/N-1 1957 (v.5)- OX/U15 1957 (v.5)- XY/N-1 1967 (v.15)-
LO/U-3

Právnik. -- Prague, 1861-

GL/U-1 Soviet Studies Branch Library 1971- LO/N-1 1960 (v.99)- LO/U-3 1949- (w. 1949 (1);1950) OX/U15 1870-97 imp., 1899- XY/N-1 1969 (Roč.108).

Pravnik: revija za pravno teorijo in prakso. -- Ljubljana, 1946-
ISSN 0032-6976

LO/N-1 LO/U-3 (w.1953 (10/12))

Právny obzor. -- Bratislava, 1918-
ISSN 0032-6984

LO/N-1 1954 (v.37)- OX/U15 1970 (Roč.53)- XY/N-1 1967 (Roč.50).
LO/U-3 1952-

Pravo: ezhediel'naya yuridicheskaya gazeta. -- Petrograd, 1898-1917

OX/U15 1899-1916 imp.

Pravovedenie. -- Leningrad, 1957-

GL/U-1 Soviet Studies Branch Library 1959-
LO/U-2 1957-69
OX/U15

Prawo kanoniczne. -- Warsaw, 1958-

LO/N-1
OX/U15
XY/N-1 1959-64 imp., 1972-

Praxis/ University of Kent Law Clinic. -- Canterbury, 1973-

AB/U-1
CB/U-1
CR/U-1
CV/U-1 1974 (no.3)-
QL/D15 1974 (no.3)-
QN/C70 1976 (no.4)-

Preliminary/ Incorporated Law Society. -- London, 1868-1879 (no.54)

LO/N-1
OX/U15

Preliminary examination journal and student's literary magazine. -- London, 1871-1875

LO/N-1
OX/U15

Preussische Anwaltszeitung see Zeitschrift für die deutsche Gesetzgebung und für einheitliches deutsches Recht

Preussische Gerichts-Zeitung see Deutsche Gerichts-Zeitung

Preussische Justiz: Rechtspflege und Rechtspolitik see Deutsche Justiz: Rechtspflege und Rechtspolitik

Preussisches Verwaltungsblatt see Deutsches Verwaltungsblatt

Prison service journal. -- Wakefield, 1960-
ISSN 0300-3558

AD/U-6
BH/U-1
BL/U-1 (w.v.1 no.4)
BT/U-1
CA/U-1
CA/U37 1962-
CC/U-1 1965-
CR/U-1 1971.
CV/U-1 1972-
DR/U-1 1960-61
ED/N-1
HL/U-1
LO/C-3 1968-
LO/N-1
LO/N27
LO-SC July 1975.
LO/U-3
LO/U11 1976-
LO/U24
LO/U28 1971-
LV-LP 1974 (no.13)-
MA/P-1 1960-70
OX/U15
QS/Q29
QW/C73
SO/U-1
XY/N-1

Probation (Croydon) see Probation journal

Probation (New York) see NCCD news

Probation journal. -- Croydon, 1974 (vol.21)-
Continues: Probation, 1929-1973 (vol.20) (ISSN 0048-539X)

AD/U-6 1966-	GL/U-2 1962-	LO/U28 1970 (v.16)-
BH/U-1 1956-	HL/U-1 1962-	NW/U-1 1956-
BL/U-1 1958- imp.	KL/U-1 1969 (v.15)-	OX/U15 1930 (v.1 no.3)-
BT/U-1 1965-	LA/U-1 1974.	QW/C73 1962 (Sept.)-
CA/U-1 1958-	LC/U-1 1953-	QW/D12 1965-73 imp., 1974 (v.21)-
CA/U37	LO/C-3 1967-	SO/U-1 1950-
CB/U-1 1955 (v.7)-	LO/C14 1959 (v.9)-	SW/U-1 1956-
CR/U-1 1962-	LO-MT 1965-	XY/N-1 1965 (v.11)-
CV/U-1 1974-	LO/N-1	
ED/N-1 1958-	LO/U11 1976-	

Probleme de medicina judiciara şi de criminalistica. -- Bucharest,

LO/N-1 1965 (v.2)-   XY/N-1 1965-69 (v.3-8)

Proceedings - American Bar Association Section of Antitrust Law
see Antitrust law journal

Proceedings - American Bar Association. Section of International and Comparative Law see International lawyer/ American Bar Association. Section of International Law

Proceedings - Association of American Law Schools. -- Washington D.C., 1950-
Continues: Minutes of the annual meeting, 1901; Proceedings, 1902-1914; Handbook and proceedings, 1915-1941; and Handbook, 1942-1949
ISSN 0066-9407

LO/U24 1928 (26th)-   OX/U15 1965-

Proceedings - Conference on labor/ New York University. -- New York, 1948-
ISSN 0069-8563

No holdings notified

Proceedings - Institute on eminent domain/ Southwestern Legal Foundation. -- New York? 1959-1969
1970 merged with Proceedings - Institute on planning and zoning to form: Planning, zoning and eminent domain institute, q.v.
ISSN 0537-975X

No holdings notified

Proceedings - Institute on mineral law/ Louisiana State University. -- Baton Rouge, 1953-
ISSN 0076-1087

No holdings notified

Proceedings - Institute on planning and zoning/ Southwestern Legal Foundation. -- Albany, N.Y., 1960-1969
1970 merged with: Proceedings - Institute on eminent domain to form: Planning, zoning and eminent domain institute, q.v.
ISSN 0537-9814

No holdings notified

Proceedings - International symposium on comparative law of the Canadian and Foreign Law Research Centre see Travaux - Colloque international de droit comparé du Centre Canadien de Droit Comparé

Proceedings - Medico-Legal Society of New South Wales. -- Sydney, 1960/62-
ISSN 0047-6587

No holdings notified

Proceedings - New York University Institute on Federal Taxation. -- Albany, 1942-

LO/U24 1970 (29th)-   XY/N-1 1972 (30th)-

Proceedings - University of Southern California, Tax Institute. -- Albany, N.Y., 1949-

LO/U24 1971 (23rd)-

Proceedings of the American Law Institute. -- Philadelphia, 1923-
ISSN 0056-9045

BL/U-1 1923-30
CA/U13 1956- imp.
LO/U24 1923-44; 1956 (33rd)-
OX/U15 1923-44;1956-
QS/S-6 1923-36

Proceedings of the American Society of International Law. -- Washington D.C., 1907-
ISSN 0066-0647

AB/U-1
AD/U-6
BH/U-1 1961-
BL/U-1 1938-52;1961-
BR/U-1 1961-
BT/U-1 1967-
CA/U-1 1907-11;1931; 1961-
CA/U13 1909- imp.
CB/U-1 1966-
CR/U-1 1938-52 imp.
CV/U-1 1963-
DN/U-1 1961-
DR/U-1 1965-
ED/U-1 1938-55 imp., 1961-
EX/U-1 1964-
GL/U-1 1938-
GL/U-2 1975-
HL/U-1 1944-45;1950-
KL/U-1 1956- imp.
LA/U-1 1959-75
LC/U-1
LD/U-1
LO-MT 1922;1931; 1956-
LO/N-1 1907-32
LO/N17 1947-
LO/S14 1970-
LO/U-1 1968-
LO/U-2 1931;1938-
LO/U-3 1907-64;1969; 1974-
LO/U11
LO/U24
LV/P-1 1944;1961-69
LV/U-1 1961-
MA/U-1
NO/U-1 (w.v.53-54)
NW/U-1 1961-
OX/U15
QS/S-6 1961-
QS/S-7
QW/D12 1974-
RE/U-1 1974-
SH/U-1 1963-
SO/U-1 1961-

Proceedings of the annual conference - Canadian Council on International Law. -- Ottawa, 1972-

LO/U24

Proceedings of the Annual Conference of the Law of the Sea Institute, University of Rhode Island <u>see</u> Law of the sea

Proceedings of the annual Institute on oil and gas law and taxation. -- Albany, N.Y. 1949-

LO/U24 1971 (22nd)- XY/N-1 1971 (22nd)-

Proceedings of the Australian and New Zealand Society of International Law. -- Melbourne, 1935.

AD/U-6
CA/U-1
ED/U-1
LO/N-1
LO/U-3
LO/U24
OX/U15

Proceedings of the... biennial conference on charitable foundations/ New York University Institute on Federal Taxation. -- Albany, 1953-

LO/U24 1969 (9th)-

Proceedings of the Canadian Bar Association <u>see</u> Yearbook of the Canadian Bar Association

Proceedings of the Canadian Society of Forensic Science. -- Ottawa, 1962-1965 (vol.4)

LO/U24 (w.v.1) XY/N-1 1964-65 (v.3-4)

Proceedings of the Colloquium on the law of outer space. Vienna, etc., 1958-
ISSN 0069-5831

CA/U13 1963 (no.4); 1964 (no.6)-
ED/U-1 1958-60;1965-
LO/S14
LO/U-2
LO/U24
OX/U15
XY/N-1 1961 (4th)-

Proceedings of the East-West Trade Conference, Stanford University <u>see</u> Stanford journal of international studies

Proceedings of the Institute of Patent Attorneys of Australia. -- Melbourne, 1918/19-

LO/N14 1920 (no.3)-

Proceedings of the Medico-Legal Society of Victoria. -- Melbourne, 1931-
ISSN 0047-6595

CA/U-1 1955-
LO/M32 1931-1966/69
LO/U24 1946/53-66/69 (v.5-11)
OX/U-1 1937-
QS/S-4 1933-38

Proceedings of the Natural Law Institute/ University of Notre Dame. -- Notre Dame, Ind., 1947-1951 (vol.5)

LO/U-3
LO/U24
OX/U15

Proceedings of the New York State Bar Association. -- Albany, 1877-1968 (vol.91)

LO/U24 1898-1968 (v.21-91) imp.   OX/U15 1966-68 (v.89-91)

Proche-Orient, études juridiques: (sub-series of) annales de la Faculté de Droit et des Sciences Economiques. -- Beirut, 1967-
ISSN 0032-9649

LO/N-1   LO/U24 1967-73 (no.17)   XY/N-1 1969 (no.6)-
LO/U14

Professional administration. -- London, 1971 (vol.1)-
Continues: Secretary, 1904-1960 (vol.57) and: Chartered secretary, 1961 (vol.1)-1971 (vol.11 no.3)

BH/P-1
BH/U-1 1920-
BR/U-1 1904-60 imp. 1961-
CA/U-1
CB/U-1 1947-71
CV/C-1 1961-71
ED/S11
ED/U-1 1939-60 imp., 1961-
GL/U-1 1949-
GL/U-2 1954-71 imp.
LA/U-1 1969-71
LC/U-1 1963-
LD/C-1 1931-52;1955-60;1961-70 (v.10);1971-
LD/P-1 1961-71
LO/C-3 1968-
LO/C-5 1965-71 (v.11 no.3) imp., 1971 (v.1)-
LO/C14 1968-70
LO-CBL last 10 years
LO-MT 1958-
LO/N-1
LO/N26 last 3 years
LO/S28 1961-
LO/U-1 1921-
LO/U-3 1925-60
LO/U24 1950 (v.47)-
LV-LP last 5 years
LV/P-1 1906-
MA/P-1 1904-70;1971-
NW/U-1 1925-61 (w.v.24)
OX/U-1
QG/C25 1971-
QM/C68 Jun.1972-Nov. 1975 imp.
QN/C70 1961-
QS/Q29 1933-43;1949-
QS/S-6 1953-
QW/D12 1961-
XY/N-1 1910-60 (v.7-57); 1965 (v.5)-

Progress in nuclear energy: series 10, Law and administration. -- London, 1959-1966 (vol.4)
ISSN 0079-6549

AD/U-6   LO/N-1   LO/U-2
CA/U-1   LO/N14   XY/N-1 1962-66 (v.3-4)

Prometheus: für Licht und Recht, Zeitschrift in zwanglosen Heften. -- Aarau, 1832-1833 (no.3)

LO/N-1

Property lawyer. -- London, 1826-1830

BH-LS   QS/S-7 1826-29   QS/S-8
LO/N-1 1826 (Jan.).

Propriété industrielle. -- Berne, 1885-
From 1962 also published in English as: Industrial property, q.v.
ISSN 0033-1430

LO/N-1   LO/U24 1921-42;1961.   XY/N-1 1972 (88e année)-
LO/N14 1885-1961

Prosecutor/ National District Attorneys' Association. -- Chicago, 1965-
Vols. 1-3 no.3 entitled: NDAA
ISSN 0027-6383

No holdings notified

Prospectus see University of Michigan journal of law reform

Provisional International Civil Aviation Organization journal see PICAO journal

Przegląd polski ustawodawstwa cywilnego i kryminalnego see Revue polonaise de législation civile et criminelle

Przegląd ustawodawstwa gospodarczego = Economic legislation review. -- Warsaw, 1948-

LO/N-1 1953 (v.4 no.3)-
LO/U-3 1950- imp.
OX/U-1 1950- imp.
XY/N-1 1954-57 imp., 1967 (Rok.20)-

Public administration. -- London, 1926 (vol.4)-
Continues: Journal of public administration, 1923-1925 (vol.3)
ISSN 0033-3298

AB/N-1
AB/U-1
AD/U-6 1926-32;1952-
BH/P-1
BH/U-1
BL/U-1 (w.1924 (v.2 no.4))
BR/U-1
BT/U-1
CA/U-1
CA/U13 1948-55;1957-
CB/U-1
CC/U-1
CR/U-1 1938-49 imp., 1950-
CV/U-1 1945 (v.23)-
DN/U-1 1946- (1949-52 imp.)
DR/U-1 1926-
ED/N-1
ED-SLC 1965-
ED/U-1 1946-
EX/U-1
GL/U-1 1925-
GL/U-2 1933- imp.
HL/U-1
KL/U-1 imp.
LA/U-1 1947-
LC/C-1 1950-
LC/U-1
LD/C-1 1928-37;1945-46;1954 (v.32)-
LD/P-1
LD/U-1 1927-
LO/C-3 1950-
LO/C-5 1955-60 imp., 1967-
LO/C14 1949 (v.27)-
LO/C15 1970-
LO/C47 1941-
LO-CBL 1954-*
LO/N-1
LO/N-5 1923-40 imp., 1941-
LO/N17
LO/N26 1924-
LO/N27 1963-
LO/N46
LO/P-6 1954-
LO/S65 1951-65
LO-TS 1973-
LO/U-1
LO/U-2 1946-
LO/U-3
LO/U12 1965- (w.1969 no.1)
LO/U24
LO/U28 1952 (v.30)-
LV-LP 1964 (v.42)- imp.
LV/P-1 1923-32;1939-
LV/U-1
MA/P-1
NW/U-1 1951 (v.29)-
OX/U-1
OX/U25
QE/C76 1960-
QM/C48 1923-57;1965- (v.1-10 microfilm)
QM/C68 1960 (v.38)-
QN/C70 1957-
QS/Q12 1929-47 imp., 1948-
QS/Q29 1923-24 imp., 1925-65;1966 imp.,1967-
QW/C73
QW/D12 1946 (v.24)-
RE/U-1
SH/U-1 1966 (v.44)-
SO/U-1 1926-
SW/U-1 1926-30;1940-
XY/N-1
YK/U-1 1963-

Public administration (Sydney) see Australian journal of public administration

Public administration in Israel and abroad <u>see</u> Israel annual of public administration and public policy

Public administration review/ American Society for Public Administration. -- Washington D.C., 1940-
ISSN 0033-3352

AB/U-1 1965-
BH/U-1 1947-
BL/U-1 1947-52
BR/U-1 1948-
BT/U-1
CA/U-1
CB/U-1 1947- (w.v.10-11,21)
CC/U-1
CV/U-1 1963-
DR/U-1 1959-
ED/U-1
EX/U-1 1958-
GL/U-1 1948-
GL/U-2
HL/U-1
KL/U-1 imp.
LA/U-1 1966-
LC/C-1 1972-
LC/U-1
LD/C-1 1970 (v.30)-
LD/U-1 1948-
LO/C25 1977-
LO/C47 1971-
LO/N-1 1963-
LO/N17 1951-71 imp.
LO/U-1 1970-
LO/U-3
LO/U28 1973-
LV-LP 1976-
LV/U-1 1945-
QN/C70 1968-
QW/D12 1965-66 (v.25-26);1969 (v.29)-
SO/U-1
SW/U-1
XY/N-1 1947-59 imp., 1963 (v.23)-
YK/U-1 1966 (March)-

Public contract law journal/ American Bar Association Section of Public Contract Law. -- Chicago, 1967-
ISSN 0033-3441

LO/U24

Public law: the constitutional and administrative law of the Commonwealth. -- London, 1956-
1958 absorbed: British journal of administrative law, q.v.
ISSN 0033-3565

AB/N-1
AB/U-1
AD/U-6
BC-UC 1964-
BH-LS
BH/U-1
BL/U-1
BR/U-1
BT/U-1 1965-66;1970-
CA/U-1
CA/U13
CB/U-1 1959-
CH-CI 1966-
CR/U-1
CV/C-1 1958-
CV/U-1
DN/U-1
DR/U-1
ED/S10 1956-69
ED/S11
ED-SLC 1958-
ED/U-1
EX/U-1
GL/U-1
GL/U-2
HL/U-1
KL/U-1
LA/U-1
LC/C-1 1958-
LC/U-1
LD/C-1 1958;1961-
LD/U-1
LO/C-3 1958-
LO/C-5
LO/C10 1958-
LO/C14 1958-
LO/C15 (w.1957)
LO/C25 1963-
LO/C27
LO/C47 1961-
LO-MT
LO/N-1
LO/N-5
LO/N17
LO/N26
LO/N46
LO/R74 1967-
LO-SC (w.1968-71)
LO-TS
LO/U-1
LO/U-2
LO/U-3
LO/U11
LO/U12 1958-
LO/U14
LO/U24
LO/U28 1965-
LV-LP 1970-
LV/P-1
LV/U-1
MA/P-1 1964-
MA/U-1
NO/U-1
NW/U-1
OX/U15
OX/U25
QE/C76
QG/C25 1964-
QL/D15
QM/C48 1958- (w.1960)
QM/C68 1958-
QN/C70
QS/Q12 1958-
QS/Q13 1958-
QS/S-4

(cont'd)

Public law: the constitutional and administrative law of the Commonwealth (cont'd).

QS/S-6	RE/U-1	XM/C10 1958-
QS/S-7	SH/U-1	XY/N-1 1958-
QS/S-8	SO/U-1	YK/U-1
QW/D12	SW/U-1	

Public utilities law anthology. -- Arlington, Va., 1974-

No holdings notified

Publicist. -- Berlin, 1845-1849

LO/N-1

Publishing, entertainment, advertising and allied fields law quarterly. -- Mundelein, Ill.; Pittsburgh, Pa., 1961-
ISSN 0555-6392

No holdings notified

Pump Court. -- London, 1883-1891 (no.12)

ED/S11	LO/N-1	OX/U15
LO-MT 1883-86	LO/U24 1883-86	QS/S-7 1883-84

Punjab record. -- Lahore, 1866- (?)

LO-MT 1898-1919 (v.33-54)	LO/U14 1896-1919 imp.	QS/S-7 1912-19 (v.54)
	OX/U15 1866-1905	

al-Qadā' (A legal journal). -- Baghdad, 1942-

LO/U14 1944-45

al-Qadā' wa'l-tashrī (A monthly law journal). -- Tunis,

LO/U14 1959 (v.1 no.4)- imp.

Quaderni di criminologia clinica. -- Rome, 1959-
Quarterly supplement to: Rassegna di studi penitenziari, q.v.
ISSN 0033-4928

CA/U37 1962-	OX/U15	XY/N-1 1962 (an.4)-
LO/U-3		

Quaderni fiorentini per la storia del pensiero giuridico moderno. -- Milan, 1972-

No holdings notified

Quaderni giuridici/ Ordine degli Avvocati di Roma. -- Milan, 1965-
ISSN 0481-1100

LO/U24

Quarterly law review <u>see</u> Kikan horitsugaku

Quarterly newsletter - American Bar Association Special Committee on Environmental Law. -- Chicago, 1974-
Continues: Occasional newsletter... 1973.
ISSN 0093-7797

LO/U24

Quarterly review of jurisprudence. -- London, (1887-88?)

LO/N-1 OX/U15

Quarterly review of socialist law <u>see</u> Review of socialist law

Queens intramural law journal <u>see</u> next entry

Queens law journal. -- Kingston, Ont., 1971 (vol.1 no.2)-
Continues: Queens intramural law journal, 1968-1970 (vol.1 no.1)
(ISSN 0048-6310)

LO/U-2 1971 (v.1 no.2). LO/U24 (w.v.1 no.1) OX/U15

Queensland Justice of the Peace and reports <u>see</u> Queensland lawyer

Queensland Law Society journal. -- Brisbane, 1971-

BL-LS LO/U24 OX/U15

Queensland lawyer. -- Brisbane, 1973-
Continues: Queensland Justice of the Peace and reports, 1907-1973 (ISSN 0033-6181)

LO/U24 OX/U15

Quis custodiet? <u>see</u> Law and justice

R.C.M.P. quarterly/ Royal Canadian Mounted Police = GRC revue trimestrielle. -- Ottawa, 1933-
ISSN 0033-6858

QW/C73

Rabels Zeitschrift für ausländisches und internationales Privatrecht. -- Berlin; Tübingen, 1961 (Bd.26)-
Continues: Auslandsrecht: Blätter für Industrie und Handel, 1919-1926 (Bd.7) and: Zeitschrift für ausländisches und internationales Privatrecht, 1927 (Bd.1)-1942; 1949-1960 (Bd.25)
ISSN 0033-7250

BH/U-1	1960-	LO/U-2	1959.	MA/U-1	1949-
CA/U13	1927-37;1939-41 imp.,1949-	LO/U-3	1927-40/42; 1949-71	OX/U15	(w.1924 nos.1-5)
ED/U-1	1967 (Bd.31)-	LO/U11	1949-	OX/U25	1949-58
EX/U-1	1966-	LO/U24	1922-23;1925- (w.Bd.11,14)	SO/U-1	1974-
GL/U-1	1973-			XY/N-1	1969 (Bd.33)-
LA/U-1	1949-76				

Rada narodowa <u>see</u> next entry

Rada narodowa, gospodarka, administracja. -- Warsaw, 1973-
Continues: Rada narodowa, 1943-1972
Absorbed: Gospodarka i administracja terenowa, q.v.

LO/N-1		XY/N-1	1973-

Radians'ke [or Radjans'ke] pravo. -- Kiev, 1958-

GL/U-1	Soviet Studies Branch Library 1964-	OX/U15	(1963-64 imp.)	XY/N-1

Rassegna della proprietà industriale, letteraria ed artistica. -- Milan, 1934-
Suspended May 1942-Apr.1946

LO/N14 imp.

Rassegna di diritto commerciale italiano e straniero. -- Turin, 1883-1889

LO/N-1

Rassegna di diritto legislazione e medicina legale veterinaria. -- Milan, 1967-
ISSN 0300-3485

XY/N-1 1967 (no.2)-

Rassegna di diritto pubblico. -- Naples, 1946-
ISSN 0033-9512

LO/U-3	1946-69 (w. 1965 no.4; 1966 no.1)	LO/U24	1951-63 (v.18 no.2)	XY/N-1	1968-72 (v.23-26:1)

Rassegna di studi penitenziari. -- Rome, 1951-
From 1959 has a quarterly supplement entitled: Quaderni di criminologia clinica, q.v.
ISSN 0033-9628

CA/U37 1962-	OX/U15	XY/N-1 1967 (v.17)-
LO/U-3		

Rating and income tax <u>see</u> next entry

Rating and valuation reporter. -- London, 1961-
Continues: Rating and income tax, 1924-1960
ISSN 0048-6817

CA/U-1 1971-	LO/U-2 1938 (July)-1976	QS/Q12 1925-41 imp.
CA/U13	LV/P-1 1954-	QS/S-6 1950-
ED/S11	LV/U-1 1971-	QS/S-7 1943-
GL/U-2 1976-	MA/P-1 1931-60 imp., 1961-	QS/S-8 1930-
LC/C-1 1971-	NW/U-1 1924-26	QW/D12 1970-
LO-MT 1927-36;1943-	OX/U15	RE/U-1 1961-64;1966-
LO/N-1	QE/C76 last 5 years	SO/U-1 1975-
LO/N26 last 5 years	QG/C25 1976-	XM/C10 1975-
LO/P-6 1956-		XY/N-1 1969 (v.9)-
LO-SC 1958-		

Real estate law journal. -- Boston, 1972-
ISSN 0048-6868

XY/N-1 1975 (v.3 no.3)-

Real property, probate and trust journal/ American Bar Association, Section of Real Property, Probate and Trust Law. -- Chicago, 1966-
ISSN 0034-0855

LO/U24

Recht der Arbeit. -- Munich, 1948-

LO/U-3	OX/U15 1953 (Bd.6)-	XY/N-1 1967 (Bd.20)-

Recht der internationalen Wirtschaft: Aussenwirtschaftsdienst des Betriebs-Beraters. -- Heidelberg, 1954-
1958 (vol.4)-1974 (vol.20) entitled: Aussenwirtschaftsdienst des Betriebs-Beraters: Recht der internationalen Wirtschaft, (ISSN 0004-8232)
Continues: Nachrichten der Studiengesellschaft für privatrechtliche Auslandsinteressen, 1949-1954

CA/U13 1964-	LO-MT 1958-	OX/U15 1954-
ED/U-1 1960 (v.6)-	LO/U-2 1954-	SO/U-1 1974-76
GL/U-1 1960-	LO/U-3	XY/N-1 1969 (Bd.15)-
LD/C-1 1974.	LO/U24 1961-62 imp., 1963 (Bd.9)-	

Recht der Schiffahrt = Maritime law review. -- Hamburg, 1957-
Text in English and German
ISSN 0034-1320

OX/U15

Recht en maatschappij. -- Assen, 1955-
ISSN 0484-0968

LO/N-1 1955-64

Recht in Japan. -- Frankfurt, 1975-

LO/U14

Recht in Ost und West: Zeitschrift für Rechtsvergleichung und innerdeutsche Rechtsprobleme. -- Berlin, 1957-
Subtitle varies slightly
ISSN 0486-1485

GL/U-1 Soviet Studies Branch Library 1970-	LO/N-1 1959-	OX/U15
	LO/N17 1961-65	XY/N-1
	LO/U24	

Recht und Wirtschaft. -- Berlin, Oct. 1911-1922

OX/U15

Rechtsgeleerd magazijn <u>see</u> next entry

Rechtsgeleerd magazijn Themis: tijdschrift voor publiek- en privaatrecht. -- Haarlem, etc., 1939-
Continues: Rechtsgeleerd magazijn, 1882-1938
Formed by union of Rechtsgeleerd magazijn with Themis, 1839-1938

CA/U13 1961-	LO/U24	XY/N-1 1969-
LO/N-1		

Rechtsherstel: maandelijke orgaan van de Raad voor het Rechtsherstel. -- The Hague, 1946-
Subtitle varies

No holdings notified

Rechtskundig tijdschrift voor België. -- Antwerp, 1897-1963

LO/U24 1960-63 (v.50-53)

Rechtskundig weekblad. -- Antwerp, 1931-1940 (vol.9), 1946 (vol.10)-
Between 1941 and 1944, replaced by: Juristenblad, q.v.

LO/U24	XY/N-1 1969 (v.33)-

Rechtsprechung. -- Vienna, 1918-1938

LO/U24 (w.v.1; v.2 imp.)

Rechtsprechung zum Wiedergutmachungsrecht. -- Munich, 1949/50-
ISSN 0342-1821

LO/U24

Rechtstheorie: Zeitschrift für Logik, Methodenlehre, Kybernetik und Soziologie des Rechts. -- Berlin, 1970-
ISSN 0034-1398

CA/U13 LO/U24 XY/N-1 1973 (Bd.4)-
LO/N-1 OX/U15

Rechtswissenschaftlicher Informationsdienst/ Deutsches Institut für Rechtswissenschaft. -- Berlin, 1952-1959
ISSN 0415-7311

LO/U24

Record of the Association of the Bar of the City of New York. -- New York, 1946-
ISSN 0004-5837

LO-MT OX/U15 (1946-47 imp.) QS/S-7 1946-68
LO/U24 QS/S-6 1946-68 XY/N-1 1973 (v.28)-

Recorder; or, Judicial and magisterial magazine. -- London, Feb.-Mar. 1816

LO/N-1

Recueil ASERJ/ Association Sénégalaise d'Etudes et de Recherches Juridiques. -- Dakar, 1970-

No holdings notified

Recueil analytique de jurisprudence et de législation <u>see</u> Recueil Dalloz de doctrine, de jurisprudence et de législation

Recueil annuel de jurisprudence belge. -- Brussels, 1949-

BL/U-1 imp. ED/U-1 1965- OX/U15

Recueil critique de jurisprudence et de législation <u>see</u> next entry

Recueil Dalloz de doctrine, de jurisprudence et de législation. -- Paris, 1945-1964
Continues: Jurisprudence générale. Recueil périodique et critique de jurisprudence, de législation et de doctrine, 1825-1923 (Title varies); Recueil Dalloz, 1924-1944, consisting of two separate series: Recueil hebdomadaire de jurisprudence... 1924-1940 which became Recueil analytique de jurisprudence et de législation, 1941-1944; and Recueil périodique et critique de jurisprudence de législation et de doctrine, 1924-1940, which became Recueil critique de jurisprudence et de législation, 1941-1944.
Feb. 1955-June 1956 issued with Recueil Sirey as Recueils Dalloz et Sirey
1965 merged with Recueil Sirey to form Recueil Dalloz Sirey, q.v.

AB/U-1 1845-1964 BH/U-1 1845-1964 BR/U-1 1950-64
AD/U-6 1953-64 BL/U-1 1845-1964 CA/U13 1845-1964

(cont'd)

Recueil Dalloz de doctrine, de jurisprudence et de législation (cont'd).

CB/U-1 1845-1964	LC/U-1 1845-1964	LO/U11 1964.
CV/U-1 1845-1964	LD/U-1 1845-1964	LO/U24 1845-1964
ED/U-1 1845-1964	LO-MT 1845-1964	OX/U15 1845-1964
EX/U-1 1845-1964	LO/N-1	SO/U-1 1908-38,1946, 1948-64
GL/U-1 1946-64	LO/U-3 1955-57	
HL/U-1 1960-64		

Recueil Dalloz Sirey de doctrine, de jurisprudence et de législation. -- Paris, 1965-
Formed by union of Recueil Sirey q.v. with Recueil Dalloz, q.v.
ISSN 0034-1835

AB/U-1	ED/U-1	LO/U-3 1965-77
AD/U-6	EX/U-1	LO/U11
BH/U-1	GL/U-1	LO/U12
BL/U-1	HL/U-1	LO/U24
BR/U-1	LC/U-1	OX/U15
CA/U13	LD/U-1	QS/S-6
CV/U-1	LO-MT	SO/U-1
DN/U-1	LO/N-1	XY/N-1 1966-
DR/U-1	LO/U-2 1965;1974-	

Recueil Dareste de législation, doctrine et jurisprudence coloniales. -- Paris, 1938 (vol.41)-1939 (vol.42)
Continues: Recueil de législation et jurisprudence coloniales, 1898-1906 (vol.3) and: Recueil de législation, de doctrine et de jurisprudence coloniales, 1907 (vol.4)-1937 (vol.40)

LO/U24	OX/U15 1938-39

Recueil de documents en matière pénale et pénitentiaire/ International Penal and Penitentiary Commission. -- Berne, 1931-1951 (vol.15)

LO/N-1	LO/U24	OX/U15 1931-40

Recueil de droit pénal. -- Paris, 1943?-1974 (vol.32)

LO/U24 1961-74	XY/N-1 1966-74 (v.24-32)

Recueil de jurisprudence du droit administratif <u>see</u> Administration publique: revue du droit public et des sciences administratives

Recueil de l'Académie de Législation de Toulouse. -- Toulouse, 1851/52-1903? 1905-1914 (2. série, vols.1-10); 1917-1920 (3. série, vols.1-4); 1920-
1905-1914 entitled Recueil de législation de Toulouse
1917-1920 entitled Bulletin de l'Académie de Législation

AD/U-6 1910-14;1917-20;1920-33; 1936;1938-42	LO/N-1 1951-70	OX/U15 1851-1903; 1949;1962; 1965.
	LO/U-3 1928/29-30/31	

Recueil de législation, de doctrine et de jurisprudence coloniales see Recueil Dareste de législation, doctrine et jurisprudence coloniales

Recueil de législation de Toulouse see Recueil de l'Académie de Législation de Toulouse

Recueil de législation et jurisprudence coloniales see Recueil Dareste de législation, doctrine et jurisprudence coloniales

Recueil de mémoires et travaux de la Société d'Histoire du Droit et des Institutions des Anciens Pays de Droit Ecrit. -- Toulouse; Montpellier, 1948-
ISSN 0583-8282

HL/U-1 1974 (v.9). OX/U15 1948;1951;1955;1958.

Recueil des cours de l'Académie de Droit International. -- The Hague, 1923-1939;1947-
ISSN 0001-401X

AB/U-1	GL/U-2	LO/U24
AD/U-6 1947-	HL/U-1 1955 (v.87)-	LV/U-1
BH/U-1	KL/U-1	MA/U-1
BL/U-1 1936,1963- imp.	LC/U-1 imp.	NO/U-1
BR/U-1	LD/U-1	NW/U-1 1923-73
BT/U-1 1923- (1926-38 imp.)	LO/C47 1968-	OX/U15
	LO-MT	OX/U25
CA/U-1	LO/N17	RE/U-1 1975-
CA/U13	LO/S14	SH/U-1 1923-60 imp., 1961-
DN/U-1	LO/U-1	
DR/U-1 1950-	LO/U-2	SO/U-1 1947-
ED/U-1 1926-	LO/U-3	XY/N-1 1963 (v.108); 1966 (v.119)-
EX/U-1 1959-	LO/U11 (w.v.34)	
GL/U-1	LO/U12 1923-72	

Recueil général de jurisprudence, de doctrine et de législation coloniales et maritimes see Penant

Recueil général des lois et des arrêts see Recueil Sirey

Recueil hebdomadaire de jurisprudence... see Recueil Dalloz de doctrine, de jurisprudence et de législation

Recueil judiciaire/Ministère de la Justice. -- Phnom-Penh, Cambodia, 1955-
ISSN 0410-4307

No holdings notified

Recueil Penant see Penant

Recueil périodique et critique de jurisprudence, de législation et de doctrine see Recueil Dalloz de doctrine, de jurisprudence et de législation

Recueil Sirey; jurisprudence, législation. -- Paris, 1950-1964
Continues: Recueil général des lois et des arrêts, 1791-1830 (Sirey chronologique), 1831-1923;
Recueil général des lois et des arrêts fondé par J.B. Sirey; Journal du Palais; Pandectes françaises périodiques, 1924-1949 (The three titles, previously issued independently, combined under one cover)
Feb. 1955-June 1956 issued with Recueil Dalloz as Recueils Dalloz et Sirey.
1965 merged with Recueil Dalloz to form Recueil Dalloz Sirey, q.v.
ISSN 0484 162X

BL/U-1 1963-64
CA/U13
ED/U-1 1951-64
LD/U-1 1962-64
LO-MT 1845-1964
LO/N-1 1801/2-1964
LO/U-3 1801/02-1964
LO/U24
OX/U15 1801/02-1964
QS/S-6

Recueils - Société Internationale de Droit Pénal Militaire et de Droit de la Guerre <u>see</u> Société Internationale...

Recueils Dalloz et Sirey <u>see</u> Recueil Dalloz de doctrine, de jurisprudence et de législation <u>and</u> Recueil Sirey

Regeringsrättens årsbok. -- Stockholm, 1909-

LO/U-3 1909-18 imp., 1946-

Regt (Recht) in Nederlandsch-Indië <u>see</u> Hukum dan masjarakat

Reich Volksordnung Lebensraum: Zeitschrift für völkische Verfassung und Verwaltung. -- Darmstadt, 1941-1943 (Bd.6)

LO/U24 Bd.1,3,5.

Reichsverwaltungsblatt <u>see</u> Deutsches Verwaltungsblatt

Reichsverwaltungsblatt und preussisches Verwaltungsblatt <u>see</u> Deutsches Verwaltungsblatt

Religion and the public order: an annual review of Church and State, and of religion, law and society. -- Ithaca, 1964-19??.
Ceased publication?
ISSN 0080-0856

AB/N-1 1969 (v.5).
BT/U-1 1969 (v.5).
CA/U-1 1964-
ED/N-1 1964-66 (1963-65);1969.
LO/U24 1968-69 (v.4-5)
XY/N-1 1964-69 (v.5)

Repertorium für die öffentliche und gerichtliche Arzeneywissenschaft. -- Berlin, 1789-1792 (Bd.3)
Continues: Magazin für die gerichtliche Arzeneikunde und medicinische Polizei, 1782-1784 (Bd.2) and: Neues Magazin für die gerichtliche Arzeneikunde, 1785-1788 (Bd.2)

LO/N-1 1782-88

Report of proceedings of the annual tax conference/ Canadian Tax Foundation. -- Toronto, 1947-
Vol.3, 1949, not published: 1969 conference not held

GL/U-1 1968-	LO/U24 1964 (17th 1963)-	XY/N-1 1967-

Report of the ... conference/ International Law Association (Until 1893 called Association for the Reform and Codification of the Law of Nations). -- London, 1873-1913;1920-
Papers for the intended 1914 conference embodied in the Reports of the Executive Council, 1913/14 & 1914/15
ISSN 0074-6738

AB/N-1 1903,1948-68 (w.1954,1964)	LC/U-1 1964-	LV/P-1 1903-52 imp.
AD/U-6 1873-1923 imp., 1924-	LD/P-1 1958-70	LV/U-1 1873-1939 imp.
BH/P-1 1873-74;1899-	LO-MT	NO/U-1 1946 (41st)-
BR/U-1 1946-	LO/N-1 (w.4th)	OX/U15 1873-74;1890-95;1903-
CA/U-1 1903-	LO/N17	QS/Q12 1910-36 imp., 1954-
CA/U13 1879- imp.	LO/R74 1960-	QS/S-4 1930-38;1948-60;1964-
CR/U-1 1930-36	LO/S14 1920-	QS/S-6 imp.
ED/U-1 1895-1947 (42nd) imp., 1956 (47th)-	LO/U-1 1882-87	QS/S-7 imp.
HL/U-1 1873-74;1899-1901;1921; 1924-26	LO/U-2 1905-56 (22nd -46th) imp., 1958 (48th)-	XY/N-1 1962 (50th)-
	LO/U-3 imp.	
	LO/U11 1912-13;1920-72	
	LO/U24 1879-99 imp., 1908-	

Report of the Canadian Bar Association <u>see</u> Yearbook of the Canadian Bar Association and minutes of proceedings...

Report of the session - Asian-African Legal Consultative Committee. -- New Delhi, 1960 (1st, 1957)-
1st report issued under earlier name: Asian Legal Consultative Committee
ISSN 0571-2726

BL/U-1 1966.	LO/U24	XY/N-1 1964 (6th)-
LO/U-3 (w.1969 (10th))	OX/U15	

Report of the session - Asian Legal Consultative Committee <u>see</u> previous entry

Res judicatae <u>see</u> Melbourne University law review

Res publica. -- Brussels, 1959-
ISSN 0486-4700

CA/U-1	LO/N-1	SW/U-1 1968-73
HL/U-1	LO/U-3	XY/N-1 1966 (v.8)-

Research, patents and trademarks. -- New York, 1954-
Continues: International bulletin of industrial property, 1947-1953

LO/N14 1949-55 (v.2-4 no.7)

Responsa meridiana. -- Capetown, 1964-
ISSN 0486-5588

CA/U13	OX/U15	XY/N-1 1969 (v.2)-
LO/U24		

Responsabilità civile e previdenza: rivista bimestrale di dottrina, giurisprudenza e legislazione. -- Milan, 1930-

LO/U-2 1965-71	LO/U24 1965 (v.30)-	XY/N-1 1971 (v.36)-

Ret og pfligt <u>see</u> Staten

Revenue, judicial and police journal. -- Calcutta, Sept. 1863-Nov.1865 (vol.5)

LO-MT v.1-4

Review - International Commission of Jurists. -- Geneva, 1969-
Merger of: Bulletin of the International Commission of Jurists, q.v., and: Journal of the International Commission of Jurists, q.v.
Editions also in French, German and Spanish
ISSN 0020-6393

AB/U-1	LD/U-1	LV/U-1
AD/U-6	LO/C25	MA/U-1
BH/U-1	LO-MT	NO/U-1
BL-LS	LO/N-1	OX/U15
BL/U-1	LO/N17	OX/U25
BR/U-1	LO/N26 last 10 years	QM/C48
CA/U13	LO/S14	QN/C70 1972-
CB/U-1	LO/U-2	QS/Q29
DN/U-1	LO/U-3	QS/S-6
DR/U-1 1969.	LO/U12	RE/U-1
ED/S10	LO/U14	SH/U-1 1969-75 (v.1-15)
ED/S11	LO/U24	
GL/U-1	LV-LP 1974 (no.13)-	SO/U-1
HL/U-1 1969 (no.1-3).		XY/N-1

Review of contemporary law = Revue de droit contemporain. -- Brussels, 1958-
Continues: Law in the service of peace: International Association of Democratic Lawyers review, 1954-1957
Editions in English and French
ISSN 0048-7473

AB/N-1 1954-70	EX/U-1 1966-70 imp.	LV/U-1 1960-70 imp.
AB/U-1 1960-	GL/U-1 1954-70	NO/U-1 1958-70 (v.17 no.1)
AD/U-6 1958-	HL/U-1 1962/63-69 (v.9-16)	
BH/U-1 1958-		OX/U15 1954 (v.2)-
BR/U-1 1958-	LD/U-1 1958-	QS/Q12 1959-69 imp.
BL/U-1 1958-	LO/N17 1963-70	QS/S-6 1954-70
CA/U-1 1961-	LO/N26 1954-69 (v.16)	QS/S-7 1958-69
CA/U13 1963-70	LO/U-2 1959-70 (v.17 no.1)	XY/N-1
DR/U-1 1958-70		
ED/S10 1962-70	LO/U24 1958-70 (v.17 no.1)	
ED/S11		

Review of Ghana law. -- Accra, 1969-
ISSN 0034-6578

BH/U-1	LO/U14	QS/S-7
CA/U13 1974 (v.6 pt.2)-	LO/U24	XY/N-1
	OX/U15	

Review of Hungarian legislation see Hungarian law review

Review of juridical sciences. -- Baghdad, 1969-

LO/N-1 1969 (v.1 nos. i & ii).	LO/U14	LO/U24 1969.

Review of law and social change see New York University review of law and social change

Review of Polish law. -- Warsaw, Nov. 1947-1950

GL/U-1 1948-50	LO/U-3	XY/N-1 1948 (June., Oct.,Dec.).
LO/S14 1948-50	OX/U15	

Review of Polish law and economics. -- Warsaw, Mar.-Dec.1928; 1930-Feb.1931

ED/U-1 1928 imp.	LO/U-3 imp.

Review of socialist law. -- Leyden, 1975-

LO/U-2	OX/U15	QE/C76
LO/U24 1976 (v.2)-		

Review on Hungarian and foreign law see Magyar jog és külföldi jogi szemle

Revija za kriminalistiko in kriminologijo. -- Ljubljana, ca 1950-
Text in Slovenian, summaries in English
ISSN 0034-690X

CA/U37 1960-	LO/N-1 1964 (v.15)-	XY/N-1 1966-67 imp., 1968 (v.19)-

Revista académica da Faculdade de direito do Recife. -- Recife, 1891-

CA/U-1 1891-98;1916-18;1921-38; 1940-43	LO/U24 1961-67 (v.60-61;63)	OX/U15 1913-18;1921-38;1940-43

Revista americana de derecho internacional see Revista de derecho internacional

Revista argentina de derecho internacional. -- Buenos Aires, 1920-1922

LO/U24

Revista centroamericana de legislación, derecho y jurisprudencia. -- San Salvador, (ca 1900-)

LO/U24 1902 (v.3).

Revista cubana de derecho. -- Havana, 1972?-

XY/N-1

Revista cubana de jurisprudencia. -- Havana, 1962-
ISSN 0484-6664

LO/N-1 1962.

Revista da Faculdade de direito/ Universidade de São Paulo. -- São Paulo, 1893-
ISSN 0080-6250

AD/U-6 1954-
BH/U-1 1954-
CA/U-1 1931-38;1948-
ED/U-1 1930-38;1953-63 imp.,1965-
GL/U-1 1935-
LO/U24 1946 (v.41)-
LV/U-1 1967-
OX/U15 1932-
XY/N-1 1912,1914/25, 1938-9 imp., 1949,1963-74

Revista da Faculdade de direito/ Universidade do Ceará. -- Ceará, 1946-

LO/U24 1946-55 (v.9); 1964-65 (v.18-19)

Revista da Faculdade de direito/ Universidade Federal do Paraná. -- Curitiba, 1953-
ISSN 0526-4308

CA/U-1 1953-54; 1956-60
LD/U-1 1954-58 imp.
LO/U24 1953-69 (v.12)
OX/U15 1953-54; 1956-60

Revista da Faculdade de direito da Universidade de Lisboa. -- Lisbon, 1917-
None published 1918-1933, 1935, 1937-1946

LO/N-1 1953-
LO/U24 1948;1964-71
XY/N-1 1967 (v.21)-

Revista da Ordem dos advogados. -- Lisbon, 1941-

LO/U24 1965 (año 25)- (w.año 27)

Revista de administração/ Universidade de São Paulo. -- São Paulo, 1947-

LO/U-3 Mar.1947-May 1963

Revista de administración de comercio y de jurisprudencia <u>see</u> Revista de jurisprudencia

Revista de administración pública. -- Madrid, 1950-
ISSN 0034-7639

LO/U-3
LO/U24 1960- (1961 imp.)
OX/U-1
XY/N-1 1966 (v.49)-

Revista de ciência política. -- Rio de Janeiro, 1967-
Continues: Revista de direito público e ciência política, 1958-1966 (ISSN 0556-5774)
ISSN 0034-8023

CC/U-1 LO/N-1 1966 (v.9). XY/N-1 1963 (v.6)-

Revista de ciencias jurídicas. -- Valparaiso, 1971-

No holdings notified

Revista de ciencias jurídicas/ Universidad de Costa Rica. -- Ciudad Universitaria Rodrigo Facio, 1963-
ISSN 0034-7787

LO/N-1 1963-72 (v.2) LO/U24 1963 (no.2)-1972 (no.21) XY/N-1 1974 (v.24)-

Revista de ciências jurídicas, econômicas e sociais/ Universidade do Pará. -- Belem, Pará, 1963-1964
ISSN 0034-7795

LO/U-3

Revista de ciencias jurídicas y sociales/ Universidad de Madrid. -- Madrid, 1918-1936

CA/U13 LO/N-1 LO/U-3 1929.

Revista de ciencias jurídicas y sociales/ Universidad Nacional del Litoral. -- Santa Fé, 1930-

LO/U-3 1945-52 LV/U-1 1936-55 imp. OX/U15 1943-53;1955.
LO/U24 1943 imp.

Revista [de] derecho. -- Caracas, 1944-

LO/N-1

Revista de derecho: segunda epoca. -- Concepción, 1971 (año 39)-
Continues: Revista de derecho, 1933-1960; and: Revista de derecho y ciencias sociales, 1961-1970
ISSN 0034-7957

LO/U24 1960 (año 28)- XY/N-1 1966 (v.34)- (w.v.38,40)

Revista de derecho comercial. -- Montevideo, 1964-
ISSN 0034-7876

No holdings notified

Revista de derecho del trabajo. -- Madrid, 1954-
ISSN 0482-5357

LO/U-3 1954-63

Revista de derecho economico. -- Santiago, Chile, 1963-
ISSN 0556-5715

LO/U24 1963 (no.2)- imp.

Revista de derecho español y americano. -- Madrid, 1956-
ISSN 0556-5723

LO/U24 1956-69 (v.14 no.24)   XY/N-1 1963 (v.8 no.2); 1969 (v.14 no.24).

Revista de derecho internacional. -- Havana, 1922- ca 1952
Continues: Revista americana de derecho internacional, 1907?-1921

LO/U-3 1922-41 imp.   LO/U24 1931 imp., 1932 (Sept.)-1943 (Sept.)   OX/U15 1928-33

Revista de derecho internacional y ciencias diplomáticas/ Universidad Nacional del Litoral. -- Santa Fé, 1949-
ISSN 0034-7892

LO/N-1 1958-61   LO/U-3 (w.1960)   XY/N-1 1964-71 (v.13-20)

Revista de derecho internacional y politica exterior. -- Madrid, 1905-1910

LO/U24 1905-08 (v.4)

Revista de derecho judicial. -- Madrid, 1960-
ISSN 0484-6893

CA/U13

Revista de derecho, jurisprudencia y administración. -- Montevideo, 1894-1933; 1937-
ISSN 0034-7906

LO/U24 1953-70 imp.   XY/N-1 1965 (v.63)-

Revista de derecho, jurisprudencia y ciencias sociales see next entry

Revista de derecho, jurisprudencia y ciencias sociales y Gaceta de los tribunales. -- Santiago, 1951-
Continues: Revista forense chilena, 1885-1902; Revista de derecho y jurisprudencia, 1903-1910; and: Revista de derecho, jurisprudencia y ciencias sociales, 1910-1950

LO/N-1 1908-10   LO/U24 1960-68 (v.65)   XY/N-1 1967-70 (v.64-67,no.6)

Revista de derecho, legislación y jurisprudencia del Colegio de Abogados de Puerto Rico see Revista del Colegio de Abogados de Puerto Rico

Revista de derecho mercantil. -- Madrid, 1946-

LO/U-3   LO/U24 1948-51 imp., 1961-   XY/N-1 1969 (no.111)-

Revista de derecho privado. -- Madrid, 1913-
ISSN 0034-7922

CA/U13 1962- LO/N-1 1950 imp. XY/N-1 1967-
LD/U-1 1947-51 imp.

Revista de derecho procesal (Madrid) see Revista de derecho procesal iberoamericana

Revista de derecho procesal. -- Santiago de Chile, 1971-

No holdings notified

Revista de derecho procesal iberoamericana. -- Madrid, 1969-
Continues: Revista de derecho procesal, 1945-1964, and: Revista iberoamericana de derecho procesal, 1964-1968
ISSN 0557-6474

LO/U24 1960- XY/N-1 1973-

Revista de derecho público. -- Madrid, 1932-1936

LO/N-1

Revista de derecho público. -- Santiago de Chile, 1963-
ISSN 0556-5758

XY/N-1 1967 (v.8)-

Revista de derecho público/ Universidad Nacional de Tucumán. -- San Miguel de Tucumán, 1949-

LO/U-3 1949-50

Revista de derecho puertorriqueño. -- Ponce, 1961-
ISSN 0034-7930

CA/U13 1961-63 (nos.1-7); 1965 (no.15)- LO/U24 XY/N-1

Revista de derecho y ciencias políticas. -- Lima, 1936-
ISSN 0034-7949

LO/U24 1955-72 imp. LV/U-1 1965. XY/N-1 1968 (v.32)-

Revista de derecho y ciencias sociales. -- Asunción, 1927-1938; 1941-

OX/U15 1933-38

Revista de derecho y ciencias sociales. -- Buenos Aires, 1952-
Suspended November 1954-Summer 1956
ISSN 0484-6931

CA/U37

Revista de derecho y ciencias sociales (Concepción) see Revista de derecho: segunda epoca

Revista de derecho y jurisprudencia <u>see</u> Revista de derecho, jurisprudencia y ciencias sociales y Gaceta de los tribunales

Revista de derecho y legislación. -- Caracas, 1911-
ISSN 0034-7965

LO/U24 1919-23 imp., 1959-65 (v.54)

Revista de derechos humanos: publicación de la Comisión de Derechos Civiles del Estado Libre Asociado de Puerto Rico. -- San Juan, 1970-

No holdings notified

Revista de direito agrário. -- Brasília, 1973-

XY/N-1

Revista de direito da procuradoria geral. -- Rio de Janeiro, 1955-
ISSN 0485-1900

OX/U15 1955-71 (w.nos.12-15,21)

Revista de direito do trabalho. -- Petrópolis, Brazil, 1973-

No holdings notified

Revista de direito e economia. -- Coimbra, Portugal, 1975-

XY/N-1

Revista de direito penal. -- Rio de Janeiro, 1971-

LO/N-1

Revista de direito público e ciência politica <u>see</u> Revista de ciência política

Revista de drept economic. -- Bucharest, 1974-

OX/U15

Revista de drept public. -- Bucharest, 1926-

LO/N-1 1937-39 OX/U-1 1927-32

Revista de drept şi sociologie <u>see</u> next entry

Revista de drept, sociologie şi economie politica. -- Bucharest, 1904 (vol.6)-
Continues: Revista de drept şi sociologie, 1898-1903

LO/N-1 1899-1904

Revista de informacão legislativa. -- Brasilia, 1964-
ISSN 0034-835X

AB/N-1 imp.
LO/U24 1965-72 imp.
OX/U15 1965-72 (w. 1967 (nos.15-16))
XY/N-1 1968 (no. 17)- imp.

Revista de jurisprudencia. -- Havana, 1856-1867
1860 entitled: Revista de administración de comercio y de jurisprudencia

LO/N-1 1856-61

Revista de jurisprudencia peruana. -- Lima, 1943-

LO/U24 1961 (v.19)-

Revista de la Academia Colombiana de Jurisprudencia. -- Bogotá, 1910-

LO/U24 1919;1960-67 imp.

Revista de la Escuela Nacional de Jurisprudencia <u>see</u> Revista de la Facultad de Derecho de Mexico

Revista de la Facultad de Ciencias Jurídicas y Sociales de Guatemala/ Universidad Nacional. -- Guatemala City, 1938-

LV/U-1 1938-41 imp.   OX/U15 1938-41;1949;1959-61

Revista de la Facultad de Derecho/ Universidad Central de Venezuela. -- Caracas, 1954-
ISSN 0041-8393

BL/U-1 1957-   LO/U24 (w.no.3)   OX/U15 1961;1963-

Revista de la Facultad de Derecho/ Universidad de Oviedo. -- San Francisco, Oviedo, 1953-
ISSN 0472-3104

LO/U24 1953-60

Revista de la Facultad de Derecho de la Universidad Complutense de Madrid. -- Madrid, 1971-
Continues: Revista de la Facultad de Derecho de la Universidad de Madrid, 1940-1951?; n.s. 1957-1971?

LO/U24 1957-   XY/N-1 1970 (v.37)-

Revista de la Facultad de Derecho de la Universidad de Madrid <u>see</u> previous entry

Revista de la Facultad de Derecho de Mexico/ Universidad Nacional de Mexico, Mexico, 1951-
Continues: Revista de la Escuela Nacional de Jurisprudencia, 1939-1950
ISSN 0539-628X

LO/U24   OX/U15 1939 (nos.2,4);1940-49 (nos.6-44)

Revista de la Facultad de Derecho y Ciencias Sociales (Buenos Aires) <u>see</u> Revista Jurídica de Buenos Aires

Revista de la Facultad de Derecho y Ciencias Sociales. -- Montevideo, 1950-
ISSN 0540-7877

LO/U24 1950-71 (v.22)

Revista de la propiedad industrial. -- Madrid, 1953-
ISSN 0482-5829

LO/N14 1953-55

Revista de la Real Academia de Jurisprudencia y Legislación. -- Madrid, 1950-62 (no.24)
ISSN 0515-1155

LO/U24 1959-61 (nos.18-23)

Revista de la Sociedad Argentina de Derecho Romano. -- Córdoba, 1954-

CA/U-1 OX/U15 1954-57/58;1961/62-

Revista de legislación universal y de jurisprudencia española. -- Madrid, 1902-1914?

LO/U24 1902-03 (v.1-2)

Revista de legislación y jurisprudencia. -- Buenos Aires, 1869-1880 (1-12)

LO/N-1 1869-72 (v.1-8)

Revista de los tribunales y de legislación universal. -- Madrid, 1878-
Title varies

LO/U24 1878-1911 imp.

Revista de medicina legal de Colombia. -- Bogotá, 1935-

LO/N-1 1935-

Revista de medicina legal y jurisprudencia médica. -- Rosario, 1937?-

LO/M32 1948-50 (v.12-14)

Revista de tribunales. -- Santiago de Chile, 1898-1907

OX/U15 1899-1904

Revista del Centro de Estudiantes de Derecho. -- Caracas, 1918-1925?

LO/U24 1919-20 (v.1) imp.

Revista del Colegio de Abogados de Buenos Aires <u>see</u> next entry

Revista del Colegio de Abogados de la Ciudad de Buenos Aires. -- Buenos Aires, 1964 (vol.35)-
Continues: Revista del Colegio de Abogados de Buenos Aires, 1921-1956 (vol.34)

LO/U24 1921-29 imp., 1930-72

Revista del Colegio de Abogados de Puerto Rico. -- San Juan, 1955-
Continues: Revista de derecho, legislación y jurisprudencia del Colegio de Abogados de Puerto Rico, 1935-Mar.1938; June 1939-Sept.1941; Feb.1944-Nov.1951; Nov.-Dec.1954
ISSN 0010-0579

No holdings notified

Revista del Colegio de Abogados del Uruguay. -- Montevideo, 1957-

CA/U13 1957-58 LO/U24 1958 imp.,1962-63

Revista del foro/ Colegio de Abogadas. -- Lima, 1914-

CA/U13 1950-61;1966- LO/U24 1950-71 imp. OX/U15 1950-51
CC/U-1 1935-36

Revista del Instituto de Ciencias Penales y Penitenciarias/ Universidad Nacional. -- Bogotá, 1953-

OX/U15 1953-56

Revista del Instituto de Derecho Aeronautico/ Universidad Nacional. -- Córdoba, 1952-

CA/U-1 1952-58; 1959-62 LO/U24 1953-54 imp. OX/U15 1952-65 imp.

Revista del Instituto de Derecho Civil/ Universidad Nacional. -- Tucumán, 1948-

CA/U13 1948-53

Revista del Instituto de Derecho Comparado. -- Barcelona, 1953-1966

CA/U13 LO/N-1 1963-66 LO/U24
LA/U-1 LO/U-3 OX/U15
LO/C47 1958-66

Revista del Instituto de Derecho Comparado. -- La Plata, 1961-

OX/U15 1961.

Revista del Instituto de Derecho del Trabajo e Investigaciones Sociales/ Universidad Central. -- Quito, 1961?-

LO/U-3 1963 (Ano 3, no.5)-

Revista del Instituto de Derecho Público y Ciencias Sociales/ Universidad Nacional del Litoral. -- Santa Fé, 1957?-

LO/N-1 1958-61 imp.

Revista del Instituto de Historia del Derecho/ Facultad de Derecho y Ciencias Sociales de la Universidad de Buenos Aires. -- Buenos Aires, 1949-

CC/U-1 1956-63 imp. LO/U-2 1950-60 imp. OX/U-1
LO/N-1 1950-68

Revista del Instituto de Investigaciones y Docencia Criminologicas. -- La Plata, 1958-

LO/U-3

Revista del Ministerio de Justicia. -- Caracas, 1952-

LO/U24 1961-67 imp.

Revista dos tribunais. -- São Paulo, 1912-
ISSN 0034-9275

LO/N-1 1962. LO/U24

Revista española de derecho canónico. -- Madrid, 1946-
ISSN 0034-9372

LO/N-1 OX/U-1 XY/N-1 1973 (v.29)-

Revista española de derecho internacional. -- Madrid, 1948-
ISSN 0034-9380

CA/U13 1960- LO/U-3 1948-70 OX/U15
LO/N-1 1955- LO/U24 XY/N-1 1966 (v.19)-

Revista española de derecho militar. -- Madrid, 1956-
ISSN 0034-9399

No holdings notified

Revista Facultad de Derecho (Tucumán) see Revista jurídica/ Universidad Nacional de Tucumán

Revista forense. -- Caracas, 1893 (nos.1-6)

LO/N-1

Revista forense. -- Rio de Janeiro, 1904-

LO/U24 1946-65 imp., 1966 (no.211)- XY/N-1 1969 (no.225)-

Revista forense chilena see Revista de derecho, jurisprudencia y ciencias sociales y Gaceta de los tribunales

Revista general de derecho. -- Valencia, 1945-

LO/U24 1960 (v.16)- XY/N-1 1969 (v.25)-

Revista general de legislación y jurisprudencia. -- Madrid, 1853-

LO-MT 1947 imp., 1949 imp. LO/N-1 LO/U24 1959 (v.107)- XY/N-1 1969 (v.118)-

Revista iberoamericana de derecho procesal see Revista de derecho procesal iberoamericana

Revista internacional del notariado. -- Madrid, 1949-

CA/U13 1959-63;1968- LO/U24 1959-70

Revista judicial. -- Tegucigalpa, 1904-07

LO/N-1

Revista jurídica. -- Rio de Janeiro, 1865-1922

LO/N-1 1865-73 (1-12)

Revista jurídica/ Faculdade Nacional de Direito, Universidade do Brasil. -- Rio de Janeiro, 1934-1935;1938-

CA/U-1 1946-53 LO/U24 1942-67 OX/U15 1944/45-54; 1959 (v.8-12, 17)

Revista jurídica/ Facultad de Derecho, Ciencias Sociales, Politicas y Económicas, Universidad Boliviana Mayor de "San Simón" (Formerly Universidad Autónoma de Cochabamba). -- Cochabamba, 1937-

CA/U13 1957-59;1966- LD/U-1 1938-39 LO/N-1 1946. LO/U24 1949-50 imp.

Revista jurídica/ Ministerio Público Federal. -- Mexico City, 1936-1939 (nos.1-25)

OX/U15 1938-39 (nos.10-23)

Revista jurídica/ Universidad Nacional de Tucumán. -- Tucumán, 1957-
Continues: Revista Facultad de Derecho (Tucumán), 1943-1956
ISSN 0496-3849

LO/C47 1957-72 LO/U24 1954-

Revista jurídica argentina: la Ley see La Ley: revista jurídica argentina

Revista jurídica de Buenos Aires. -- Buenos Aires, 1957-
Continues: Revista de la Facultad de Derecho y Ciencias Sociales, 1907-1932;1946-1956; and: Boletín mensual del Seminario de Ciencias Juridicas y Sociales, 1932-1944
ISSN 0034-9747

CC/U-1 1956-63 imp.
LO/N-1 1959-69
LO/U-2 1963-66
LO/U-3 1954-56
LO/U24 1957-69
OX/U-1 1936-37
OX/U15 1946-48;1958; 1965-67

Revista jurídica de Cataluña. -- Barcelona, 1895-

LO/U24 1950-
XY/N-1 1966-

Revista jurídica de Córdoba. -- Buenos Aires, 1947-

LO/U24 1947-52 (no.14)

Revista jurídica de la Universidad de Puerto Rico. -- Rio Piedras, 1932-

BL/U-1 1963-
CA/U13 1934-36; 1947- imp.
LO/U24 1943 imp., 1944-
OX/U15 1934-38
XY/N-1 1966 (v.35)-

Revista jurídica de la Universidad Interamericana de Puerto Rico. -- Hato Rey; Santurce, 1964-
ISSN 0041-851X

LO/U24 1971 (v.6)-
XY/N-1 1976 (v.11)-

Revista jurídica del Peru. -- Lima, 1950-
ISSN 0484-7784

LO/U24 1961 (v.12)-

Revista jurídica dominicana. -- Ciudad Trujillo, 1939-1960

LO/N-1 1939-60
LO/U24 1957-60

Revista jurídica interamericana <u>see</u> Inter-American law review

Revista jurídica Panameña: organo de la Facultad de Derecho y Ciencias Políticas de la Universidad de Panamá. -- Panama, 1973-
ISSN 0302-6655

LO/U24

Revista jurídico-criminal. -- Bogotá, 1938 (no.1)-1939 (no.14/15)

LO/N-1 1-13

Revista mexicana de derecho internacional. -- Mexico City, 1919-1923

LO/N-1
LO/U-3
LO/U11 1920 (v.2, nos.2-4).
OX/U15 1919-22

Revista mexicana de derecho penal. -- Mexico City, 1933- (ca 1934)

LD/U-1 1933-34 imp.	OX/U15 1934.

Revista penal y penitenciaria. -- Buenos Aires, 1936-

CA/U37 1945-	OX/U15 1944;1947-	XY/N-1 1964 (v.29)-
LO/N-1 1943-54;1959-63;1967-		

Revista peruana de derecho internacional. -- Lima, 1941-
ISSN 0035-0370

LO/U24 1946-47 imp., 1950 (v.10)- (w.v.25-28)	XY/N-1 1968 (v.27)-

Revista română de drept. -- Bucharest, 1967 (vol.23)-
Continues: Justiţia nouă, 1945-1966 (vol.22)
ISSN 0035-0435

CA/U13 1969-71 imp., 1972-	LO/N-1 1954-	OX/U15 1963-
	LO/U-3 1953- imp.	XY/N-1 1963-

Revista trimestral de jurisprudencia. -- Rio de Janeiro, 1957-
ISSN 0035-0540

No holdings notified

Revista uruguaya de derecho internacional. -- Montevideo, 1972-

XY/N-1 1972-73 (v.2)

Revoliutsiia prava: zhurnal. -- Moscow, 1927-1929
1930 merged with: Sovetskoe pravo: zapiski, q.v.

LO/U-2

Revue administrative. -- Paris, 1948-
ISSN 0035-0672

AB/U-1 1966-	KL/U-1 1965 (v.18)-	LO/U-3
BR/U-1 1961-	LV/U-1 1962-76	LO/U24 1960 (v.13)-
EX/U-1 1957-	LO/N-1	XY/N-1 1966 (v.19)-

Revue administrative et juridique du Burundi. -- Bujumburu, 1967-
Continues: Revue juridique de droit écrit et coutumier du Rwanda et du Burundi, 1961-1966 (ISSN 0484-887X)
ISSN 0556-7133

LO/U14 1961-66 imp., 1967-	LO/U24 1961-74

Revue aéronautique internationale. -- Paris, 1931-1939 (vol.9)

CA/U13 1931-38	LO/U-3	XY/N-1
LO/N-1 1938-39	LO/U24	

Revue "al qanoun wal iqtised" = Droit et économie politique. -- Cairo, 1931-

CA/U13 1967-	LO/U14 1935-39;1941; 1944-	OX/U-1 1948;1949 (nos. 3-4)-1956
LO/U-3 1931-56		XY/N-1 1970-72 (v.40-42)

Revue "al-ulum al-qanuniya wal-iqtisadiya" = Revue des sciences juridiques et économiques/ Ain Shames University. -- Cairo, 1959-
ISSN 0542-190X

CA/U-1 1963-	LO/U14	OX/U-1 1959-65 (no.1); 1966-72

Revue algérienne des sciences juridiques, politiques et économiques. -- Algiers, 1964-
Continues: Bulletin judiciaire de l'Algérie, 1877-1884; Revue algérienne et tunisienne de législation et de jurisprudence, 1885-1912; and: Revue algérienne, tunisienne et marocaine de législation et de jurisprudence, 1913-1962
ISSN 0035-0699

CA/U13 1956-62 imp., 1964-65	LO/U-3 1964-73	LO/U24 1964-72 (v.9 no.3)
LO/N-1 1877-1921; 1952-62	LO/U14 1927-62 imp., 1964-	OX/U-1 1964-70
		XY/N-1 1964-70 imp.

Revue algérienne et tunisienne de législation et de jurisprudence <u>see</u> previous entry

Revue algérienne, tunisienne et marocaine de législation et de jurisprudence <u>see</u> Revue algérienne des sciences juridiques, politiques et économiques

Revue allemande de droit aérien et spatiale <u>see</u> Zeitschrift für Luft- und Weltraumrecht

Revue asienne de droit comparé = Asian comparative law review. -- Saigon, 1963.
ISSN 0556-7211

CA/U13	LO/U14	OX/U15
HL/U-1	LO/U24	

Revue belge de droit international = Belgian review of international law = Belgisch tijdschrift voor internationaal recht. -- Brussels, 1965-
ISSN 0035-0788

BH/U-1 1974-	LO/N17	MA/U-1
CA/U13	LO/U-1 1970-72	NO/U-1
ED/U-1 1972-	LO/U-2	OX/U15
LO-MT	LO/U-3	XY/N-1 1967-
LO/N-1 1965-70	LO/U24	

Revue belge de droit maritime. -- Brussels, 1924-1925

LO/N-1

Revue bibliographique de droit et de jurisprudence. -- Paris, 1869-1870

LO/N-1

Revue bibliographique des ouvrages de droit, de jurisprudence, d'économie politique.... -- Paris, 1894-1939 (vol.46), 1951-

BL/U-1 1952- imp. LD/U-1 1937-69 imp. XY/N-1 1966-
GL/U-1 1951- OX/U-1 1951-57 (June)

Revue bibliographique et critique de droit français et étranger. -- Paris, 1853-1857
Absorbed by: Revue historique de droit français et étranger, q.v.

LO/N-1 1853 (1). OX/U-1

Revue camerounaise de droit. -- Yaoundé, 1972-

LO/U14

Revue canadienne: philosophie, histoire, droit. -- Montreal, 1864-1922 (vol.80 = new (i.e. 5th) series vol.27)

LO/N-1 1881- OX/U-1

Revue canadienne de criminologie <u>see</u> Canadian journal of criminology and corrections

Revue canadienne du droit de commerce <u>see</u> Canadian business law journal

Revue catholique des institutions et du droit. -- Grenoble; Lyon, 1872-

LO/N-1 1874-1939 LO/U-3 1873-99 imp.

Revue congolaise de droit <u>see</u> Revue zaïroise de droit

Revue critique de droit international <u>see</u> next entry

Revue critique de droit international privé. -- Paris, 1947 (vol.36)-
Continues: Revue de droit international privé et de droit pénal international, 1905-1921 (vol.17); Revue de droit international privé, 1922 (vol.18)-1933 (vol.28) and: Revue critique de droit international, 1934 (vol.29)-1946 (vol.35)
ISSN 0035-0958

AD/U-6 ED/U-1 1967- LC/U-1 1949-
BL/U-1 1923-24 EX/U-1 1976- LO/C-5 1973-
CA/U13 GL/U-1 1948- LO-MT 1963 (v.52)-
(cont'd)

Revue critique de droit international privé (cont'd).

LO/U-2 1965-
LO/U-3 1957-73
LO/U11 1950-
LO/U24 (w.v.32 & 33; v.34 imp.)
OX/U15
XY/N-1 1968 (v.57)-

Revue critique de jurisprudence belge. -- Brussels, 1947-
ISSN 0035-0966

ED/U-1 1967-
LO/U24
OX/U15
XY/N-1 1969 (v.23)-

Revue critique de la jurisprudence en matière civile <u>see</u> next entry

Revue critique de législation et de jurisprudence. -- Paris, 1851-1914;1924-1939
1851-1852 entitled: Revue critique de la jurisprudence en matière civile.
1853 absorbed: Revue de législation et de jurisprudence, q.v.

CA/U-1 1851-69
ED/S11 1851-1914
GL/U-1 1851-59
LO/N-1 1851-1914
OX/U15
OX/U25 1851-61

Revue critique de législation et de jurisprudence du Canada. -- Montreal, 1871-1875

LO-MT
OX/U15
QS/S-6

Revue d'histoire diplomatique. -- Paris, 1887-
ISSN 0035-2365

BR/U-1
CA/U-1
CB/U-1 1964-
DN/U-1 1965-
ED/U-1 1939-
LC/U-1 (w.1940-66)
LO/N-1
LO/U-3 1969-
LO/U19
LO/U24 1890-91; 1904-07
LV/U-1 1887-1936; 1954-
OX/U-1
XY/N-1 1970 (v.84)-

Revue d'histoire du droit <u>see</u> Tijdschrift voor rechtsgeschiedenis

Revue de criminologie et de police technique <u>see</u> Revue internationale de criminologie...

Revue de doctrine et de jurisprudence coloniales <u>see</u> Revue mensuelle de doctrine...

Revue de droit/ Université de Sherbrooke. -- Sherbrooke, Que., 1970-

LO/U24
OX/U15 1971 (v.2)-

Revue de droit administratif et de droit fiscal. -- Lausanne, 1945-

LO/U-3 1955-
XY/N-1 1969 (v.25)-

Revue de droit canonique. -- Strasbourg, 1951-
ISSN 0556-7378

CA/U-1 1957 (v.7)- OX/U-1 XY/N-1 1972 (v.22)-

Revue de droit comparé. -- Montreal, 1964-
ISSN 0080-2514

No holdings notified

Revue de droit contemporain <u>see</u> Review of contemporary law

Revue de droit et de jurisprudence du Katanga <u>see</u> Revue juridique du Zaïre: droit écrit et droit coutumier

Revue de droit familial. -- Brussels, 1955-1972

OX/U15 1970-72 (v.11-13)

Revue de droit français et étranger. -- Paris, 1844-1850
Continues: Revue étrangère de législation et d'économie politique, 1833-1835 (vol.2) and: Revue étrangère et française de législation, 1836 (vol.3)-1843 (vol.10)

ED/U-1 1844-49 LO/U-3 OX/U15 1833-49
LO/N-1

Revue de droit hongrois. -- Budapest, 1958-
Continues: Revue de la législation hongroise, 1954-1956 (no.6) (ISSN 0482-7759)
For English edition <u>see</u> Hungarian law review
ISSN 0556-7386

LO/N-1 1958-60 OX/U15 1956 (no.5)- 1960 XY/N-1 1959;1968 (no.2)-
LO/U-3 1958-60

Revue de droit industriel et de sécurité sociale <u>see</u> Droit du travail et sécurité sociale

Revue de droit intellectuel: l'ingénieur-conseil. -- Brussels, 1911-
1911-1935 entitled: L'Ingénieur-conseil
ISSN 0035-1083

LO-MT 1958 LO/N14 1911- (v.4 & 5 imp.) XY/N-1 1964 imp.

Revue de droit international. -- Paris, 1927-1940 (vol.25)

CA/U-1 1939. LO/U-3 OX/U15
CA/U13 1927-38

Revue de droit international (Tokyo) <u>see</u> Kokusaihō gaikō zasshi

Revue de droit international de sciences diplomatiques et politiques: the international law review. -- Geneva, 1923-
Title varies slightly. English title added with vol.4
ISSN 0035-1091

BH/U-1 1974-	LO/U24 1927-30 imp.,	OX/U15
BL/U-1 1923-65 imp.	1950-51 imp.,	QS/S-7 1923-39
ED/U-1 1923-35	1952-67	XY/N-1 1966 (v.44)-
LO/U-3 1923-72	LV/U-1 1923-35	

Revue de droit international et de droit comparé. -- Brussels, 1949 (vol.26)-
Continues: Revue de l'Institut de Droit Comparé, 1908-1914 (vol.7); Bulletin trimestriel - Institut Belge de Droit Comparé, 1922 (vol.8)-1924 (vol.10) and: Revue trimestrielle - Institut Belge de Droit Comparé, 1925 (vol.11)-1939 (vol.25)
ISSN 0035-1105

BH/U-1 1961-	LD/U-1 1949-	OX/U15
CA/U-1 1908.	LO-MT 1958 (v.35)-	QS/Q12 1950-56;1957-
CA/U13 1908-14;1949-	LO/U-3	61 imp.
CV/U-1 1967 (v.44)-	LO/U24	QW/D12 1973-
ED/S10 1908-13	MA/U-1 1949- imp.	XY/N-1 1966 (v.43)-

Revue de droit international et de législation comparée. -- Brussels, 1869-1940

AD/U-6 1869-1914	LD/U-1 1922-39	LO/U24 1869-1904;
CA/U-1	LO-MT	1920-39 imp.
CA/U13	LO/N-1	LV/U-1 1932-37
ED/S11	LO/N17 1869-1914;	OX/U15 1869-82
ED/U-1	1920-39	OX/U25
GL/U-1 1880-82;	LO/U-1 1869-1937	QS/S-7
1931-39	(1933 imp.)	
KL/U-1 1889-1911	LO/U-3 1904-31 imp.	
imp.		

Revue de droit international pour le Moyen-Orient. -- Paris, 1951-1959 (vol.8 no.1)
ISSN 0482-7686

LO/N-1	LO/U14 1951-58	OX/U15
LO/U-3	(v.7 no.1)	

Revue de droit international privé (et de droit pénal international) see Revue critique de droit international privé

Revue de droit maritime comparé. -- Paris, 1923-1940 (vol.40)
Continues: Revue internationale du droit maritime, 1885-1922

CA/U13	LD/U-1 1923.	OX/U15 1923-40
ED/U-1 1928-33 imp.	LO-MT 1885-1931	OX/U25 1885-1900
GL/U-1 1923-31 imp.	LO/N-1 (w.v.6-8)	QS/S-7 1885-1910
HL/U-1 1923-33 imp.	LO/U-3 1923-40	

Revue de droit pénal et de criminologie. -- Brussels, 1907-
ISSN 0035-4384

BH/U-1 1961/62-
CA/U37
ED/U-1
LD/U-1 1960-
LO/U-3 1952-
LO/U24 1960 (v.41)-
OX/U15 1950-
XY/N-1 1965 (v.46)-

Revue de droit pénal militaire et de droit de la guerre. -- Brussels, 1962-
ISSN 0556-7394

BH/U-1
LO/U11
LO/U24
MA/U-1 1966 (v.5)-
OX/U15
XY/N-1 1969 (v.8)-

Revue de droit social = Tijdschrift voor sociaal recht. -- Brussels, 1962-
Continues: Jurisprudence du louage d'ouvrage: revue des conseils de prud'hommes, 1929-1947, and: Revue de droit social et des tribunaux du travail, 1948-1961
ISSN 0035-1113

GL/U-1 1971-
LO/U-3 (w.1944/45)
OX/U15 1968-

Revue de droit social et des tribunaux du travail <u>see</u> previous entry

Revue de droit suisse <u>see</u> Zeitschrift für schweizerisches Recht

Revue de droit uniforme = Uniform law review. -- Rome, 1973-
Merger of: L'Unification du droit: annuaire, q.v., and: Jurisprudence de droit uniforme = Uniform law cases

BL/U-1
ED/U-1 1974-
LD/U-1
LO/N17
LO/U24
OX/U15
XY/N-1 1975 (no.2)-

Revue de l'administration et du droit administratif de la Belgique. -- Liège; Brussels, 1854-

LO/N-1 1854-65
LO/U-3 1898-1921 imp.

Revue de l'arbitrage. -- Paris, 1955-
ISSN 0556-7440

OX/U15
XY/N-1 1967-

Revue de l'enregistrement des hypothèques du timbre et du domaine <u>see</u> Revue de l'enregistrement et des impôts

Revue de l'enregistrement et des domaines. -- Brussels, 1937-

No holdings notified

Revue de l'enregistrement et des impôts. -- Paris, 1960-
Continues: Revue de l'enregistrement des hypothèques du timbre et du domaine, 1891-1959

LO/N-1 1894-

Revue de l'Institut de Droit Comparé _see_ Revue de droit international et de droit comparé

Revue de la législation hongroise _see_ Revue de droit hongrois

Revue de la sécurité sociale. -- Paris, 1948-1969

OX/U15 1965-69

Revue de la Société des Juristes Bernois _see_ Zeitschrift des bernischen Juristenvereins

Revue de législation ancienne et moderne française et étrangère _see_ Revue historique de droit français et étranger

Revue de législation et de jurisprudence. -- Montreal; Quebec, 1845-1848

LO-MT	OX/U15	QS/S-7
LO/N-1		

Revue de législation et de jurisprudence. -- Paris, 1834-1853 (vol.46)
Absorbed by: Revue critique de législation et de jurisprudence, q.v.

ED/U-1 1835-53	LO/N-1	OX/U15 1847-53

Revue de législation ouvrière et sociale. -- Paris, 1897-1898

LO/N-1

Revue de médecine légale. -- Paris, 1914.
Continues: Revue de médecine légale et de jurisprudence médicale, 1893-1913
Title sometimes appears on title page as: Médecine légale et jurisprudence médicale, travaux, rapports et jugements

AD/U-6 1905-14 imp.

Revue de médecine légale et de jurisprudence médicale _see_ previous entry

Revue de science criminelle et de droit pénal comparé. -- Paris, 1936-
ISSN 0035-1733

AD/U-6 1953-	GL/U-1 1949-	LO/U24 1961-
BL/U-1 1967-	LD/C-1 1973-	OX/U15 1945-
CA/U37	LD/U-1 1967 (no.2).	SO/U-1 1974-
ED/U-1 1968-	LO/N-1 1950-	XY/N-1 1966-
EX/U-1 1968-	LO/U-3 1936-77	

Revue des droits de l'homme: droit international et droit comparé = Human rights journal: international and comparative law. -- Paris, 1968-
1968 (vol.1) entitled: Droits de l'homme
ISSN 0035-1989

AD/U-6	ED/U-1	NO/U-1
BH/U-1	LO/N17	OX/U15
BL/U-1	LO/S14	QW/D12 1975 (v.8)-
CA/U13	LO/U-3	SH/U-1
CB/U-1	LO/U11 1970 (v.3)-	SO/U-1
DN/U-1	LO/U24	XY/N-1
DR/U-1 1969-	MA/U-1 1969 (v.2)-	

Revue des lois, décrets et traités de commerce. -- Brussels, 1923-1946
1923-1926 (vol.2) entitled: Revue trimestrielle des lois...

LO/U-3

Revue des sciences juridiques et économiques <u>see</u> Revue "al-ulum al-qanuniya wal-iqtisadiya

Revue des sciences sociales, série économie- sciences juridiques. -- Bucharest, 1956-1963 (vol.7)
Continued in part by: Revue roumaine des sciences sociales, série de sciences juridiques, q.v.
ISSN 0484-8640

LO/U-3	OX/U-1

Revue des sociétés: jurisprudence, doctrine, législation française et étrangère. -- Paris, 1883-
1975 absorbed: Journal des sociétés civiles et commerciales: revue pratique de jurisprudence, de doctrine et de législation, q.v

LD/U-1 1972 (no.1).	LO/U-3 1947-

Revue "Droit et économie politique" <u>see</u> Revue "al qanoun wal iqtised"

La Revue du Barreau de la Province de Québec <u>see</u> next entry

La Revue du Barreau du Québec. -- Montreal, 1967 (vol.27)-
Continues: La Revue du Barreau de la Province de Québec, 1941-1966

AD/U-6 1956-	LO/U24	QS/S-7 1941-45; 1956-61
CA/U13 1959 (v.19)-	OX/U15	XY/N-1 1972 (v.32)-
LO-MT 1955-		

Revue du droit. -- Quebec, 1922-1939 (vol.17)

LO/U24	OX/U15	OX/U25 1932-34 imp.

Revue du droit bancaire. -- Paris, 1922-1936

LV/U-1 1928-30 imp.

Revue du droit du travail. -- Montreal, 1963-
ISSN 0035-256X

No holdings notified

Revue du droit public et de la science administrative see Epitheoresis demosiou dikaiou kai dioiketikou dikaiou

Revue du droit public et de la science politique en France et à l'étranger. -- Paris, 1894-
ISSN 0035-2578

AB/U-1 1961 (v.77)-
AD/U-6 1965-
BR/U-1 1965-
BT/U-1 1969-72
CA/U-1 1894-95; 1897-1903
CA/U13 1903-31 imp., 1950-
CC/U-1 1963-
CV/U-1 1963 (v.79)-
DN/U-1 1961-
DR/U-1 1949-
ED/U-1 1904-
EX/U-1 1962-
GL/U-1 1959-
GL/U-2 1965-70
HL/U-1 1961-66 (v.82); 1968 (v.84)-
KL/U-1 1951-
LC/U-1 1950-73
LD/U-1 1964-
LO/C-5 1972-
LO/C10 1972 (v.88)-
LO-MT 1961-
LO/N-1
LO/U-2 1961-
LO/U-3 1904;1928- imp.
LO/U12 1966-
LO/U14 1964-
LO/U24 1915-55 imp., 1958-
MA/U-1 1946 (v.62)- imp.
NO/U-1 1965 (v.81)-
NW/U-1 1950-72
OX/U15 1953-
RE/U-1 1958 (v.74)-
SH/U-1 1960-
SO/U-1 1974-
XY/N-1 1966 (v.82)-

Revue du Maghreb see Revue marocaine de droit

Revue du Marché Commun. -- Paris, 1958-
ISSN 0035-2616

AB/U-1 1973-
BH/U-1
BL/U-1 1964-
BR/U-1 1966-
BT/U-1 1958,1964/65,1968-
CA/U13 1958;1959-61 imp.,1962-
DR/U-1 1974 imp.
ED/U-1 (1959-61 and 1963 imp.)
GL/U-1 1970-
LC/U-1 1964-
LD/C-1 1973-
LD/U-1 1959-67 imp., 1968-
LO-MT 1971 (v.140)-
LO/N17 1975-
LO/N26 last 5 years
LO/S14
LO/U-2
LO/U-3
LO/U24
MA/P-1 Nov.1958-
NO/U-1 1968-73
OX/U-1
RE/U-1 1964 (v.7)-
SO/U-1 1958,1964-65;1968-
XM/C10 1970-

Revue du notariat. -- Montreal, 1898-
ISSN 0035-2632

BH/U-1 1962-
LO/U24

Revue du notariat belge. -- Brussels, 1971-
Merger of: Revue pratique du notariat belge, 1871-1970, q.v.
and: Annales du notariat et de l'enregistrement, 1896-1970, q.v.

No holdings notified

Revue égyptienne de droit international. -- Alexandria; Cairo, 1945-
ISSN 0080-259X

CA/U13 1947;1949; 1957-	LO/N17 1945-74	LO/U24 1945-72
ED/U-1	LO/S14 1946;1955-	OX/U15
	LO/U-3 1945-72	XY/N-1 1963-

Revue étrangère de législation et d'économie politique <u>see</u> Revue de droit français et étranger

Revue étrangère et française de législation <u>see</u> Revue de droit français et étranger

Revue française de droit aérien. -- Paris, 1947-
ISSN 0035-287X

CA/U13 1954-	LO/U24	XY/N-1 1966 (v.20)-
LO/U-2 1948-	OX/U15 1948;1950-	

Revue générale d'administration. -- Paris, 1878-1928

LO/N-1	LO/U-3

Revue générale de droit. -- Ottawa, Ont., 1970-
Continues: Justinien, 1964-1969 (vol.5) (ISSN 0449-4504)
ISSN 0035-3086

LO/U24	OX/U15	XY/N-1 1973 (v.4)-

Revue générale de droit aérien <u>see</u> Revue générale de l'air et de l'espace

Revue générale de droit commercial. -- Paris, 1938-1943

LO/U11 1938-39 (v.2)

Revue générale de droit international public. -- Paris, 1894-
ISSN 0035-3094

AB/N-1 1924-49;1951-	GL/U-1 1930-	LO/U24 1910-18;1925-30;1956;1959;1961-
BH/U-1 1971-	LC/U-1 1925-	LV-LP 1974 (v.78)-
BL/U-1 1966-76	LD/U-1 1922-	NO/U-1 1966 (v.70)-
BR/U-1 1929-	LO-MT	OX/U15
CA/U-1	LO/N-1	OX/U25 1905-
CA/U13 (w.1962)	LO/N17 imp.	XY/N-1 1966 (v.37, 3e sér.)-
DR/U-1 1970-	LO/S14 1941/45-	
ED/U-1 1970-	LO/U-2 1927-	
EX/U-1 1965-	LO/U-3	

Revue générale de l'air <u>see</u> next entry

Revue générale de l'air et de l'espace. -- Paris, 1964 (vol.27)-
Continues: Revue juridique de la locomotion aérienne, 1910-1928 (vol.12); Droit aérien, 1929 (vol.13)-1931 (vol.15); Revue générale de droit aérien, 1932 (vol.1)-1939 (vol.8) and: Revue générale de l'air, 1946 (vol.9)-1963 (vol.26)
ISSN 0035-3108

CA/U13 1910-39 imp.
ED/S11 1910-13
GL/U-1 1914-31
LO/N17 1911-14; 1923-31
LO/U-3 1910-31 imp., 1932-
LO/U24 1924 (v.8 March)- (w.1930 (v.14))
OX/U-1 1946-74 (w. 1951, v.14 no.2)
XY/N-1 1961 (v.24)-

Revue générale des assurances terrestres. -- Paris, 1929-
ISSN 0035-3167

LO/U24 1962 (v.33)-
OX/U15 1947-
XY/N-1

Revue générale du droit, de la législation et de la jurisprudence en France et à l'étranger. -- Paris, 1877-1938

CA/U13
ED/U-1
LO/N-1
OX/U15 1928-38

Revue hellénique de droit international. -- Athens, 1948-
ISSN 0035-3256

CA/U-1 1949-50;1953-
CA/U13
GL/U-1 1954-
LO/C47 1954-69
LO/U-3 (w.15e année, no.3/4)
LO/U24
OX/U15
XY/N-1 1966-

Revue historique de droit français et étranger. -- Paris, 1855-
1st series, 1855-1869 (15 vols) has current title.
2nd series, 1870-1876 (6 vols) entitled: Revue de législation ancienne et moderne française et étrangère.
3rd series, 1877-1921 (45 vols) entitled: Nouvelle revue historique de droit français et étranger.
Original title resumed with 4th series, 1922- .
No. 39 omitted in numbering of 3rd series.
ISSN 0035-3280

AB/U-1 1944-
AD/U-6 1907-
CA/U-1
DR/U-1 1969-
ED/S11 1882-1902
ED/U-1 1903-
GL/U-1 1889-(w.v.41)
LA/U-1 1965-
LD/U-1 1946-
LO-MT 1855-69
LO/N-1
LO/U-2 1922-
LO/U24 1877-1934; 1962-
LV/U-1 1877-1976
MA/U-1 imp.
OX/U15 1870-
OX/U25 1877-
QS/S-5 1937-
RE/U-1 1922-38;1959-63;1966-
XY/N-1 1953;1969 (v.47)-

Revue hongroise de droit et de jurisprudence see Magyar jogi szemle

Revue internationale de criminologie et de police technique. -- Geneva, 1953-
Continues: Revue de criminologie et de police technique, 1947-1952
ISSN 0035-3329

AD/U-6 1962-
CA/U37
GL/U-1 1954-
LO/N27 1972-
LO/U-3
LV/P-1 1962-75
OX/U15
XY/N-1 1964 (v.18)-

Revue internationale de droit comparé. -- Paris, 1949-
Continues: Bulletin de la Société de Législation Comparé, 1872 (1869/72)-1948 (vol.71) (Individual issues entitled: Bulletin mensuel... then Bulletin trimestriel...)
ISSN 0035-3337

AD/U-6
BH/U-1 1928 (v.58)-
BL/U-1 1964-
BR/U-1 1977-
CA/U13
CV/U-1
DN/U-1 1949-
ED/S11 1887-1916
ED/U-1
EX/U-1 1964-
GL/U-1
HL/U-1 1949-72 (v.24)
LC/U-1 1949-
LD/C-1 1973 (v.25)-
LO/C10 1949-
LO/C47
LO-MT 1884-88;1890-
LO/N-1
LO/U-1 1922-
LO/U-2
LO/U-3 1885-88;1897-1929 (1923 imp);1949-
LO/U11 1949-
LO/U12 1974-
LO/U24
LV/U-1 1869-1976
MA/U-1 1949-
OX/U15 1929 (v.59)-
QS/S-7 1869-1939
SH/U-1
XY/N-1 1966 (v.18)-

Revue internationale de droit pénal. -- Paris, 1924-June 1939; Jan.-June 1940;1946-

CA/U37 1924-64 (v.35)
ED/S11 1951-53
ED/U-1 1959-
LO/U-3 imp.
LO/U24 1951- imp.
OX/U15 1955-
SH/U-1 1973 (v.44)-
XY/N-1 1974 (v.45)-

Revue internationale de la Croix-Rouge. -- Geneva, 1919-
For ed. in English see International review of the Red Cross (1961-)
ISSN 0035-3361

CA/U-1 1952-61
CA/U13 1952-
LO/U-3 1919-61 imp.
LO/U24 1954-60
XY/N-1 1928-52 imp.

Revue internationale de la propriété bâtie. -- Rome, 1934-1939

LO-MT 1936-39
LO/N-1
LO/U-3
OX/U-1 1936-39

Revue internationale de la propriété industrielle et artistique. -- Paris, 1890-
ISSN 0035-337X

LO/N14 1922-

Revue internationale de la radio-électricité. -- Paris, 1924-1949 (vol.18)
1924-1933 entitled: Revue juridique internationale...
None published 1940-1947

LO/N-1

Revue internationale de la théorie du droit... = Internationale Zeitschrift für Theorie des Rechts. -- Brno; Zurich, 1926-1939

ED/U-1 1926-38	LO/U-3	OX/U15
LO/N-1	LO/U24	OX/U25

Revue internationale de législation et de jurisprudence musulmanes. -- Cairo, 1895-1896

LO/N-1

Revue internationale des droits de l'antiquité. -- Brussels, 1948-1952 amalgamated with: Archives d'histoire du droit oriental (q.v.) to form: Archives d'histoire du droit oriental: revue internationale des droits de l'antiquité.
1954 reverted to original title and continues both periodicals
ISSN 0556-7939

AD/U-6 1949-	LD/U-1 1949-50	MA/U-1
BL/U-1 1960-	LO/N-1	OX/U15
CA/U-1	LO/U-2	OX/U25
CA/U13 1963-67	LO/U14	QS/S-5
ED/U-1	LO/U24 1963 (v.10)-	XY/N-1 1967 (v.14)-
GL/U-1		

Revue internationale des sciences administratives. -- Brussels, 1928-1939;1947-
For English ed. (1957-) <u>see</u> International review of administrative sciences

CC/U-1 1948-56	KL/U-1 1950 (v.16)-	LO/U-3
DR/U-1 1954-	LO/N-1 1947-56	XY/N-1
EX/U-1 1955-61		

Revue internationale du droit d'auteur. -- Paris, 1953-
ISSN 0035-3515

CA/U-1 1953;1955.	LO/N14	OX/U15 (w.1953-54 (nos.2-3))
CB/U-1 1970 (no.63)-	LO/U-3	
LO/N-1	LO/U24 1954 (no.5)-	

Revue internationale du droit des gens. -- Paris, etc., 1936-1940; 1947-1957;1959-
1936-1961 entitled: Revue internationale française du droit des gens
ISSN 0484-8853

CA/U13 1936-39;1947-54;1957.	LO/U24 1936 (v.1 no.1); 1960 (v.29)-1962	OX/U15 1936 (t.1 no. 5)-1964;1966; 1969.
LO/U-3 1936-39;1964.		

Revue internationale du droit maritime <u>see</u> Revue de droit maritime comparé

Revue internationale française du droit des gens <u>see</u> Revue internationale du droit des gens

Revue ivoirienne de droit. -- Abidjan, Ivory Coast, 1969-
ISSN 0048-816X

CA/U13 1972/73- LO/U14 XY/N-1 1970-73 imp.
CB/U-1 1969-

Revue judiciaire congolaise. -- Léopoldville, 1962-1963 (vol.2)
Absorbed by: Revue juridique du Congo, <u>afterwards</u> Revue juridique du Zaïre, q.v.
ISSN 0484-8861

LO/U14 LO/U24

Revue judiciaire des cours et des tribunaux. -- Montpellier, 1856-1875
1865-1868 entitled: Revue judiciaire du Midi
1869-1870 entitled: Revue judiciaire des cours impériales

LO/N-1

Revue judiciaire des cours impériales <u>see</u> previous entry

Revue judiciaire du Midi <u>see</u> Revue judiciaire des cours et des tribunaux

Revue judiciaire libanaise. -- Beirut, [ca 1945]-

LO/U14 1960 (v.16)- imp.

Revue juridique de droit écrit et coutumier du Rwanda et du Burundi <u>see</u> Revue administrative et juridique du Burundi

Revue juridique de l'Afrique Centrale <u>see</u> Revue juridique du Zaïre: droit écrit et droit coutumier

Revue juridique de la locomotion aérienne <u>see</u> Revue générale de l'air et de l'espace

Revue juridique de Madagascar. -- Paris, 1951-1954 (no.4)
ISSN 0482-8275

LO/U14 1951 (no.1). LO/U24

Revue juridique du Congo <u>see</u> Revue juridique du Zaïre: droit écrit et droit coutumier

Revue juridique du Congo Belge <u>see</u> next entry

Revue juridique du Zaïre: droit écrit et droit coutumier. -- Lumumbashi, 1971 (vol.47 no.2)-
Continues: Revue de droit et de jurisprudence du Katanga, 1924-1927; Revue juridique du Congo Belge, 1927-1960; Revue juridique de l'Afrique Centrale, 1960-1963 and: Revue juridique du Congo, 1964-1971.
1964 absorbed: Bulletin des tribunaux coutumiers, q.v. and: Revue judiciaire congolaise, q.v.

LO/U14 1954-	NW/U-1 1964 (v.40)-1971 (v.47)	XY/N-1 1969 (v.45)-
LO/U24 1964 (v.40)-		

Revue juridique et économique du Sud-Ouest: annales de la Faculté de Droit et des Sciences Economiques de l'Université de Bordeaux, série juridique. -- Bordeaux, 1950-1971 (vol.20)
1950-1955 entitled: Annales de la Faculté de Droit, Université de Bordeaux. Continued from 1971 (vol.21) as: Revue économique du Sud-Ouest; holdings of this title not recorded
ISSN 0035-3566

CA/U-1	LO/U-3	OX/U15
GL/U-1 1950-56	LO/U24 1950-59 imp., 1960-71	XY/N-1 1966-71 (v.17-20)
LD/U-1 1955-57		

Revue juridique et politique: indépendance et coopération. -- Paris, 1947-
1947-1958 entitled: Revue juridique et politique de L'Union française
1959-1963 entitled: Revue juridique et politique d'outre-mer
ISSN 0035-3574

BL/U-1 1947-50 (w.v.4 no.1)	LO/N-1	LV/U-1 1947-49
CA/U-1 1947-50	LO/N17 1949-52;1959.	MA/U-1 imp.
DR/U-1 1948-49	LO/S14	OX/U15
GL/U-1 1947-49	LO/U-3	XY/N-1 1948-49 imp., 1966 (v.20)-
LD/U-1 (w.1948 (t.2 nos.1-2))	LO/U11 1967-75	
	LO/U14 1948-58	
	LO/U24	

Revue juridique et politique d'outre-mer see previous entry

Revue juridique et politique de l'Union française see Revue juridique et politique: indépendance et coopération

Revue juridique internationale de la radio-électricité see Revue internationale de la radio-électricité

Revue juridique Thémis de l'Université de Montréal. -- Montreal, 1966 (vol.1)-
Continues: Thémis: revue juridique, 1951-1965 (vol.15)
ISSN 0556-7963

LO/U-2 1953-70	OX/U15	XY/N-1 1971 (v.6)-
LO/U24 1951-52 (v.2) imp., 1952 (v.3)-		

Revue légale. -- Montreal, 1869-1892;1895-
From 1907 (n.s. vol.13) contains only reports of cases.
ISSN 0035-3604

LO-MT 1955-59 LO/U24 1880;1895- QS/S-6 1869-92
LO/N-1 OX/U15 1895- QS/S-7 1869-92

Revue marocaine de droit. -- [Casablanca], 1949-1965 (vol.17)
Continues: Revue marocaine de législation, doctrine, jurisprudence chérifiennes, 1935-1939 (vol.3).
1939 (année 3, no.9) entitled: Revue du Maghreb

LO/U14 1949-65 imp. LO/U24 1961-65 (v.13-17)

Revue marocaine de législation, doctrine, jurisprudence chérifiennes <u>see</u> previous entry

Revue mensuelle de doctrine et de jurisprudence coloniales. -- Brussels, 1924-1940
1924-1931 entitled: Revue de doctrine et de jurisprudence coloniales

LO/N-1 1924-26 imp.

Revue néerlandaise de droit international <u>see</u> Netherlands international law review

Revue pénale suisse <u>see</u> Schweizerische Zeitschrift für Strafrecht

Revue pénitentiaire <u>see</u> Revue pénitentiaire et de droit pénal et études criminologiques

Revue pénitentiaire de Pologne. -- Warsaw, 1926-1931

LO/U-3 1927-29 imp.

Revue pénitentiaire et de droit pénal <u>see</u> next entry

Revue pénitentiaire et de droit pénal et études criminologiques. -- Paris, 1931 (vol.55)-
Continues: Bulletin de la Société Générale des Prisons, 1877-1892; Revue pénitentiaire, 1892-1908 and: Revue pénitentiaire et de droit pénal, 1908-1930
ISSN 0035-3825

ED/U-1 1955. LO/U-3 1949- XY/N-1 1956-
LO/N27 1960- imp. OX/U15 1921-22;1925; 1962.

Revue polonaise de législation civile et criminelle = Przegląd polski ustawodawstwa cywilnego i kryminalnego. -- Warsaw, 1922-1932.
Issued in 2 sections: Ustawodawstwo cywilne = Législation civile, 1928-1931 (vol.4) and: Ustawodawstwo kryminalne = Législation criminelle, 1922-1932 (vol.3/4)

BH/U-1 1928-30 LO/U-3 1928-32 imp.

Revue pratique de droit français. -- Paris, 1856-

LO/N-1

Revue pratique des sociétés. -- Louvain, 1970 (vol.69)-
Continues: Revue pratique des sociétés civiles et commerciales, 1889-1969?

LO-MT 1970 (v.70)-

Revue pratique des sociétés civiles et commerciales <u>see</u> previous entry

Revue pratique du notariat belge. -- Brussels, 1871-1970
Merged with: Annales du notariat et de l'enregistrement to form: Revue du notariat belge, q.v.

No holdings notified

Revue roumaine des sciences sociales, série de sciences juridiques. -- Bucharest, 1964 (vol.8)-
Continues in part: Revue des sciences sociales, série économie-sciences juridiques, q.v.
ISSN 0035-4023

BH/U-1	LO/U-3	OX/U15 1964 (v.8)-
CA/U13	LO/U24 1964 (v.8)-	XY/N-1

Revue sénégalaise de droit. -- Dakar, 1967-
ISSN 0035-4112

LA/U-1 1967-75	LO/U24	XY/N-1 1967- (w.no.3 Jun.1968)
LO/U14	OX/U15 1967.	

Revue suisse de jurisprudence <u>see</u> Schweizerische Juristen-Zeitung

Revue suisse de la propriété industrielle et du droit d'auteur <u>see</u> Schweizerische Mitteilungen über gewerblichen Rechtsschutz und Urheberrecht

Revue togolaise de droit et des relations internationales. -- Benin, [ca 1971]-

LO/U14 1974 (v.3)-

Revue trimestrielle - Institut Belge de Droit Comparé <u>see</u> Revue de droit international et de droit comparé

Revue trimestrielle de droit civil. -- Paris, 1902-

AD/U-6 1955-	EX/U-1 1959-	LO/U11 1968-
BH/U-1 1966-	GL/U-1 1950-	LO/U12 1969-
BL/U-1 1969-	LC/U-1 1970 (v.68)-	LO/U24 1920 (v.19)-
CA/U-1 1902-07	LD/C-1 1974-	OX/U15
CA/U13	LO/C10 1972 (v.70)-	SH/U-1 1963 (v.61)-
CV/U-1 1971 (v.70)-	LO-MT 1963 (v.61)-	SO/U-1 1968-
ED/U-1	LO/U-2 1967-73	XY/N-1 1966 (v.65)-

Revue trimestrielle de droit commercial. -- Paris, 1948-
ISSN 0048-8208

BL/U-1 1974-
CA/U13 1967-
DN/U-1
EX/U-1
GL/U-1 1973-
LC/U-1
LD/C-1 1974-
LO/C10 1972-75
LO/C47 1960-
LO-MT 1958 (v.11)-
LO/U-2 1948-73
LO/U-3
LO/U12
LO/U24 1959 (v.12)-
MA/U-1 1971 (v.24)-
OX/U15
SO/U-1 1970-
XY/N-1 1966 (v.19)-

Revue trimestrielle de droit européen. -- Paris, 1965-
ISSN 0035-4317

AB/U-1
BH/U-1
BR/U-1 1975 (v.11)-
CA/U13
CB/U-1
CR/U-1
ED-SLC
ED/U-1
EX/U-1
GL/U-1
LC/U-1
LD/C-1 1973 (v.9)-
LD/U-1
LO-MT
LO/N-5
LO/N17
LO/U-3 1978-
LO/U11 1966-75
LO/U12
LO/U24
LV/U-1 1965-76
NO/U-1
OX/U15
QN/C70 1972-
QW/D12
SH/U-1
SO/U-1
XY/N-1 1968 (v.4)-

Revue trimestrielle des lois, décrets et traités de commerce
see Revue des lois, décrets...

Revue tunisienne de droit. -- Tunis, 1953-
ISSN 0482-8429

LO/U14 1953-58 (v.6, no.2); 1966/67.
LO/U24 1963/65-

Revue zaïroise de droit. -- Kinshasa-N'gombe, 1971 (vol.2 no.2)-
Continues: Revue congolaise de droit, 1970-1971 (vol.2 no.1)

LO/U14

Revue živnostenského vlastnicitví. -- Prague, 1935-1939 (vol.5 no.5)

LO/N14

Rheinische Zeitschrift für Zivil- und Prozessrecht des In- und Auslandes. -- Mannheim, 1909-1925

LO/U24 1909-12 (v.4)

Rheinisches Archiv für das Civil- und Criminalrecht der königlich preussischen Rhein-Provinzen. -- Cologne, 1820-1901
1820-1899 (Bd.94) entitled: Archiv für das Civil- und Criminalrecht...

LO/N-1

Rheinisches Museum für Jurisprudenz. -- Bonn, 1827-1835

CA/U13
OX/U15 1833-35
QS/S-7

Rhode Island Bar journal. -- Providence, 1952-
ISSN 0556-8595

No holdings notified

Rhodesia and Nyasaland law journal <u>see</u> next entry

Rhodesian law journal. -- Salisbury, 1961-
1961-1963 (vol.3) entitled: Rhodesia and Nyasaland law journal
ISSN 0035-483X

AB/U-1 1969-	EX/U-1	OX/U15
AD/U-6 1968-	LO/N17 1961-71	SH/U-1 1961-72
BL/U-1	LO/U14	SO/U-1 1965-
CA/U13	LO/U24	XY/N-1 1974 (v.14)-

Rivista del diritto commerciale e del diritto generale delle obbligazioni. -- Milan, 1903-
1903-1909 entitled: Rivista di diritto commerciale, industriale e marittimo
ISSN 0035-5887

CA/U13 (w.1954-56)	LO/U-3 1903-12 imp., 1922-39 imp., 1957-	OX/U15 (w.1912,1921)
GL/U-1 1973-		RE/U-1 1936-40;1942-43 imp.
LO-MT 1962-		
LO/N-1 1903 imp.	LO/U24 1960 (v.58)-	XY/N-1 1969 (v.67)-

Rivista del diritto della navigazione. -- Rome, 1935-1972?
ISSN 0035-5895

LO/U-3 1954-72	OX/U15	XY/N-1 1969 (v.35)-
LO/U24 1960 (v.26)-		

Rivista del diritto matrimoniale e dello stato delle persone. -- Milan, 1958-1968 (vol.10)
ISSN 0483-1411

LO/U24

Rivista della proprietà intellettuale ed industriale. -- Milan, 1928-1937;1946-1962

LO/N14 (w.v.1 nos.1-2;v.11)

Rivista delle società. -- Milan, 1956-
ISSN 0035-6018

CA/U13 1960- imp.	LO/U-3 1956-64	OX/U15
LO/C47 1959-65	LO/U24	XY/N-1 1969 (v.14)-

Rivista di difesa sociale. -- Genoa, 1947-1956

CA/U37

Rivista di diritto agrario. -- Florence, 1922-

LO/U-3 1955 (v.34)-	XY/N-1 1967 (v.46)-

Rivista di diritto civile. -- Rome, 1955-
ISSN 0035-6093

GL/U-1 1973-
LO-MT 1962-
LO/U24
OX/U15
XY/N-1 1969 (v.15)-

Rivista di diritto commerciale, industriale e marittimo <u>see</u> Rivista del diritto commerciale e del diritto generale delle obbligazioni

Rivista di diritto del lavoro. -- Milan, 1926-31;1949-
ISSN 0035-6107

LO/U-3 1949-

Rivista di diritto ecclesiastico <u>see</u> Diritto ecclesiastico

Rivista di diritto europeo. -- Rome, 1961-
ISSN 0035-6123

BH/U-1
CA/U13
ED/U-1
EX/U-1 1974-
GL/U-1
KL/U-1 1968-74 (v.8-14)
LO-MT
LO/N-1
LO/N-5
LO/U-3 1961 (v.1 no.2)- 1973
LO/U24
MA/U-1
OX/U15
QN/C70 1972 (v.12)-
QW/D12 1973-
RE/U-1 1964-67 imp.
SO/U-1
XY/N-1 1966 (v.6 no.3)-

Rivista di diritto finanziario e scienze delle finanze. -- Padua; Milan, 1937-1943; 1949-
1949 absorbed: Rivista italiana di diritto finanziario, q.v.
ISSN 0035-6131

LO/U-3
XY/N-1 1966 (v.25)-

Rivista di diritto industriale. -- Milan, 1952-
ISSN 0035-614X

LO-MT 1958 (v.7)-
XY/N-1 1968 (v.17)-

Rivista di diritto internazionale. -- Rome; Milan, 1906-1943;1953-
ISSN 0035-6158

CA/U-1 1929-40
CA/U13 1933-39;1953-
ED/U-1 1970-
LO/N-1
LO/U-3 1906-43 imp., 1953-72 imp.
LO/U24 1920 (n.s.v.8)- (w.1941-43)
LV-LP 1975-
MA/U-1 1937 (v.16)-
OX/U15 1906;1908-10; 1921-
RE/U-1 1966-67 imp.
XY/N-1 1966 (v.49)-

Rivista di diritto internazionale e comparato del lavoro. -- Bologna, 1953-
ISSN 0035-6166

LO/U-3
LO/U24 1961 (n.s.v.1)-
OX/U15
XY/N-1 1964 (v.4)-

Rivista di diritto internazionale privato e processuale/ Università di Milano. Istituto di Diritto Internazionale Privato. -- Padua, 1965-
ISSN 0035-6174

CA/U13 LO/N-1 OX/U15
GL/U-1 1973- LO/U24 XY/N-1 1965 imp., 1967 (v.3)-

Rivista di diritto penitenziario. -- Rome, 1930-1942

CA/U37

Rivista di diritto privato. -- Padua, 1931-1939 (vol.9)

CA/U13 OX/U25

Rivista di diritto processuale. -- Padua, 1946-
Continues: Rivista di diritto processuale civile, 1924-1943 (vol.20)
ISSN 0035-6182

LO/U24 1924-36 imp., 1959- RE/U-1 1936-41 XY/N-1 1969 (2a ser. v.24)-

Rivista di diritto processuale civile <u>see</u> previous entry

Rivista di diritto processuale penale. -- Milan, 1954-1957 (vol.4)
Merged with: Rivista italiana di diritto penale, q.v. to form: Rivista italiana di diritto e procedura penale, q.v.

No holdings notified

Rivista di diritto pubblico e della pubblica amministrazione in Italia. -- Rome, 1909-1923 (vol.15); ser.2, 1924 (vol.16)-1950 (vol.41)?
1924 absorbed: Giustizia amministrativa, q.v., vol.16 of Rivista being vol.35 of Giustizia.

LO/U-3 1909-28

Rivista di diritto svizzero <u>see</u> Zeitschrift für schweizerisches Recht

Rivista di storia del diritto italiano. -- Rome, 1928-

AD/U-6 1934 (vol.7 fasc.3). GL/U-1 1971- OX/U15
LO/N-1 1928-1969/70 XY/N-1 1971 (v.44)-
CA/U13 (w.1940-43) MA/U-1 1961 (v.34)-

Rivista giuridica del lavoro e della previdenza sociale. -- Rome, 1949-

CA/U13 1962- imp. LO/U-3 1949-77

Rivista internazionale di filosofia del diritto. -- Rome; Milan, 1921-
ISSN 0035-6727

AD/U-6 1952-
CA/U13 1960-
ED/U-1 1951-
GL/U-1 1973-
LO/N-1 1932-43;1947-
LO/U24 1930-43 imp., 1953 (v.30)-
OX/U15
RE/U-1 1934-37; 1939-42
XY/N-1 1932;1968 (v.45)-

Rivista italiana di diritto e procedura penale. -- Milan, 1958 (n.s. vol.1)-
Merger of: Rivista italiana di diritto penale, q.v. and: Rivista di diritto processuale penale, q.v.
ISSN 0557-1391

CA/U13 1960-65
ED/S11
LO/U24
XY/N-1 1968 (v.11)-

Rivista italiana di diritto finanziario. -- Milan, 1937-1949
Absorbed by: Rivista di diritto finanziario e scienze delle finanze, q.v.

LO/U-3 1937-43

Rivista italiana di diritto internazionale privato e processuale. -- Genoa, 1931-1932

LO/U24
OX/U25 1931.

Rivista italiana di diritto penale. -- Milan, 1929-1943; n.s. 1948-1957 (vol.10)
Merged with: Rivista di diritto processuale penale to form: Rivista italiana di diritto e procedura penale, q.v.

ED/S11 1948-57
LO/U24 1951-57 (v.4-10)

Rivista italiana di diritto sociale. -- Rome, 1961-
ISSN 0035-6824

XY/N-1 1971.

Rivista italiana per le scienze giuridiche. -- Rome, 1886-1921; 1926-40;1947-

AD/U-6 1952-62
CA/U13 1926-29;1963-
LO/N-1 1886-1919
LO/U24 1926-40 imp., 1947-
OX/U15 1947-
XY/N-1 1969 (n.s.v.23)-

Rivista penale: rassegna di dottrina, legislazione, giurisprudenza. -- Rome; Padua; etc., 1874-
1874-1929 entitled: Rivista penale di dottrina, legislazione, giurisprudenza
ISSN 0035-7022

LO/N-1 1874-1940;1961-
OX/U15 1941-43;1948-60;1962-

Rivista penale di dottrina, legislazione giurisprudenza <u>see</u> previous entry

Rivista trimestrale di diritto e procedura civile. -- Milan, Mar. 1947-

CA/U13 1960-	LO-MT 1958 (v.12)-	OX/U15
ED/U-1 1969-	LO/N-1	XY/N-1 1966 (v.20)-
GL/U-1 1973-	LO/U24 1953 (v.7)-	

Rivista trimestrale di diritto pubblico. -- Milan, 1951-
ISSN 0557-1464

LO/U-3	OX/U15	XY/N-1 1966 (v.16)-
LO/U24 1960 (v.10)-		

Rocky Mountain law review see University of Colorado law review

Rocky Mountain Mineral Law Institute. -- Albany, N.Y., 1955-
ISSN 0557-1987

LO/U24 1970 (16th)- XY/N-1 1969 (15th)-

Rostrum: rivista giuridica, edita a cura della Camera degli Avvocati di Malta. -- Valletta, 1955-1960 (vol.4)

LO/U24

Ruch prawniczny ekonomiczny i socjologiczny. -- Poznan, 1921-
ISSN 0035-9629

XY/N-1 1966 (v.28)-

Rundschau für gewerblichen Rechtsschutz. -- Berlin-Charlottenburg, 1928-

LO/N14 1928-33 (Bd 1 no.4- Bd.7 no.3)

Rutgers Camden law journal. -- Camden, N.J., 1969-
ISSN 0036-0449

LO/U24

Rutgers journal of computers and the law. -- Newark, N.J., 1970-
ISSN 0048-8844

BL/U-1 1973-	LO/N-1 1977-	OX/U15 1971 (v.2)-
CB/U-1 1971 (v.2)-	LO/U24	XY/N-1

Rutgers law review. -- Newark, N.J., 1947-
1947-1948 entitled: Rutgers University law review
ISSN 0036-0465

BL/U-1 1963-	OX/U15	XY/N-1 1970 (v.25)-
LO/U24	QM/C48 1975 (v.29)-	

Rutgers University law review see previous entry

SCOLAG bulletin/ Scottish Legal Action Group. -- Dundee, 1975-

CA/U13 DN/U-1 OX/U15

SVLR bulletin <u>see</u> ASDA bulletin

Sächsisches Archiv für bürgerliches Recht und Prozess <u>see</u> Archiv für Rechtspflege in Sachsen, Thüringen und Anhalt

Sächsisches Archiv für Rechtspflege <u>see</u> Archiv für Rechtspflege in Sachsen, Thüringen und Anhalt

St. John's law review. -- Brooklyn, N.Y., 1926-
ISSN 0036-2905

BL/U-1 1963-65
CA/U13 1972-
EX/U-1 1975-
LO/C10 1969 (v.44).
LO/U24
OX/U15
XY/N-1 1972 (v.47)-

Saint Louis law review <u>see</u> Washington University law quarterly

Saint Louis University law journal. -- St. Louis, Mo., 1949-
First three issues of vol.1 entitled: Intramural law review
ISSN 0036-3030

BL/U-1 1964-
CA/U13 1967 (v.12)-
LO/C47 1976-
LO/U24
OX/U15 1952 (v.2)-
XY/N-1 1969 (v.14)-

St. Mary's law journal. -- San Antonio, Tex., 1969-
ISSN 0581-3441

LO/U24

Salesianum. -- Turin, 1939-
ISSN 0036-3502

XY/N-1 1972 (v.34)-

San Diego law review. -- San Diego, Cal., 1964-
ISSN 0036-4037

LO/U24 OX/U15 XY/N-1

Santa Clara law review. -- Santa Clara, Cal., 1975 (vol.16)-
Continues: Santa Clara lawyer, 1961-1975 (ISSN 0581-6106)

AB/U-1 1972-
LO/U11 1973-75 (v.13 no.2-v.15 no.1)
LO/U24 1972 (v.12)-
XY/N-1 1967 (v.8)-

Santa Clara lawyer <u>see</u> previous entry

Saskatchewan Bar review <u>see</u> next entry

Saskatchewan law review. -- Saskatoon, 1967 (vol.32)-
Continues: Saskatchewan Bar review, 1936-1966 (vol.31)
ISSN 0036-4916

BL/U-1 1958- OX/U15 1953- XY/N-1 1970 (v.35)-
LO/U24

Scandinavian studies in criminology. -- Oslo, 1965-
ISSN 0085-5936

AD/U-6
BH/U-1
BL/U-1
BR/U-1
CA/U-1
CB/U-1
DR/U-1 1968-71
ED/N-1
ED/U-1
HL/U-1 1965-74
LO/C15
LO/N-1
LO/U-2
LO/U-3
LO/U24 1965-71 (v.3)
LO/U28
OX/U15
OX/U25
RE/U-1 1965-68
SO/U-1 1971-
XY/N-1

Scandinavian studies in law. -- Stockholm, 1957-
ISSN 0085-5944

AB/U-1
AD/U-6
BH/U-1
BL/U-1 1959;1975-
BR/U-1
CA/U13
CB/U-1
CR/U-1
CV/U-1
DN/U-1
DR/U-1
ED/U-1
EX/U-1 1958-
GL/U-1
HL/U-1 1957-73
LC/U-1
LD/U-1
LO/C15
LO/C25 1957;1970-75 imp.
LO/C47
LO/N-1
LO/R74
LO/U-2
LO/U-3
LO/U11 1958-
LO/U12
LO/U24
LV/U-1
NO/U-1
NW/U-1 1957-60
OX/U15
OX/U25
QN/C70
QW/D12
RE/U-1
SH/U-1
SO/U-1
XY/N-1 1967 (v.11)-

Schaffen und Wettbewerb. -- Prague, 1928-1935 (vol.8)-
German edition of: Soutez a tvorba, q.v.
No more published?

LO/N14 1933-35 (v.6-8)

Schlesisches Archiv für die practische Rechtswissenschaft. --
Breslau, 1837-1848 (Bd.6)

LO/N-1

Schmollers Jahrbuch für Gesetzgebung, Verwaltung und Volkswirtschaft <u>see</u> Zeitschrift für Wirtschafts- und Sozialwissenschaften

Schöffe: Zeitschrift für Schöffen und Schiedskommissionen. --
Berlin, D.D.R., 1954-
ISSN 0036-6250

LO/N-1 LO/U24 XY/N-1 1967 (Jg.14)-

School of Law review/ University of Toronto <u>see</u> University of Toronto Faculty of Law review

Schriften zum internationalen Steuerrecht <u>see</u> Cahiers de droit fiscal international

Schweizerische Juristen-Zeitung = Revue suisse de jurisprudence. -- Zurich, 1904-
ISSN 0036-7613

LO/U24	OX/U15 1942 (Jg.39)-	XY/N-1 1967 (Jg.63)-

Schweizerische Mitteilungen über gewerblichen Rechtsschutz und Urheberrecht = Revue suisse de la propriété industrielle et du droit d'auteur. -- Zurich, 1928-

LO/N14 1951-	LO/U-3 1928-76	XY/N-1 1973-

Schweizerische Vereinigung für Luft- und Raumrecht Bulletin <u>see</u> ASDA bulletin

Schweizerische Zeitschrift für Sozialversicherung. -- Berne, 1957-
ISSN 0036-7877

LO/U-3 1957-76 imp.	XY/N-1 1967 (Jg.11)-

Schweizerische Zeitschrift für Strafrecht = Revue pénale suisse. -- Berne, 1896-
Continues: Zeitschrift für schweizer Strafrecht, 1888-1895
ISSN 0036-7893

ED/U-1 1968-	LO/U24 1888-1923 (Bd.36); 1966 (Bd.82)-	OX/U15 1950-
LO/U-3 1888-1946		XY/N-1 1967 (Bd.83)-

Schweizerisches Jahrbuch für internationales Recht = Annuaire suisse de droit international. -- Zurich, 1944-

CA/U13	LO/U-2 1955.	OX/U15
ED/U-1	LO/U-3 1944-71	XY/N-1 1964 (Bd.21)-
LO/N-1	LO/U24	

Scientia juridica: revista bimestral portuguesa e brasileira. -- Braga, 1951-
ISSN 0559-1422

LO/U24 1960 (v.9)-	XY/N-1 1969 (v.18)-

Scots law chronicle <u>see</u> Law chronicle: or, Journal of jurisprudence

Scots law times. -- Edinburgh, 1893-
Absorbed: Law Society of Scotland newsletter, 1951, q.v.
ISSN 0036-908X

AB/N-1 1947-64	BH-LS 1925-	CB/U-1
AB/U-1 1903-	BH/U-1	DN/U-1
AD-A	BL/U-1 1959-	DR/U-1
AD/U-6	BR/U-1 1897 (v.5)-	ED/S10
BC-UC 1895-1931; 1950-71 imp.	CA/U-1 1899-	ED/S11
	CA/U13	ED-SLC (cont'd)

Scots law times (cont'd).

ED/U-1
EX/U-1
GL/U-1
GL/U-2
HL/U-1 1961-
KL/U-1 1962-65
LC/U-1 1893-95; 1900/01-
LD/U-1 (w.1944-57)
LO-MT
LO/N-1
LO/R74 1965-
LO-SC 1907-
LO-TS 1948-
LO/U-2 1957;1959-70;1972-
LO/U-3 1920-
LO/U11
LO/U24
LO/U28 1908-
LV/U-1 1902/03-
MA/U-1
NO/U-1 1893-1905; 1959- (w.v.10)
NW/U-1 1962-
OX/U15
QE/C76
QM/C68 1893/94- 1974
QN/C70 1960-
QS/S-4 1897-
QS/S-6
QS/S-7 1924-
QS/S-8
QW/D12
RE/U-1 1902-
SH/U-1 1893-1909;1949-
SO/U-1 1925-
XM/C10 1972-
XY/N-1 1967-

Scottish law gazette. -- Edinburgh, 1933-
ISSN 0036-9314

AD-A
AD/U-6
BL/U-1 1964-
CA/U-1 1968-
CA/U13 1959-
DN/U-1 1955-74
ED/S10
ED/S11 1945-
ED-SLC
ED/U-1
GL/U-1 1957-
GL/U-2 1960 (v.28)-
LO-MT
LO/N-1
LO-SC 1977-
LO/U24 1933-38 (v.6); 1941-50 imp., 1951-
OX/U15
QS/S-8
XY/N-1 1967 (v.35)-

Scottish law journal and Sheriff Court record <u>see</u> next entry

Scottish law magazine and Sheriff Court reporter. New series. -- Glasgow, 1862-1867 (vol.6)
Continues: Scottish law journal and Sheriff Court record, 1858-1861 (vol.3).
Absorbed by: Journal of jurisprudence and Scottish law magazine, q.v.

AD/U-6
CA/U-1 1862-67
ED/S11
LO/N-1 1865-67
OX/U15

Scottish law review and Sheriff Court reports. -- Glasgow, 1885-1963 (vol.79)

AB/N-1 1915.
AB/U-1
AD-A
AD/U-6
BC-UC 1959-63
CA/U13
DN/U-1
ED/S10
ED/S11
ED/U-1
GL/U-1
GL/U-2 1887 (v.3)-1963
LC/U-1
LO-MT
LO/N-1
LO-SC
LO/U24
LV/U-1
OX/U15

Scottish Legal Action Group bulletin <u>see</u> SCOLAG bulletin

Scuola positiva: rivista di diritto e procedura penale. -- Milan, 1891-1972
Not published 1944-1946

CA/U37
LO/U-3 1910-56
RE/U-1 1934-37

Séances et travaux - Académie Diplomatique Internationale. -- Paris, 1927-1940 (année 13, 1939)
Ceased publication

LO/U-3 1928-38
XY/N-1 1930-39 (années 3-13) (w.1934 (année 8))

Secretary <u>see</u> Professional administration

Securities law review. -- Albany, N.Y., 1969-
ISSN 0080-8474

BH/U-1
HL/U-1
MA/U-1
SO/U-1 1969-72
XY/N-1 1973 (v.5)-

Securities regulation law journal. -- Boston, 1973-
ISSN 0097-9554

XY/N-1

La semaine juridique: Doctrine, jurisprudence, textes = Juris-classeur périodique. -- Paris, 1926-
ISSN 0049-0156

CA/U13 1945-
CV/U-1 1970 (44e an.)-
ED/U-1 1974-
LO/C-5 1972-
LO/U12 1972-
LO/U24 1946 (20e an.)-
OX/U15 1946-
XY/N-1 1976 (50e an.,no.33/6)-

Seminar: annual extraordinary number of 'The jurist'. -- Washington D.C., 1943-1956 (vol.13)

AD/U-6 (w.1953)
CA/U-1
LO/U-2
LO/U24
LV/U-1 1943-53
OX/U15
OX/U25

Seton Hall law review. -- Newark, N.J., 1970-
ISSN 0586-5964

No holdings notified

Sexual law reporter. -- Los Angeles, 1975-

No holdings notified

Shenaton ha-mishpat ha-'ivri/ Institute for Research in Jewish Law, Hebrew University. -- Jerusalem, 1974-

LO/U14

Shingle/ Philadelphia Bar Association. -- Philadelphia, 1938-
ISSN 0037-377X

No holdings notified

Singapore law review: journal of the University of Singapore Law Society. -- Singapore, 1969-
Continues: Me judice, 1958-1967 (vol.8)
ISSN 0080-9705

LO/U24 1960-61 imp., 1962-70
OX/U15 1958 imp., 1959-71/72 (v.3 n.s.)

Smith's law journal <u>see</u> Law journal/ ed.Smith (London)

Sociaal-economische wetgeving. -- Zwolle, 1952-
ISSN 0037-7597

ED/U-1 1967-
GL/U-1 1973-
LO/U24 1962 (v.10)-
OX/U15 1956 (v.4)-
SO/U-1 1974-76
XY/N-1 1959-

Social and labour bulletin/ International Labour Office. -- Geneva, 1974-

No holdings notified

Social meaning of legal concepts. -- New York, 1948-1953 (no.5)

CA/U13
LO/U24
OX/U15

Socialist thought and practice. -- Belgrade, 1961-
ISSN 0583-7200

CA/U-1
LA/U-1 1969-
LO/N17 1969-
LO/U-3
LO/U24
OX/U-1
XY/N-1

Société Internationale de Droit Pénal Militaire et de Droit de la Guerre. Congrès international (Proceedings). -- Strasbourg, 1960 (1er congrès, 1959)-
ISSN 0583-8657

LO/N-1 1966 (3rd).
LO/U24
OX/U15

Sociologia del diritto. -- Milan, 1974-

BL/U-1

Sociologie et droit slaves. -- Paris, 1945-1950

LO/U-3
OX/U-1

Solicitor <u>see</u> next entry

Solicitor quarterly. -- London, 1962-1965 (vol.4)
Continues: Solicitor, 1934-1961 (vol.28)
ISSN 0584-0724

AB/N-1
AB/U-1 1944-46; 1962-65
BC-UC 1946-51; 1960-61
BH-LS 1953-61
BH/U-1 1934;1962-65
BL/U-1 1962-65
CA/U13
CR/U-1 1962-65
ED/S11
EX/U-1 1951-65
HL/U-1 1934-37; 1957-65
LC/U-1 (cont'd)

Solicitor quarterly (cont'd).

LO-MT
LO/N-1
LO/N-5 1962-65
LO-SC 1935-47
LO-TS 1964-65
LO/U-2 1934-36 imp., 1947;1949-65
LO/U11 1934-57
LO/U24
OX/U15
QS/Q12
QS/S-7 1962-65
QS/S-8 1934;1942-65
RE/U-1
SH/U-1 1962-65
SO/U-1 1964-65

Solicitors' clerks' gazette <u>see</u> Solicitors' managing clerks' gazette

Solicitors' journal. -- London, 1857 (vol.1)-
Continues: Legal observer and solicitors' journal, 1830-1856 (vol.52), of which subtitle varies.
1857-1906 (vol.50) entitled: Solicitors' journal and reporter.
With vol.51, 1906 absorbed: Weekly reporter and until 1927 (vol.71) entitled: Solicitors' journal and weekly reporter
ISSN 0038-1047

AB/N-1 1912-
AB/U-1 1907-15;1926-
AD-A last 5 years
AD/U-6 1956-
BH-LS
BH/P-1
BH/U-1 1830-38;1857-
BL-LS 1857-
BL/U-1 1956-59;1965-
BR/U-1 1911 (v.56)-
BT/U-1 1955-65;1975.
CA/U-1 1830-56;1930- imp.
CA/U13 1857-
CB/U-1 1940-66 imp., 1967-
CH-CI 1857-
CR/U-1 1927- imp.
CV/C-1 1973-
CV/U-1 1877 (v.22)- (w.v.86;89-92)
DN/U-1 1970-
DR/U-1 1857-1965 imp., 1966-
ED/S10 1941- imp.
ED/S11
ED-SLC 1966-
ED/U-1 1830-35;1965-
EX/U-1 1899-1912;1946-58 imp.,1964-
GL/U-2 1973-
HL/U-1 1947-
KL/U-1 1973 (v.117)-
LC/C-1 1965-
LC/U-1 1925-
LD/C-1 1960-71
LD/U-1 1875-88;1921-
LO/C-3 1973-
LO/C-5 1969- imp.
LO/C14 1968-
LO/C15 1921-39;1941-
LO/C18 1952-3;1968 (v.112)-
LO/C25 1968-
LO/C47 1971-
LO-CBL 1955-*
LO-MT
LO/N-1
LO/N-5 1950-
LO/N27 1906-
LO/N46 1906-
LO/P-6 1955-
LO/R74 1965 (v.109)-
LO/S28 1924-72
LO-SC 1857-1949 imp., 1951-
LO-TS 1891-
LO/U-1 1913-36;1950-
LO/U-2 1966-
LO/U-3 1967-
LO/U11 1968-
LO/U12 1949-(1949-50;1958 imp.)
LO/U24 1830-32;1857-
LO/U28 1906-11;1925-30;1934-39; 1948-
LV-LP last 5 years
LV/P-1 1973-
LV/U-1 1925/26-
MA/U-1 1883- imp.
NO/U-1 1969-
NW/U-1 1969-
OX/U15
OX/U25 1857-
QE/C76 1968-
QG/C25 1968-
QL/D15 1920-
QM/C48 1962-
QM/C68 1977-
QN/C70 1960-
QS/Q12 1950-
QS/Q13 1962 (July)-
QS/S-4 1857-
QS/S-6 1857-
QS/S-7
QS/S-8
QW/C73 1949-
QW/D12 1967 (v.111)-
RE/U-1 1875-
SH/U-1 1962-
SO/U-1 1948-
XM/C10 1973-
XY/N-1 1912-14 (v.57-58); 1963 (v.107)-

Solicitors' journal and reporter <u>see</u> previous entry

Solicitors' journal and weekly reporter <u>see</u> Solicitors' journal

Solicitors' managing clerks' gazette. -- London, 1941-1962
Continues: Solicitors' clerks' gazette, 1921-1940
Continued by: The Legal executive, q.v.

AB/N-1 1921-28
LO/N-1
OX/U15 1921-36

Sotsialisticheskaia zakonnost': organ prokuratury SSSR. -- Moscow, 1935-
ISSN 0038-1691

GL/U-1 Soviet Studies Branch Library 1939-
LO/U-2 1936-40; 1956-70
LO/U-3 1949-54;1958- (w.1962 no.1)
OX/U15 1935-55 imp., 1957-
XY/N-1 1958-

Sotsialistichesko pravo. -- Sofia, 1952-
ISSN 0489-7714

LO/N-1
LO/U-3 imp.
XY/N-1 1969-

Soutez a tvorba. -- Prague, 1928-
Publication suspended 1940-1945.
1928-1935 also issued in German under title: Schaffen und Wettbewerb, q.v.

LO/N14 1936-50 (v.9 no.5/6-v.21)

South African journal of criminal law and criminology = Suid-Afrikaanse tydskrif vir strafreg en kriminologie. -- Cape Town, 1977 (vol.1)-
Continues: Crime, punishment and correction = Misdaad, straf en hervorming, 1972-1976 (vol.5)

CA/U37
LO/U24
XY/N-1

South African law journal. -- Cape Town, 1901 (vol.18)-
Continues: Cape law journal, 1884-1900 (vol.17)
ISSN 0038-2388

AB/U-1
AD/U-6
BH/U-1 1956-
BL/U-1 1960-
BR/U-1 1901-50 imp. 1967-
CA/U13
CR/U-1 1950-
CV/U-1 1967 (v.84)-
DN/U-1 1956-
ED/S11 1930-59
ED/U-1
HL/U-1
LC/U-1 1947- (w.v.68 no.1;v.69 no.2)
LO-MT 1901-
LO/S65 1907-76 imp.
LO/U12 1956- (w.1959 nos.3-4)
LO/U14 1958-66 imp., 1967-
LO/U24
MA/U-1 1895- imp.
NO/U-1
OX/U15
OX/U25 1906-
QS/S-4 1946-
QS/S-7 1928-
RE/U-1 1974-
SO/U-1 1948-
XY/N-1 1967 (v.84)-

South African law times. -- Johannesburg, 1932-1936 (vol.5)

CA/U13
LO/N-1
LO/U24
OX/U25

South African yearbook of international law. -- Pretoria, 1975-

LO/U24

South Carolina law quarterly see next entry

South Carolina law review. -- Columbia, 1962 (vol.15)-
Continues: South Carolina law quarterly, 1948-1962 (vol.14)
ISSN 0038-3104

CA/U13 1968-
LO-MT 1970 (v.22)-
LO/U24
OX/U15
XY/N-1 1970 (v.22 no.3)-

South Dakota Bar journal. -- Pierre, 1932-
ISSN 0038-3244

LO/U24 1965 (v.34)-

South Dakota law review. -- Vermillion, 1956-
ISSN 0038-3325

LO/U24 1972 (v.17)-
OX/U15
XY/N-1 1972 (v.17)-

South Pacific law review. -- Sydney, 1948-1950 (vol.1 no.8)

GL/U-2
LO/U-3
LO/U14 (w.1948 (v.1 no.5), 1949 (v.1 no.7))
LO/U24
OX/U15
QN/C70

South Texas law journal. -- Houston, 1955-
ISSN 0038-3546

LO/U24

Southern California law review. -- Los Angeles, 1927-
ISSN 0038-3910

BL/U-1 1964-
CA/U13 1958-
LO/U24
OX/U15
XY/N-1 1970 (v.43)-

Southern Illinois University law journal. -- Carbondale, Ill., 1976-

No holdings notified

Southern law quarterly see Tulane law review

Southern law review. -- St. Louis, Mo., 1875 (n.s.)-Feb. 1883
Continues: Southern law review and chart of the Southern law and collection union, 1872-Oct.1874
Absorbed by: United States law review, q.v.

LO/N-1 1875-76 (n.s.1-2 no.3)
OX/U15 (w.1878-79 (v.7))

Southern law review and chart of the Southern law and collection union see previous entry

Southern University law review. -- Baton Rouge, La., 1974-

No holdings notified

Southwestern law journal. -- Dallas, 1947-
1947 (vol.1) entitled: Texas law and legislation
ISSN 0038-4836

LO/U24
OX/U15 1950-
XY/N-1 1964 (v.18)-

Southwestern law journal and reporter. -- Nashville, 1844.

OX/U15

Southwestern University law review. -- Los Angeles, Cal., 1916/17-
Not published 1919-1970

LO/U24
XY/N-1 1972 (v.4)-

Sovetskai͡a iustitsii͡a: organ NKI͡U SSSR i Verkhovnogo Suda SSSR.
-- Moscow, 1930-
Continues: Ezhedel'nik sovetskoi iustitsii, 1922-1929
ISSN 0038-5115

BH/U-1 1939.
CA/U37 1965-
CC/U-1 1960-
GL/U-1 Soviet Studies Branch Library 1957-
LO/N-1 1938-40;1958-
LO/U-2 1922-41; 1957-70
LO/U-3 1925-31 imp., 1957- imp.
MA/U-1 1964-
OX/U15 1922-41;1957-
XY/N-1 1957-

Sovetskie finansy see Den'gi i kredit

Sovetskii ezhegodnik mezhdunarodnogo prava = Soviet year-book of international law. -- Leningrad, 1958-
ISSN 0584-5335

AD/U-6 (w.1960)
CA/U13 1960-
CC/U-1 (w.1960)
GL/U-1 Soviet Studies Branch Library
LO/N-1
LO/N17 1958; 1960; 1966/67; 1968/69.
LO/U-2 1958-60;1962-
LO/U-3
LO/U24 1959- imp.
OX/U15
XY/N-1 1959;1968-

Sovetskoe gosudarstvo i pravo. -- Moscow, 1930-
ISSN 0038-5204

BT/U-1 1968-77
CA/U-1 1946-
CA/U37 1965-
CC/U-1 1946-
DR/U-1 1947-71 imp., 1972-
GL/U-1 Soviet Studies Branch Library 1939-41;1946-
LO/N-1
LO/S14 1946-
LO/U-2 1930-61;1963-65;1973.
LO/U-3 1931- imp.
MA/U-1 1946- imp.
OX/U-1 1947-
OX/U15 1940;1946-
SW/U-1 1963-74
XY/N-1 1946-
YK/U-1 1966-

Sovetskoe pravo. -- Tallin, Estonia, 1967-

LO/U-2 1967-70

Sovetskoe pravo: zapiski. -- Moscow, 1929-1930
Continues: Sovetskoe pravo: zhurnal Instituta sovetskogo prava, 1922-1928.
1930 merged with: Revoliutsiia prava, q.v.

LO/U-2 1929-30

Sovetskoe pravo: zhurnal Instituta sovetskogo prava see previous entry

Soviet law and government. -- New York, 1962-
ISSN 0038-5530

AB/N-1	ED/U-1 Summer 1965-	LO/N-1
BH/U-1	GL/U-1 Soviet Studies Branch Library 1968-70	LO/U-2
BL/U-1 1964- (w.v.12 no.2)	HL/U-1 1973 (v.12)-	LO/U-3
BT/U-1		LO/U24
CA/U13		XY/N-1
CC/U-1 1967-		YK/U-1

Soviet year-book of international law see Sovetskii ezhegodnik mezhdunarodnogo prava

Speculum juris: annual journal of the Faculty of Law and Juridical Society of the University College of Fort Hare. -- Fort Hare, South Africa, 1965-
ISSN 0584-8652

BL/U-1	LO/U14 1967.	OX/U15
CA/U13	LO/U24	XY/N-1
DR/U-1 1968-		

Ssu-fa chuan-k'an (Judicial monthly). -- Taipei, 1951-
ISSN 0561-7634

No holdings notified

Der Staat. -- Berlin, BRD, 1962-
ISSN 0038-884X

ED/U-1 1962-	LO/N-1	LV/U-1 1966-76
HL/U-1 1966-75 (Bd.14)	LO/U-3 1962-63 (v.1-2)	OX/U-1
LC/U-1	LO/U24 1964 (Bd.3)-	SW/U-1 1962-73
		XY/N-1 1967 (Bd.6)-

Staat und Recht. -- Berlin, DDR, 1952-
ISSN 0038-8858

LO/N-1 1954-	LO/U24 1960 (Jg.9)-	XY/N-1 1966 (Jg.15)-
LO/U-3 (w.1953)	OX/U15	

Staatshandbuch für Gesetzgebung, Verwaltung und Volkswirtschaft des Norddeutschen Bundes see Annalen des Deutschen Reichs für Gesetzgebung, Verwaltung und Volkswirtschaft

Das Standesamt. -- Frankfurt am Main, 1948-
Continues: Der Standesbeamte, 1874-1920 and: Zeitschrift für Standesamtswesen, 1921-1944

LO/U24 1968 (Jg.21)-

Der Standesbeamte <u>see</u> previous entry

Stanford journal of international studies. -- Stanford, Cal., 1968 (vol.3)-
Continues: Proceedings of the East-West Trade Conference, Stanford University, 1966-1967 (vol.2)
ISSN 0081-4326

AD/U-6	LO/U24	XY/N-1
HL/U-1 1970 (v.5).		

Stanford law review. -- Stanford, Cal., 1948-
ISSN 0038-9765

AB/U-1	LD/U-1	QN/C70 1970-
BL/U-1 1965-	LO-MT 1959-	QS/Q12 1948-49 imp.
CA/U13	LO/N-1 1951-	QS/S-4 1959-
CR/U-1	LO/U12	SH/U-1 1973 (v.26)-
CV/U-1 1967 (v.20)-	LO/U24	SO/U-1 1965-
ED/U-1	OX/U15	XY/N-1 1962 (v.15)-
HL/U-1 1948/49- 71/72 (v.24)	OX/U25	
	QM/C48 1976-	

Stát a právo. -- Prague, 1956-
ISSN 0585-0967

LO/N-1	LO/U-3 1960 (v.6)-	XY/N-1 1960 (v.6)-

State and law <u>see</u> Pánstwo i prawo

State Bar journal of the State Bar of California <u>see</u> California State Bar journal

State Bar review/ Washington State Bar Association. -- Seattle, 1934-1936 (vol.2)
Absorbed by: Washington law review, q.v.

No holdings notified

Staten. -- Copenhagen, 1859-1862
1859-1860 entitled: Ret og pfligt

LO/N-1

Steuer und Wirtschaft. -- Stuttgart, etc., 1921-1944;1947-

LO/U-3 1921-44	OX/U15 1941 (Jg.20(2))-	XY/N-1 1962 (Jg.39)-

Strafhervormingnuus <u>see</u> Penal reform news

Straits law journal. -- Singapore, 1888-1892 (vol.5 no.12)

LO/N-1 imp.

Studi di diritto industriale. -- Rome, 1921-1942 (anno 21)

LO/N14 LO/U-3

Studi e documenti di storia e diritto. -- Rome, 1880-1904 (vol.25)

LO/N-1 OX/U15 QS/S-5 1880-98

Studi economico-giuridici/ Università di Cagliari. -- Cagliari, 1909-

LO/U-2 1963/4-1971/2 OX/U15 1914-46 imp.,1951/52-

Studi parmensi/ Università di Parma. -- Milan, 1951-
ISSN 0562-2646

AD/U-6 1951. GL/U-1 OX/U-1

Studi sassaresi/ Università di Sassari, Società Sassaresi per le Scienze Giuridiche. -- Sassari, Sardinia, 1901-

AD/U-6 1938-59;1963; 1965 (fasc.3-4). LO/U-3 1946-67 LV/U-1 1901-09 imp.

Studi senesi/ Università di Siena. -- Siena, 1884-
ISSN 0039-3010

AD/U-6 1950-
LO/U-2 1967-74
LO/U-3 1884-1973 imp.
OX/U15 1884;1887-1901;1936-
RE/U-1 1968-70 (v.17-19 no.2)
XY/N-1 1916 (v.32).

Studia et documenta historiae et juris. -- Rome, 1935-

AD/U-6
CA/U-1
CA/U13
ED/U-1 1963-
LC/U-1 1959 (v.25).
LO/N-1 (v.1-6)
LO/U-2
LO/U24
MA/U-1
OX/U15
OX/U25 1954-
XY/N-1 1969 (v.35)-

Studia juridica/ Towarzystwo Naukowe w Toruniu (Scientific Society of Torun). -- Torun, 1962-
ISSN 0081-6671

LO/N-1 XY/N-1 1964 (t.5 no.2); 1967 (t.7 no.3).

Studia juridica/ Universidad Central de Venezuela. -- Caracas, 1957-
ISSN 0491-273X

LO/U24 XY/N-1 1973 (no.3).

Studia juridica auctoritate universitatis Pécs publicata. -- Budapest, 1958-
ISSN 0562-2824

LO/N-1 1959 (no.5)- XY/N-1 1969 (no.66)-

Studia nad historia pǎnstwa i prawa: (series 2). -- Warsaw, 1954-
ISSN 0562-2921

LO/N-1	OX/U-1	XY/N-1 1954-61 imp.

Studia prawnicze/ Polska Akademia Nauk. Institut Nauk Prawnych. -- Warsaw, 1962-
ISSN 0039-3312

LO/N-1	XY/N-1 1969 (no.21)-

Studia universitatis Babes-Bolyai. Series jurisprudentia. (Series III, 2). -- Cluj, Rumania, 1958-
ISSN 0578-5464

CA/U-1	LO/N-1	OX/U-1 1962-
DR/U-1 1964-	NW/U-1 1964-69	OX/U15
GL/U-1 1962-		

Studie z mezinárodního práva. -- Prague, 1955-
ISSN 0562-3138

OX/U15

Studies en voordrachten/ Freie Universiteit te Brussel. -- Brussels, 1962-1964;1970
Ceased publication?
ISSN 0524-7969

AD/U-6	GL/U-1	MA/U-1
CA/U-1	LO/U-3	OX/U15
ED/U-1 (w.1964 (II))	LO/U24	

Studies in law and economic development see Journal of international law and economics

Studies on international fiscal law see Cahiers de droit fiscal international

Studii şi cercetări juridice. -- Bucharest, 1956-
ISSN 0039-4041

CA/U13 1956-63	LO/U-3	XY/N-1 1958-9 imp., 1964 (anul 9)-
LA/U-1 1964-	OX/U15	
LO/N-1 1957-		

Sudan law journal and reports. -- Khartoum, 1956-
ISSN 0585-8631

AB/N-1 1956-66; 1968-69	EX/U-1 1957-70 imp.	LO/U24
	LO/N-1	OX/U15
BL/U-1	LO/U12 1956-65	QS/S-7 1958-62
CA/U13	LO/U14	XY/N-1 1965-69
DR/U-4		

Süddeutsche Juristenzeitung. -- Heidelberg, 1946-1950 (Jg.5)
Merged with: Deutsche Rechtszeitschrift, q.v., to become: Juristenzeitung, q.v.

CA/U13 1949-50
LO/U11
LO/U24
OX/U15 (w.1946)

Suffolk University law review. -- Boston, 1967-
ISSN 0039-4696

LO/U24 1971 (v.6)-
XY/N-1 1969 (v.4)-

Suid-Afrikaanse tydskrif vir strafreg en kriminologie <u>see</u> South African journal of criminal law and criminology

Summary of proceedings [etc.]- ... conference of the International Bar Association. -- The Hague, 1948-1968 (12th)

AD/U-6 1962 (no.9).
LO/U-2 1950-68 (nos.3-12)
LO/U24 1950-68 (nos.3-12)

Supreme Court journal. -- Mylapore, 1950-
Continues: Federal law journal of India, 1937-1943, and: Federal law journal, 1944-1949

CA/U13
LO/N-1 1951.
LO/N17 1937-69 (v.41)
LO/S55 (w.v.5 nos.2; 8-10)
LO/U14 1943-
OX/U13 1959-
OX/U15 1937-49 (v.12)
XY/N-1 1972 (v.46)-

Supreme Court monthly review. -- Lahore, 1968-

OX/U15

Supreme Court review. -- Chicago, 1960-
ISSN 0081-9557

AB/N-1 1963-67;1971-
BL/U-1 1964-
CA/U-1 1969-
CB/U-1 1966-
CC/U-1 1963-
CV/U-1 1967-
ED/U-1 1960;1962-
GL/U-1 1962-
HL/U-1 1966-
LO-MT 1961;1964; 1966;1971-
LO/U-2 1962.
LO/U-3
LO/U24
LV/U-1 1961.
NO/U-1 1963-
OX/U15
QN/C70 1970-
RE/U-1
SW/U-1 1960;1962-
XY/N-1 1963-

Survey of California law. -- Santa Clara, 1953-
Continues: Annual survey of California law, 1948-53

No holdings notified

Svensk juristtidning. -- Stockholm, 1918-
ISSN 0039-6591

CA/U13 1954-
LO/U24 1918;1928- (w.1934;1940-42)
XY/N-1 1969 (Årg.54)-

Sydney law review. -- Sydney, 1953-
ISSN 0082-0512

AB/U-1 1954 (v.1 no.2)-
BH/U-1
BL/U-1 1954 (v.1 no.2)-
CA/U13
CB/U-1 1965 (v.5)-
LC/U-1 1965 (v.5)-
LD/U-1 1954 (v.1 no.2)-
LO/N-1 1963 (v.4 no.2)- imp.
LO/U-3 1965-
LO/U12 1954 (v.1 no.2)-
LO/U24
MA/U-1
NO/U-1
OX/U15
QS/S-4
SH/U-1
XY/N-1 1959 (v.3)-

Symposium - St. Louis University Student Bar Association. -- St. Louis, 1973-
ISSN 0093-1136

No holdings notified

Syndicat National des Auteurs et Compositeurs de Musique: le bulletin des auteurs <u>see</u> SNAC: le bulletin des auteurs

Syracuse journal of international law and commerce. -- Syracuse, N.Y., 1972/73-
ISSN 0093-0709

LO/U24
XY/N-1

Syracuse law review. -- Syracuse, N.Y., 1949-
ISSN 0039-7938

BL/U-1 1953-74
CA/U13
LO/U24
OX/U15
XY/N-1 1969 (v.21)-

TVVS: maandblad voor ondernemingsrecht. -- Deventer, 1971 (vol.14)-
Continues: Tijdschrift voor vennootschappen, verenigingen en stichtingen, 1958-1970 (vol.13) (ISSN 0041-4743)

OX/U15 1966 (v.9)-

Table: journal of the Society of Clerks-at-the-Table in Commonwealth Parliaments. -- London, 1953 (vol.22)-
Continues: Journal of the Society... Empire Parliaments, 1932-1952 (vol.21)

BH/U-1
BR/U-1 1953 (v.22)-
CA/U-1 1953 (v.22)-
CA/U13
ED/N-1
HL/U-1 1955;1959-73 (v.42)
LO/N-1
LO/N26
LO/N46
LO/U-3
LO/U11 1932;1936-
LO/U24
SW/U-1 1961-71

Tasmanian University law review <u>see</u> University of Tasmania law review

Tax adviser. -- New York, 1970-
ISSN 0039-9957

No holdings notified

Tax counselor's quarterly. -- Chicago, Ill., Mar.1957-
ISSN 0040-0009

No holdings notified

Tax haven review <u>see</u> Tax planning international

Tax law review. -- New York, Oct.1945-
ISSN 0040-0041

BL/U-1 1968-	LO/U24	SO/U-1 1964-
CR/U-1 1971-	OX/U15	XY/N-1 1966 (v.22)-
LD/U-1		

Tax lawyer: bulletin of the Section of Taxation, American Bar Association. -- Washington D.C., 1967 (vol.21)-
Continues: Bulletin - A.B.A. Section of Taxation, 1947-1967 (vol.20)
ISSN 0040-005X

LO/U24

Tax memo/Canadian Tax Foundation. -- Toronto, 1954-
ISSN 0576-6230

LO/U24 1965-69

Tax news service/ International Bureau of Fiscal Documentation. -- Amsterdam, 1965-
Loose-leaf
ISSN 0040-0076

CA/U13 1972-	LO-MT 1972-	QM/C68 1975-
DN/U-1 1972-	LO/N26 1976-	QS/S-6
ED/U-1 1974-	LO/U-2 1974-76	SO/U-1 1971-
EX/U-1 1969-	LO/U24	XM/C10 1971-
GL/U-1	OX/U15	XY/N-1 1976-
HL/U-1 1973-	QL/D15 1974-	

Tax planning international. -- London, 1976 (vol.3)-
Continues: Tax haven review, 1974-1976 (vol.2)

CA/U-1 1976 (v.3)-	OX/U-1 1976 (v.3)-	XY/N-1 1976 (v.3 no.9)-
ED/N-1 1976 (v.3)-		

Taxation. -- London, 1927-
ISSN 0040-0149

AB/N-1	CH-CI 1958-	EX/U-1 1975-
AD/U-6 1968/69-	DN/U-1 1961-75	GL/U-1 1960-
CA/U-1	ED/S11	GL/U-2 1956- imp.
CA/U13 1964-	ED/U-1 1961-	LA/U-1 1969-

(cont'd)

Taxation (cont'd).

LC/C-1 last 5 years	LV/P-1 Apr.1944-	QM/C68 1975-
LD/U-1 1951-62	LV/U-1 1949-	QN/C70 1966-
LO/C14 1967/68- imp.	MA/P-1	QS/Q29 last 3 years
LO/C25 1973-	OX/U-1	QW/D12 last 3 years
LO/C47 last 3 years	QG/C25 1968-	RE/U-1 1974 (v.93)- (v.93 imp.)
LO-CBL 1952-	QL/D15 1962 (v.69); 1963 (v.71)-	SH/U-1 1939-44;1946-
LO/N-1	QM/C48 1975 (v.96 no.2503)-	XM/C10 1972-
LO/N26 1959-		XY/N-1
LO/P-6		
LO-SC 1936-40;1947-49;1950-		

Taxes: the tax magazine/ CCH. -- Chicago, 1923-
ISSN 0040-0181

LO/C14 1968-74 LO/U24 1972 (v.50)- XY/N-1 1966 (v.44)-

Taxpayer. -- Cape Town, 1952-
ISSN 0040-0270

OX/U15 imp.

Technik und gewerblicher Rechtsschutz. -- Bremen, 1928-1932 (Bd.5)

LO/N14

Tehran University law review. -- Tehran, [ca 1969]-

LO/U14 1973 (no.12)-

Tel-Aviv University law review = Iyunei mishpat. -- Tel-Aviv, 1971-

OX/U15

Tel-Aviv University studies in law. -- Tel-Aviv, 1975-

OX/U15

Telegram. -- London, 1859-1879

LO/N-1 OX/U15

Temi: eco dei tribunali. -- Venice, 1876-1908 (vol.33)?
1876 (vols.1-4) entitled: Temi veneti

LO/N-1 1876-85

Temi veneti <u>see</u> previous entry

Témis: revista de ciencia y técnica jurídica. -- Zaragoza, 1957-
ISSN 0495-0674

CA/U13 OX/U15

Templar: or, Monthly register of legal and constitutional knowledge. -- London, 1788-Jan.1789

LO/N-1 OX/U-1 QS/S-7

Temple law quarterly. -- Philadelphia, 1927-
1938 (vol.13)-1945 (vol.19 no.2) entitled: Temple University law quarterly
ISSN 0040-2974

BL/U-1 1954-	NO/U-1 1942-44,1948; 1952-54 imp.	XY/N-1 1946-48; 1970 (v.43 no.2)-
CA/U13 1947-	OX/U15	
LO/U24		

Temple University law quarterly <u>see</u> previous entry

Tennessee law review. -- Knoxville, Nov.1922-
ISSN 0040-3288

LO/U24	OX/U15	XY/N-1 1970 (v.37 no.2)-

Texas Bar journal. -- Austin, Texas, 1938-
ISSN 0040-4187

LO/U24 1972 (v.35)-	XY/N-1 1975 (v.38)-

Texas international law forum <u>see</u> next entry

Texas international law journal. -- Austin, Tex., 1971 (vol.7)-
Continues: Journal of the University of Texas International Law Society, 1965, and: Texas international law forum, 1965 (vol.1 no.2)-1971 (vol.6)

CA/U13	NO/U-1 1966 (v.2)-	XY/N-1 1969 (v.5 no.2)-
LO/U24	OX/U15 1966 (v.2)-	

Texas law and legislation <u>see</u> Southwestern law journal

Texas law review. -- Austin, Texas, Dec.1922-
ISSN 0040-4411

BL/U-1 1970-	LO/U24	QN/C70
CA/U13 1965-	OX/U15	XY/N-1 1966 (v.45)-

Texas Southern intramural law review <u>see</u> next entry

Texas Southern University law review. -- Houston, 1971-
Continues: Texas Southern intramural law review, 1970-1971
ISSN 0092-3559

No holdings notified

Texas Tech law review. -- Lubbock, Tex., 1969/70-
ISSN 0564-6197

LO/U24

Thémis: ou, Bibliothèque du jurisconsulte. -- Paris; Brussels, 1824-1831 (vol.9)

LO/N-1

La Thémis: revue de législation, de droit et de jurisprudence. -- Montreal, 1879-1884 (vol.5)

LO/U24 OX/U15

Thémis: revue juridique (Montreal) see Revue juridique Thémis de l'Université de Montréal

Themis: verzameling van bijdragen tot de kennis van het publiek en privaatrecht. -- The Hague, 1839-1938 (deel 99)
1939 merged with: Rechtsgeleerd magazijn to form: Rechtsgeleerd magazijn themis, q.v.

LO/N-1

Themis: Zeitschrift für Doctrin und Praxis des römischen Rechts. -- Göttingen, 1838-1841
Continues: Themis: Zeitschrift für praktische Rechtswissenschaft, 1827-1830 (Bd.2)

LO/N-1

Themis: Zeitschrift für praktische Rechtswissenschaft see previous entry

Themis polska. -- Warsaw, 1828-1830; ser.2, 1913 (vol.1)-1918 (vol.8); ser.3, 1928 (vol.1)-1937 (vol.9)?

LO/N-1

Tidskrift för lagskipning see Nytt juridiskt arkiv

Tidskrift för lagstiftning see Nytt juridiskt arkiv

Tidskrift för lagstiftning, lagskipning och förvaltning. -- Stockholm, 1864-1888 (vol.25)

LO/N-1

Tidskrift för Sveriges advokatsamfund. -- Stockholm, 1935-
ISSN 0040-6902

LO/U24 1936 (Årg.2)- XY/N-1 1970 (Årg.36)-

Tidskrift utgiven av Juridiska föreningen i Finland. -- Helsinki, 1864-
ISSN 0040-6953

LO/N-1 1910 (v.46)- LO/U24 1951 (v.87)-

Tidsskrift for Grønlands retsvaesen. -- Copenhagen, 1965-
ISSN 0040-6880

LO/N-1 LO/U24 XY/N-1 1970 (Årg.6)-

Tidsskrift for rettsvitenskap. -- Oslo, 1888-
ISSN 0040-7143

LO/N-1 1888-89 LO/U24 XY/N-1 1968-

Tijdschrift van het recht see Hukum dan masjarakat

Tijdschrift voor bestuurswetenschappen en publiek recht. -- Brussels, 1946-
ISSN 0040-7437

No holdings notified

Tijdschrift voor buitenlandsche en koloniale wetgeving en Regtspraak. -- Amsterdam, 1856 (vol.1).

LO/N-1

Tijdschrift voor milieu en recht. -- Zwolle, 1975?-

No holdings notified

Tijdschrift voor privaatrecht. -- Ghent, 1964-
ISSN 0082-4313

CA/U13
LO/U24
OX/U15
XY/N-1 1969 (Jg.6 no.3)-

Tijdschrift voor rechtsgeschiedenis = Revue d'histoire du droit. -- Haarlem, 1918-1941;1950-

AB/U-1 1951- imp.
AD/U-6 1918;1922-
CA/U13
ED/U-1 1923-41;1950-
GL/U-1 1919-
LO/N-1
LO/U-2
LO/U24
MA/U-1 1958 (v.26)-
OX/U15
OX/U25
XY/N-1 1969 (v.37)-

Tijdschrift voor sociaal recht see Revue de droit social

Tijdschrift voor strafrecht see Delikt en delinkwent

Tijdschrift voor vennootschappen, verenigingen en stichtingen see TVVS

Title news/ American Title Association. -- Washington, D.C.,1922-
ISSN 0040-8190

No holdings notified

Trade mark record. -- New York, 1886-1914 (vol.38)

LO/N14 1905-13

Trade-mark reporter. -- New York, June 1911-
1941 absorbed Bulletin of the United States Trade-mark Association, q.v.
ISSN 0041-056X

LO/N14 imp. LO/U24 1971 (v.61)-

Transactions of the Grotius Society. -- London, 1915-1958/59
From 1961 incorporated in: International and comparative law quarterly, q.v.

AB/N-1 1918-57	EX/U-1 1916-59	NO/U-1
AB/U-1	GL/U-1	NW/U-1
AD/U-6	HL/U-1	OX/U15 (w.1915)
BH/P-1 1945-59	LC/U-1	OX/U25
BH/U-1	LD/U-1	QL/D15 1923-50; 1952-59
BL/U-1 1940-59	LO-MT	QN/C70
BR/U-1	LO/N-1	QS/Q12 1919-59 imp.
CA/U-1	LO/N17	QS/S-4
CA/U13	LO/N46 1927-59	QS/S-7
CB/U-1	LO/S14	QS/S-8
CH-CI	LO/U-2	QW/D12
DN/U-1	LO/U-3	RE/U-1
DR/U-1	LO/U11	SH/U-1
ED/S10 1916-56	LO/U24	SO/U-1
ED/S11	LV/U-1	XY/N-1 imp.
ED/U-1	MA/P-1	

Transactions of the International Law Association. -- London, 1925 (1873-1924).

CA/U-1	LO/U-3	LO/U24
LO/N-1	LO/U11	OX/U15

Transactions of the Medico-Legal Society see Medico-legal journal

Transactions of the Society for Jewish Jurisprudence, English branch. -- London, 1926-1933?

LO/N-1 1926-29 LO/U-2 1926-29 LO/U24 1926-29

Transactions of the Society for Promoting the Amendment of the Law. -- London, 1857-1863

LO-MT QS/S-7

Transpatent. -- Düsseldorf, 1949-
ISSN 0041-1310

LO/N14

Transportation law journal. -- Atlanta, Ga., 1969-
ISSN 0049-450X

XY/N-1

Transportation law seminar: papers and proceedings. -- Washington D.C., 1971-

XY/N-1 1971-72

Trauma: medicine, anatomy, surgery for lawyers. -- Albany, N.Y., 1959-
ISSN 0564-1470

XY/N-1 1971 (v.13 no.2)-

Travaux - Colloque international de droit comparé du Centre Canadien de Droit Comparé = Proceedings - International symposium on comparative law of the Canadian and Foreign Law Research Centre. -- Ottawa, 1963-
ISSN 0588-3172

LO/U24 OX/U15

Travaux de l'Association Henri Capitant des amis de la culture juridique française. -- Paris, 1945-
1945-1959 (tom.13) entitled: Travaux de l'Association Henri Capitant pour la culture juridique française

BL/U-1 1967 (t.19).
CA/U13
LD/U-1 1955-57 (t.9-11); 1959-63 (t.13-15); 1965-68 (t.17-20)
LO/U11
LO/U24
OX/U15 (w.1953 (t.8))
XY/N-1 1966 (t.18)-

Travaux de l'Association Henri Capitant pour la culture juridique française <u>see</u> previous entry

Travaux du Comité français de droit international privé. -- Paris, 1934-

CA/U13
LO/U-3
LO/U24
OX/U15
OX/U25 1934-37
XY/N-1 1966 (27 an.)-

Travaux et conférences de la Faculté de Droit de l'Université Libre de Bruxelles. -- Brussels, 1954-1967
1965 not published
ISSN 0524-7977

AD/U-6
CA/U-1
CA/U13
ED/U-1 (w.1954)
GL/U-1
LO/U-1
LO/U-3 1955-59; 1963-67
LO/U24
OX/U15

Travaux et recherches de la Faculté de Droit et des Sciences Economiques de Paris. Série "Droit privé". -- Paris,
ISSN 0078-9801

No holdings notified

Travaux et recherches de la Faculté de Droit et des Sciences Economiques de Paris. Série "Droit public". -- Paris, 1964-
ISSN 0078-981X

LO/N-1 1964-71 (v.5)

Travaux juridiques et économiques/ Université de Rennes. -- Rennes, 1906-1941;1954-

LO/U-3 1906-12
OX/U15 1930-41;1954.
XY/N-1 1967-71 (t.28-31)

Trent law journal. -- Nottingham, 1977-

OX/U15 QS/S-8

Trial/ American Trial Lawyers Association. -- Boston, Mass., 1965-
ISSN 0041-2538

BH/U-1 1965-68 imp., 1969-   LO/U24 1966-70 imp., 1971-   XY/N-1

Trial judges' journal <u>see</u> Judges' journal

Trial lawyer's guide. -- Chicago, Ill., 1957-
ISSN 0041-2546

No holdings notified

Trial lawyers quarterly. -- New York, 1964-
ISSN 0041-2554

LO/U24 1971 (v.8)-   XY/N-1 1973 (v.9)-

Tribunal/ Howard League for Penal Reform. -- London, 1932;1950-1951
ISSN 0493-900X

CA/U-1 1950-51   LO/U-3 1950-51   LV/U-1 1950-51
ED/N-1 1950-51   LO/U24 1950-51   OX/U15
LO/N-1

Tribune des colonies et des protectorats <u>see</u> Penant

Trudy - Vsesoyuzny iuridichesky zaochny institut. -- Moscow, 1961?-

GL/U-1 Soviet Studies Branch Library 1966-

Trudy Vsesoyuznogo nauchno-issledovatel'skogo instituta sovetskogo zakonodatel'stva. -- Moscow, 1974-

GL/U-1 Soviet Studies Branch Library

Trust bulletin <u>see</u> next entry

Trust letter/ American Bankers' Association. -- New York, 1971 (no.1)-
Continues: Trust bulletin, 1921-1970 (vol.50 no.4)

LO/U24 1938-49 imp., 1949 (v.29)-   XY/N-1 1963 (v.43)-

Trusts and estates. -- New York, 1904-
1904-1938 (vol.67) entitled: Trust companies magazine
ISSN 0041-3682

CA/U13 1968- imp.   LO/U24 1972 (v.111)-   XY/N-1 1966 (v.105 no.11)-

Trust companies magazine <u>see</u> previous entry

Tulane civil law forum. -- New Orleans, 1973-

No holdings notified

Tulane law review. -- New Orleans, 1929 (vol.4)-
Continues: Southern law quarterly, 1916-1918 (vol.3)
ISSN 0041-3992

AB/U-1
AD/U-6 1955-
BH/U-1 1942-
BL/U-1 1956-
BR/U-1
CA/U13
CH-CI
CR/U-1
DN/U-1 1931-
DR/U-1 1951-
ED/S11 1950-
ED/U-1 1929-
EX/U-1 1968-
GL/U-1 1973-
HL/U-1 1935-39
KL/U-1
LA/U-1 1947-76
LC/U-1
LD/U-1 1945-
LO/C14 1962-74
LO-MT 1970-
LO/U-2 1966-
LO/U-3 1936-
LO/U12 1945-
LO/U24
MA/U-1 1949-
NO/U-1
OX/U15
OX/U25 1947-
QE/C76 1974-
QN/C70 1971-
QW/D12
RE/U-1 1975-
SH/U-1 1957-
SO/U-1 1916-18;1929-42;1953-
XY/N-1 1945 (v.20)-

Tulane Tax Institute/ Tulane University. -- New Orleans, 1951-
ISSN 0564-4402

LO/U24 1972 (21st).

Tulsa law journal/ University of Tulsa College of Law. -- Tulsa, Okla., 1964-
ISSN 0041-4050

BL/U-1 1964-75
LO/U24
XY/N-1 1969 (v.6)-

Tydskrif vir die Suid-Afrikaanse reg = Journal of South African law. -- Cape Town, 1976-

LO/U24

Tydskrif vir hedendaagse romeins-hollandse reg = Journal of contemporary Roman-Dutch law. -- Durban, 1937-1946;1948-

AD/U-6 1937-42; 1945-50; 1951-57 imp.
CA/U13 1960-
ED/U-1 1959-
LO/N-1
LO/U14 1968-
LO/U24
OX/U15
XY/N-1 1937;1969 (Bd.32)-

Tydskrif vir regsvergelyking en internasionale reg van suidelike Afrika <u>see</u> Comparative and international law journal of southern Africa

U.B.C. legal notes see University of British Columbia law review

U.B.L.S. law journal/ Law Society, University of Botswana, Lesotho and Swaziland. -- Roma, Lesotho, 1970-

LO/U14

U.C.D. law review see University of California, Davis law review

U.C.L.A.-Alaska law review. -- Los Angeles, 1971-

No holdings notified

U.C.L.A. intramural law review see next entry

U.C.L.A. law review/ University of California Los Angeles. -- Los Angeles, 1953 (vol.1)-
Continues: U.C.L.A. intramural law review, 1952-1953 (ISSN 0500-8743)
ISSN 0041-5650

BL/U-1 1969-
BR/U-1 1975 (v.23)-
CA/U13 1953-
CR/U-1
LO/U12 1953-
LO/U24
OX/U15
QN/C70 1970-
SO/U-1 1973-
XY/N-1

U.M.K.C. law review/ University of Missouri, Kansas City. -- Kansas City, 1969 (vol.37)-
Continues: Kansas City law review, 1932-1938 (vol.6); University of Kansas City law review, 1938-1963 (vol.31), and: University of Missouri at Kansas City law review, 1964-1968 (vol.36)
ISSN 0047-7575

BL/U-1 1964-
EX/U-1 1964-
LO/U24
OX/U15
XY/N-1 1970 (v.39)-

Übersicht der gesammten Staats- und Rechtswissenschaftlichen Literatur. -- Berlin, 1868-1914 (Jahrg.47)

LO/N-1
LO/U-2 1871-80; 1882;1885.
LO/U24
OX/U-1

Uchenye zapiski - Vsesoiuznii Institut Iuridicheskikh Nauk see next entry

Uchenye zapiski - Vsesoiuznii Nauchno-issledovatel'skii Institut Sovetskogo Zakonodatel'stva. -- Moscow, 1964 (vol.1)-
Continues: Uchenye zapiski - Vsesoiuznii Institut Iuridicheskikh Nauk, 1940-1963 (2nd series, vol.17)

LO/U-2 1963 (2nd series vol.16)-1973 (no.28) imp.

Uganda law focus. -- Kampala, 1972-

LO/U14 LO/U24 1972-74 (v.2 no.1)

Ugeskrift for retsvaesen. -- Copenhagen, 1867-

LO/N-1 1966- OX/U15 XY/N-1 1969-
LO/U24 1874- imp.

Ügyvédszövetséti közlöny (Hungarian Bar review). -- Budapest, 1914?-

LO-MT 1927-33 (v.4-10)

Ulsterview: magazine of the no.2 region of the International Police Association. -- Belfast, 1965-1974

OX/U15 (w.1969)

Unauthorized practice news/ American Bar Association, Standing Committee on Unauthorized Practice of the Law. -- Chicago, 1934-
ISSN 0041-6452

LO/U24 1961 (v.27)-

L'Unification du droit: annuaire = Unification of law: yearbook. -- Rome, 1948-1971
Merged with: Jurisprudence de droit uniforme = Uniform law cases, to become: Revue de droit uniforme, q.v.

BL/U-1 LD/U-1 LO/U24
CA/U13 LO/C47 1963-71 OX/U15
ED/U-1 1948;1954-71 LO/N17 1950-71 XY/N-1 1969-71
LC/U-1 1966-68

Unification of law: yearbook <u>see</u> previous entry

Uniform law review <u>see</u> Revue de droit uniforme

Union law review. -- Johannesburg, 1910-1911 (vol.2)

LO/U24 OX/U15

United Nations juridical yearbook. -- New York, 1962-
ISSN 0082-8297

AB/N-1 ED/S11 LO/U-3
AD/U-6 1967- ED/U-1 1963- LO/U11
BH/P-1 GL/U-2 1971- LO/U24 1963-
BH/U-1 KL/U-1 MA/P-1 1963-
BL/U-1 1964- LO/C47 1963-72 NO/U-1 1963-
CA/U-1 1963- LO/N-1 OX/U15
CA/U13 LO/N-5 QS/Q29
CB/U-1 1963- LO/N17 SO/U-1 1963-
CV/U-1 1963- LO/S14 XY/N-1 1965-
DR/U-1 1965- LO/U-2 1963.

United Nations law reports. -- New York, 1966-
ISSN 0503-4582

CA/U13	MA/P-1 1966-69 imp.	SH/U-1
LO/S14 1966 (Sep.)- 1975 (Aug.)	OX/U15	SO/U-1

United States Air Force JAG law review <u>see</u> Air Force law review

United States jurist. -- Washington D.C., 1871-1873 (vol.2)

LO/N-1

United States law journal and civilian's magazine. -- New Haven, 1822-1823;1826 (vol.2)
Title varies

LO/N-1 1822-23

United States law review. -- New York, July 1929 (v.63 no.3)-1940 (vol.74)
Continues: American law review, 1866-May 1929 (vol.63 no.2).
1883 absorbed: Southern law review, q.v.
1884 absorbed: Western jurist, q.v.
1929 absorbed: New York law review.
1940 (vol.74) resumed title: New York law review

CA/U13 1866-1938	LO/N-1	LV/U-1 1909-40
ED/S11	LO/U24 imp.	OX/U15
LO-MT		

United States monthly law magazine <u>see</u> Livingston's monthly law magazine

Universitas: ciencias jurídicas y socio-economicas. -- Bogotá, 1951-
Sub-title varies
ISSN 0041-9060

LO/U24 1954 (no.6)- (w.no.28)	XY/N-1 1962 (no.22)-

University Law College journal/ Rajputana University. -- Jaipur, 1954-

LO/U14 1954 (v.1 no.1).

University law review. -- New York, 1893 (vol.1)-1897 (vol.3)
Continues: Intercollegiate law journal, 1891-1893 (vol.2)

LO/U24 1893-97 (v.1-3)	OX/U15 1893-97 (v.1-3)

University of Baltimore law review. -- Baltimore, Md., 1971-
ISSN 0091-5440

No holdings notified

University of British Columbia law review. -- Vancouver, 1959 (vol.1)-
Continues: U.B.C. legal notes, 1949-1958 (vol.2) (ISSN 0497-2910)
ISSN 0068-1849

BH/U-1 1959-
BL/U-1 1964-
BR/U-1 1975 (v.10)-
CA/U13 1959-
DN/U-1 1959-
LO/U24
NO/U-1 1970 (v.5)-
OX/U15
XY/N-1 1961 (v.1 no.4)-

University of British Columbia law review: centennial edition [and] Cahiers de droit: édition du centenaire/ Université Laval. -- Quebec, 1967
Special joint issue of both journals

BH/U-1
BL/U-1
CA/U13
LO/N-1
LO/U24
OX/U15

University of California, Davis law review. -- Davis, 1969-
ISSN 0502-9414

LO/U24

University of California at Los Angeles-Alaska law review <u>see</u> UCLA-Alaska law review

University of Ceylon law review. -- Peradeniya, 1958.

LO/N-1
OX/U15

University of Chicago law review. -- Chicago, 1933-
ISSN 0041-9494

AB/U-1
BL/U-1 1964-
BR/U-1
CA/U-1 1970-
CA/U13
CB/U-1 1966-
CR/U-1
CV/U-1
DR/U-1 1950-
ED/S11 1950-70
ED/U-1
LC/U-1 1944 (v.12)-
LO/C15 1971-
LO-MT 1946-
LO/R74 1967 (v.35)-
LO/U-2
LO/U-3 1953- (w.1958 no.4)
LO/U12 (w.1973 no.1; 1974 nos.1-2)
LO/U24
LO/U28
LV/U-1 1971-74 (v.39-41)
MA/U-1 imp.
NO/U-1
OX/U15
QN/C70 1967-
SH/U-1
SO/U-1 1965-
XY/N-1 1949 (v.17)-

University of Chicago Law School record <u>see</u> Law School record/ University...

University of Cincinnati law review. -- Cincinnati, 1927-1942; 1948-
ISSN 0009-6881

LO/U24
OX/U15

University of Colorado law review. -- Boulder, Col., 1962 (vol.35)-
Continues: Rocky Mountain law review, 1928-1962
ISSN 0041-9516

BL/U-1 1964-   OX/U15   XY/N-1 1970 (v.39)-
LO/U24

University of Detroit journal of urban law. -- Detroit, 1976 (vol.54)-
Continues: University of Detroit law journal, 1931-1966 (vol.43) and: Journal of urban law, 1966 (vol.44)-1976 (vol.53). After vol.18, 1954/55, numbering changes to vol.33, 1955/56

BL/U-1 1963-   CR/U-1 1970-   OX/U15 1963 (v.41)-
CA/U13 1969 (v.47)-   LO/U24   XY/N-1 1971 (v.48 no.2)-

University of Detroit law journal <u>see</u> previous entry

University of Florida law review. -- Gainesville, 1948-
ISSN 0041-9583

BL/U-1 1964-   LO/U24   XY/N-1 1967 (v.20)-
CA/U13 1948-50; 1967 (v.20)-   OX/U15

University of Ghana law journal. -- Legon, 1964-
ISSN 0041-9605

AB/N-1 1964-70   CR/U-1 1972-   OX/U15
BL/U-1 1965-   LO/U14   SH/U-1 1964-75
CA/U13   LO/U24   XY/N-1

University of Illinois law bulletin <u>see</u> Illinois law quarterly

University of Illinois law forum. -- Champaign, 1949-
ISSN 0041-963X

BL/U-1 1969-   CR/U-1   OX/U15
CA/U13 1966-   LO/U24   XY/N-1 1968- (as Law Forum)

University of Kansas City law review <u>see</u> U.M.K.C. law review

University of Kansas law review. -- Lawrence, Kan., 1952-
ISSN 0083-4025

LO/U24 1971 (v.20)-   OX/U15 1953 (v.2)-   XY/N-1 1971 (v.19 no.4)-

University of Malaya law review <u>see</u> Malaya law review

University of Miami law review. -- Coral Gables, Fla., 1957 (vol.12)-
Continues: Miami law quarterly, 1947-1957
ISSN 0041-9818

BL/U-1 1963-
CA/U13 1966-
LO/U24
OX/U15
QS/S-4 1952-
XY/N-1 1969 (v.24)-

University of Michigan journal of law reform. -- Ann Arbor, 1970 (vol.4)-
Continues: Prospectus: a journal of law reform, 1968-1970
ISSN 0033-1546

LO/U24
OX/U15
XY/N-1

University of Missouri at Kansas City law review <u>see</u> U.M.K.C. law review

University of New Brunswick law journal. -- St. John, N.B., 1952-
Continues: University of New Brunswick Law School journal, 1947-1951 (vol.4)
ISSN 0077-8141

BL/U-1 1964-
LO/U24
OX/U15
XY/N-1 1970 (v.20)-

University of New Brunswick Law School journal <u>see</u> previous entry

University of New South Wales law journal. -- Kensington, N.S.W., 1975-

CA/U13
LO/U24
OX/U15

University of Newark law review. -- Newark, N.J., 1936-1942 (vol.7)

No holdings notified

University of Pennsylvania law review. -- Philadelphia, 1944 (vol.93)-
Continues: American law register, 1852-1907 (vol.55, o.s.), and: University of Pennsylvania law review and American law register, 1908-1944 (vol.92)
Numbering irregular from 1861 to 1910
ISSN 0041-9907

AB/U-1 1960-
BL/U-1 1952-
BR/U-1 1975 (v.124)-
CA/U13 1900-
CR/U-1 1949-
CV/U-1 1966 (v.115)-
DR/U-1 1950-
ED/U-1 1974 (v.123)-
LC/U-1 1944 (v.93)-
LD/U-1 1965-
LO-MT 1852-96;1950.
LO/N-1
LO/U-2
LO/U12 1936-
LO/U24 1861-
MA/U-1 1926-
NO/U-1 1902 (v.51)-
OX/U15
QN/C70 1970-
QS/S-7 1866-89
SH/U-1 1960 (v.109)-
SO/U-1 1919-
XY/N-1 1966 (v.115)-

University of Pennsylvania law review and American law register <u>see</u> previous entry

University of Pittsburgh law review. -- Pittsburgh, 1935-1942;1947-
ISSN 0041-9915

BL/U-1 1964-
CA/U13 1966-70;1973-
LO/U24
OX/U15
XY/N-1 1966 (v.28)-

University of Queensland law journal. -- St. Lucia, Queensland, 1948-
ISSN 0083-4041

AB/U-1 1971-
AD/U-6
BL/U-1
CA/U13 1956-67;1970-
DN/U-1 1968- imp.
DR/U-1 1951 imp., 1952-
LO/N-1 1948 (v.1 no.3)-
LO/S65
LO/U12 1961-
LO/U24
NO/U-1 1951-
OX/U15
SO/U-1 1961-
SW/U-1 1968-
XY/N-1 1970 (v.7)-

University of Richmond law notes see next entry

University of Richmond law review. -- Richmond, Va., 1968 (vol.3)-
Continues: University of Richmond law notes, 1958-1967
ISSN 0566-2389

LO/U24
XY/N-1

University of San Fernando Valley law review. -- Sepulveda, Cal., 1967-
ISSN 0042-000X

LO/U24

University of San Francisco law review. -- San Francisco, 1966-
ISSN 0042-0018

BL/U-1 1970-
CR/U-1
LO/U24
XY/N-1

University of Tasmania law review. -- Hobart, 1964 (vol.2)-
Continues: Tasmanian University law review, 1958-1963
ISSN 0082-2108

BH/U-1
BL/U-1
CA/U13
GL/U-1 1958-70
LD/U-1
LO/C47 1971-
LO/U-2
LO/U12
LO/U24
LV/U-1
NO/U-1 1974 (v.4 no.3)-
OX/U15
XY/N-1 1967 (v.2 no.4)-

University of Toledo intramural law review. -- Toledo, Ohio, 1967-1968 (vol.1)
No more published

LO/U24

University of Toledo law review. -- Toledo, Ohio, 1969-
ISSN 0042-0190

LO/U24
XY/N-1

University of Toronto Faculty of Law review. -- Toronto, 1973 (vol.31)-
Continues: School of Law review, 1942-1955 (vol.13) and: Faculty of Law review, 1956-1972 (vol.30)

BL/U-1 1965-
LO/U24
OX/U15
XY/N-1

University of Toronto law journal. -- Toronto, 1935-
ISSN 0042-0220

AB/N-1 1935-52
AB/U-1
BH/U-1
BL/U-1 1965-
BR/U-1 1972 (v.22)-
CA/U-1 1938-52
CA/U13
CB/U-1 1975-
CV/U-1 1970 (v.20)-
DN/U-1 1937-57 imp., 1958-
ED/S10 1935-40
ED/S11 1939-52
ED/U-1 (w.v.5 no.2)
EX/U-1
HL/U-1
LC/U-1 1941/42; 1957/58-
LO/C25 1977-
LO/N-1 1938-
LO/N46
LO/S65 1947-76
LO/U-3
LO/U11 1935-57
LO/U12 1969-
LO/U24
MA/U-1 1943-
NO/U-1 1936 (v.1 no.2)-
OX/U15
OX/U25
QM/C48 1968 (v.18)-
SH/U-1 1957-
SO/U-1 1965-
XY/N-1 1957 (v.12)-

University of West Los Angeles law review. -- Culver City, Cal., 1969-
ISSN 0083-4068

No holdings notified

University of Western Australia law review. -- Nedlands, W.A., 1960 (vol.5)-
Continues: Annual law review, 1948-1959 (vol.4)
ISSN 0042-0328

AB/U-1 1951-
BH/U-1
BL/U-1
BR/U-1 1976 (v.12)-
CA/U13
DR/U-1 1951-53
EX/U-1 imp.
ED/U-1
GL/U-1
LO-MT 1948-53
LO/N-1
LO/S65 1948-76
LO/U-1 1948-74 (1973-74 imp.)
LO/U12 1965-
LO/U24
LV/U-1 1948-53
MA/U-1
NO/U-1
OX/U15
QS/S-7
SH/U-1 1957 (v.4)-
SO/U-1 1973-

University of Western Ontario law review. -- London, Ont., 1976 (vol.15)-
Continues: Western law review, 1961-1966 (vol.5) and: Western Ontario law review, 1967 (vol.6)-1975 (vol.14) (ISSN 0083-8950)

BL/U-1
LO/U24
OX/U15
XY/N-1

University of Zambia law bulletin. -- Lusaka, [ca 1970]-

LO/U24 1971 (v.2 no.1).

Untersuchungen zur deutschen Staats- und Rechtsgeschichte. -- Aalen, 1878-1940 (n.150); 1962 (n.f.)-
ISSN 0083-4572

AD/U-6 1890 (n.34);1891 (n.37); 1910 (n.100);1972 (n.f.n.17).
CA/U-1
LO/N-1 1962-75
OX/U15

Up against the law. -- London, 1973-

CA/U-1 1973 (no.2)-
ED/N-1 1974 (no.2)- (w.nos.3,6)
LO/N-1
OX/U15 1973-75 imp.
QW/C73 1974-

Upper Canada jurist. -- Toronto, 1844-1848

LO/U24
OX/U15
QS/S-6
QS/S-7

Upper Canada law journal <u>see</u> Canada law journal

Upper Canada law journal and local courts' gazette <u>see</u> Canada law journal

Urban law annual. -- St. Louis, 1968-
ISSN 0566-3377

LO/U24 1971-

Urban lawyer: the national quarterly on local government law/ American Bar Association, Section of Local Government Law. -- Chicago, 1969-
ISSN 0042-0905

LO/U24
XY/N-1

Urheberrechtliche Abhandlungen. -- Munich, 1957-
ISSN 0500-7151

LO/N14
XY/N-1

Utah Bar journal. -- Salt Lake City, 1973-
ISSN 0091-9691

No holdings notified

Utah law review. -- Salt Lake City, 1949-
ISSN 0042-1448

BL/U-1 1962-70
LO/U24
XY/N-1 1971 no.2-

Valparaiso University law review. -- Valparaiso, Ind., 1966-
ISSN 0042-2363

CR/U-1 LO/U24 OX/U15

Vanderbilt international: bulletin of the Vanderbilt International Law Society <u>see</u> next entry

Vanderbilt journal of transnational law. -- Nashville, Tenn., 1971 (vol.5)-
Continues: Vanderbilt international: bulletin of the Vanderbilt International Law Society, 1967/68-1971 (ISSN 0042-2525)
ISSN 0090-2594

LO/N-1 1977-
LO/U24
OX/U15
XY/N-1

Vanderbilt law review. -- Nashville, Tenn., 1947-
ISSN 0042-2533

CA/U13 1958-
LO/U24
NO/U-1 1960-72
OX/U15
XY/N-1 1966 (v.20)-

Verdict/ Oxford University Law Society. -- Oxford, 1964-1969
ISSN 0507-7060

BH/U-1 1966-69
CA/U13 (w.1964 (v.1 no.1))
DR/U-1 v.5 imp.
LO-MT
LO/N-1
LV/U-1 1966-69
OX/U15
QS/S-4 imp.
QS/S-6 1964-68 imp.
QS/S-7 1964-68

Verfassung und Recht in Übersee. -- Hamburg, 1968-
ISSN 0506-7286

LO/U14 LO/U24 XY/N-1 1974-

Verhandlungen des Deutschen Juristentages. -- Berlin, 1860-

LO/U24 1860- (w.v.17;19)

Verhandlungen des Schweizerischen Juristenvereins = Actes de la Société Suisse des Juristes = Atti della Società Svizzera dei Giuristi. -- Basel, 1861-1947 (vol.81)
From 1883 the proceedings are also included in, and from 1948 published only in: Zeitschrift für schweizerisches Recht, q.v.

LO/U24 1874 (v.13)-1947 (v.78)

Verkehrsrechtliche Abhandlungen und Entscheidungen. -- Berlin, 1936-1944 (Bd.16)

LO/N-1

Verkehrsrechtliche Mitteilungen. -- Bielefeld, 1954-

OX/U15 1955 (Bd.2)-

Vermont law review. -- South Royalton, Vt., 1976-

No holdings notified

Veröffentlichungen - Vereinigung der deutschen Staatsrechtslehrer. -- Berlin, 1924-

OX/U15

Veröffentlichungen des Instituts für das Recht der Wasserwirtschaft an der Universität Bonn. -- Munich; Cologne, 1955-

OX/U15

Versicherungsrecht. -- Karlsruhe, 1950-
ISSN 0506-7782

No holdings notified

Versicherungsrundschau. -- Vienna, 1946-

LO/U-3 1949- XY/N-1 1973 (Jg.28)-

Versicherungswissenschaft, Versicherungspraxis, Versicherungs-Medizin see Deutsche Versicherungszeitschrift für Sozialversicherung und Privatversicherung

Verwaltungsarchiv: Zeitschrift für Verwaltungslehre, Verwaltungsrecht und Verwaltungspolitik. -- Cologne, 1893-1943;1957-
1957-1964 (Bd.55) issued as quarterly supplement to Deutsches Verwaltungsblatt, q.v.
ISSN 0042-4501

ED/U-1 1968-
LO/U-3 1957-
LO/U24 1960 (Bd.51)-
OX/U15 1957-
XY/N-1 1965 (Bd.56)-

Vestnik - Seriya 10, Pravo see next entry

Vestnik - Seriya 12, Pravo/ Moskovsky universitet. -- Moscow, 1966-
Continues: Vestnik - Seriya 10, Pravo, 1960-1965
Continues in part: Vestnik - Seriya ekonomiki, filosofii i prava, 1956 (n.s.)-1959 (ISSN 0541-0789)
ISSN 0027-1357

BH/U-1 1960-
CC/U-1 1960-
GL/U-1 Soviet Studies Branch Library
LO/U-3
OX/U-1 1956-59
OX/U15 1960-
XY/N-1 1956-59 imp., 1960-

Vestnik - Seriya ekonomiki, filosofii i prava/ Leningradsky universitet. -- Leningrad, 1956-
ISSN 0024-0818

CA/U-1
DR/U-1 1957 imp.
GL/U-1 Soviet Studies Branch Library
LO/U-3
OX/U15
SW/U-1 1964-
XY/N-1 1956-59 imp., 1965-

Vestnik - Seriya ekonomiki, filosofii i prava (Moscow) see Vestnik - Seriya 12, Pravo

Victoria University College law review see next entry

Victoria University of Wellington law review. -- Wellington, N.Z., 1957 (vol.2 no.3)-
Continues: Victoria University College law review, 1953-1957
ISSN 0042-5117

BH/U-1	LO/U12 1955-	SO/U-1
BL/U-1 1964-	LO/U24	XY/N-1 1953-57 (v.2 no.3)
CA/U13	OX/U15	
LC/U-1 imp.		

Vierteljahresschrift für die gerichtliche und öffentliche Medizin see Zeitschrift für Rechtsmedizin

Vierteljahresschrift für gerichtliche Medizin und öffentliches Sanitätswesen see Zeitschrift für Rechtsmedizin

Villanova law review. -- Villanova, Pa., 1956-
ISSN 0042-6229

BL/U-1 1964-	NO/U-1	OX/U15
CA/U13 1968-	LO/U24	XY/N-1 1969 (v.15)-

Virgin Islands Bar journal. -- Christiansted, St. Croix, V.I., 1967-
ISSN 0507-0317

No holdings notified

Virginia Bar Association journal. -- Richmond, 1975-
ISSN 0360-3857

No holdings notified

Virginia journal of international law. -- Charlottesville, Va., 1963 (vol.3)-
Continues: Journal of the John Bassett Moore Society of International Law, 1960-1962
ISSN 0042-6571

CA/U13 1966- imp.	LO/U24	OX/U15
CV/U-1	MA/U-1 1966 (v.7)-	SH/U-1 1966-
DR/U-1 1963-	NO/U-1	XY/N-1 1966 (v.7)-

Virginia law journal. -- Richmond, Va., 1877-1893 (vol.17)

LO/N-1 1877-79

Virginia law review. -- Charlottesville, Va., 1913-
ISSN 0042-6601

BL/U-1 1970- | LO/U12 | QN/C70 1970 (v.56)-
CA/U13 1969- | LO/U24 | SO/U-1 1974-
CB/U-1 1973 (v.59)- | NO/U-1 1961-72 | XY/N-1 1966 (v.52)-
CR/U-1 1950- | OX/U15

Völkerbund und Völkerrecht. -- Berlin, 1934-1938 (Bd.4)

LO/N-1 | LO/U24

Voprosy izobretatel'stva. -- Moscow, 1966-
ISSN 0507-3480

LO/N14 | XY/N-1 1967-

Vyavahara nirnaya. -- Delhi, 1952-
ISSN 0506-2780

LO/U14 1953-62 (v.2-7 no.1)

Vynálezy see Vynálezy a zlepšovací navrhy

Vynálezy a normalisace see Vynálezy a zlepšovací navrhy

Vynálezy a ochranna znamky see next entry

Vynálezy a zlepšovací navrhy. -- Prague, 1973-
Continues: Vynálezy a normalisace, 1957-1959; Vynálezy, 1960-1969 and: Vynálezy a ochranna znamky, 1970-1972

LO/N14 1957-69 | XY/N-1 1958 (v.2)-

W.G.O. Monatshefte für osteuropäisches Recht: Die Wichtigsten Gesetzgebungsakte in den Ländern Ost- und Südeuropas und in den ostasiatischen Volksdemokratien. -- Hamburg, 1959-
ISSN 0509-5212

GL/U-1 Soviet Studies Branch Library | LO/U-3 | OX/U15
LO/U24 1968 (v.10)- | XY/N-1 1973 (v.15)-

Wage-price law and economics review. -- Washington D.C., 1975-
ISSN 0361-6665

XY/N-1

Wake Forest intramural law review see next entry

Wake Forest law review. -- Winston-Salem, N.C., 1970 (vol.7)-
Continues: Intramural law review of Wake Forest College, 1965-1967 (ISSN 0539-2144), and: Wake Forest intramural law review, 1968 (vol.4)-1970
ISSN 0043-003X

LO/U24 1971 (v.8)- OX/U15 1975 (v.11)- XY/N-1 1974 (v.10)-

Warasan ratthaprasasanasat. -- Bangkok, 1960-
ISSN 0509-6278

LO/N-1

Waseda hogaku = Waseda law review. -- Tokyo, 1922-

LO/U14 1924- imp.

Waseda law review <u>see</u> previous entry

Washburn law journal. -- Topeka, Kan., 1960-
ISSN 0043-0420

BL/U-1 1965- LO/U24 XY/N-1 1966 (v.6)-

Washington and Lee law review. -- Lexington, Va., 1939-
ISSN 0043-0463

AB/U-1 1972 (v.29)- LO/U24 XY/N-1 1975 (v.32)-
BL/U-1 1964- OX/U15

Washington law review. -- Seattle, 1919-
With vol.11 no.4, 1936 absorbed: State Bar review, q.v., and from then until 1961 (vol.36) entitled: Washington law review and State Bar journal
ISSN 0043-0617

BL/U-1 1964- OX/U15 XY/N-1 1970 (v.45)-
LO/U24

Washington law review and State Bar journal <u>see</u> previous entry

Washington University law quarterly. -- St. Louis, Mo., 1936 (vol.22)-
Continues: Saint Louis law review, 1915-1936
ISSN 0043-0862

BL/U-1 1964- LO/U24 1936 (v.22)- XY/N-1 1968-

Wayne law review. -- Detroit, Mich., 1954-
ISSN 0043-1621

BL/U-1 1963-76 LO/U24 OX/U15

Weekblad voor fiscaal recht. -- Deventer, 1872-
ISSN 0043-1796

No holdings notified

Weekblad voor privaatrecht, notariaat en registratie. -- 's-Gravenhage, 1975 (jaarg.106)-
Continues: Weekblad voor privaatrecht, notaris-ambt en registratie, 1870-1974

LO/U24 OX/U15 1944/45-77 (Jg.75/6-108) XY/N-1 1969-

Weekblad voor privaatrecht, notaris-ambt en registratie <u>see</u> previous entry

Weekly jurist. -- Bloomington, Ill., 1879-1881
Continues: Monthly western jurist, 1874-1877 (vol.3) and: Monthly jurist, 1877-1879 (vols.1 & 2)

No holdings notified

Weekly law magazine. -- London, 1842-1843
Vol.1, nos.1-20, entitled: Law clerks' magazine

CA/U-1 imp. LO/N-1 OX/U15
ED/S11

West Indian law journal. -- Kingston, 1977-
Continues: Jamaica law journal, 1970-1977 (Oct.1975)

LO/U24 OX/U15 1972 (June)-

West Publishing Co.'s Docket <u>see</u> The docket

West Virginia Bar <u>see</u> West Virginia law review

West Virginia law quarterly <u>see</u> West Virginia law review

West Virginia law quarterly and the Bar <u>see</u> next entry

West Virginia law review. -- Morgantown, 1949 (vol.52)-
Continues: West Virginia Bar, 1894-1895; Bar/ West Virginia Bar Association, 1896 (vol.3)-1917; West Virginia law quarterly and the Bar, 1917 (vol.25)-1925, and: West Virginia law quarterly, 1925 (vol.32)-1949
ISSN 0043-3268

BL/U-1 1963-76 OX/U15 1948 (v.51)- XY/N-1 1971 (v.74)-
LO/U24

Western jurist. -- Des Moines, Iowa, 1867-1883 (vol.17)
Absorbed by: American law review, <u>afterwards</u> United States law review, q.v.

LO/N-1

Western law review <u>see</u> University of Western Ontario law review

Western law times <u>see</u> next entry

Western law times of Canada. -- Winnipeg, 1890-1895 (vol.6)
Vols.1, 2 and 5 entitled: Western law times

OX/U15

Western Ontario law review <u>see</u> University of Western Ontario law review

Western Reserve law review <u>see</u> Case Western Reserve law review

Western State University law review. -- Anaheim, Cal., 1972-
ISSN 0095-568X

No holdings notified

Westminster Hall chronicle and legal examiner. -- London, 1835-1836
Continues: Legal examiner (London), 1831-1833, q.v., and: Legal examiner and law chronicle, 1833-1835

BH-LS 1836.	GL/U-1 1833-34	OX/U15 1833 (v.1 nos. 1-10);1835-36
CA/U-1	LO/N-1	QS/S-7 1833-34
ED/S11	MA/P-1	
ED/U-1 1833-34		

Wettbewerb in Recht und Praxis. -- Frankfurt am Main, 1955-
ISSN 0508-6205

LO/N14	LO/U24 1959 (Jg.5)-

Willamette law journal. -- Salem, Ore., 1959-
ISSN 0043-5562

LO/U24 1971 (v.7)-

William and Mary law review. -- Williamsburg, Va., 1957-
ISSN 0043-5589

EX/U-1 1970-	OX/U15	XY/N-1 1973 (v.15)-
LO/U24		

William Henry Ballantyne lecture/ International Association for the Protection of Industrial Property, British Group. -- London, 1953-
ISSN 0510-4807

LO/N-1	LO/N14

Wirtschaft und Recht: Zeitschrift für Wirtschaftspolitik und Wirtschaftsrecht mit Einschluss des Sozial- und Arbeitsrechtes. -- Zurich, 1949-
ISSN 0043-6135

CA/U13 1949-52	LO/U-3	XY/N-1 1966 (Bd.18)-

Wirtschaft und Wettbewerb = Competition and trade regulation = Concurrence et marché. -- Düsseldorf, 1951-
ISSN 0043-6151

CA/U13 1964-
ED/U-1 1951-60;1964-
GL/U-1 1973-
LO/U-3 imp.
LO/U24 1960 (Bd.10)-
OX/U15
XY/N-1 1966 (Bd.16)-

Wisconsin Bar bulletin. -- Madison, Wis., 1948-
Continues: Bulletin of the State Bar Association of Wisconsin, 1927-1948
ISSN 0043-6380

LO/U24 1971 (v.44)-

Wisconsin law review. -- Madison, 1920-
ISSN 0043-650X

BL/U-1 1964-
CA/U13 1959-
CR/U-1 1960-
CV/U-1 1959- (w.1962 no.2)
ED/U-1 1971-
LO/U-2 1941-54
LO/U-3 1922-
LO/U24
OX/U15
XY/N-1 1970-

Wochenschrift für die gesammte Heilkunde <u>see</u> Zeitschrift für Rechtsmedizin

Women lawyers journal/ National Association of Women Lawyers. -- Chicago, Ill., 1911-
ISSN 0043-7468

LO/U24 1972 (v.58)-
OX/U15 1972 (v.58)-

Workmen's compensation law review. -- Buffalo, N.Y., 1974-
ISSN 0094-3436

XY/N-1

World law review/ World Conference on World Peace through the Rule of Law. -- Washington, [ca 1970]-
Continues: World peace through law: [papers presented]/ World Conference on World Peace through the Rule of Law, 1963-[ca 1970] (ISSN 0084-215X)
ISSN 0091-1437

No holdings notified

World peace through law: [papers presented]/ World Conference on World Peace through the Rule of Law <u>see</u> previous entry

Wyoming law journal <u>see</u> Land and water law review

Yale law journal. -- New Haven, Conn., 1891-
ISSN 0044-0094

AB/U-1
AD/U-6
BC-UC 1963-73 imp.
BH/U-1
BL/U-1
BR/U-1
BT/U-1 1940-
CA/U13
CB/U-1
CH-CI
CR/U-1
CV/C-1 1962-
CV/U-1
DN/U-1 1930-
DR/U-1 1951-
ED/U-1
EX/U-1
GL/U-1 1944-
GL/U-2 1966-
HL/U-1
KL/U-1
LC/C-1 1970-
LC/U-1
LD/C-1 1973/74 (v.83)-
LD/U-1 1953-
LO/C-3
LO/C10 1949 (v.59)-
LO/C14 1962/63-
LO/C15 1945-
LO/C25 1959-
LO/C47 1969-
LO-MT
LO/N-1 1891-1918; 1925-28/29; 1952/53-
LO/U-2
LO/U-3 1915-
LO/U11 1959/60-
LO/U12 1916-
LO/U24
LO/U28 1966 (v.76)-
LV-LP 1972 (v.82)-
LV/U-1 1950/51-
MA/U-1 1916-
NO/U-1 1916 (v.26)-
NW/U-1 1933-
OX/U15
OX/U25 1932-
QE/C76
QL/D15 1973/74-
QM/C48 1975-
QM/C68 1949/50-73/74;1977-
QN/C70 1923 imp.-
QW/D12
RE/U-1
SH/U-1
SO/U-1 1949-
XM/C10 (w.1974)
XY/N-1 1949 (v.59)-
YK/U-1 1962-76

Yale review of law and social action. -- New Haven, Conn., 1970-
ISSN 0044-0132

LO/N-1 1977-
XY/N-1

Yale studies in world public order. -- New Haven, Conn., 1974/75-

BL/U-1 1975 (v.2)-
LO/U24 1975/76 (v.2)-
LV-LP 1975 (v.2)-

Yearbook - Association of the Bar of the City of New York. -- New York, 1908-
Continues: its Annual report, 1879-1907

CA/U-1 1927-44;1946-
LO-MT 1910;1923-
LO/U24 1900-66
QS/S-6 1946-67
QS/S-7 1951-63 imp.

Yearbook - International Association for the Protection of Industrial Property <u>see</u> Jahrbuch - Internationale Vereinigung für Gewerblichen Rechtsschutz

Yearbook - International Copyright Society <u>see</u> Jahrbuch - Internationale Gesellschaft für Urheberrecht

Yearbook - Supreme Court Historical Society. -- Washington D.C., 1976 (1975)-

LO/U24

Yearbook - United Nations Commission on International Trade Law. -- New York, 1970 (1968/70)-

AB/N-1
CA/U-1
LO/N-5
LO/N26
LO/S14
LO/U-3
LO/U24
LV/P-1 1972 (v.3)-
MA/P-1
OX/U15
QM/C68 1972 (v.3).
SO/U-1
XY/N-1 1972 (v.3)-

Yearbook, commercial arbitration. -- Deventer, 1976-

LO/U24

Yearbook of air and space law = Annuaire de droit aérien et spatial/ McGill University Institute of Air and Space Law. -- Montreal, 1965-1967
Ceased publication
ISSN 0084-3636

AD/U-6
CA/U-1
CA/U13 (w.1966)
ED/U-1
LO/U-2
LO/U11
LO/U24
OX/U15
XY/N-1 1967.

Yearbook of the A.A.A. <u>see</u> Annuaire de l'A.A.A.

Yearbook of the Association of Attenders and Alumni... <u>see</u> Annuaire de l'A.A.A.

Yearbook of the Canadian Bar Association and minutes of proceedings of its annual meeting. -- Ottawa, 1946 (28th)-
Continues: Minutes of proceedings of the annual meeting... 1915-1944 (27th).
1915 also entitled: Report of the Canadian Bar Association

ED/S11 1923- imp.
HL/U-1 1955-73
LO/U-2 1943;1947; 1949-52
LO-MT
LO/U24 1915-70;1974-
OX/U15
OX/U25 1971-73
QS/S-7 1952-70
SO/U-1 1966,1968-

Yearbook of the European Convention on Human Rights, the European Commission and European Court of Human Rights. -- The Hague, 1959 (vol.1, 1955/57)-
Vol.1 entitled: Documents and decisions - European Commission of Human Rights
ISSN 0071-2701

AB/U-1
AD/U-6
BH/U-1
BL/U-1
BR/U-1 1958-
BT/U-1
CA/U-1
CA/U13
CB/U-1 1965-
CR/U-1
DN/U-1
DR/U-1
ED/U-1 1958-
EX/U-1 1958-
GL/U-1
HL/U-1 1958-60 (v.3); 1962 (v.5)-
LA/U-1 1970-
LC/U-1
LD/U-1 1958/59-
LO-MT
LO/N-1
LO/N17
LO/N26 1958/59-
LO/N27
LO/R74
LO/S14
LO/U-2 1955-57;1962-
LO/U-3
LO/U11
LO/U12 1958-(w.1961)
LO/U24
LV/U-1 1964.
NO/U-1 1958 (v.2)-
NW/U-1 1968 (v.11)-
OX/U15

(cont'd)

Yearbook of the European Convention on Human Rights, the European Commission and European Court of Human Rights (cont'd).

QE/C76
QS/Q29
QS/S-7 1959-
QW/D12 1968 (v.11)-
RE/U-1 1955/57-60 (v.3)
SH/U-1
SO/U-1
XY/N-1 1966 (no.9)-

Yearbook of the International Court of Justice. -- The Hague, 1947 (1946/47)-
ISSN 0074-445X

AB/N-1
AB/U-1
AD/U-6 w.1948/49 and 1964/65
BH/P-1
BH/U-1
BL/U-1 1946/47-49/50;1967/68.
BR/U-1
BT/U-1 1958/59;1963/64;1965/66-
CA/U-1
CA/U13 (w.1948/49)
CB/U-1
CV/U-1 1963/64.
DR/U-1 1950/51-
ED/N-1
ED/U-1
EX/U-1 1952-
GL/U-2 1967 (v.22)-
KL/U-1 1955/56 (v.10)-
LC/U-1
LD/P-1
LD/U-1 1946/47-64/65
LO/C15 1961/62-64/65;1966/67-
LO/C47 1971-
LO-MT
LO/N-1
LO/N-5 1970-
LO/N17
LO/N26
LO/P-6 current year
LO/R74 1964-
LO/S14
LO-SC 1946/47-48/49;1950/51;1953/54-63/64
LO/U-1
LO/U-2 1947-
LO/U-3
LO/U11
LO/U24
LV/U-1 (w.1949/50;1959/60)
MA/P-1 (w.1957/58;1964/65;1968/69-1972/73)
MA/U-1
NO/U-1 1946/47-1948/49;1954/55-1956/57;1972/73-
NW/U-1 1947-
OX/U15
OX/U25
QM/C68 1973-74.
QS/Q12
QS/Q29 1946/47-62/63;1964/65-
QS/S-4
QS/S-6
QW/D12 1974-
RE/U-1 1973/74-
SH/U-1 1956/57.
SO/U-1 1953- imp.
XY/N-1 1946-52 (v.1,4-6);1968-70 (v.23-24)

Yearbook of the International Law Commission. -- New York, 1956 (1949)-

AB/N-1
AB/U-1
AD/U-6
BH/U-1
BL/U-1 1949-61
BR/U-1 1949-62;1971-
CA/U-1
CA/U13
CB/U-1
CV/U-1
DN/U-1 1962-
ED/U-1
EX/U-1
GL/U-1 1964-
GL/U-2 1964;1967- imp.
KL/U-1 1973-
LA/U-1 1967-
LC/U-1
LD/U-1
LO/C15 1962-
LO/N-1
LO/N-5 1970-
LO/N17
LO/N26
LO/R74 1963-
LO/S14
LO/U-2
LO/U-3
LO/U11
LO/U12 1970-
LO/U24
MA/P-1
NO/U-1
NW/U-1
OX/U15
QS/Q12 1949-65
QS/Q29
QS/S-6 1967-
SH/U-1
XY/N-1

Yearbook of the New Jersey State Bar Association. -- Camden, 1899-

OX/U15 1915-16

Yearbook on human rights. -- New York, 1947 (vol.1, 1946)-
ISSN 0084-4098

AB/N-1	ED/U-1 1964-	LO/U-1
AB/U-1 1946-60	EX/U-1	LO/U-2
AD/U-6 1946-50;1961-	GL/U-1	LO/U-3
BH/U-1 1946-1948;	HL/U-1	**LO/U11
1956-	LC/U-1 1946.	**LO/U24
BL/U-1 1946-53;1957-	LD/P-1 1947-	**MA/P-1 (w.1969)
60;1968.	LD/U-1	NO/U-1 1966-
BR/U-1 1946-54	LO/C25 1970-	OX/U-1
BT/U-1	LO-MT 1959-	OX/U15
CA/U-1	LO/N-1	QS/Q12
CA/U13 (w.1953)	LO/N17	**QS/Q29
CB/U-1	LO/N26	**SH/U-1 1955-
CV/U-1	LO/P-6 1946-72	SO/U-1 1958-
DR/U-1 1946;1953;	LO/R74 1961-	XY/N-1 1946-52;
1959.	LO/S14	1957-59;1961-
ED/S11	LO-SC 1946;1948-70	

** known to have the 1959 Supplementary volume

Yugoslav law. -- Belgrade, 1975 (no.1)-
Continues: New Yugoslav law, 1950-1967 (vol.18), (ISSN 0028-7946)

AD/U-6 1951-52 imp.	LO/C47 1956-67 imp.	LO/U24 1950-52 imp.,
1953-67	LO-MT 1975-	1956-
BH/U-1 1951-	LO/N-1	LV/U-1 1950;1956-
BL/U-1 1976-	LO/U24 1956-	OX/U15
CA/U-1	LO/S14 1950-67	QS/S-6 1950-67 imp.
CA/U13 imp.	LO/U-2 1956-67 imp.	QS/S-7 1950-67
ED/S11 1952-	LO/U-3	XY/N-1 1975-
GL/U-1 1950-67	LO/U11 1956-62;1975-	

Zambia law journal. -- Lusaka, 1969-
ISSN 0514-8448

AD/U-6	LO/N-1 1969 (v.1	LO/U24
BL/U-1	no.1).	OX/U15
CR/U-1 1970-	LO/U14	XY/N-1
ED/U-1		

Zbornik Pravnog Fakulteta u Zagrebu. -- Zagreb, 1948-

GL/U-1 Soviet Stud-	LO/N-1	OX/U15
ies Branch	LO/U-3 1948-77 imp.	XY/N-1 1953-59
Library 1966-	LO/U11 1956-	(G.3-9)

Zbornik Radova Pravnog Fakulteta u Splitu. -- Split, 1963-

LO/N-1

Zbornik znanstvenih razprav/ Univerza v Ljubljani. Pravna-Ekonomska Fakulteta. -- Ljubljana, 1921-

LO/N-1 (w.1939/40 (L.16))
LO/U-3 imp.
OX/U15 1921-39 imp.
XY/N-1 1956;1962 (L.30)-

Zeitschrift der Akademie für Deutsches Recht. -- Berlin, 1934-1944
1936 absorbed: Deutsche Juristen-Zeitung, q.v.

CA/U13 1935-38
LO/U-2 1934-37 imp.
LO/U-3 imp.
LO/U24 1934-43 imp.
OX/U15 1934-44 (1941 imp.)

Zeitschrift der Savigny-Stiftung für Rechtsgeschichte, Germanistische Abteilung. -- Weimar, 1880-1944, 1947-
ISSN 0084-5264

AB/N-1 1882;1898-1915 imp., 1924;1935.
AB/U-1 1880- imp.
AD/U-6
CA/U-1
CA/U13
CB/U-1 1969-
GL/U-1 1960-
LO-MT 1880-1911 (v.32) imp.
LO/N-1
LO/U-2 1907-70
LO/U24 1940-44;1959-
LV/U-1 1880-1944; 1947-74
OX/U15
OX/U25
XY/N-1 1966 (Bd.83)-

Zeitschrift der Savigny-Stiftung für Rechtsgeschichte, Kanonistische Abteilung. -- Weimar, 1911-1944;1947-
ISSN 0084-5264

AD/U-6
CA/U-1
CA/U13 1932-
CB/U-1 1969-
DN/U-1 1940-51 imp., 1953-
GL/U-1 1960-
LO/N-1
LO/U-2 1911-70
LO/U24 1940-44;1959-
LV/U-1 1911-44; 1947-74
OX/U-1
OX/U25
XY/N-1 1969 (Bd.86)-

Zeitschrift der Savigny-Stiftung für Rechtsgeschichte, Romanistische Abteilung. -- Weimar, 1880-1944;1947-
Continues: Zeitschrift für Rechtsgeschichte, 1861-1878 (Bd.13)
ISSN 0084-5264

AB/U-1 1880- imp.
AD/U-6
CA/U-1
CA/U13
ED/U-1 1880-
GL/U-1 1880-
LC/U-1 1963 (Bd.80)-
LD/U-1 1880-
LO/N-1
LO/U-2
LO/U24
LV/U-1 1880-1944; 1947-74
MA/U-1 1967-
OX/U15
OX/U25
QS/S-5
XY/N-1 1969 (Bd.86)-

Zeitschrift des Bernischen Juristenvereins = Revue de la Société des Juristes Bernois. -- Berne, 1864-
ISSN 0044-2127

LO/U24 1966 (Jg.102)-
OX/U15 1939 (Jg.75)-
XY/N-1 1967 (Jg.103)-

Zeitschrift für Arbeitsrecht und Sozialrecht. -- Vienna, 1966-
ISSN 0044-2321

XY/N-1 1969 (Jg.4)-

Zeitschrift für ausländisches öffentliches Recht und Völkerrecht. -- Berlin, etc., 1929-1944; 1950-
ISSN 0044-2348

BH/U-1 1974-
CA/U13
ED/U-1 1963-
GL/U-1 1970-
LO/N-1 1964-66
LO/N17 1929-40;1970-
LO/S14 1950-
LO/U-2 1929-42/43; 1959/60-
LO/U-3
LO/U24
NO/U-1 1961 (Bd.21)-
OX/U15
RE/U-1 1961-70
XY/N-1 1966 (Bd.26)-

Zeitschrift für ausländisches und internationales Privatrecht
see Rabels Zeitschrift für ausländisches und internationales Privatrecht

Zeitschrift für Bergrecht. -- Bonn; Cologne, 1860-

LO/N-1 1860-1930
XY/N-1 1973 (Bd.114)-

Zeitschrift für Civil- und Criminalrecht. -- Heidelberg, 1833-1845

LO/N-1

Zeitschrift für Civilrecht und Prozess. -- Giessen, 1828-1844 (Bd.20); N.F. 1845 (Bd.1)-1865 (Bd.22)

EX/U-1 1840-65
LO/N-1

Zeitschrift für das gesamte Familienrecht: Ehe und Familie im privaten und öffentlichen Recht. -- Bielefeld, 1962 (Jg.9 no.5)-
Continues: Ehe und Familie im privaten und öffentlichen Recht, 1954-1962 (Jg.9 no.4)
ISSN 0044-2410

ED/U-1 1969-
LO/U-3
LO/U24 1960 (Jg.6)-
OX/U15
XY/N-1 1967 (Jg.14)-

Zeitschrift für das gesamte Handelsrecht und Wirtschaftsrecht. -- Stuttgart, 1858-1944; 1946-
Title varies slightly
ISSN 0044-2437

BH/U-1 1871;1887-1902
ED/U-1 1968-
GL/U-1 1967-
LO-MT 1958 (v.121)-
LO/N-1
LO/U-3 1871-1916; 1938- (w.1976 no.2)
LO/U24 1961 (Bd.124)-
OX/U15 1948-
OX/U25 1888-93 imp.
XY/N-1 1969 (Bd.132)-

Zeitschrift für das gesamte Luftrecht. -- Berlin, 1926-1928 (Bd.2 Hft.1)

CA/U13
OX/U15

Zeitschrift für das Privat- und öffentliche Recht der Gegenwart. -- Vienna, 1874-1916 (Bd.42)

CA/U-1 1874-79 imp.
ED/S11
LO/N-1
LO/U24
OX/U15 1886-90;1905.

Zeitschrift für das Recht und die Politik der Kirche. -- Leipzig, 1847 (Bd.1-2).

LO/N-1

Zeitschrift für deutschen Zivilprozess see Zeitschrift für Zivilprozess

Zeitschrift für deutsches bürgerliches Recht und französisches Zivilrecht. -- Mannheim, 1900 (Bd.31)-1907 (Bd.38)
Continues: Zeitschrift für französisches Zivilrecht, 1870-1899 (Bd.30)

LO/N-1 LO/U24

Zeitschrift für deutsches Recht und deutsche Rechtswissenschaft. -- Leipzig, 1839-1861 (Bd.20)

CA/U-1 LO/N-1

Zeitschrift für deutsches Strafverfahren. -- Karlsruhe; Darmstadt, 1841-1843 (Bd.3); N.F. 1844 (Bd.1)-1847 (Bd.4)

LO/N-1

Zeitschrift für die Criminal-Rechts-Pflege in den preussischen Staaten... -- Berlin, 1825-1833 (Bd.24)

LO/N-1

Zeitschrift für die deutsche Gesetzgebung und für einheitliches deutsches Recht. -- Berlin, 1872 (Bd.6)-1875 (Bd.8)
Continues: Preussische Anwaltszeitung, 1862-1866 and: Zeitschrift für Gesetzgebung und Rechtspflege in Preussen, 1867 (Bd.1)-1871 (Bd.5)

LO/N-1

Zeitschrift für die freiwillige Gerichtsbarkeit und die Gemeindeverwaltung in Württemberg. -- Stuttgart, 1862-
Continues: Monatsschrift für die willkürliche Gerichtsbarkeit und das Notariat in Württemberg, 1859-1861 (Jg.3)
1920 absorbed: Jahrbücher der württembergischen Rechtspflege, q.v.

LO/U11 1923-36

Zeitschrift für die gesamte Staatswissenschaft. -- Tübingen, 1844-1944;1948-
ISSN 0044-2550

AD/U-6 1952-68
GL/U-1 1966-
HL/U-1 1966-75 (Bd.131)
LO/N-1
LO/U-1
LO/U-3
OX/U-1
XY/N-1 1961 (Bd.117)-

Zeitschrift für die gesamte Strafrechtswissenschaft. -- Berlin, 1881-1944;1950-
ISSN 0084-5310

ED/U-1 1967-
LO/U24 (w.v.11; 53-63)
OX/U15 1950-
OX/U25 1885-93
XY/N-1 1966 (Bd.78)-

Zeitschrift für die gesamte Versicherungswissenschaft. -- Berlin, 1899-
ISSN 0044-2585

LO/U-3 1930-41/42;1960-
XY/N-1 1973-

Zeitschrift für die Landeskultur-Gesetzgebung der preussischen Staaten. -- Berlin, 1874-1918 (Bd.40)

LO/N-1

Zeitschrift für evangelisches Kirchenrecht. -- Tübingen, 1951-
ISSN 0044-2690

CA/U-1
OX/U-1
XY/N-1 1973 (Bd.18)-

Zeitschrift für französisches Zivilrecht <u>see</u> Zeitschrift für deutsches bürgerliches Recht und französisches Zivilrecht

Zeitschrift für Gerichtsvollzieher <u>see</u> Zeitschrift über Vollstreckungsrecht und Zustellungswesen

Zeitschrift für geschichtliche Rechtswissenschaft. -- Berlin, 1815-1850 (Bd.15)

ED/U-1 1815-48
GL/U-1
LO/N-1
LO/U24
OX/U15

Zeitschrift für Gesetzgebung und Rechtspflege in Preussen <u>see</u> Zeitschrift für die deutsche Gesetzgebung und für einheitliches deutsches Recht

Zeitschrift für Gesetzkunde und Rechtspflege, zunächst in Ungarn, Kroatien, und Slawonien, Siebenbürgen, Serbien und dem Temeser Banat. -- Pressburg, 1855-1860

LO/N-1

Zeitschrift für Handelsgesetzgebung... -- Nürnberg, 1857 (Bd.1).

LO/N-1

Zeitschrift für Handelsrecht. -- Berlin, 1852-1853 (No.3)

LO/N-1

Zeitschrift für Industrierecht. -- Berlin, 1906-Sept.1922 (Bd.15)

LO/U-3 1906-19

Zeitschrift für internationales Privat- und öffentliches Recht <u>see</u> Niemeyers Zeitschrift...

Zeitschrift für internationales Privat- und Strafrecht <u>see</u> Niemeyers Zeitschrift...

Zeitschrift für internationales Recht <u>see</u> Niemeyers Zeitschrift...

Zeitschrift für Kirchenrecht <u>see</u> Deutsche Zeitschrift für Kirchenrecht

Zeitschrift für Kirchenrechts- und Pastoralwissenschaft. -- Regensburg, 1842-1848

LO/N-1

Zeitschrift für Luft- und Weltraumrecht = German journal of air and space law = Revue allemande de droit aérien et spatiale. -- Berlin, 1975 (Jg.24 Hft.2)-
Continues: Zeitschrift für Luftrecht, 1952-1959 and: Zeitschrift für Luftrecht und Weltraumrechtsfragen, 1960-1975. English and French titles added with Jg.25, 1976

LO/U-2 LO/U24 XY/N-1 1964 (Jg.13)-
LO/U-3 1952-77 OX/U25

Zeitschrift für Luftrecht <u>see</u> previous entry

Zeitschrift für Luftrecht und Weltraumrechtsfragen <u>see</u> Zeitschrift für Luft- und Weltraumrecht

Zeitschrift für Miet- und Raumrecht. -- Düsseldorf, 1948-

OX/U15 1952 (Bd.5)- XY/N-1 1973 (Bd.26)-

Zeitschrift für öffentliches Recht <u>see</u> Österreichische Zeitschrift für öffentliches Recht und Völkerrecht

Zeitschrift für österreichische Rechtsgelehrsamkeit und politische Gesetzkunde <u>see</u> Österreichische Zeitschrift für Rechts- und Staatswissenschaft

Zeitschrift für osteuropäisches Recht. -- Berlin, 1925-1927 (Jg.3); N.F. 1934-1944 (Jg.11)
1927 merged with: Ostrecht, q.v., to form: Zeitschrift für Ostrecht (see next entry).
Original title resumed with new series

LO/U-3 1925-39

Zeitschrift für Ostrecht. -- Berlin, 1927-1934 (Jg.8)
Continued by new series of: Zeitschrift für osteuropäisches Recht (see previous entry)

LO/U-3

Zeitschrift für Praxis und Gesetzgebung der Verwaltung see Fischers Zeitschrift für Verwaltungsrecht

Zeitschrift für Recht und Gesetzgebung in Kurhessen. -- Cassel, 1836-1837 (Bd.2)

No holdings notified

Zeitschrift für Rechtsgeschichte see Zeitschrift der Savigny-Stiftung für Rechtsgeschichte, Romanistische Abteilung

Zeitschrift für Rechtsmedizin = Journal of legal medicine. -- Berlin, 1970-
Contines: Kritisches Repertorium für die gesammte Heilkunde, 1823-1833; Wochenschrift für die gesammte Heilkunde, 1833-1851; Vierteljahresschrift für die gerichtliche und öffentliche Medizin, 1852-1871; Vierteljahresschrift für gerichtliche Medizin und öffentliches Sanitätswesen, 1872-1921 and: Deutsche Zeitschrift für die gesamte gerichtliche Medizin, 1922-1969
ISSN 0044-3433

AD/U-6 1882-1937	LO/M32 1950-54;1966; 1968-69	NW/U-1 1962-69 (v.53-65)
CA/U-1 1859-	LO/N-1	XY/N-1 1914-28;1958 (Bd.48)-
GL/U-1 1852-78		

Zeitschrift für Rechtspflege in Württemberg. -- Reutlingen, 1859-1860 (Bd.2)

LO/N-1

Zeitschrift für Rechtspflege und Verwaltung see Fischers Zeitschrift für Verwaltungsrecht

Zeitschrift für Rechtspolitik. -- Munich, 1968-
Supplement to Neue juristische Wochenschrift, q.v.
ISSN 0514-6496

BL/U-1 1974-	GL/U-1 1969-	OX/U15
CA/U13	LO/U12 1969-70 imp. 1971- (1975 imp.)	SO/U-1 1970 (v.3)-
CV/U-1	LO/U24	XY/N-1 1969 (Bd.2 Hft.3)-
ED/U-1		
EX/U-1 1975-		

Zeitschrift für Rechtsvergleichung. -- Vienna, 1960-
ISSN 0514-275X

CA/U13	LO/U24	OX/U15
LO/U11	MA/U-1	XY/N-1 1967 (Bd.8)-

Zeitschrift für Rechtsvergleichung und internationales Recht des südlichen Afrika see Comparative and international law journal of southern Africa

Zeitschrift für schweizer Strafrecht see Schweizerische Zeitschrift für Strafrecht

Zeitschrift für schweizerische Gesetzgebung und Rechtspflege. -- Zürich, 1875-1882 (Bd.5)

LO/N-1

Zeitschrift für schweizerisches Recht = Revue de droit suisse = Rivista di diritto svizzero. -- Basle, 1852-
From 1883 contains: Verhandlungen des Schweizerischen Juristenvereins (also issued separately 1861-1947)

LO/N-1 1852-1920
LO/U11 1964- imp.
LO/U24 1882 (N.F. Bd.1)-
OX/U15 1924-
XY/N-1 1967 (N.F. Bd.86)-

Zeitschrift für soziales Recht. -- Vienna, Oct.1928-1934 (Bd.6)

No holdings notified

Zeitschrift für Standesamtswesen see Das Standesamt

Zeitschrift für Strafrechtspflege in den preussischen Staaten. -- Königsberg, 1839-1840 (Bd.2)

LO/N-1

Zeitschrift für Unternehmens- und Gesellschaftsrecht. -- Berlin, 1972-

OX/U15

Zeitschrift für vergleichende Rechtswissenschaft einschliesslich der ethnologischen Rechtsforschung. -- Stuttgart, 1878-1942;1953-

AB/N-1 1900;1906-23
AD/U-6 1953-
CA/U-1
CA/U13 1960-
ED/U-1 1878- (w.v.54 (3);55 (1-3))
LO/N-1
LO/U14 1916 (Bd.34 Hft.3); 1933 (Bd.47 Hft.2-3); 1934-
LO/U24 (w.Bd.25-55)
NW/U-1 1960-72
OX/U15
QS/S-7 1878-1914
XY/N-1 1967 (Bd.69)-

Zeitschrift für Verkehrsrecht. -- Vienna, 1956-
ISSN 0044-3662

XY/N-1 1973-

Zeitschrift für Versicherungsrecht. -- Leipzig, 1865-1866 (Bd.2)

No holdings notified

Zeitschrift für Völkerrecht. -- Breslau; Berlin, 1906-1944 (Bd.26 Hft.3)
1906-1913 (Bd.6) entitled: Zeitschrift für Völkerrecht und Bundesstaatsrecht.
1938 absorbed: Niemeyers Zeitschrift für internationales Recht, q.v.

AB/N-1
BH/U-1 1938-44
BL/U-1 1926-39 imp.
CA/U-1
CA/U13 1906-41 (Bd.25)
ED/U-1 1924-36 imp.
LO/N-1 1908-14 imp., 1938-44
LO/U-3
LO/U24 1906-41 (Bd.24) (Bd.16,20,22 imp.)
LV/U-1 1926-39 imp.
OX/U15 1916-18; 1931-44

Zeitschrift für Völkerrecht und Bundesstaatsrecht <u>see</u> previous entry

Zeitschrift für Wasserrecht. -- Cologne, 1963-
ISSN 0044-3735

XY/N-1 1973 (Bd.12)-

Zeitschrift für Wehrrecht. -- Berlin, Munich, 1936-

LO/U24 1942-44 (Bd.7-8)

Zeitschrift für Wirtschafts- und Sozialwissenschaften. -- Berlin, 1972 (Bd.92)-
Continues: Jahrbuch für Gesetzgebung, Verwaltung und Rechtspflege des Deutschen Reiches, 1871-1876 (Bd.4); Jahrbuch für Gesetzgebung, Verwaltung und Volkswirtschaft im Deutschen Reiche, N.F. 1877 (Bd.1)- 1912 (Bd.36), and: Schmollers Jahrbuch für Gesetzgebung, Verwaltung und Volkswirtschaft, 1914-1944;1949-1971 (ISSN 0036-6234)

AD/U-6 1952-61
BH/U-1 1899;1901-19; 1921
CA/U-1
ED/U-1 1871;1913-
LO/U-3 1877-1944; 1949-
LO/U24 1871-1914 (N.F. Bd.38); 1939 (Bd.63).
OX/U-1
XY/N-1 1963 (Bd.83)-

Zeitschrift für Zivilprozess. -- Cologne, 1950 (Bd.64)-
Continues: Zeitschrift für deutschen Zivilprozess, 1879-1943 (Bd.63).
Bd.25-48 have subtitle: und das Verfahren in Angelegenheiten der freiwilligen Gerichtsbarkeit

LO/N-1 1879-1914
LO/U24 (w.Bd.35-60; 63)
OX/U15 1950-
OX/U25 1887-91 imp.
XY/N-1 1950 (Bd.64)-

Zeitschrift über Vollstreckungsrecht und Zustellungswesen. -- Berlin, 1894 (Bd.8) -1901 (Bd.15)
Continues: Zeitschrift für Gerichtsvollzieher, 1887-1893 (Bd.7)

LO/N-1

Zentralblatt der Rechtswissenschaft. -- Stuttgart; Berlin, 1881-1913 (Bd.33)
1881-1910 (Bd.29) entitled: Centralblatt (later Zentralblatt) für Rechtswissenschaft

CA/U-1 1881-1912 LO/N-1 OX/U-1 1881-1906

Zentralblatt für Jugendrecht und Jugendwohlfahrt. -- Berlin, Apr. 1909-
Publication suspended 1944-1949.
Title varies

LO/U24 1933-36 (Jg.25-27) XY/N-1 1967 (Jg.54 Hft.6)-

Zentralblatt für Rechtswissenschaft see Zentralblatt der Rechtswissenschaft

Zhengfa yanjiu see Cheng fa yen chiu